Living LANGUAGE & LITERATURE

**George Keith
and
John Shuttleworth**

Hodder & Stoughton

Orders: please contact Bookpoint Ltd, 39 Milton Park, Abingdon, Oxon OX14 4TD. Telephone:
(44) 01235 827720, Fax: (44) 01235 400454. Lines are open from 9.00 – 6.00, Monday to Saturday,
with a 24 hour message answering service. Email address: orders@bookpoint.co.uk

British Library Cataloguing in Publication Data
A catalogue record for this title is available from The British Library

ISBN 0 340 77175 5
First published 2000
Impression number   10 9 8 7 6 5 4 3 2
Year   2005 2004 2003 2002 2001

Cover photo ©1999 Roy Export Company Establishment.
Typeset by Fakenham Photosetting Limited, Fakenham, Norfolk NR21 8NN
Printed in Great Britain for Hodder & Stoughton Educational, a division of Hodder Headline Plc,
338 Euston Road, London NW1 3BH by J. W. Arrowsmith Ltd, Bristol.

Contents

Preface

Who are you?

If you are reading this book, then you:

- are probably studying English Language and Literature at AS and/or A2 level
- already have some experience in studying English Language and Literature
- are aware of some of the relevant terms and concepts.

Obviously *Living Language and Literature* is primarily intended as an introduction to AS and A level English Language and Literature. However, it will also be useful if you are studying either English Literature or English Language. For a more direct focus on English Literature, you should read *Living Literature* by Frank Myszor and Jackie Baker and for English Language, you should read *Living Language* by George Keith and John Shuttleworth.

In this introduction we explain:

- the differences between GCSE and A level
- how this book relates to the Assessment Objectives for the English Language and Literature specifications
- key skills.

Bridging the Gap: from GCSE to A level

You will find that moving from GCSE to A level is a big step, but not a step that you are unprepared for, nor one that will be too great for you. This is because there is an intermediate stage in A level study which means that everyone has to sit an Advanced Subsidiary (AS) examination before proceeding to A level. Many people will take this examination at the end of the first year of their course, but it can be taken at other times, depending on how your course is organised. The AS exam is pitched at a standard in between A level and GCSE, so that, at the beginning of your A level course, you are faced with less of a mountain to climb. You do not have to move on from AS to A level unless you wish to do so. You cannot, however, take A level without already having taken AS level.

Your exams are now connected like this:

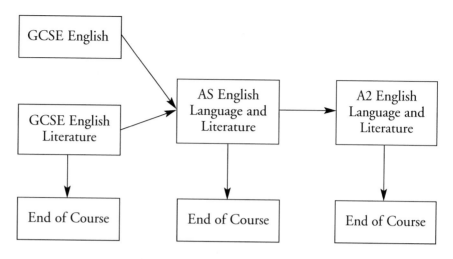

GCSE English

Shakespeare
Prose ⎤ one of these has to
Poetry ⎦ be pre-1914
Non-fiction texts
Media texts
A range of speaking and
listening activities
A range of writing
activities

GCSE English Literature

Shakespeare
Prose
Poetry
Drama
Comparisons between texts
Literary tradition
Cultural contexts

AS English Language and Literature

This requires you to show knowledge and understanding of:
- a minimum of two literary texts covering prose, poetry or drama, one of which must have been written before 1900
- a range of non-literary texts including both spoken and written language
- literary–critical concepts and terminology related to genre, style and structure and how to apply these to texts
- linguistic concepts and frameworks for the study of both written and spoken language and how to apply these to texts

- the ways that variations in language can shape and change meanings and forms

In addition you need to be able to:
- write appropriately and accurately for a variety of audiences and purposes and comment on what you have produced

A level English Language and Literature (in addition to AS requirements)

This requires you to show knowledge and understanding of:
- two further literary texts, one of which must have been written before 1770, which ensures that all three genres (prose, poetry and drama) have been covered by the end of A level
- a wider range of both spoken and written non-literary texts and the ways in which meanings and forms in language are shaped by variations in mode, use, time or place
- the ways in which spoken and written texts relate to the contexts in which they were received and created

In addition you need to be able to:
- compare texts and evaluate different analytical approaches to their study, bearing in mind cultural and historical factors
- demonstrate your knowledge of the ways in which the study of language and of literature inform each other

So how is GCSE different from AS and A level? The answer to this depends on whether you are discussing English or English Literature GCSE. One thing to remember is that because you will have studied a lot of literature in GCSE English, you don't need to have studied GCSE English Literature in order to go on to AS/A level in Language and Literature. Naturally, there is continuity with English Literature GCSE, as you would expect. There you had to show some knowledge of the historical and cultural context in which a text was written as well as an understanding of the literary tradition. Both of these feature again at AS and A level.

There is also continuity with GCSE English. There you had to write pieces for different purposes and had to study a range of non-fiction and non-literary texts. These, too, feature again at AS and A level, but, in addition, you will be studying some spoken texts. You will also be studying how the spoken and written languages are structured and organised.

In general terms, to succeed beyond GCSE you obviously need to enjoy studying literature and language. You will also need to be prepared to study literary and non-literary texts from outside your own time and culture, thus expanding your horizons. As you continue your studies, the methods you use will become as important as the content of the course. This is why *how* you approach a text is just as important as *what* you say about it. Above all, you will need to be able to make your own judgements about what you read and hear, coming closer to being an *independent informed reader and listener* as you progress through the course.

The course you are following is already an excellent one designed to test your knowledge, understanding and skills in English Language and Literature. However, the government has stipulated that there should also be a number of Assessment Objectives whose objective is to assess whether you have achieved AS or A level standard and therefore whether you deserve an award in the subject. The mark you achieve in each component of the course depends *entirely* on how well you have demonstrated your ability to meet these Assessment Objectives, whether in coursework or in an end of module examination. It's as well, therefore, to know what these Assessment Objectives are.

Here they are in full for AS and A level. The right hand column of the chart offers some explanations.

Assessment Objectives		Explanation
AO1	communicate clearly the knowledge, understanding and insights gained from the combination of literary and linguistic study, using appropriate terminology and accurate written expression	write accurately and use technical terms
AO2i	in responding to literary and non-literary texts, distinguish, describe and interpret variation in meaning and form	be able to show how texts vary in their meanings and organisation
AO2ii	respond with knowledge and understanding to texts of different types and from different periods, exploring and commenting on relationships and comparisons between them	as above, but also write about old texts and about different types, looking at their similarities and differences
AO3i	respond to and analyse texts, using literary and linguistic concepts and approaches	use literary and linguistic ways of writing about texts
AO3ii	use and evaluate different literary and linguistic approaches to the study of written and spoken language, showing how these approaches inform their reading	as above, but also comment on how useful the methods you used to study the texts were
AO4	show understanding of the ways contextual variation and choices of form, style and vocabulary shape the meanings of texts	write about why texts vary in meaning
AO5	identify and consider the ways attitudes and values are created in speech and writing	show how attitudes and values are created in texts

Assessment Objectives		Explanation
AO6	demonstrate expertise and accuracy in writing for a variety of specific purposes and audiences, drawing on knowledge of literary texts and features of language to explain and comment on the choices made	write a variety of your own texts and a commentary on them

AO2 and AO3 are split into two parts. The first part applies only to AS level and the second part only to A level.

Key skills

The National Qualification in Key Skills requires all AS and A level students to take the following Key Skills:

- Application of Number
- Communication
- Information Technology

English Language and Literature is relevant to two of these: Communication and Information Technology.

The **Communication** unit includes:

- discussion
- making a presentation
- selecting and synthesising information (**reading**)
- writing different kinds of text.

The **Information Technology** unit includes:

- plan and use **different sources** to search for and select information
- explore, develop and exchange **information** and derive new information
- **present information**, including text, numbers and images.

You can be credited with Key Skills through any of the A levels or GNVQs that you are studying.

1 Learning about Language in Five Birthdays

1 A level English language and literature

The course on which you are now set, a new millennium course if ever there was one, has long been overdue. It is a very odd state of affairs that 'Language' and 'Literature' ever became separated in the first place, since you couldn't have one without the other. There are still communities in the world (there used to be many, many more) whose languages do not have a written form, there being no social need for writing. Even so, you can detect fictional, poetic, playful and religious uses of the oral language that have much in common with the stuff of literature (e.g. gods, heroes, monsters, myths and legends, sex and death) all of which are in fact important sources of the 'Literature' now studied by A level students. A good deal of this book is devoted to the remarkable things that are created by this ancient mixture of language and imagination, some comic and lighthearted, others serious and tragic.

To begin in humorous vein, consider the case of Wallace and Gromit and the tale of *Anoraknophobia* (Hodder & Stoughton, 1998) (Fig. 1.1).

Wallace's Ping Pong O'Matic Automated Home Leisure System has hiccupped badly during field trials. When next door's pigeons then ruin Gromit's washing, man and dog face a hefty repair bill. Thus they enter an Invention Convention sponsored by the shadowy Acme Corporation ... First Prize: £100.

So begins *Anoraknophobia*, which brings the pair face-to-eyepatch with the sinister Herr Doktor Count Baron Napoleon von Strudel, inventor of the Acme Utility Anorak, and his hypnotic, spider-taming wife Queenie. The so-called von Strudels seem strangely familiar to Wallace, however. And man and dog soon find themselves entangled in Operation S.P.A.R.R.O.W, a thoroughly evil plan to brainwash the cream of British brainpower – with serious implications for the future of table tennis and other indoor sports.

Wallace and Gromit are characters created by Nick Park for Television. The world they live in, the things they do, and especially the way Wallace talks (thanks to the distinctive voice of actor Peter Sallis), very quickly gained household familiarity and a place in modern comic mythology. You may loathe them, you may find them lovable, but you can't not know them. It is not, however, just the visual power of TV animation that gives them life, it is the use of language too, as indicated in the introduction above to one of their cartoon adventure books. They are entirely made up,

Fig 1.1 Page 1 of Anoraknophobia

daft fictions that give a lot of people much enjoyment. Such is the power of language and imagination combined.

Once, a ten-year-old schoolgirl said to some researchers investigating what ideas children had about language: 'If you didn't have language, you wouldn't be able to tell lies'. It's a brilliant remark, much wiser than she could ever have known. The whole of English Literature is constructed, not exactly of lies, but of fictions – of things that never happened and people who never were: the Wife of Bath, Hamlet, Moll Flanders, Oliver Twist, Alice in Wonderland, Sherlock Holmes, and so on; each one created by that special blend of imagination and language.

Your course then, has not been designed for students who don't want 'too much' Literature or 'too much' Language; it has a clear dual focus of its own. First of all it has been designed to give you a *linguistic perspective on Literature*. This means not taking language for granted but looking more closely at the rich resources that make literature an everyday communication possible. Second, the course will give you a *literary perspective on Language*. This means understanding the creative processes and the finished products of poets, playwrights and storytellers, and also of writers in some other genres. And that includes *you and your coursework*, and everybody else who chooses to use language in that special way, generally recognised as 'literary', whether for play, jokes and entertainment or for serious reflections on human life, love, fortune and death – which is what Literature is mostly about.

2 Abstract nouns: beware!

Look at the following conversation from Act One of the play, *Loot*, by Joe Orton.

SHE: I ask for nothing. I am a woman. Only half the human race can say that without fear of contradiction.

   (SHE kisses him)

    Go ahead, ask me to marry you. I have no intention of refusing. On your knees. I am a great believer in traditional positions.

HE: The pains in my legs . . .

   (HE kneels)

SHE: Exercise is good for them. Make any kind of proposal you like. Try to avoid abstract nouns.

Loot is an absurdist play: a mixture of the daft, the blackly comic and the disconcertingly perceptive. It is full of the clever language-play illustrated above. Notice for example, that while it may be literally true that half the human race can claim to be women, there is an implied, jokey meaning here as well, i.e. that it cannot be contradicted that women never ask for anything. Notice too, how the woman being proposed to is in charge of the situation, dictating terms, the man on his knees looking, and probably feeling, slightly foolish.

The final joke about abstract nouns deserves some explanation. Indeed, abstract nouns in matters of romantic love are more likely to be the rule than the exception. In other walks of life however, there is a suspicion about abstract nouns. Great rallying cries have consisted of abstract nouns e.g. 'Liberte, Egalite, Fraternite', 'Long live the revolution', 'Death to tyranny'. Often they are written with initial capitals to emphasise them: Liberty, Equality, Brotherhood, Sisterhood, The Revolution, Tyranny, Loyalty, the Faith, 'may the Force be with you'. Note the definite article, sometimes used to emphasise the noun and suggest more precision than it deserves. Note too, that many abstract nouns end in 'ism': e.g. Patriotism, Socialism, Consumerism, defeatism. If you question them: 'What revolution?'. What do you mean by 'Loyalty'? – good, bloody-minded responses – you may be imprisoned or executed if the regime is a repressive one, on the grounds of another popular abstract noun for trumped-up charges, namely 'treason', or should that be 'Treason' with a capital T? Note also, the inverted commas, which are a handy device to signal caution when using abstract nouns.

Business managers, engineers and social workers are advised to avoid abstract nouns in their reports. 'He has a drink problem' contains a vague abstract noun phrase which, in a report, would say very little. 'He drinks two bottles of whisky a day' is far more informative for being concrete. Note too that the word drink is used in the second example as a verb. It is a useful exercise, now and then, to convert what you are about to say, or have just read as an abstract noun phrase into an equivalent verb: 'I'm an extrovert I suppose' becomes 'I like being with other people' since 'extrovert' could also mean 'bossy big head'.

Poets and novelists use abstract nouns with extreme caution, preferring the vivid and movingly concrete. It is unfortunate that the antonym for 'abstract', namely 'concrete', has such hard edged, even brutal connotations nowadays, when it originally meant something more organic, i.e. 'growing together'. 'Real' is still a good modern synonym especially in literary contexts. Not unconnected, is the way in which 'real!' is used in everyday conversation as an adjective meaning, 'terrific', 'great', or as an adverb, albeit overused, 'it really gets to you'. Note also the well known 1990s saying, 'Get real!'. What on earth might, 'Get abstract!' mean?!

Abstract nouns mean something or nothing, anything and everything. Sometimes there seem to be as many meanings as there are users of any abstract noun you care to mention. Lasting friendships can be made when you meet somebody who means exactly the same as you do by nouns such as: fairness, efficiency, sharing, trust, honesty, faithfulness, truth, optimism, romance, and the biggest one of all, *love*.

The joke in Orton's play is that proposals of marriage, declarations of love and invitations to lifelong or even temporary partnership are bound to raise a few abstract nouns. The woman wishes to avoid them, yet even the most commonplace ones have many meanings: love? marriage? partnership? And it is highly likely that 'trust' and 'heart' (in the metaphorical sense, not the anatomical!) will not be far away in such a context.

ACTIVITY 1

Will you marry me?
What verbal conventions do people use nowadays in real life to propose? Think of some

examples. Are there still formal or semi-formal proposals? What influences the ways in which language is used on these occasions, e.g.

nervousness? momentousness? dread? careful thought? calculation?

Now get a copy of Joe Orton's *Loot* and compare the whole of this scene with (a) Jack's proposal to Gwndolen in Act One of *The Importance of Being Earnest* and (b) the balcony scene in *Romeo and Juliet* which, if not exactly a proposal, is a declaration and a swearing of true love.

With help from your teacher you could also search out two or three more literary proposals and declarations of love. There's Mr Collins in *Pride and Prejudice*, Angel Clare in 'Tess', to start with. Include also examples from popular literature or other sources that you know. How, for example do people propose in soaps? Kevin Webster to Alison for example, in *Coronation Street*?

There are loads of proposals/declarations of love in novels and in teenage girls' comic style, love stories. You might even come across a Victorian or Edwardian manual of advice for young men and women on the etiquette of love and relationships.

This activity will give you an idea of what a 'linguistic perspective on literature' feels like. Don't look at plot themes or characterisation, look at what is said and at the verbal conventions and the contexts in which the words are spoken.

How 'true to life' do your examples seem? What is the mixture of ardour/romance and hard-headedeness? What ideas, feelings and attitudes of the writer do you detect behind the words he/she puts into the mouths of the characters?

3 The language half

The title of your A level course consists of two particularly huge abstract nouns, joined by the disarmingly simple conjunction, 'and'. Beware all phrases joined together in that way until you or the author have made it absolutely clear what is meant. Throughout this book we shall do our best to explain what we mean by the words we use, and by the end of your course, you must ensure that you can explain what you mean by a word, and not leave an examiner to guess. One of the surest ways to earn a mark or two, when you have used a particularly 'heavy' word, in an exam answer, e.g. 'alienation', 'foregrounding', 'tone', or a word that is too easy to take for granted, e.g. 'irony' or 'dialect', is to follow it with something like: 'What I mean here by alienation is …' or ' "Alienation" in this instance means …'. It doesn't matter too much if the examiner disagrees with your point of view, she still has marks to give you for your communicativeness and your determination to be understood.

The chief aim of the rest of this chapter is to begin to get some clear, systematic ideas about the nature and functions of language in life, before exploring specific uses of language in literature.

ACTIVITY 2

Response statements
Take the two abstract nouns *Language* and *Literature* and write, underneath each, ten statements beginning 'Literature is …' or 'Language is …'. Don't think you are writing definitions because you have used the verb 'is'. You are writing descriptions which will give

you much more scope than definitions. Both are useful but descriptions can be personal or general, wide ranging or limited, negative as well as positive. Unlike definitions, they don't have to cover everything, just enough to be useful. Here are some examples to start you off:

Literature

– is uplifting stuff
– is boring
– is anything written down
– is not just anything written down
– is highbrow entertainment

In later chapters you will be exploring in much more detail just what you and others mean by the word 'literature'. We take it to be the case that without language there would not be any

Language

– is used only by humans
– is stuff for thinking with
– is communication
– is good for helping people with
– is good for hurting people with

kind of writing at all, and that it makes sense to look first at the very stuff out of which literature is made. The next activity starts you off by considering different kinds of writing.

ACTIVITY 3

Varieties of writing

Under the general heading of *Writing* make two lists (about ten items in each), one of varieties of writing you would call English Literature in the A level sense of the word, and writing of any other kind. Here's a start:

Writing

A level Eng Lit stuff
The plays of Shakespeare
Keats' *Ode to Autumn*
Waiting for Godot

Other stuff
Renault car manual
Biology textbook
The *Sun* newspaper

COMMENTARY

It is likely that the bulk of your first list consisted of plays, poems and novels. You may also have included biographies and travel writing, though some may have excluded these on the grounds that they are 'fact' not 'fiction'. Those who included them may have done so on the ground that the examples chosen were 'well written'. These are all issues that need to be explored and argued but for the moment, let's go on intuition.

Your second list could go on for ever, so great is the variety of non-fictional, functional, factual, non-literary forms of written English – call them what you will.

To say that both lists have language in common seems pathetically obvious, yet even a superficial comparison of some of the language features they have in common – words, grammar, forms and functions – will soon suggest significant differences. There are also significant contextual differences, and underlying these, a very significant distinction in language itself between speech and writing, that has many implications for the ways in which we understand meanings.

Here's a diagram to start with, of the relationship between Language and Literature (in the A level senses of those words) that you can use as a working model. As you go through the activities in the book you will gradually modify and refine the model. A note of explanation follows the diagram.

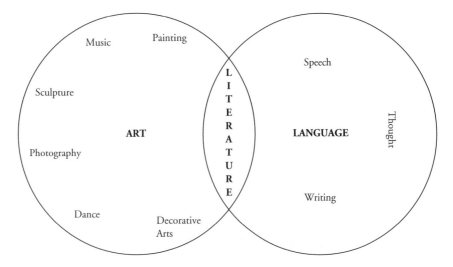

Think of the distinguishing feature of 'Literature' as *Art*, that is to say language used for artistic purposes. Some linguists use the term 'Verbal Art' as a description of poems, plays, and prose fiction and also of certain kinds of advertising, religious practices and performances to entertain or persuade.

Not all the arts of course are linguistic e.g. painting, photography, sculpture, music. In a later chapter you will explore what are referred to as the four modes of language use, namely: listening, speaking, reading and writing. For the moment, take note of the dividing line we have drawn between literacy (reading and writing) and oracy (speaking and listening). We do not wish to separate literature too much from its oral origins, though this will need explanation later.

4 Out of the mouths of babes

Already the terms 'language' and 'literature' become less abstract as they are given shape by making distinctions and citing examples. One way of understanding some important aspects of the nature and functions of language is to study it as it grows and develops in infancy and through childhood to maturity. It is a very concrete way of focusing the huge generality of the term 'language' and of giving it a recognisably human face and voice. It will in fact be your own face and your own voice, for despite the fact that all English speakers have their own, personal versions of the language, just as they have their own personal faces and fingerprints, they all go through remarkably similar stages of language acquisition in the early years. Thus, studying your language life-history is a way of studying all the structures and functions of the language itself. The story of you and your language is a story shared with millions of others, but it is also the story of your individual development. You share your dialect with the people you are born into and live among, your dialect is your own, personal version of language.

ACTIVITY 4

You and your language

You will need a couple of friends to help you with this activity, so that you can compare experiences, plus a little family help to corroborate details. Think about and answer the following questions.

1 When and what was (or might have been) the first word you spoke?
   Were you considered a noisy, talkative, babbling baby, or a quiet one?

2 When do you think you started (or are known to have started) talking in joined-up words (they may not have been conventional sentences, that doesn't matter)?

3 What are your earliest recollections of talking, being talked to, being read to, listening?

4 Do you have any recollections of favourite 'baby talk' in the family? Special words for things? 'Funny' sayings?

5 What do you remember as your earliest reading? Books? Labels? Anything else?
   At what age do you think you started reading on your own? Can you remember anyone teaching you to read? Have you saved any of your baby/early childhood books?

6 What is your earliest memory of writing anything? What was it? Who was it for? Why do you think you wrote it? How has your handwriting grown? What differences are there between your handwriting and that of your friends? Where do the differences lie? In size? Neatness? Vowel letters? Consonants? Which of you is the 'best' or 'worst' speller?

7 What did you most enjoy reading as a child? What do you read mostly now? Do you recollect ever writing a story, a poem or a letter, for the sheer doing of it? Did you ever keep a diary? Do you still?

8 Who makes you laugh quite a lot by the things they say? What kind of humour is it?

Compare your three sets of responses and see if you can make any reasonable generalisations about language development from infancy onwards, and in particular, about factors that influence language development and reading enjoyment.

We are going to look now at a series of birthdays from nought to age five. As we go through them we shall illustrate first, some important aspects of language for everyday living and then suggest their significance for a fuller understanding of literature. Each birthday should be seen as a notional staging point, a statistic, observable in the behaviour of large numbers of children. They are not a single, narrow ladder everybody climbs at the same speed and in exactly the same order. Everybody is that bit different, yet patterns are observable when statistics are collated. Some children do some things sooner, some later, than others. Environmental factors and individual purposes have a great deal of influence on language development. Don't assume it's a matter of innate intelligence any more than it is just a matter of imitating adults. There are of course physiological factors that take their own natural growth time in all children. An infant is not likely to utter dental sounds if it does not yet have teeth to make the dental sounds with. The sound that begins and ends the word 'judge', because of the combinations required to say it, is generally observed to come at the end of the process whereby children acquire a full set of English pronunciations (by about the age of five or six).

5 From birth to first birthday: an introduction to English phonology

Babies are born communicators. They leave us in no doubt that they have arrived in the world and are well equipped with strong lungs, a diaphragm and vocal cords. They can produce pain and pleasure sounds immediately. Aaaaaaaaaagh! is the first vowel sound, almost primeval; mmmmmmmmm! is the first consonant, expressing comfort and satisfaction.

Babies are also born listeners. All the bones of their bodies are soft to allow for physical growth (notice how the bones of the skull do not join up until later), except for the three bones in the middle ear (the ossicles) that transmit sounds to the aural nerve system. They are still capable of growth but must be hard from the start in order to to carry the vibrations in the air. You probably know already that an important part of post-natal care is observing whether or not a child shows a physical response to sounds from different directions, especially from behind. It is a standard test for deafness.

Through the early months, children grow in language as well as in body, noticing where sounds come from, recognising familiar, repeated sounds, from mother and other close ones, responding positively to friendly, reassuring sounds, and reacting negatively to unfriendly, frightening sounds, e.g. the loud voice of an otherwise affectionate stranger who cannot understand why he has made the baby cry. Babies show an early ability to distinguish human speech sounds from other sounds in the environment; they are tuned in, if you like, to language. They burble and babble, begin to notice their own vocal sounds and repeat some of them, often laughing with delight. They also like appreciative adults and older children who babble along with them interactively. Explicit meanings are of course out of the question but much bonding and many unspoken meanings are made without the use of recognisable words. By the time they are about six months old, babies in English speaking families and communities have acquired a distnctive English intonation pattern, long before they know any English words to say with it. It sounds like the chant, 'da de da de da de da', and is the basis of such familiar, everyday speech patterns as 'You put the kettle on, I'll make some lunch'. This is an iambic pentameter line (ten syllables with a distinctive stress pattern) and is also frequent in English poetry, 'I met a traveller from an antique land' or 'Shall I compare thee to a summer's day?'

French babies, on the other hand, acquire quite different intonation patterns, corresponding to the patterns of French adult speakers. So too, do infants of other languages all over the world, which partly explains why, when you are learning a second language, it is the intonation patterns of native speakers that make understanding difficult even when you know the individual words used and their grammatical construction.

By the time a child has reached its first birthday it will have begun to acquire the phonology of the English language. This means that it will be on the way to using the 44 sounds (a mixture of vowels and consonants) that make up the sound system of spoken English in the British Isles. This needs a little explanation.

Human speech sounds, and the combinations in which they occur, vary from language to language across the world. All manner of sounds may be produced by the human voice, some of which may be regarded as comic, rude, offensive, or non-verbal expressions of feeling, others work together to form the recognised meaning system of that language. Some philosophers of the Ancient World attempted to explain the origin of speech in onomatopoeia but common sense shows that for every word in English that sounds like the thing it represents, there are tens of thousands that don't. Words such as 'splash', 'crack' and 'clang' do have an onomatopoeic character, but how would you explain a word like 'tree'? Moreover, when you consider the French and German equivalents, 'arbre' and 'baum' it would be farcical to try and argue which version sounded most like the thing represented. (There are possibilities here for a comedy script, possibly set in Brussels!)

Out of the world repertoire of possible speech sounds, each different language has selected its own set and uses them as sound symbols to make meaningful words. A term given to these individual, meaningful sounds is 'phoneme'. Phonology is the study of the phonemes of a particular language and the range of combinations and variations that express meaning. Do remember that phonology is a study of how meanings are made. Phonetics, on the other hand, is the study of speech sounds as such, regardless of the language spoken. Speech therapists from all over the world, for example, will have a great deal in common so far as their work is concerned, but may speak entirely different languages. Articulatory phonetics is concerned with speech production (a science of special interest to speech therapists); auditory phonetics is concerned with how speech sounds are received (a science of special interest to hearing specialists); acoustic phonetics is a pure science that investigates the noise speech sounds make (of special interest to recording engineers and manufacturers of voice controlled security systems, for example).

The International Phonetic Alphabet (IPA) makes it possible for linguists, speech therapists, modern language teachers and dictionary compilers to indicate accurately the pronunciation of a particular sound or word. It is better than phonetic spelling in that it is not dependent on previous knowledge of a language. Such phonetic spellings as 'Roight mite' (Right mate) and 'Avyernot' (Have you not) would help an English speaker recognise a Londoner and a Blackburnian in print but a Scandinavian or a Nigerian reader might well have some difficulty. If, however, they are written in IPA, there is no doubt.

At first you will find IPA odd, but it is an easy thing to refer to, when you need it. The IPA symbols for the 44 phonemes of English are set out in *Figure 1.2*. You don't need to learn these by heart (unless you wish to!) for you will never be tested on them in an exam. However, using them now and again in a transcript, to show exactly how a word or phrase was spoken, will raise A level English coursework distinctly out of the amateur class.

ACTIVITY 5

IPA transcription

Using the IPA symbols (see *Figure 1.2* below) write out your name and address. Don't be fooled by the conventional spelling.

You can give yourself more practice by working with a partner. Send each other one-sentence messages.

What details are you beginning to notice about English spelling when the written symbols are compared with the actual sounds?

The International Phonetic Alphabet is given below along with examples of each sound in English words. The small (r) symbol indicates vowels that are known as 'r' controlled, that is they blend with an 'r' sound. Look at the examples and say them aloud, listening for the 'r'. The slanting lines are traditionally used to indicate a phoneme – a sound unit that has a distinct meaning.

The consonant sounds of English are:

/p/	as in *part*	/f/	as in *food*	/h/	as in *has*
/b/	as in *but*	/v/	as in *voice*	/m/	as in *mat*
/t/	as in *too*	/θ/	as in *thing*	/n/	as in *not*
/d/	as in *did*	/ð/	as in *this*	/ŋ/	as in *long*
/k/	as in *kiss*	/s/	as in *see*	/l/	as in *let*
/g/	as in *get*	/z/	as in *zoo*	/r/	as in *red*
/tʃ/	as in *chin*	/ʃ/	as in *she*	/j/	as in *yes*
/dʒ/	as in *joke*	/ʒ/	as in *measure*	/w/	as in *will*

The vowel sounds of English are:

(long vowels)		(short vowels)		(diphthongs)	
/ɪː/	as in *each*	/ɪ/	as in *it*	/eɪ/	as in *day*
ɑː $^{(r)}$/	as in *car*	/e/	as in *then*	/ar/	as in *by*
/ɔː $^{(r)}$/	as in *more*	/æ/	as in *back*	/ɔɪ/	as in *boy*
/uː/	as in *too*	/ʌ/	as in *much*	/əʊ/	as in *no*
/u: $^{(r)}$/	as in *word*	/ɒ/	as in *not*	/aʊ/	as in *now*
		/ʊ/	as in *put*	/ɪə$^{(r)}$/	as in *near*
		/ə/	as in *again*	/eə$^{(r)}$/	as in *there*
				/ʊə$^{(r)}$/	as in *truer*

Figure 1.2 The International Phonetic Alphabet

Think of phonemes as a set of sound symbols more useful to listeners than to speakers. Each is a kind of norm that enables a listener to recognise the meaning of a sound even when the speaker may have an accent quite different from the listener's. We said earlier that everybody has a personal language profile. It's called an idiolect. All manner of physiological, psychological and cultural factors have made your way of speaking the way it is so that the very sound of your voice has a 'you ness' about it that everybody knows and loves – well, almost everybody. The actual speech sounds you produce are properly called 'allophones', and it is the difference in the speaking of those allophones that accounts for much of the difference heard between two voices saying the same words.

The following words are each made up of three phonemes:

Bit fit git hit kit lit nit pit sit tit wit zit

You will notice that the middle vowel phoneme and the final consonant phoneme remain the same for each word, only the initial consonant phoneme changes BUT that single change makes all the difference to the meaning of each word.

Exploring English phonology

The meanings of words are symbolised in a far more sophisticated way than onomatopoeia could ever explain.

1 Look again at the list of words above. Keeping the first and last phonemes constant, go through the remaining vowels (a, e, o, u) and substitute for the 'I,' each one of the other four. Put on one side any new combination, e.g. lat, wat, that does not appear to be a known word. Check in a large dictionary. Just use the initial consonants we have given you above.

2 Now choose any vowel other than 'i' and see if other initial consonants will form a word. Keep the final consonant constant.

3 Now choose another vowel. Keep the initial consonants we gave you but change the final consonant. Go through the letters of the alphabet sequentially, putting on one side 'words' you are not sure about.

4 There is no need to follow the logic of this activity exhaustively. You will soon begin to see how many possibilities there are for slight changes of sound to result in huge changes of meaning.

5 Now select some of the words, and working with a partner, listen for the allophonic

differences in your pronunciations of the words. A final phoneme may be omitted, an initial one may be more stressed. Pay particular attention to the differences in vowel pronunciation. Listen carefully. Then try a few polysyllabic words where differences of pronunciation will become more noticeable.

6 Select any five words you have looked at and see if the IPA spelling would correspond with the English alphabetical spelling. It will for some but not for others. Notice, for example that the short 'a' in 'bat' would be written as an æ as in b æ t.

7 Test the accuracy of your IPA transcription by giving it as an 'unseen' for a partner to translate. You will find the vowels a little more difficult than the consonants.

8 Finally, if you have the opportunity to work with a student who speaks another language as well as English, compare some of the sounds in the two languages, noting pronunciation features that may cause difficulty. Look particularly for consonant combinations that are 'difficult' and vowel sounds that are unfamiliar. Listen also for rhythms and intonation patterns, i.e. sequences of rising and falling tone.

COMMENTARY You have just looked at a mere fragment of the English vocabulary and at some of the sounds it uses. You may also have had an opportunity to explore a sound system other than English phonology.

Phonemes are a useful way of sorting out all the variants of a particular meaning sound but they are essentially for the use of ears rather than mouths. You probably noticed pronunciation variations between you and the person(s) you worked with. Accent is a useful term here. Accent is the pronunciation characteristic of an individual and of particular groups. Regional dialects contain distinctive pronunciations of certain common words and these pronunciations collectively add up to an accent. Regional accents are a familiar element in people's idiolects. Equally important are accents created in communities of bilingual speakers. What people actually speak are allophones. Don't think of phonemes as 'the perfect English accent'. There is bound to be some correspondence between phonemes and Received Pronunciation but allophonic variations are noticeable even between same age/same gender/same social class/same regional origins speakers.

You will also have noticed that the spellings of English words frequently do not correspond to IPA. The /k/ sound at the beginning of a word like 'cat' is a case in point. This is an issue we shall return to at a later birthday.

We started this section focusing on an infant at the very beginning of life. Any babysitter, brother, sister, parent will have noticed the earnest expressivness, the energy with which children use grunts, wa wa sounds, goo goos and bagabagbagas as an early kind of talk. It is observable both as play and as real communication. Then we looked at the sound system into which children initiate themselves with a little help and encouragement from adults. It is important to recognise that children learn language by doing things with it, however little they may appear to have. They don't collect the phonemes, like language miles, so that they can then make a meaning or two when they have a full set. Research evidence shows that babies use what sounds they have in systematic ways. A sound like 'na na' will be used to mean one particular thing, e.g. to express annoyance or displeasure, whereas 'ne ne', with a big smile, expresses play and pleasure. Punctuation is important right from the start . Babies soon get the message that speech sounds are important to adults, good for communicating with and good for playing with.

There follows a summary of the implications of that first year of your language life for understanding now the nature and functions of language. This in turn will be followed by a summary of implications for an understanding of literature.

Language

1 Language originates as speech and has distinct physical/physiological characteristics. Primary experiences and emotions are embedded and encoded in speech patterns and accompanied by physical behaviour – cuddling, hugging, smiling, smacking, tickling, touching, feeding, etc.
2 Intonation – the tunes of words and phrases – carry meaning in addition to dictionary meanings. All kinds of emotions, affections, implications are carried by the sounds as distinct from the dictionary meanings.
3 Our first experiences of language are interpersonal and closely bound to social and cultural contexts.
4 Personal growth and language growth are closely interwoven. The way you speak is partly governed by biological factors but also by cultural influences evident in accent.
5 English phonology consists of a relatively small number of sounds capable of generating a huge number of words. Patterns, alliterative coincidences, close similarities rhymes, repeated vowel sounds (assonance) are bound to be frequent, but meaning differences can be both subtle and vast.
6 Speech and early vocalisation both vary in a number of ways: pace, volume, pitch, duration, stress. A prolonged utterance by a twelve-month-old gives delight because, while you haven't a clue what is meant, it will appear to be an adult sentence.
7 Language development from the cradle to the grave is a fascinating mixture of creative urge to fulfil your own purposes with whatever resources you've got, and imitation of what is going on in the immediate environment.

Literature

1 Throughout this book you will be reminded that writing does not have the physical presence, the interactive immediacy or the spontaneous time scale of spoken language. Even when a work of literature is very exciting and full of characters shouting at each other, it takes place inside a reader's head. The reader has activated it, but it's still a put-up job compared to the authenticity of two real life speakers who, unlike characters in fiction, have no idea what they are going to say next. Yes, you can curl up with a good book, but reading is essentially an intellectual activity; it is ideational (goes on inside your head) whereas talk is interpersonal. The distinction between ideational and interpersonal is a useful one. Another is the distinction between spectator language, where you are apart from actions and speech in fiction, watching and listening, and participant language, where you are involved in real actions with real people.

2 It is very easy to read conversation in a novel or play, or to read a poem, without actually hearing or listening to it. If, as we have seen in a child's first year of life, intonation is so important, then it is highly likely that literature is written to be heard as well as read. Public poetry readings, radio dramatisations of novels, can be wonderful experiences but it is also necessary to hear books with an inner ear to catch nuances of meaning and to enjoy them to the full.

3 Despite the important differences between speech and writing indicated above (there's a phrase you can't use in speech – 'indicated above'!) literary works are frequently rooted in primary experiences of the spoken language. Playscripts and dialogue in novels are two obvious examples. The huge repertoire of storylines upon which many writers draw, stretches back into ancient, oral traditions that predate written versions by as much as thousands of years. The Bible and other religious texts are written versions of much older tales handed down through memory. Narrative poetry descends from spoken sagas, while the very term 'lyric' reminds us that poetry originated in song. Paradoxically, the spoken word lies at the heart of literature.

4 The frequent use of the terms 'voice' and 'tone' in literary criticism to describe particular personal qualities and nuances of expression, remind us again that literature is not entirely disembodied. One of the main concerns for creative writing coursework is 'finding the right voice' or making what you write 'sound right', yet further evidence of how easily we talk about writing in speech, or phonological, terms.

5 Even before their first birthday, children show an awareness of rhythm and sound repetition, both important elements in poetry. The notion that young children are closer to the spirit, and the fun of poetry as sound is not entirely a fanciful one.

6 All the elements of everyday speech sounds are crucial raw material for poetry, which transforms them into amusing, moving, curious artistic meanings.

7 Just as a child learns to use the sounds of English to make meanings by a mixture of creative urge and approximate imitation, so creative writers express their own 'original' visions and ideas by stretching existing verbal resources and by modifying genre conventions.

6 Now we are one: entering the world of words

Sometimes 'baby's first word' comes at about the time of the first birthday; sometimes even before. But certainly in the second year of life babies are expected to be able to combine speech sounds into an increasing number of words that become more and more recognisable as familiar English pronunciations. Having discovered that speech sounds are important in life, they soon discover that you can achieve vastly more with complete words. It will not be surprising that the naming of things plays an important part in this stage, hence the number of nouns in a child's early vocabulary, reflecting some of the vast number of noun words in any English dictionary. Do not suppose however that their word development is a mere recital or rehearsal of names. There will also be other kinds of words in evidence. Here are some examples:

Again = do it again
Here (accompanied by pointing)
Down (as child sits down).

Clearly there are more to these words than meets the ear. They are surrounded by an invisible grammar that a child is not yet ready to make explicit. That will come later. Even when single noun words are used, the context makes it clear that a child is saying something and not merely practising vocabulary. Here are some examples:

Dada (said as he enters) means 'Here comes dada'
Door (as mother closes it) means 'Mama closes the door'.

Just as babies begin to acquire the sound system of English early in the first year of life (a process that carries on for three or four years more) so in the second year they rapidly build up a personal vocabulary learned through experience. The English vocabulary (also referred to as 'lexis') is not a system in the way that phonology is. It is a massive accumulation of native and acquired words, too highly diversified to be systematic in itself but held together and made usable by grammar as we have already seen. Words enable you to carry the world round in your head, to talk about things that don't exist, to label things, to insult people, make them laugh, cheer them up, talk rubbish or write great poetry. They can have many meanings in themselves as well as in different contexts. Grammar keeps the words tidy.

First though, an activity to get you thinking about words.

ACTIVITY 7

Early words

1 Discuss with a partner the kinds of words adults use with very young children, e.g. Naughty! Make a list, and then sketch a word picture of a child's view of the world gained from significant words used by adults:

Good boy! No! Bad doggie! and so on. Notice how words are loaded with approval, disapproval, menace, humour, encouragement.

2 In recent years, educationists have debated the value of adults using baby-talk. Some

deplore it, others approve. Here are some examples; din din, jim jams, choo choo, beddy-byes, wee wee. Think of some examples you know and discuss:

– why adults do it
– what effect you think it has on children
– why some adults might disapprove
– whether it matters.

3 If you have access to a young child aged between one and two and a half, make notes of the words the child uses and how they are being used, e.g. in what context? For what purpose? Also try out some words of your own to see how the child responds. Make sure you put them in a context, e.g. play a game (Peep Bo) or introduce a toy or animal. If the child is already at the two-word stage you could try adjective noun pairs, e.g. big cat/little cat; red ball/green ball.

4 Notice also words that amuse children. These may be made-up words or dictionary words.

There are four aspects of word acquisition (word power!) that have implications for a general understanding of the nature and functions of language.

1 Children encounter a large number of words through speech, long before they can read. They seem to find it very easy to make these words their own, to wear them comfortably, to use them confidently. In adult life too, many words are encountered through speech in social contexts, on specific occasions.

ACTIVITY 8

Nice words and naughty words

With a partner, consider occasions when you encountered (not necessarily as a child) a new word.

Does it make a difference that a word is encountered in the spoken rather than the written medium?

Are there words that belong to the spoken language rather than the written language? Think of some examples, e.g. slang and so-called colloquialisms.

When you have discussed this, consider the kinds of censorship or disapproval that some adults place on young children's innocent uses of 'rude' words. What do you think a child learns about life through approval or disapproval of the words it utters?

Are there words of which you have come to disapprove or dislike strongly?

2 Young children learn the words of their families and local/regional communities. Social class will also play a part. Early words and experiences of language are learned in usually intimate, familiar contexts which bond the words and the speakers very closely. Distinctive words are a feature of all dialects whether regional, social or occupational. Key dialect words usually refer to basic things: kinds of food and drink; feeling ill; locations (e.g. ginnel/alley/snicket); games; feeling happy. If you add these special, everyday words and phrases to the intonation patterns being acquired you can see how early in life the accents and vocabulary of a regional dialect are acquired.

ACTIVITY 9

Dialect words

Make a list of what would be considered dialect words in your part of the world. Make your list into a little dictionary for visitors. Be humorous if you wish; dialect seems to bring out both good and bad humour in people. Make sure your humour is good humour. Dialects are 'funny' but so are people. There is a saying: Mess with my dialect and you mess with me!

When you have looked at your region's dialect words, compare them with another part of the country. You can do this by consulting other people and by looking at an English dialects atlas. Why do you think dialect words continue to exist? Where do the old ones come from? Can you think of any new ones, not necessarily regional, but peculiar to new generations of children?

3 It is useful to think of your personal vocabulary in two parts. One is your active vocabulary, words you use very frequently in speech and words that most likely spring to mind unbidden when you write informally. It is a very handy mental arrangement that there are plenty of ever-ready words just waiting to be used. People have lots of ever-ready words in common but there are always variations. Just ask any two English speakers to give you the plot of a set book and instantly you will see what we mean. The problem with ever-readiness is that the words become habits; they start to use you rather than your using them.

4 The other kind of vocabulary is referred to as a passive vocabulary, much of which will be received through reading, formal lectures and media talk. This is the one you rummage in, hoping to find an alternative or the 'right' word when you are writing something thoughtful.

Like travel, new words broaden the mind; they are indeed 'language power'. Children acquire new words at a remarkable rate (don't be fooled by a child who doesn't seem to say much; watch how she listens). Children grow up into a vast language in which the words themselves have life histories of their own. Clearly a young child does not reflect on this, but you are now in a position to do so. Language acquisition is a lifelong process and A levels mark a very significant new stage of accelerated word learning.

It helps to understand that the English vocabulary originated from Germanic roots which can be seen clearly in texts written in Old English (aka Anglo Saxon). Following the Norman Conquest, Old English became mixed with a huge number of French words so that by the time of Chaucer's death (1400) the two languages were blended. You should note too that many words of Latin origin came into English via French pronunciations and spellings. Some Latin came in directly through the Church but by no means all of it. French originated as a Romance (i.e. Latin) language, not Germanic, which goes a long way to explaining the spelling peculiarities children encounter when they begin to write English.

At the time of the Renaissance and the new interest in Ancient World science texts, there was a considerable influx of Greek words (Appendix 2 at the end of this chapter gives examples of how the English vocabulary has grown and how its spellings have been affected).

Into the modern world, word borrowings by English have been on a massive, worldwide scale.

ACTIVITY 10

Etymologies and synonyms

1 Working with a partner, make a list of some new words used in English that you have recently learned. They do not have to be A level English words. Write down a definition of your own, then check in a dictionary.

2 Now look up the origin of the words. You will need a dictionary that gives etymologies at the bottom of the entry. (There are dictionaries that just give etymologies.) The code will be explained in the introductory section, e.g. ON = Old Norse; Ar = Arabic; ME = Middle English and so on.

3 Think about someone you know and see if there are some favourite or typical words that spring to mind. Are there some words you use a lot (though you may be the last to know!).

4 Why do you think some words are longer than others? You need to look at four or five long words to see just how they are constructed.

5 Bookshops usually have two or three different dictionaries of English synonyms on their shelves. They sell well. Linguists say however, that strictly speaking there are no synonyms in English because each set will have slightly different nuances of meaning, and that it is the nuances that make all the difference. Collect some pairs, trios, quartets of synonyms, e.g. strange, odd, alien, outlandish and explore just what the nuances are that make a person choose one in a particular context as opposed to any of the others.

The poet T. S. Eliot talked about 'the intolerable wrestle with words' as an inevitable process creative writers go through. Katherine Mansfield said about one of her short stories, 'There mustn't be one word out of place, or one word that could be taken out. That's how I aim my writing. It will take some time to get anywhere near there.' The significance of word acquisition for your understanding of literary texts is to make sure you acquire them rather than they acquire you. This is especially true of the coursework you write, if you are to be in control of it.

ACTIVITY 11

Missing words

The following poems have had certain words removed. Replace them with suitable alternatives. You may choose the same one as the poet, sometimes; you may never choose the same one. The aim of this activity is not to choose the 'right' words but to compare your choices with those of the poets. Word choice is an influential factor on literary style.

This activity will draw attention to distinctive word choices. Stylistics is a matter of not taking words for granted, and of exploring the effects of the ones chosen out of many possibilities.

You will find the complete texts of these poems in Appendix 1 at the end of the chapter.

At Night

To W.M.

Home, . . . from the horizon . . . and . . .,
Hither the soft wings . . .;
. . . of the memories of the . . .
The . . . doors of sleep.

Oh, which are they that . . . through . . . light
Of all these . . . birds?
Which with the . . . and the . . . flight?
Your . . . to me, your . . .!

Alice Meynell

Especially when the October wind

Especially when the October wind
With . . . fingers . . . my hair,
Caught by the . . . sun I walk on . . .
And cast a shadow . . . upon the land,
By the . . . side, hearing the . . . of birds,
Hearing the raven . . . in winter . . .,
My . . . heart who . . . as she talks
Sheds the . . . blood and drains her . . . .

Dylan Thomas

Poetic voices

Below are two excerpts from longer poems. One is by John Milton, the other by William Barnes. You can look up their dates and details later; just concentrate on their choices of vocabulary and comment on the differences.

Since I noo mwore do zee your feace,
Up steairs or down below,
I'll zit me in the lwonesome pleace
Where flat-bough'd beech do grow:
Below the beeches' bough, my love,
Where you did never come,
An' I don't look to meet ye now,
As I do look at hwome.

Since you noo mwore be at my zide,
In walks in zummer het,
I'll goo alwone where mist do ride,
Drough trees a- drippen wet:
Below the rain-wet bough, my love,

Where you did never come,
An' I don't grieve to miss ye now,
As I do grieve at hwome.

Wm Barnes

Where were ye, Nymphs, when the remorseless deep
Closed o'er the head of your loved Lycidas?
For neither were ye playing on the steep
Where your old bards, the famous Druids, lie,
Nor on the shaggy top of Mona high,
Nor yet where Deva spreads her wizard stream.
Ay me, I fondly dream,
Had ye been there! – for what could that have done?
What could the Muse herself that Orpheus bore,
The Muse herself, for her enchanting son
Whom universal nature did lament,
When by the rout that made the hideous roar
His gory visage down the stream was sent,
Down the swift Hebrus to the Lesbian shore.

John Milton

The first of these uses features of a regional dialect as it would be spoken. Is it possible that the second one is a special kind of literary dialect?

ACTIVITY 13

Keywords

With the aid of IT, linguists can easily compile concordances (i.e. systematic lists) of words occurring in the works of a particular novelist – their favourite words.

Look at the novel(s) you studied for O level or GCSE (or any other literature exam) and scan through to see if you can spot any words or phrases that are characteristic of the book – key words, if you like. They don't have to be frequent ones.

You can repeat this exercise with Shakespeare plays.

If you wish, you could play a game of collecting a group of significant words from a well known book (not names, of course) and asking a partner to guess the book. You could reveal the clues one at a time. Here are some fairly easy ones:

battle/dagger/blood/witches = *Macbeth*

Quite/absolutely indifferent/notorious domesticity/handbag = *The Importance of Being Earnest.*

7 Now we are two: joined up thinking

Psychologists and linguists agree that the first three years of language learning are an intellectual achievement unequalled by anything else in life, so far as sheer quantity and speed of learning are concerned. It helps to think of a child as a highly observant, experimental scientist constantly noticing things, guessing, trying again, playing with the raw data, making errors and learning from them, beginning to recognise 'rules' and spotting exceptions (of which there are so many in English), looking for patterns and irregularities. Just listing the range of mental activities that go on in language learning makes your head spin!

The very speed of the process, coupled with so much intelligent guesswork, makes imitation of adults a very unlikely explanation. True, English phonology and vocabulary learning have a large element of imitation in them, but when it comes to grammar – the stuff that holds together the phonology and the words so that they make meanings – innate programming remains the best explanation so far. Humans, says Noam Chomsky, are programmed to be grammatical. It's a part of DNA. The actual grammar rules they adopt will be determined by the language into which they are born, but if they did not have the grammatical instinct to start with, they could not acquire communicative competence in language as we now know it.

The great high spot then, in language learning, is not so much the first word, welcome and delightful as that is, but the first putting together of two words. If words are to make meanings they have to be joined together by invisible but nevertheless controlling grammatical patterns or rules. This grammatical connection between words is what is meant by 'syntax'. Syntax is joined-up language, if you like, and it is not stretching the point too far to describe syntax as joined-up thinking as well.

During the second year of life, roundabout 18 months, babies start to generate what are referred to as 'two-word utterances', hence the term 'two-word stage' to distinguish it from the 'one-word stage' earlier. The third year of life, and onwards to the next two birthdays, is characterised not just by verbalising but by sentence making. At the one-word stage, we said that single words are embedded in grammar. They have to be if they are to fulfil a purpose, and a child's use of language, like an adults, is ninety-nine per cent of the time purposeful. Two-word utterances reveal the grammar a little more explicitly. Here are some examples:

Baby chair = The baby is sitting on the chair
Doggie bark = The dog is barking
Ken water = Ken is drinking water
Hit doggie = I hit the doggie
Daddy hat = Daddy's hat.

The above examples have not been made up; they are data from a language acquisition study in which the researcher observed carefully the context of the language use in order to interpret accurately the child's meaning. The grammatical relation between each pair of words can be described as follows:

Agent–location (the baby is the agent but the verb is omitted in favour of its location)
Agent–action (this time the verb is stated)
Agent–object (again, the verb is unstated but an object is stated)

Action–object (this time the agent of the action is unstated but the verb and its object are stated)

Possessor–possessed (the apostrophe 's', signifying possession has been omitted).

You can see that grammar here is not simply a matter of being 'correct' or 'proper', but a matter of expressing important concepts such as: who does what? to whom? where? and who owns or possesses what. And there are many more possibilities for a child to express as it grows day by day.

Some years ago a serious and influential research paper was published called, 'How Little Sentences Grow Into Big Ones', a title which describes exactly the process through which young children's language development goes from the second birthday onwards.

ACTIVITY 14

Grammatical words

Look at the examples below of utterances collected from studies of different children between the ages of 28 months and 34 months. Guess at the likely meaning and write out a grammatically complete or explicit version; e.g. play ball = play ball with me.

Big drum
Lost shoe

Allgone milk
What name (said in a questioning tone)
Chair broken
I good boy
Where teddy?
Car make noise
I got bikky
Mine car.

COMMENTARY

Occasionally you may have had to supply a verb, and it is likely to have been a form of the verb 'to be' or 'to have', the most frequently used verbs in the English Language, e.g. is, been, was, am, have, had.

You will also have had to supply other kinds of grammatical words such as: the, a, my, this, that, your.

Grammatical words don't have any content meaning in themselves but they help other words like verbs and nouns to have meaning. Just look, for example, at how the meaning of a commonplace word like 'get' can be changed radically by the addition of little grammatical words; get off with; get by; get over it; get on with; get away; get out; getup (as in 'You aren't going in that getup are you?'); get up; get down; get off; get along.

ACTIVITY 15

Sentences

Sentences are not just strings of words; they are structures in which there are places for the words and every word needs to be in its place. This is especially true of English. Remember how, in the first year of life, babies acquire intonation patterns without knowing any words to put in them. Grammatical structures are also shapes and patterns that will accommodate appropriate words, and they match to a considerable extent, intonation patterns. The simplest structure of all is a list of items: e.g. blanket, torch, water bottle, map, compass, whistle. This makes sense by inference, i.e. it sounds like a list of things (nouns) you would take with you on a hike. The following list, however, is merely a string of words, with no grammatical pattern and no other connection that can be inferred: although, when, giraffe, therefore, blue, probably, but.

ACTIVITY 16

Grammar and rhythm

The American avant garde composer John Cage once remarked: 'I have nothing to say and I am saying it, and that is poetry.'

If you think about this for a while it is not as nonsensical as it might first appear. The poet Edwin Morgan gave it a great deal of thought and wrote a poem entitled *Opening The Cage*, which consists of John Cage's words rearranged fourteen different ways.

Read the poem through first, and then read each line separately using rhythm, emphasis and pauses to make the line mean something. It can be done with nearly all of them if you persist, and is an object lesson on how grammar and rhythm are related. It is true, some lines have a word order that seems to defeat grammatical sense, but not many.

Opening the Cage

(Fourteen lines on fourteen words)

I have to say poetry and is that nothing and am I saying it

I am and I have poetry to say and is that nothing saying it

I am nothing and I have poetry to say and that is saying it

I that am saying poetry have nothing and it is I and to say

And I say that I am to have poetry and saying it is nothing

I am poetry and nothing and saying it is to say that I have

To have nothing is poetry and I am saying that and I say it

Poetry is saying I have nothing and I am to say that and it

Saying nothing I am poetry and I have to say that and it is

It is and I am and I have poetry saying say that to nothing

It is saying poetry to nothing and I say I have and I am that

Poetry is saying I have it and I am nothing and to say that

And that nothing is poetry I am saying and I have to say it

Saying poetry is nothing and to that I say I am and have it

Edwin Morgan

You can discover some of the grammatical principles or 'rules' that bind English word orders together by playing the following game with a partner. Each of you write a longish sentence (say, 10 words or more) and then write it down in a jumbled word order. First, see how long it takes to unscramble each sentence *then* write down the 'rules' that told you where each word belonged. (Remember that questions can be written in the word order of statements if you forget to put the question mark in!)

As you do this activity, you will in fact be making a start on writing down the rules of English syntax.

COMMENTARY   Like English phonology, English grammar is a system. If it were not systematic, it would be of no use to humans wanting to make meanings with it. There is plenty of room for originality of expression but there are also outer limits which must be observed if communication is to work effectively. Being able to include knowledge of grammar in your repertoire of approaches to text analysis is an important part of a Language and Literature course. An outline of English grammar is given in Chapter Six of *Living Language* (Keith and Shuttleworth, 2000).

For the moment, just concentrate on sentences. So far you have considered how infants move through sounds, then words, then grammar in their acquisition of language. Remember, that we are still only concerned with speaking and listening. Literacy (reading and writing) is not on the horizon just yet. The grammar of sentences, or sentence grammar as it is sometimes called, will be your main concern when investigating texts to see how they are constructed and how meanings are made. Grammar can be divided into two principal areas of study: MORPHOLOGY and SYNTAX. Morphology is the study of how single words are constructed and how their structure may be changed to do a grammatical job within the sentence. Syntax is the study of how two or more words are combined. It's about joined-up words and the rules for joining them. Ultimately, it's about joined-up thinking. Children's 'mistakes' are very instructive clues to English morphology. Examples such as the following show that a child can apply one rule in a general way, but needs to know more about irregular forms and exceptions.

1 Them mens
2 We buyed some mices
3 Mine car
4 I runned home
5 Mummy car (i.e. That is mummy's car).

Don't get hooked on the obvious errors, notice that in each case the child is applying a general rule that isn't however completely regular. By the time you were five or six you would have worked out many of the irregularities in English. You now know what is going wrong above:

Child **1** uses plurals but wrong pronoun form and wrong noun form
Child **2** uses past tense and plural, but again wrong forms
Child **3** singular noun but wrong pronoun form
Child **4** past tense conveyed but wrong verb form
Child **5** possession implied but not indicated by the final 's' sound (in speech) or the apostrophe 's'.

Essentially, English morphology is about fastening bits of words (bound morphemes) onto free-standing words (free morphemes). These 'bits' are technically referred to as 'morphemes' or 'affixes' or 'prefixes and suffixes'. Occasionally, you come across an 'infix' as in (man/men or woman/women), a fairly self-explanatory term.

Sometimes you will find interesting morphological features in poetry. Look at the poem *Ozymandias* by Shelley for example (page 263). In it you will notice three words ending with the suffix '-less' (trunkless, lifeless, boundless). Is this an accident, or does the repeated suffix add something to the meaning of the poem?

ACTIVITY 17

Noticing more about everyday grammar
Grammatical choices are made intuitively but their effects sometimes deserve closer scrutiny. Below are ten sentences: seven spoken or written by adults, three spoken by children aged about three. Each sentence is followed by a question to point you in the direction of a grammatical choice. Your task is to say what effect that choice has. You may find some examples of non-standard grammar; don't just say they are wrong, ask why the term non-standard exists? Who says so? And why do we seem to need the term?

1 To err is human: to forgive, divine.
   (What is the effect of the two infinitives? Why the colon? Why the comma? Where would you expect language like this to occur?)

2 I ain't no good at that sort of thing, me.
   (What is the effect of the first person pronoun? Are tag pronouns used in your part of the country? Why do you think they are ingrained in some dialects? What's your view on double negatives?)

3 Actually, I need to give the greenhouse a good clearout.
   (Why do people often front their sentences with an adverb like 'actually', which is such a common one that children of six or seven use it? Notice the two compound nouns.

Compounding is a distinct feature of English word building. Think of some others. Why do we do it?)

4 Your country needs you.
   (What is the effect of statements that use the second person voice?)

5 I would if I could, but I can't.
   (What is the effect of using what are called 'modal verbs', i.e. 'would', 'could' and 'can't'?)

6 I don't want put in chair.
   (What is the missing morphology?)

7 Nobody don't likes me.
   (Again, what's happening to the morphology?)

8 What I would say to you is this: this is the best chance for peace we have ever had.
   (spoken in an interview)
   (What is the effect of prefacing a remark in this way? What effect, additionally, does the modal have?)

9 No, I don't want to sit seat?
   (How do you make sense of this?)

10 Even though you have come early for once and done your best in difficult circumstances, it still isn't good enough.
   (The main point of this sentence [its subject and main verb] come after the comma. Why do we construct sentences sometimes, with so much modification at the beginning?)

Birthday number three

If you look in Appendix 3 at the end of this chapter you will see a summary of pioneer researches by Howard Lenneberg, an American researcher of language acquisition in young children. You will see that by the age of three a remarkable amount has been achieved. Look especially at the summaries for thirty months and for three years. Remember though, that these are statistical generalisations.

Without tying language development too much to specific ages, it is reasonable to view young children as progressing through three major dimensions of language: first, the sound system, next the wordhoard (an Anglo-Saxon term for vocabulary), and then grammar, though we have already seen that the word stage and the grammar stage overlap, just as the phonological stage goes on into the school years. Once the three elements, sounds, words and grammar, are acquired and developing rapidly in all manner of personal and social contexts, the rest of the language learning story is all *pragmatics*. This needs some explanation because it is a key concept in understanding language use whether in everyday life or in literature. It is an aspect of language acquisition that is certainly lifelong and will play a considerable part in your own progress as an A level student.

Pragmatics, as linguists understand it today, began as a study of how speakers and listeners understand each other, especially when so many meanings in everyday talk are implied meanings, dependent upon context as much as on word meaning and grammar. Words cannot be taken at face, or 'ear', value; agendas can be hidden ones; texts have subtexts. Everywhere there is a concern about lack of communication, misreading, and of saying the wrong thing. Think how familiar are such sayings as: Do you get my meaning? What I mean to say is …. Do you see what I mean? You've got to say what you mean and mean what you say (easy advice to give, difficult to put into *practice* [same word family as ' pragmatics']).

Young children have to learn through language a wide range of social attitudes and behaviour encoded in the language. Pragmatics is very much a matter of knowing the code, whether at an interview or trying to read a particularly obtuse poem. A young child who replies, 'Yes, he is', to a question on the telephone, 'Is your daddy in?', and then puts the phone down, doesn't realise that the question really means, 'I want to speak to your daddy'. That's pragmatics. You learn it through social experience for phone calls and reading experience for poetry.

We shall look more closely at pragmatics in life and literature when exploring conversations in Chapters 4 and 5.

ACTIVITY 18

Saying the right thing

Pragmatics is very much a matter of understanding the rules or the codes that govern whatever kind of conversation in which you are participating. Meanings are exchanged more by implication than explicitly. Most of the time humans are extraordinarily cooperative.

Working with a partner, write a short sketch for two or three people in which one is clearly not on the same wavelength as the others and isn't picking up the inferences. The dramatist Harold Pinter is a good example of this kind of writing. Some of the sketches by The Two Ronnies are also good examples.

ACTIVITY 19

Double meanings

Language has a life of its own; it can use you without your even noticing, just as much as you use it. Words have many meanings, as any dictionary will reveal. Everyday misunderstandings are common enough, resulting in good humour, bad humour, embarrassment, and deep hurt.

There is a familiar vocabulary to cover varieties of double (multi) meanings: ambiguity, irony, puns, double entendres, implied meaning, sarcasm, inference. You could even include metaphor, since people do not literally 'kick the bucket', 'bite the bullet' or 'eat their hearts out'. Euphemisms too, are ways of being ultra polite, of not saying literally what you mean: 'I am going to the bathroom' or 'She's passed over'.

The modern concern for political correctness is an example of pragmatic awareness of how the names people are called by, can imply, intentionally or otherwise, devaluation, offence, unfair discrimination and all manner of prejudices.

Choose two ways in which meanings are implied by writers/inferred by readers (e.g. puns, irony, euphemism, political correctness) and think of examples from both life and literature. Advertising and politics are good sources in everyday life, Shakespeare, Hardy and Blake are good sources in literature.

Where would you place comedians (one of the most obvious sources)? Somewhere between life and literature?

The process in which a young child begins to 'read' implied meanings and to recognise that words, like things, are sometimes not what they seem, continues throughout life. In an important sense, babies are born readers, not in the sense that they can read print, but in the sense that they very early on search for meanings in their immediate environment. Focusing on a mother's face, for example, and recognising familiar gestures and noises as 'friendly' ones, sensing moods and learning to respond are all evidence of a child's ability to read the world it has been born into.

Ferdinand de Saussure (1857–1913) a linguist who has been extremely influential on the development of our understanding of the nature of language, viewed language as a sign system embedded in other kinds of sign and signal systems operating in all aspects of our everyday lives. Many meanings are communicated without words: body language, facial expression, dress codes, flags, badges, mathematical symbols, logos, map symbols, musical notation. Even buildings communicate impressions of power, wealth, importance, besides being useful for a specific function. The way in which a room is decorated and furnished (and whether it is tidy or not!) will communicate signals to a receptive observer. The general word used to describe the many sign and signal systems in any social context is *semiotics*. The key concept here is *meaning*: the signs communicate meanings. Notice the family connection between 'semiotics' and 'semantics'. Semantics is the study of how meanings are made and communicated. Saussure classified verbal language under the heading of semiotics. Another linguist, Michael Halliday, describes language as a 'social semiotic' which sounds a bit of a mouthful. All it means is that language is a system for making meanings that other people can understand and share. It is a sign system that binds people together in a communication network that can be taken for granted most of the time.

In the next three activities you are going to explore ways in which language combines with non-verbal sign systems to make additional, implicit meanings, first in everyday life, then in film and TV and finally in plays and novels.

ACTIVITY 20

Reading people
Life is full of close encounters of the language kind, rich in pragmatics. Think of pragmatics here as guessing rightly or wrongly what someone actually means, falling out for no apparent reason, being unable to say what you want to say or saying the wrong thing, getting on like a house on fire with a perfect stranger.

With a partner, look at the following statements, and choose two or three where you have experienced something very similar. Discuss social, psychological and any other factors that would explain the situation in which such statements are likely to occur. Draw on your own experience but make your explanation as objective as possible.

Write up one of your explanations as an example of pragmatics in action for an encyclopaedia article.

1 Why is it you always twist what I say?
2 You can never get a word in edgeways.
3 I just don't believe a word he says.
4 You've got to get them on your wavelength.
5 I can read your mind.
6 Stop repeating everything I say.
7 Don't go on and on about it. Let it drop, can't you.
8 I'm just a girl who can't say 'No'.
9 I knew you weren't listening. What have I just said?
10 That's right! Walk away. You never talk.
11 Look at me when I am talking to you.
12 Watch my lips.

Next, make a list of the kinds of non-verbal signs and signals (personal and contextual) that assist words to make their meanings. You could also list signs and signals that inhibit verbal communication.

ACTIVITY 21

The moving image
The last activity was concerned with interactive situations in which you could draw on your experience as a participant. This activity focuses on the ways in which you read two dimensional signs and signals purely as a spectator of films and television. Some of the questions and tasks below require you to look closely at a video you have taped or acquired beforehand; others may be discussed with a partner from recollected experience.

1 What are the non-verbal signs and signals early on in a film that tell you who is a 'goody' and who is a 'baddy'. (Physical build? Kind of smile? Gesture or habit? Associated objects? Clothes? Setting?) You may include tone of voice on the grounds that it is not so much what is said as the way in which it is said.

2 You could extend the above question to other themes such as: How do you know that two people will fall in love before the film ends? What makes you guess that a character will turn out weak? Treacherous? Or become a victim? How do you know which one will get the woman or the man in the end? Or who has got to die?

3 Get hold of any video of a film you have not seen before and watch the first seven minutes. Then guess, from the clues you have already read in the characters' behaviour and from the story so far, how the film will turn out. You may not be very accurate about actual plot details but note such unspoken things as mood, atmosphere, pace, contrasts. Remember that you are watching actors, a director and a set designer at work.

4 Videotape a discussion programme and observe in detail the non-verbal signs and signals that affect your response or reaction to the words anybody actually says. Observe in particular smiles and laughter (there are many different kinds), body posture, hand movements, angle of the head. You will of course be very much in the hands of a camera crew as to whether you will have any chance to see participants listening, yet listeners also send out signals.

5 In some films, the images of gesture, face, clothes and setting combine to give a line of dialogue a special significance (note the family connection between the words 'sign', 'signal' and 'significance'). The line is made memorable, 'Here's looking at you, kid' and 'Play it, Sam' are well known examples from *Casablanca*. 'Make my day' is another from *Dirty Harry*.

6 Think of a film you have enjoyed and recollect a significant line of dialogue. Then visualise all the images and contextual features that contribute to the significance of the line of dialogue. Tone of voice will also need to be considered.

ACTIVITY 22

Use your imagination

The worlds of film and TV seem so realistic, natural and spontaneous, yet even the briefest introduction to media studies will show how everything you see is framed by the camera and contextualised by a script. This is not to deny that great art can be achieved in both media, but they remain closed worlds, peephole pictures of real life. It is the imagination of both creators and viewers that gives them their significance and their scope.

Novels are, on the face of it, even more closed worlds, relying entirely on words, yet many would argue that the very absence of the visual element allows the imagination much freer rein. Much depends on the implicit relationship established between the writer and the reader, often created by subtle nuances in the language. It is the nuances of style as well as the content that will determine whether or not you are going to get on with a book. Content can raise high expectations in a reader; style will either fulfil them or be a let-down. If you have no style as a storyteller, children will be disappointed. And this is where pragmatics comes in again.

1 Read the following three novel openings and then write down your impressions of the voice that is telling you the story. 'What tone of voice do you hear? What emotion, or lack of it? How are you being addressed? Ask yourself also, such questions as 'What is the author making me look at?' 'Is anything being taken for granted?' 'What shifts of focus occur?'

Details of the authors and their stories will be found on page 39.

(a) 'Come home, Tenar! Come home!'
In the deep valley, in the twilight, the apple trees were on the eve of blossoming; here and there among the shadowed boughs one flower had opened early, rose and white, like a faint star. Down the orchard aisles, in the thick, new, wet grass, the little girl ran for the joy of running; hearing the call she did not come at once, but made a long circle before she turned her face towards home. The mother waiting in the doorway of the hut, with the firelight behind her, watched the tiny figure running and bobbing like a bit of thistledown blown over the darkening grass beneath the trees.

(b) The Blackbird told himself he was drinking too much because he lived in this hotel and the Silver Dollar was close by, right downstairs. Try to walk out the door past it. Try to come along Spadina Avenue, see that goddamm Silver Dollar sign, hundreds of light bulbs in your face, and not be drawn in there. Have a few drinks before coming up to this room with a ceiling that looked like a road map, all the cracks in it. Or it was the people in the Silver Dollar talking about the Blue Jays all the time that made him drink too much. He believed it was time to get away from here, leave Toronto and the Waverley Hotel for good and he wouldn't drink so much and be sick in the morning. Follow one of those cracks in the ceiling.

(c) About fifteen years ago, on a date late in August or early in September, a train drew up at Wilsthorpe, a country station in Eastern England. Out of it stepped (with other passengers) a rather tall and reasonably good-looking man, carrying a handbag and some papers tied up in packet. He was expecting to be met, one would say, from the way he looked about him: and he was, as obviously, expected.

The stationmaster ran forward a step or two, and then, seeming to recollect himself, turned and beckoned to a stout and consequential person with a short round beard who was scanning the train with some appearance of bewilderment. 'Mr Cooper', he called out – 'Mr Cooper, I think this is your gentleman', and then to the passenger who had just alighted, 'Mr Humphreys, sir? Glad to bid you welcome to Wilsthorpe. There's a cart from the Hall for your luggage, and Mr Cooper, what I think you know.'

Some additional questions to bear in mind as you think about these excerpts: Which contains clues to its country of origin? Which is the earliest of the three texts? Which one was written for young readers?

COMMENTARY We have given you novel openings to look at because no previous knowledge of the plot is required, so everybody starts from the same point. It's a bit like greeting someone for the first time. Traits of the author's storytelling style are immediately apparent, just as styles of dress are immediately apparent on first meeting someone.

Because storytelling is such a natural, seductive human activity the pragmatic features are easily taken for granted by readers. Stylistics reads just a bit below the surface and notices what is being taken for granted.

Pronouns are a good place to start. Text (a) is written in the third person, which means that you and the author share the same vantage point on the characters – the third persons. Note though, that the very first words are spoken by a character – we are not sure who until we have read on. The author then chooses to direct the reader's attention to the setting and the actions of a little girl. There are countless other choices that could have been made here but it is significant that describing the scene is a particularly popular opening strategy.

Pragmatics is about people in action and in relationships through language. Notice how the little girl's mother is referred to by the definite article 'the mother'. What difference would it make if the author had written 'her mother' or just 'mother'? The oddity of this is a clue to the genre of the story.

Two pragmatic features then, that we can notice here are the pronoun reference and the immediate use of speech which gives active status in the reader's imagination to one of the characters. Notice too that the speech takes the form of a command sentence repeated. Tension and potential conflict are introduced right at the start. Add to this the slightly disquieting use of the adjective 'darkening' in the last sentence, and your forebodings are likely to be confirmed by the next paragraph:

By the corner of the hut, scraping clean an earth-clotted hoe, the father said, 'Why do you let your heart hang on the child? They're coming to take her away next month. For good. Might as well bury her and be done with it.'

Text (b) is also written in the third person yet seems to come from inside a character's head. As a result, strong impressions of character are given to the reader, but there is also a distinct sense of place. Note too, the use of '*this* hotel', '*this* room' and 'get away from *here*' all create a sense of the here and now. Both texts in fact give quite specific time signals; 'twilight' in (a), while the forward reference to 'in the morning' implies that Text (b) is set in the evening. Always be alert to forward and retrospective references in a text. Sometimes, when you have lost the plot, you physically flip the pages back to check something, but here the author is creating anticipation rather than reminding you of something. Two technical terms here, if you fancy them, are 'anaphoric reference' and 'cataphoric reference'. The first refers to references back, e.g. 'Upset by the events of the previous day, she decided to go away' or 'See Section Three'. The second is anticipatory. In children's storytelling (spoken or written) you often come across, 'This is what we did:' a classic strategy for setting up both the story and the listener.

Text (c) also begins with time signals to the reader (these three texts were chosen entirely at random, by the way) and is again, written in the third person. Notice however, the remark 'one would say' which raises the question of just who is 'one'. We get the impression of a slightly reticent narrator who puts the reader almost in the position of a traveller who might be idly noticing fellow travellers for no particular reason. The second paragraph begins: 'The relation in which these personages stood to each other can be explained in a very few lines.' Notice how the word 'personages' echoes other old fashioned words and phrases, signalling to a modern reader a gap of fifty years or so between text (c) and the other two.

A very simple look beneath the surface of these texts reveals three important kinds of pragmatic information which writers and readers must share with each other: What time is it? Where are we? And Who's who?

In addition to these specific pragmatic features of storytelling, you should consider too, the influence in your imagination of all the visual associations set off by 'deep valley' in (a), 'hundreds of light bulbs' in (b), and 'a country station in Eastern England' in (c). In a small number of words, each author has triggered off in the reader's mind pictures and feelings that would require hundreds of words to express.

Semiotics galore

A significant change that has occurred in A level English Literature over the past fifteen years or so is a stronger recognition of the fact that Shakespeare's plays were primarily written for stage performance. This is reflected in the setting of questions that ask about performance aspects of a play as well as about themes, character and poetry. Modern film and television versions, and new theatre productions, have added much to our understanding. There have of course, been some modern productions that have not only deconstructed the play as we know it, but entirely deconstructed any possibility of enjoying it in production!

For this activity, you will need to get hold of two video versions of the same Shakespeare play. Choose a soliloquy or section of dialogue that interests you and compare in detail the different presentations. Clearly, aspects of tone and voice qualities (e.g. power, sexiness, attractiveness, warmth, declamation) will be important influences on how you respond to what is said, but consider also the messages you are getting from other sources:

- facial expressions (note changes)
- hand movements
- body posture
- dress
- whole body movement (e.g. walking about)
- location (props, scenery)
- camera angles
- music or sound effects
- any other feature of the production or acting style.

You may of course be critical of the way some of these aspects feature in a particular version, but in the first instance, concentrate on what the effects are before you consider your approval or disapproval. You might even suggest some semiotic improvements. Remember that non-verbal signals rarely go unnoticed, but you may not realise you have noticed them!

Birthday number four

In this section you are going to look in more detail at language functions. You may recollect that we said earlier that infants start to 'have a go' at language (by using a limited number of sounds) because they are driven by purpose. By the time children are four they have acquired huge quantities of language and language experience. Their physical, intellectual, social and emotional development have also gone on apace, so that there are many more things they can and want to do with language. Look again at the developmental milestones according to Lenneberg (see Appendix at end of chapter) for thirty months to three years and add to that all the interactive things that adults and three-year-olds can do together, e.g. storytelling, going shopping, watching telly, playing with toys, looking out of the window, bath time, mealtimes, falling out, seeing to cuts and bruises, talking, talking, talking.

Research into what children can do with language soon reveals that their repertoire of language functions is hardly different from that of adults; less sophisticated it may be, and less educated or practised, but still effective for living with. In other words they are competent language users very early on. They are also capable of making their language do a number of things at once. For example a child could tell you something in a slightly whinging way but imply that you should do something about it. There's three functions to start with: informing, self-expression of feeling and persuading an adult. The same child, playing in a rather bossy way with another child, may be self-assertive, instructive and persuasive, all in the same single utterance, 'No! That goes there, see?' The 'see' can be both a question and a directive.

Primary schoolchildren exploring what people use language for, will come up with interesting observations once they get the general idea. You can use language for making people laugh, for hurting people, for telling people, for talking to yourself, ('My granny does that a lot.'), for asking questions, for reading, for telephoning, for being rude, for telling lies, and so on. These are not immature ideas but extremely perceptive. They are, however, *ad hoc*. Professional investigators of language have attempted to be more systematic in describing the range of language functions. None of them though, would exclude the examples just quoted and would indeed commend the children's insight. Here are some examples of a more systematic approach. You will be able to see overlap; the important thing is to trust your own intuitions and use the experience and ideas of others when it is helpful. In other words, don't be afraid of constructing your own model. In your original writing for example, you will need to be clear what its primary purpose or function is, but in your commentary you will need to be able to recognise any additional functions, intended or otherwise (see Chapter 6 on 'The Craft of Writing').

In everyday life nobody would bother to classify language functions, you just get on and do them. But some kinds of research require you to stop and think about why language is being used in the way that it is. The anthropologist, Bronislav Malinowski (1884–1942), for example, had a very pressing need to sort out language functions, because in order to study the social lives of the Trobriand Islanders, among whom he was engaged in extensive fieldwork, he needed to understand their language. He discovered that conventional dictionary meanings and word-for-word translations were quite useless unless you understood the whole way of life in which the language functioned. Meaning would only become clear when you understood the specific way in which the words were being used. Identical words could have quite different meanings in different contexts. Think how confusing everyday English idioms and metaphors can be to intelligent adults learning English as a second language:

'Our lecturer threw a wobbler today.'
'Well, I'll go to our house!'

The following list shows how Malinowski classified the language functions of one particular Polynesian community:

1　The Pragmatic Function – language for getting things done; practical action.

2 The Magical Function – language as a means of controlling the environment; religion.

3 The Narrative Function – language as a storehouse (remenber the Anglo-Saxon term for language, 'the wordhoard') filled with useful and necessary information, e.g. the people's history.

4 Phatic Communion – speech that creates or maintains 'bonds of sentiment' between people, e.g. passing the time of day, chatting about the weather, and greetings such as 'Hi', 'How are you?'

See Malinowski (1923) 'The Problem of meaning in Primitive Languages' in *The Meaning of Meaning* edited by C. K. Ogden and I. A. Richards (Routledge). Not difficult to find and is itself a good example of how an anthropologist uses language. Another of his writings, *Coral Gardens and their Magic* (1935, Allen and Unwin) can also be found through library loan services, and is enjoyable.)

The term 'primitive language' is questioned by linguists nowadays on the grounds that if a language can be used effectively, it can hardly be called primitive, since it must have all the necessary components of sound, vocabulary, grammar and pragmatics.

An English linguist, J. R. Firth (1890–1960) took up the notion of language function as a prime guide to meaning and it was further developed by one of his followers, Michael Halliday: 'The nature of language is closely related to the functions it has to serve' (see 'Language Functions and Language Structures' in 'New Horizons in Linguistics', edited by John Lyons (Penguin, 1970).

When Halliday came to study language acquisition in detail, he worked on the basis of seven language functions, which he describes in his book *Learning How To Mean* (1970). They are summarised below:

1 Instrumental: the 'I want' function by which a child (and adult) satisfies material needs.

2 Regulatory: the 'do that' function by which other people's behaviour can be regulated.

3 Interactional: the 'me and you' function by means of which we interact with others. Adults might put it more politely because they have been socialised; 'you and me'.

4 Personal: the 'here I come' function by means of which we express our own uniqueness.

5 Heuristic: the 'tell me why or what or how' and the 'let's find out' function by which children learn and explore the environment.

6 Imaginative: the 'let's pretend' function whereby playtime and imagined worlds are enjoyed.

7 Informative: the 'I've got something to tell you' function as a means of conveying information. Halliday observes that this function normally comes last in children's language development, round about the second birthday.

An educational researcher at Leeds University, Joan Tough, also needed to systematise language functions so that teachers in different parts of the country could report their observations of infants using language, with some consistency. See, for example, *Focus on Meaning* (Ward Lock,1972), a very readable collection of transcripts and commentaries, and a good model for coursework. She describes language functions as follows:

1 Self-maintenance (i.e. using language to assert your own existence and to reassure yourself).
2 Directing others (i.e. getting people to attend to you and to do what you ask, politely or otherwise).
3 Reporting the scene (i.e. telling what is going on; offering information).
4 Predicting (i.e. talking about what hasn't happened yet; referring to the future).
5 Projecting (i.e. putting yourself in other people's shoes, e.g. 'It must have hurt you').
6 Reasoning (i.e. thinking things through and engaging in arguments).
7 Imagining (e.g. playtime language, e.g. 'I'm a big horse').

ACTIVITY 24

Making your own functions model: for life and literature

1 First, look at the three models given above and think of examples that you think would fit each function. Work through Malinowski, Halliday and Tough in turn.
2 Look at the overlaps and see if any model has an element in it, not in the others. You may decide that the differences are mainly differences of terminology; you may see a distinction.
3 Put the models to one side and brainstorm the idea of language functions. Write down as many as you can; at least thirty. You could in fact think of fifty quite easily, once you get going. Be imaginative!
4 Now sort out your examples and see which models help you most. Aim to construct a model of your own that profits from the work of others but has something of you in it. This is the model that will most help you in examinations.
5 Ask yourself where novels, poems and plays fit in. Do they fulfil lots of language functions or just one?
6 Make a list of special functions observable in literary writing (verbal art), e.g. describing characters, writing dialogue, making words rhyme, choosing a metaphor, inventing a plot. When you have got a list of examples, tidy it up into a useful model, with examples along the lines of Halliday or Tough.
7 What sorts of connections might there be between Malinowski's idea of a magical function and the idea of imaginative function in Halliday and Tough? And what do adults share with young children through the imaginative function, even though they may enjoy quite different things?

Birthday number five

And so, at last, we reach the aspect of language development on which all A level English courses are founded: literacy, that great shift from the world of speaking and listening to the world of the written word. Some chlidren start to read before the age of five, but it is noticeable that the vast majority start somewhere after their fifth birthday. They gain some idea of what a book might be for, they learn the alphabet and they begin to cope with that peculiar set of sight-and-sound misfits, known as English spelling!

For the purpose of this book we are not concerned with the mechanics of reading as decoding but rather with reading as cultural practice. 'Cultural practice' is an especially useful term for a Language and Literature course because it includes the following ideas:

- motivation (What drives you to read voluntarily? What do you enjoy most/least?)
- shared experience (through reading we learn and share hundreds of stories, myths and characters)
- acquiring moral values and beliefs (the goodies and the baddies again)
- growth of the imagination (enjoying/understanding other lives and worlds than our own)
- the teaching of reading and writing in schools.

The onset of reading is synonymous with the beginning of schooling. The two together cause a vast language explosion in the mind, and childhood reading experiences in school and at home are very formative for good or ill. In Hallidayan terms, the move into reading (and writing) is a move from interpersonal uses of language to ideational uses, i.e. interaction not with people but with a printed page which really means language inside the head. The last activity of this chapter will give you an opportunity to look back on your own reading experience up to the age of eleven.

ACTIVITY 25

Reading with attitude
Attitudes toward books, and expectations, are formed early, and they are usually only changed by the strong influence of another person or by a chance discovery on a bookshelf. In this activity, which is an extended questionnaire, you will need to answer each question first and then compare your experiences with those of a partner.

1 Do you have an early memory of being read to? By whom?
2 What is your earliest recollection of reading a book yourself? How much do you remember? The title?
3 What kinds of fiction did you most enjoy as a child? Least enjoy?
4 Do you still read children's fiction with pleasure (even if you wouldn't admit it to some of your friends)?
5 Do you ever remember enjoying poems as a child? How important was hearing and saying them and not just reading them?

6 Make a list of the nursery rhymes and stories you would be able to tell to a four/five-year-old. You may surprise yourself by how many you have never forgotten.
7 If you had to buy five stories for a child aged nine or ten, what would you choose and why?
8 There is a generally accepted view that reading literature is 'good' for children. What good do you think it does?
9 What features of language most put you off a book when you were a child?
10 How would you describe the attitudes you have acquired in childhood toward reading the following: plays, short stories, very long stories, poems, fantasy tales, realistic tales, fiction written pre-1900 (abridged or complete), comics. Have any of your attitudes changed?

ACTIVITY 26

A cautionary tale
We began this chapter with two well known cartoon characters. The final activity looks at a cartoon-like poem by Andrew Stibbs.

Read the poem, which we hope will amuse you. What does it say about language acquisition? What is effective about the format in which it is presented?

What does it suggest about differences between speech and writing?

Write a letter – serious but with a light touch – to the child's mother explaining where she is going wrong.

If We Taught Kids To Speak Like We Teach Them To Write

KID (in kitchen)	MUM (in next room)
Mummy, mummy (pause)	
Mummy, mummy!	Don't repeat yourself dear.
A big cat's just comed in the window.	Grammar!!!
Now puss on stove.	Don't use slang dear. The word is 'cat'.
Now cat in frying pan.	Good!
Fish comed out of pan.	What's the good of my correcting your speech if you take no notice?
Pan falled over. Fire in pan.	That's not a proper sentence, dear.
Now fire in hanged up clothes by chimbly.	Pronunciation!! The word is 'chimney'. Say it out ten times.
Chimney, chimney, chimby, chimly, chimbly … Now fire in granny!!	Try to vary the shape of your sentences, dear.
Now granny in fire!	Better! But make your speech more interesting by using better words.
See how the pretty yellow flames lick round the frail and combustible granny, like the greedy, angry tongues of hungry tigers, which seem … AAAAAAAAAAAAAAGGGGHHHH!!!	Why is this sentence not finished?
	Five out of ten.

Andrew Stibbs

Summary

Necessity, it is sometimes said, is the mother of invention. When humans started to live together in social groups, thousands and thousands of years ago, they invented language because they needed it. They invented it first in the form of speech (writing came much, much later) and they invented it for all kinds of communication purposes, including being able to think. Like all inventions, the rest of the history of language is a story of variations on a theme, and ever more sophisticated and technological developments. When writing was first developed, chalk and slate were every bit as much state-of-the art technology as voice readers are in today's IT world.

Observing the first five years of a child's language development is rather like studying a miniaturised, accelerated version of language evolution in which vital aspects of language are clearly displayed. The summary below lists key concepts, and is followed by a comparative listing of examples of language use in both life (the everyday kind) and literature (the verbal art kind). We are only introducing the concepts in this chapter; your understanding of them will develop as you work your way through the book. The inter-related concepts, e.g. of function and structure, will need to become second nature to your thinking.

Serious misunderstanding or unawareness will show up, for example, in examination answers and cost you valuable marks. They are central to Assessment Objectives and underpin Mark Schemes of all Examination Boards.

1 You have observed five overlapping and interacting features of language in use:
   – Phonology
   – Words (or Lexis or Vocabulary)
   – Grammar (language fastened together)
   – Pragmatics (language in action)
   – Literacy (significantly different from speech in a variety of ways)

2 Language users are primarily meaning makers guided by purposes (or functions). Phonology, words and grammar are the structures acquired in order to make meanings, to make the words do what you want them to do. Structures is another word for 'forms'.

3 It takes at least two to make a meaning: an addresser who creates, originates an utterance or a sentence, and an addressee who receives it. All social uses of language work on that principle, though using language to think with means that you are both addresser and addressee.

4 Along with Structure and Function, there is a third factor to take into account, and that is Effect. When discussing a text in an examination for example, you will need not only to show a knowledgeable understanding of functions in the text, and of the structures used, but also to evaluate the effects achieved on you, the actual reader, and any likely effects on different readers.

5 Babies learn language not in the abstract but in social contexts which contribute influential signs and signals to the meanings of the words used. This awareness continues throughout life and is equally relevant to reading and enjoying literature.

6 Meanings are not always explicit but operate in the form of codes and implications. Completely literal meanings seem to be unsatisfactory to humans, who use metaphors, figures of speech, ambiguities, symbols, analogies and codes as much in everyday life as they do in literature.

7 Language learning is formed in the melting pot of speaking and listening, which are our prime experiences of language. Literacy not only requires a new set of language skills, it is also an initiation into cultural traditions. Undoubtedly there are important connections between speech and writing but there are significant psychological and social differences. In Hallidayan terms, the shift in mode from speaking to writing is a shift from the interpersonal, with all the semiotic support systems that accompany speech, to the ideational, that often lonely existence where all the language happens, whether reading or writing, inside your own head.

Language at work (some examples)

	In life	In literature
Phonology	How an authoritative tone can make a bogus argument persuasive.	Some readers find Jane Austen's tone irritating while others are charmed by it.
	How accent and your personal and group identities are linked.	What accent do you hear when you read non-dialect poetry? Or read dialogue in novels?
Lexis	The amazing frequency with which new words come into everyday use.	Novels, plays and poems become repositories of words we used to use in an age that used to be.
	Your own habitual words and phrases – a help, or a hindrance to your original or creative writing.	Recurring words and groups of related words (semantic fields) in plays by Shakespeare, e.g. 'blood' in *Macbeth*; references to speaking and listening in *Othello*.
Grammar	Adding a tag question to your statements: Does it mean you are inviting a response? Unsure of yourself? Just a creature of habit?	The elegant sentence structure of a short story writer like Katherine Mansfield (see *Miss Brill*).
	The distinction between verbs used actively and verbs used passively.	The advantages and disadvantages of telling a story in the first person.
Pragmatics	The unspoken politeness rules for turn-taking and interrupting in everyday conversations.	Who is talking to whom in the first twenty lines of T. S. Eliot's *The Waste Land*?
Literacy	The problem of getting the tone right in a letter, or an essay.	Being able to read between the lines and detect irony in such different texts as plays by Shakespeare and Beckett.

Sources for Activity 22

(a) *The Tombs of Atuan*, Ursula le Guin, Puffin 1972.
(b) *Killshot*, Elmore Leonard, Penguin 1989.
(c) *Mr Humphreys and His Inheritance*, M. R. James, in *Ghost Stories*, orignally publ. 1931 Penguin.

Appendix 1

At Night
To W. M.
HOME, home from the horizon far and clear,
　Hither the soft wings sweep;
Flocks of the memories of the day draw near
　The dovecote doors of sleep.

Oh, which are they that come through the sweetest light
　Of all these homing birds?
Which with the straightest and the swiftest flight?
　Your words to me, your words!
　　　　　　　　　　　　　　　Alice Meynell

Especially when the October wind

ESPECIALLY when the October wind
With frosty fingers punishes my hair,
Caught by the crabbing sun I walk on fire
And cast a shadow crab upon the land,
By the sea's side, hearing the noise of birds,
Hearing the raven cough in winter sticks,
My busy heart who shudders as she talks
Sheds the syllabic blood and drains her words.
　　　　　　　　　　　　　　　Dylan Thomas

Appendix 2: A series of historical accidents

Below is a very brief outline chronicle of English spelling, with a number of examples of specific words. Read through it and then think about language investigation possibilities it suggests for coursework.

597 – Latin speaking/writing Christian missionaries land in Kent. Begin to write Old English (a Germanic tongue) using Latin alphabet plus a few other symbols eg Runic.

602 – King Athelbert issues first law book written in Old English.
　　Typical OE letter combinations: knife, knee, knuckle (initial 'k' pronounced)
　　　　　　　　　　sky, skill, skate, skin
　　　　　　　　　　hedge, badge, edge, nudge
　　　　　　　　　　batch, catch, ditch, fetch
　　　　　　　　　　crackle, pickle, heckle
　　　　　　　　　　cattle, fettle, bottle, kettle
　　　　　　　　　　dish, mash, flash, bash

Typical OE prefixes: ablaze, asleep, alive　　Typical OE suffixes: kindly, northerly, happily
　　　　　　　become, belong, believe　　　　　　　　　　　bossy, misty, sandy
　　　　　　　　　　　　　　　　　　　　　　　　　　darkness, fairness, idleness

1066 – Norman Conquest. Over next 200 years Norman French, derived from Latin (a Romance rather than a Germanic tongue), began to mix with OE and in time, change spellings.

OE cwen became queen　　　　　　OE hus became house
OE niht became night　　　　　　　OE kirk became church

Soft 'g' introduced as in gentle, generous, ginger
Soft 'c' introduced as in cell, celery, city

Typical NF prefixes:　　　　　　　　Typical NF suffixes:
　　admit, adopt, advice, adhere　　　　　adversity, diversity, iniquity
　　conclude, confirm　　　　　　　　　addition, condition, admission
　　investigate, instinct, indecisive, inconclusive
　　postpone, postscript, postmortem
　　prevent, prepare, prescribe
　　provide, promote, progress

1150– Period of middle English (ME) begins. OE words and NF words well and truly mixed by the time of Chaucer. English beginning to lose three distinctive OE alphabet symbols: þ, ð and æ.

1400 – Chaucer, who wrote his works in ME, dies.

1450 – Period of Early Modern English begins. Considerable influx of Greek words from literary/scientific sources.

Hard 'k' as in chaos, crisis, criterion	Use of 'ph' for 'f' as in catastrophe, philosophy, pharmacy
Initial silent 'p' as in pneumonia, psychology	Initial 'rh' as in rhythm, rhyme, rhombus
Initial silent 'm' as in mnemonic	Use of 'rrh' as in catarrh, haemorrhage, diarrhoea
Use of 'y' for 'i' as in analysis, syllable, synagogue	

1474 – First book printed in English appears. Henceforth, printers will have great influence on the dissemination of standardised forms of English spelling (from sixteenth century onwards especially).

During next three generations or so, considerable changes in pronunciation of English occur, e.g. gradual dropping of initial 'k;' in 'kn–' words; consistently different vowel pronunciations (the great vowel shift).

1551 – John Hart writes 'The opening of unreasonable writing of our Inglish toung'. He points out 'the divers vices and corruptions which use (or better abuse) maintaineth in our writing' and criticises in particular, 'superfluite' which he defines as 'the use of more letters than the pronunciation neadeth of voices'.

1582 – Richard Mulcaster, English 'scholmaistre' writes his 'Elementarie', containing 7,000 English words and how to spell them properly. He also advocates getting rid of unnecessary letters, e.g. doubled consonants, and invented the magic 'e' rule whereby preceding consonants are lengthened, e.g. mad/made; rid/ride; hop/hope.

1600 onwards – English pronunciation and spelling come to correspond less and less. Silent letters actually introduced to give appearance of a Latin origin rather than Germanic: e.g. debt (debitum), reign (regnum) island (insula).

1658 – Edward Phillips publishes 'The New World of English Words', 'As for orthography (Greek word for 'spelling'), it will not be requisite to say more than may conduce to the readers direction in the finding out of words'

On whether the Latin prefix 'prae' may be rendered as English 'pre', he says:

'Whether this innovation of words deprave, or inrush our English tongue is a consideration that admits of various censures, according to the different fancies of men. Certainly as by invasion of strangers, many of the old inhabitants must needs to be either slain, or forced to fly the land; so it happens in the introducing of strange words, the old ones in whose room they come must needs in time be forgotten, and grow obsolete...'

1755 – Dr Johnson's Dictionary of English appears, in the Preface of which, Johnson has much to say about spelling: e.g.

'In adjusting the orthography, which has been to this time unsettled and fortuitous, I found it necessary to distinguish those irregularities that are inherent in our tongue, and perhaps coeval with it, from others which the ignorance or negligence of later writers has produced. Every language has its anomalies, which, though inconvenient, and in themselves once unnecessary, must be tolerated among the imperfections of human things, and which require only to be registered, that they may not be increased, and ascertained, that they may not be confounded: but every language has likewise its improprieties and absurdities, which it is a duty of the lexicographer to correct or proscribe.'

'As language was at its beginning oral, all words of necessary or common use were spoken before they were written; and while they were unfixed by any visible signs, must have been spoken with great diversity, as we now observe those who cannot read to catch sounds imperfectly, and utter them negligently. When this wild and barbarous jargon was first reduced to an alphabet, every penman endeavoured to express as he could, the sounds which he was accustomed to pronounce or to receive, and vitiated in writing such words as were already vitiated in speech. The powers of the letters, when they were applied to a new language, must have been vague and unsettled, and therefore different hands would exhibit the same sound by different combinations.'

1828 – Noah Webster publishes his 'American Dictionary of the English Language' (see Section 1 of this chapter) in which there are consistent variations from British English spelling (see also Encarta) e.g. center, fiber, theater, labor, color, vigor, defense, offense, pretense.

1837 – Isaac Pitman invents a system of phonetic shorthand.

1908 – The British Simplified Spelling Society is founded.

1957 – George Bernard Shaw finances a competition for the designing of a new English alphabet.

1959 – Sir James Pitman publishes 'i.t.a.', the initial teaching alphabet to help young readers.

2000 – Computer age words and spellings e.g. program, byte, giga, modem.

Appendix 3: Developmental milestones in motor and language development

At the completion of:	*Motor development*
12 weeks	Supports head when in prone position; weight is on elbows; hands mostly open; no grasp reflex
16 weeks	Plays with rattle placed in hands (by shaking it and staring at it); head self-supported; tonic neck reflex subsiding
20 weeks	Sits with props
6 months	Sitting: bends forward and uses hands for support; can bear weight when put into standing position, but cannot yet stand without holding on. Reaching: unilateral. Grasp: no thumb apposition yet; releases cube when given another
8 months	Stands holding on; grasps with thumb apposition; picks up pellet with thumb and finger tips
10 months	Creeps efficiently; takes side-steps, holding on; pulls to standing position
12 months	Walks when held by one hand; walks on feet and hands – knees in air; mouthing of objects almost stopped; seats self on floor
18 months	Grasp, prehension, and release fully developed; gait stiff, propulsive, and precipitated; sits on child's chair with only fair aim; creeps downstairs backward; has difficulty building tower of three cubes
24 months	Runs, but falls in sudden turns; can quickly alternate between sitting and stance; walks stairs up or down, one foot forward only
30 months	Jumps up into air with both feet; stands on one foot for about two seconds; takes a few steps on tiptoe; jumps from chair; good hand and finger coordination; can move digits independently; manipulation of objects much improved; builds tower of six cubes
3 years	Tiptoes 3 yards; runs smoothly with acceleration and deceleration; negotiates sharp and fast curves without difficulty; walks stairs by alternating feet; jumps 12 inches; can operate tricycle
4 years	Jumps over rope; hops on right foot; catches ball in arms; walks line

Vocalisation and Language

Markedly less crying than at 8 weeks; when talked to and nodded at, smiles, followed by squealing–gurgling sounds usually called *cooing*, which is vowel-like in character and pitch-modulated; sustains cooing for 15–20 seconds	12 weeks
Responds to human sounds more definitely; turns head; eyes seem to search for speaker; occasionally some chuckling sounds	16 weeks
The vowel-like cooing sounds begin to be interspersed with more consonantal sounds: labial fricatives, spirants, and nasals are common; acoustically, all vocalisations are very different from the sounds of the mature language of the environment	20 weeks
Cooing changing into babbling resembling one-syllable utterances; neither vowels nor consonants have very fixed recurrences; most common utterances sound somewhat like *ma, mu, da,* or *di*	6 months
Reduplication (or more continuous repetitions) becomes frequent; intonation patterns become distinct; utterances can signal emphasis and emotions	8 months
Vocalizations are mixed with sound-play such as gurgling or bubble-blowing; appears to wish to imitate sounds, but the imitations are never quite successful; beginning to differentiate between words heard by making differential adjustment	10 months
Identical sound sequences are replicated with higher relative frequency of occurrence, and words (*mamma* or *dadda*) are emerging; definite signs of understanding some words and simple commands (*Show me your eyes*)	12 months
Has a definite repertoire of words – more than three, but less than fifty; still much babbling but now of several syllables, with intricate intonation pattern; no attempt at communicating information and no frustration at not being understood; words may include items such as *thank you* or *come here*, but there is little ability to join any of the lexical items into spontaneous two-item phrases; understanding progressing rapidly	18 months
Vocabulary of more than fifty items (some children seem to be able to name everything in environment); begins spontaneously to join vocabulary items into two-word phrases; all phrases appear to be own creations; definite increase in communicative behaviour and interest in language	24 months
Fastest increase in vocabulary, with many new additions every day; no babbling at all; utterances have communicative intent; frustrated if not understood by adults; utterances consist of at least two words – many have three or even five words; sentences and phrases have characteristic child grammar – that is, are rarely verbatim repetitions of an adult utterance; intelligibility not very good yet, though there is great variation among children; seems to understand everything said within hearing and directed to self	30 months
Vocabulary of some one thousand words; about 80 percent of utterances intelligible even to strangers; grammatical complexity of utterances roughly that of colloquial adult language, although mistakes still occur	3 years
Language well established; deviations from the adult norm tend to be more in style than in grammar	4 years

2 Moving On

It's more than likely that if you're using this book and reading these early chapters you've recently completed your GCSE studies which will, of course, have included English. Many of you will have gained good qualifications not only in English but also in the companion subject, English Literature. We'll leave the discussion of why there should be two subjects in English until later in this and in subsequent chapters and, indeed, why there should be a separate subject called English Literature at all. Why are there not GCSEs in, for example, English Advertising or English Journalism? What is it about English Literature that warrants it being a separate subject both at GCSE and at A level? Indeed, a further question: why is this book called *Living Language and Literature* and not simply *Living English*? The division of English into two 'subjects' raises important questions and issues that will occupy us throughout the book. It may be that the reason for the division is to be found in the way society regards the type of writing that is called or classified as 'literature'. Literature may be specially privileged in our society and seen as being more important than any other type of writing. Another way of viewing literature is that it is but one particular way of using language. After all, writers of both 'English' and 'English Literature' use the English language to achieve their effects and purposes.

Your GCSE course will have made you familiar with what are sometimes called the four modes of language: Reading, Writing, Speaking and Listening and these four modes formed the basis of all your work for GCSE. Your coursework will have involved you in producing a folder of *writing*; you will have been assessed on your ability to both *speak* and *listen* and you will also have had to produce *written* work in your examination papers. Much of this written work will have been produced in response to what you have *read* and some of what you had to read will have been classified as 'literature'. This will have included at least one Shakespeare play, a selection of poems by British writers considered to be important and some work by writers from 'other cultures'. But you probably don't want to be reminded of what you've just left behind! However, on reflection, you'll realise that these four modes of language – reading, writing, speaking and listening – cover all the ways that everybody uses language, though you might also want to include thinking, as most thinking involves using language. In fact, the production of what you are reading at this very minute has involved these four (or five) modes. This section of the book is the result of our reading (of current GCSE syllabuses), our thinking (the planning of this chapter and the whole book) our speaking and listening (our discussions) and, of course, our writing. In the rest of this chapter we want to examine these modes more closely. We'll start with reading.

Reading

ACTIVITY 27

1 Make a list of the literature that you read for GCSE English and, if you took the subject, English Literature as well. You should include both any complete novels and short stories and plays you read, together with any excerpts from longer works or selections from the work of poets.
2 Now make a second list, this time of the books that you have read in the past year and which you chose to read for pleasure. No teacher made you read them. You read them because you wanted to. Be honest! Don't worry whether they count as 'literature' or not, but don't include any non-fiction in your list.
3 Discuss your list with another member of your class. Were there any similarities? Do you think that any works from the second list could have been included in the first for study at GCSE? Were there any differences between the lists from girls and those from boys? How would you classify the types of book that appeared on the second list? For example, they might include such types or genres as science-fiction, comics, horror and so on.

COMMENTARY The striking difference between the two lists is, of course, the fact that you had no choice in what appeared on the first one. The books you read for GCSE were chosen by someone else. That 'someone else' is, in fact, a combination of your teacher, the exam board that decides what books should appear on its syllabus and the Government who dictate which authors are suitable for study by the nation's 16-year-olds. The nation's 16-year-olds are, naturally, not consulted. Clearly it is thought that certain books and authors are worth studying and that in some mysterious way are 'good' for you. These are the ones that are often labelled 'literature' whereas some of those that might have appeared on your second list are not accorded such an accolade. There may, however, have been some overlap between your two lists. You might have wanted, for example, to read more by a writer you studied at GCSE or go to productions of other Shakespearean plays than the one you read.

Even if there were some overlap, there are still very likely to be some works that you read during the year that wouldn't ever appear on the GCSE list as 'literature'. Nevertheless, you read them for pleasure and enjoyment. There are, of course, many reasons people choose to read: to wile away the time on a long train journey; to escape from their everyday routine into a world of romance or fantasy; or to gain insight into how people behaved in the past, are just three of many that we could have cited.

Amongst the many books of fiction published each year, only a few are allowed fully into the 'house of literature'. These issues of why some books are welcomed in with open arms, why some are barred from entry for ever and have to spend all their time out in the cold and why some are allowed into the hall, but not into the important rooms, are ones we shall return to later. Like everyone else you will probably read books that are inside and some that are outside the house.

Of course, for many people, if not for you, the second list might have been a very short one indeed, or even non-existent. Many choose not to read any books at all, claiming pressure of work (or GCSE study!), the difficulty of concentrating or that books are boring. For many, the attractions of TV, computer games and other forms of entertainment are just too strong and books come a decidedly second or third best. You, however, will not feel like this, as you've chosen to become a student of English Language and *Literature* at A level. But why? What exactly do you expect to gain from studying this subject? The next activity will help you to assess your interest in studying literature.

ACTIVITY 28

Below are 13 reasons for choosing to study literature. Next to each one is a value scale running from 1 to 6.

1 For each reason decide what is the value you place on it.

> 1 = I strongly agree with this
> 6 = I don't agree with this at all.

The reason I am studying English Literature at A level is because:

I got good grades at GCSE in
English Literature   1 2 3 4 5 6
I enjoy reading   1 2 3 4 5 6
I think it will improve my skills
in reading, writing and speaking   1 2 3 4 5 6
I couldn't think of another
subject to do   1 2 3 4 5 6
It will allow me to learn about
how people think, feel and act   1 2 3 4 5 6
I can learn about how people
lived and thought in the past   1 2 3 4 5 6

It will enable me to go to
university   1 2 3 4 5 6
There's not as much to learn as
in harder subjects   1 2 3 4 5 6
I like writing poems and stories   1 2 3 4 5 6
I like the English teachers at
school and college   1 2 3 4 5 6
It will help me discover more
about myself   1 2 3 4 5 6
I can learn about present
and past culture and society   1 2 3 4 5 6
It gives you a touch of class   1 2 3 4 5 6

2 Now write down any of your reasons that are missing from the list.

3 Rank all the reasons in order from the most to the least important.

4 Discuss these lists in a group and see if you can arrive at an agreed order.

COMMENTARY

This activity should have made clearer to you just why you and other people choose to read 'literature' and why it is sometimes seen as an important type of reading. It will, however, form only a small part of the reading that you do during your everyday life. Indeed, it would be impossible to conduct your normal life without reading. Our society depends on print and our ability to read to keep it running smoothly. It was not always so, of course. Until the late nineteenth century the ability to read and write was restricted, in the main, to the upper and the middle classes. With the introduction of the *1870 Education Act*, more and more people gained the ability to read and write with confidence, fluency and understanding. Britain became a literate society. Not surprisingly, therefore, it was at this time that many newspapers designed to appeal to this newly literate audience, were founded. The *Daily Mail* and the *Daily Mirror*, for example, date from this time. It is telling that *The Times, Daily Telegraph* and *The Observer*, all papers with a predominantly middle- and upper-class readership, were founded before this onset of mass education and literacy.

It is clear that people who cannot read are at a severe disadvantage in twenty-first century Britain. Similarly, those who are not *computer* literate will also be disadvantaged. For example, what you are reading at this moment had to be presented to the publisher not as a hand-written manuscript, but on a computer disk. This would not have been the case for the majority of books written in the twentieth century. A further illustration: many of the jobs and professions that you will apply for will require you to be computer literate. If you are not, the job will go to someone who is. You will easily be able to think of numerous other illustrations of the necessity of computer literacy. It is not surprising that Information and Communication Technology plays such a dominant role in our schools and colleges and that there are many adults who voluntarily attend evening classes to acquire these skills. People who are not computer literate are unlikely to be able to participate fully in society in the new millennium. They may become an underclass, much as those who are not conventionally literate have been since the late nineteenth century in Britain.

This next activity will indicate just how important reading is in our society.

ACTIVITY 29

1 Here are 20 examples of just some of the material that you might choose to read or might encounter as part of everyday life. For each one, note down whether you (a) frequently (b) sometimes (c) seldom (d) never read such material.

the ingredients list on a frozen food package
a bank statement
an advertisement hoarding
a train timetable
a newspaper
junk mail
a holiday brochure
a web page
a contract of employment
a dictionary
a shopping list
road direction signs
teletext
a recipe
a sports magazine
The Highway Code
the Bible (or similar religious text)
a letter or postcard
washing instructions on a garment
a bus.

2 Compile a list of a further 20 types of text that you encounter during your daily life.

3 Compare your list with those compiled by other members of the group.

COMMENTARY　You will have seen from this activity just how dependent we are on our reading skills and that even if we never choose to read the texts that are classified as literature at all, we must still interact with written or printed texts throughout our daily life. In a very real sense, we live in a literate society in which to be illiterate is a major handicap. We don't, though, read every text we encounter in exactly the same way. Francis Bacon wrote in the seventeenth century that 'some books are to be tasted, others to be swallowed and some few to be chewed and digested' and though he was writing primarily about books, what he had to say is applicable to the many different texts that we encounter constantly. There are some texts that we merely skim (newspaper headlines, brand names on tins of baked beans, for example); some that we read, but without paying much attention to (a football report not involving the team that we support, the small print on an airline ticket, perhaps); some that we read quite carefully (a college prospectus or the duplicated letter enclosed with the annual Christmas card from friends we seldom see, maybe); some that we read very carefully (questions on an exam paper or a job advertisement) and some that we return to time after time until we might even know them by heart (a love letter or a favourite poem, perhaps). So you can see that the term 'read' can encompass a wide range of activity; it's no wonder that we have many other terms that refer more precisely to the different types of reading we can engage in – *skim, peruse, pour over, glance at, study* are just some of these. How many more can you think of?

There is a further distinction that we can draw. Not only are there many ways of reading, but there are also texts that we *must* read, whether we really want to or not. I might *enjoy* reading a magazine about rock-climbing, but I *have* to read the annual tax return form that is kindly sent to me by the Inland Revenue. You might choose to read an account of Oxfam's work in helping refugees, but not want to read this text book. Your teacher may well have forced you to do so!

ACTIVITY 30

Discuss, with a partner, what differences in meaning there are between the following sentences. The words in italics are *modal* verbs or *modal auxiliaries*. Their function in a sentence or utterance is to add something extra to its straightforward meaning. In other words, they add the attitude of the speaker or writer to what she is saying or writing. For instance, there is a clear difference between 'everyone reads' (no modality) and 'everyone should read' (modality). What differences of meaning are there between:

everyone *should* read
everyone *must* read
everyone *will* read
everyone *may* read
everyone *shall* read
everyone *can* read
everyone *ought to* read
everyone *might* read
everyone *could* read
everyone *would* read.

COMMENTARY You will have seen that modality adds attitudes that include possibility, probability, uncertainty, intention, necessity, obligation, insistence, ability, definiteness and permission.

What we have done so far is to tease out what is involved in the act of reading and to highlight the many types of text that there are. Literature is but a small part of what is written, as a visit to any large bookshop will swiftly confirm. In fact, many bookshops now seem to sell not just books, but reading. The introduction of coffee bars and reading lounges into bookshops is one way of encouraging customers to remain longer on the premises. Of course, 'selling reading' will, in the end, result in larger sales of books.

ACTIVITY 31

In this activity you are going to examine the reading habits of one particular group of people.

1 Working with three or four others, choose a target group whose reading habits and patterns you want to investigate. The following are only suggestions and there may be other groups that interest you or to whom you have access.

   year 4 girls in a primary school
   year 4 boys in a primary school
   the English teachers in your school or college
   retired people attending a local day centre
   the staff where you have a part time job.

2 Discuss how you are going to obtain the necessary information. For example, will you ask them questions face to face? Will you ask them to fill in a questionnaire or a survey sheet? Will you leave them the questionnaire for a few days to complete? Here are a few, but important, matters for you to consider:

- how many people will you need to ensure that your information is representative?
- how will you phrase your questions so that there is no possibility of the respondents misunderstanding what you want?
- you may need to test the questions out to ensure that they are as clear and unambiguous as possible.
- will the questions be open-ended, multiple choice or yes/no ones?

- do you need information about age, gender, occupation, educational achievement and so forth?

3 Design the questions/questionnaire/survey sheet. Remember that your aim is to discover as much as you can about what, why, when and where people read.

4 Collect the information. This is probably easier said than done!

5 When you have gathered in the results of your work, you will need to process the information you have obtained. This could well lead to a very interesting piece of original writing that you might want to use as part of your coursework folder. For example, you might produce:

- a magazine article that contains not only your statistical results presented clearly and interestingly, but interviews with, and pen portraits of, some of your respondents
- the script of a radio documentary about 'Changing Reading Habits'. You could submit the tape of your programme as part of your folder
- a series of articles on 'A Reading Day in the Life of . . .' in which you write about very different readers. They could be different in terms of age, gender, occupation or they could be three or four generations of the same family.

There is a similar activity for 'Writing' on page 53.

Just as there are many different types of text, so writers can have different intentions when they produce them and the texts may achieve different effects on their readers. Activity 28 on page 46 will have suggested some, but only some, of the reasons for reading literary texts, but to pin down the intention of writers of such texts can be very tricky. Ask a novelist when she is writing a novel or a poet when he is writing a poem what are their purposes and intentions and they may find it very difficult to answer you. But ask an advertising copywriter, for example, the same question and the answer should come more swiftly and be more clear: to *persuade* you to buy that particular brand of washing powder, to vote for this political party or to choose to shop at Tesco rather than Safeway.

ACTIVITY 32

The aim of this activity is to introduce you to the many different purposes that texts may serve.

1 In pairs, compare the lists of texts that you compiled for Activity 27. For each text discuss:
   (a) what you think is its primary purpose

   (b) whether you think it would succeed in achieving that purpose.

2 In the light of your discussions, draw up a list of the main purposes writers can have when they produce texts.

COMMENTARY

It's likely that your list would have included amongst the purposes: *to persuade, to instruct, to advise* and *to inform*, though it may well have been more detailed than these suggestions. You might, for example, have *to warn* or *to demonstrate*. What might also have become apparent is that the same text could well have more than one purpose, though there will usually have been one primary purpose. Advertisements (such as the well-known Heineken campaigns for beer that reaches the parts other beers don't) can be amusing and entertaining, though their primary purpose is to *persuade* you, in this case to buy and drink more Heineken. A recipe from a well-known chef in a glossy cookery book whose primary purpose is to instruct and possibly to advise may also very well be entertaining and informative. And what about an advertisement that contains a recipe?

ACTIVITY 33

1 Collect as many advertisements from the print media as you can that are amusing and entertaining, as well as persuasive.

2 Make a display of these in your classroom.

Writing

We're now going to turn to the second of the four modes of language and one that occupied a great deal of your time at GCSE. Both English and English Literature will have involved you in a lot of writing, but other subjects will have also demanded that you put pen to paper or finger to keyboard fairly frequently. This distinction is quite an important one to make. Many people think of writing only as the activity that you engage in when you are holding a pen or pencil in your hand and transferring the marks that these instruments can make to a sheet of paper. This, of course is true but a variety of tools can be used that enable thoughts to be transferred from your head to another medium. The most common alternative at the moment is the word-processor where thoughts are transferred to a computer screen via a keyboard and may or may not be subsequently printed. Some forms of electronic writing remain solely on screen. For instance, the contents of e-mail or chat rooms are rarely transferred to paper. Alternatives to pen and paper in the recent past have included the typewriter, Morse code and inscriptions on stone and, in the more distant past, wax tablets and papyrus. Other cultures have other 'writing' systems. Think of Indian (native American) smoke signals, for instance. However, we'll concern ourselves with the more conventional forms of writing!

Your writing in school is likely to have included such things as note taking, reports on experiments, essays, translations, plans for assignments, coursework – and many others.

In GCSE English your writing skills were specifically assessed and you were tested on your ability to write for a variety of purposes. For example you may have been asked to:

>   *argue* for or against a point of view in a letter to a newspaper
>   *instruct* someone just beginning a part-time job
>   *entertain* by writing a short story.

You'll be able to remember many more of the writing tasks that you performed for English and English Literature, as you did them quite recently. So you'll know you were asked to write for a variety of audiences, for a variety of purposes and in a variety of forms or genres. The GCSE syllabus at the time of producing this book required you to write to:

explore	imagine	entertain
inform	explain	describe
argue	persuade	instruct
analyse	review	comment.

So, all the writing you did at GCSE either in the exam or as part of your coursework will have been designed to enable you to fulfil one of these 12 purposes. However, do you think that these 12 cover all the purposes that writing can be asked to perform? Where, for example, does writing a shopping list, planning an essay or filling in an application form fit in?

ACTIVITY 34

In a small group, brainstorm as many other purposes for writing as you can. Then give one example of a text that would be likely to fulfil each purpose.

COMMENTARY No doubt you managed to come up with many different purposes in addition to the 'GCSE 12' and were probably able to supply lots of examples of types of writing that would achieve these purposes. You may even have given as some of your examples the types of text that formed part of the list on page 47. In that activity you'll remember you were considering the various purposes of reading, not writing. It wouldn't be all that surprising, though, if you did come up with some of the same examples, or at least very similar ones, as reading and writing are very closely related. They are the two sides of the same coin. You can't really have reading without writing and vice versa. The writer of a text, whether it be a shopping list or a novel, expects to have a reader (or readers) even though in the case of a shopping list or maybe a diary, the reader may well be the writer him or herself. Though in the case of a diary, the reader could be a much older version of the writer! It could be very illuminating or perhaps even chastening to read your diary five, ten or maybe even forty years on. 'Was it really me who did/felt/thought that?' A novel that isn't read can hardly have been worth writing, unless it were written as a therapeutic or cathartic exercise. Novels need readers.

Neither does any text you read write itself. Behind every text there is always a writer (or writers) who has thought about, planned and executed it. The popular image of the lonely writer in his garret slaving away over his great work, never speaking to anyone at all and only emerging when the magnum opus is complete may be true for a very, very few writers, but the reality is that the vast majority need people to talk to. They need people with whom they can discuss their work, test out their ideas and rely on to give a true opinion of the work in progress. Some texts, for example poems or government bills, may well have gone through draft after draft before they are let loose on the reading public. In the case of government bills, examination syllabuses, film scripts and some books, for example, more than one writer may have been involved and the finished product may bear little resemblance to the first draft. Nor does this take into account the work of editors, committees and so on. You yourself may well have written a number of drafts before you were satisfied enough with your GCSE coursework to hand in the final version to your teacher. You'd be in good company, for Robert Graves, the poet, was of the opinion that a writer's best friend is his waste paper basket!

This interplay between writer and reader, or addresser and addressee as they are sometimes referred to, can be summed up in one of the most useful pieces of advice that an A level English student can be given: 'read as a writer; write as a reader'. In other words, when you write, always take account of the fact that you will have a particular audience and when you read, always be aware that you are encountering what *someone* has written for specific purposes and audiences and that 'writerly' choices of language and approach lie behind the text. More of this later in the book.

In the section on 'Reading' we suggested that much of what people actually read is very different from what you were required to read for GCSE. This next activity considers what people actually write and the purposes for which they use it. Because most of you using this book are still within the education system in some way and therefore very likely to be continuing many of the types of writing you encountered at GCSE, the activity looks at people other than yourselves and the ways they use writing in their daily lives.

ACTIVITY 35

1 Remind yourself of the hints you were given on page 49 about collecting information from surveys or questionnaires.

2 Again, decide on a target group of informants whose writing habits and patterns you want to investigate. It might very well be the same group as before or you might like to work with a contrasting or different one.

3 Design your survey or questionnaire. Remember to make it as easy as possible to administer and also as clear as possible, so that the respondents can understand what you want without any difficulty.

4 Collect your information and then process it. Again, you could use what you have obtained as the basis for a piece of original writing.

If your class conducts both these surveys on reading and writing, you will have completed a significant and valuable piece of research into contemporary literacy.

COMMENTARY

It will be interesting to compare the findings from your survey with some of the functions of writing as outlined by Florian Coulmas in his book *The Writing Systems of the World* (1989). He identified:

The mnemonic function: If something is written down, it can be 'recalled', more or less exactly for ever. Thus writing can be an aid to memory (this is what mnemonic means). Thanks to this mnemonic function, history becomes possible as well as the storage and accumulation of knowledge. Without writing, there would be no books, no libraries and therefore no knowledge. Whilst this might be an oversimplification, especially in the age of electronic data storage, it does point to the vital importance of this function of writing. Even the humble shopping list can be said to be mnemonic.

The distancing function: Writing allows communication to take place and messages to be sent over time and space. You don't need to be in the same place as the writer, nor even in the same century to read what he or she has written. You can read in the comfort of your own armchair what Dickens wrote in 1854 and it will be *exactly* what he wrote, word for word. Of course, technology means that his work can be reproduced an infinite number of times, so it can be read in two thousand years' time, or in Australia. Think how different this is from speech. Until very recently, unless they were using the telephone, speakers had to be in close proximity to each other, so that messages could be sent and, if necessary, immediately responded to. It's very hard to speak to someone in Australia without using a telephone!

Modern technology has meant that this has changed somewhat. Speech, even on the telephone, used to be entirely ephemeral, but it can now be captured and preserved by using answering machines or tape and video recorders. Whilst speech used to be the only immediate, interactive form of communication and written communication needed to be thought about and responded to at a later time, the Internet has changed all this. People can sit at their computer keyboards and e-mail each other or conduct real-time conversations on chat lines. Though these communications are 'written' on screen, they have many of the features of spoken language interaction. For instance, the language used is often very informal, the grammar is more like that of speech and 'mistakes' are sometimes left uncorrected. However, even when all this has been taken into consideration, speech still remains the main means of immediate interactive communication and writing still retains its 'distancing function'.

The social control function: 'Can I have that in writing?' You often hear that kind of request when people want to be certain about something. It's as if they trust what's written, because it can be permanent, rather than what is spoken, which is, by its nature, evanescent. There's also a related belief that if something's in print, it must be true. So those things that society expects to be permanent – the law, acts of parliament, traffic regulations, for example – are all written and printed. Our lives are controlled by what is written: you will already possess a birth certificate and will certainly have a death certificate issued in your name at some, as yet, unknown date! At some stage in your life you are likely to have a National Insurance number, a voter registration, a mortgage contract and so on. You can see from this that our lives are regulated and controlled by what is written down.

The interactional function: This function is linked to the previous one in that various types of writing are intended to influence our behaviour by the messages that they convey. For example, we might be influenced to wear a particular style of clothing by what we read in a fashion magazine, to drink a particular variety of white wine by what a wine writer has to say about it or to apply to a particular university by what the prospectus said.

The aesthetic function: Literature is, of course, the prime example of the aesthetic (concerned with the fine arts) function of writing. Virtually all of our literature, our verbal art, is written. We can't really conceive of a novel, a play or a poem that isn't written and published and that therefore can be read by us when and where we choose. Of course, plays are primarily oral and visual experiences, but most playscripts are now published. You might even have read your GCSE Shakespeare play without ever having seen a performance of it either in the theatre or on tape or film.

Much of early English poetry, such as Chaucer, was aural. It was written down, but was actually designed to be read aloud and many of the people who first encountered Chaucer's stories in *The Canterbury Tales* would have done so as listeners not as readers. It wasn't until Caxton introduced printing into England in the mid-fifteenth century that many people would have been able to see the text of what Chaucer had written. Indeed, in the pre-print age, the majority of people didn't need to be literate, because there was very little to read. You relied for entertainment on good oral story tellers. You were also very reliant on those people who could read. For example, lawyers and priests made a good living out of reading texts, because most of their 'customers' couldn't. Something of that still persists even in the twenty-first century. Lawyers (and to some extent, priests) remain powerful readers who can see the 'magic' meanings in texts that ordinary people can't. We go to them to find out what the (written) law really means and many of their arguments in court are over the precise interpretation of what to most people are rather difficult and abstruse written texts. It's little wonder that we are constantly enjoined to 'read the small print'.

The aural tradition of entertainment still exists. Indeed, there's been a renaissance recently in this tradition, with performance poets like John Hegley and Benjamin Zephaniah attracting large and enthusiastic audiences.

Speaking and listening

We've already referred to speech and talk in the previous section on 'Writing' and shown how some of the traditional barriers between the two modes, speech and writing, are beginning to break down because of the impact of the new technologies. Though it's worth stressing again that, despite the prestige that is accorded to the written and printed word in all literate societies, the vast majority of communication between people, even in these societies, is via the spoken word. Even the briefest of pauses for thought will suffice to remind you that you spend far more time speaking and listening then you do reading and writing. You will, for example, spend much more of your day at school or college talking to friends, discussing issues in class, answering teachers' questions and so on, than you will writing notes and essays or reading newspapers, magazines or books. Though we do live in a literate society, we still rely very heavily on the spoken word to enable us to function. It's quite surprising for people like ourselves who live in such a society (one in which the ability to read and write is of the utmost importance) and who find it impossible to conceive of what it must be to live in a society where there is *only* spoken language, to realise that even today there are hundreds of languages in active use that are never written at all, because no one has worked out an effective way to write them. It's been estimated that of all the thousands and thousands of languages that have been spoken during the course of human history only about 106 of them have ever developed writing to a sufficient extent to produce what we call literature. There are about 3000 languages spoken in the world today; of these, a mere 78 have a written literature. That's not to say that these languages don't give rise to stories and poetry, but they remain as oral stories and poetry. There are authors whose works we now encounter as written texts who conceived them as texts to be listened to. We've already seen that many people who enjoyed the works of Chaucer in the late fourteenth century did so as a listening experience. There's also general agreement that the 'Homer' who 'wrote' the classical Greek epics *The Iliad* and *The Odyssey* was basing the works on a much earlier oral tradition.

So there is strong support for the view that language is first and foremost oral, though in the present GCSE syllabuses that you have just experienced only 20 per cent of the marks are give to Speaking and Listening! We saw earlier that reading and writing (or readers and writers) are an inseparable twosome; the same is true of speaking and listening. Though the National Curriculum, of which GCSE is a part, sees 'Speaking and Listening' as one, many linguists regret this lumping together. They stress that the role of the listener is an important one and that it has a set of skills, just as the other modes (speaking, reading and writing) do. We have to learn to read and write; we have also to learn how to listen. However, it is a rare situation in which someone speaks without having a listener, though we do from time to time 'talk to ourselves'. This might be when we want to give ourselves encouragement to perform a particularly difficult, challenging or hazardous task or when we are trying to sort out a problem or a plan of action in our minds. The majority of our talk, however, is conducted with a listener or listeners other than ourself. It's impossible to be a listener without there being someone speaking.

ACTIVITY 36

1 Discuss with a partner and list the types of speaking and listening activities that you did for GCSE and for which you were assessed. These might have included such tasks as giving a formal talk or being 'hot-seated' as a character from a set text.

2 Now, discuss and list as many as you can of the normal everyday talk activities that you participate in. These could range from telling jokes to asking questions; from planning your evening's entertainment with friends to telling lies.

3 What differences, if any, are there between the two lists? Think about contexts (where did the talk take place and with whom?), purposes (why were you talking?), and topics (what were you talking about?).

COMMENTARY

We would expect that your second list would have contained not only a greater variety of speech situations and contexts, but that most of these would have been a good deal less formal than those for GCSE assessment. That's not to say that you won't find yourself in formal speech situation outside GCSE, of course. We're all likely to have to face an interview from time to time. The GCSE syllabus categorised the purposes of talk as being to:

explain	describe	narrate
explore	analyse	imagine
discuss	argue	persuade.

How appropriate do you think these categories are to cover the talk in your second list? Or your first?

In these first two chapters, we have looked at language in childhood and then at your own recent experiences of language at GCSE. In this chapter, we have examined the four modes of language (speaking, listening, reading and writing) and have seen in particular that people's reading consists of much more than what is commonly called 'literature'. Indeed, we have seen that literature plays little or no part in many people's reading lives.

You, however, are embarking on a course whose title 'English Language and Literature' suggests that these are two separate entities, that there is 'English Language' and 'English Literature' and that they are both worthy of study at an advanced level. In the next chapter, we will explore what we mean by 'literature' and whether the two Englishes are separable.

3 What's in a Name?

In the first two chapters we moved from your very early language experiences in childhood (Chapter 1) to more recent ones at the conclusion of your compulsory education (Chapter 2). Having reached the stage where you were, at the very least, certified as being competent in English and English Literature, you are now ready to tackle more advanced study in the subject. One of the main aims that all such advanced courses share is that you should be able 'to show knowledge and understanding of a range of literary and non-literary texts'. This isn't quite as straightforward as it might seem because you have, naturally, to be able to recognise just what is a 'literary' or a 'non-literary' text. This next activity will help you to do just this.

ACTIVITY 37

1 Working in small groups, read the following 13 short texts carefully. Discuss them and decide which should be placed in the 'literary' and which in the 'non-literary' category.
2 For each text, write down the reasons that enabled your group to decide on its category.

3 Now, as a class, collect together all these reasons and discuss them. Try to list them in order of importance, beginning with the one that was most helpful to you in reaching your decision.

---

1 *From Mr Lydekker; FRS, Hertfordshire*   *6 February 1913*

Sir,

    While gardening this afternoon I heard a faint note which led me to say to my under-gardener, who was working with me, 'Was that the cuckoo?' Almost immediately afterwards we both heard the full double note of a cuckoo repeated either two or three times – I am not quite sure which. The time was 3.40; and the bird, which was to the westward – that is to say, to windward – appeared to be about a quarter of a mile away. There is not the slightest doubt that the song was that of a cuckoo.

    The late Professor Newton, in the fourth edition of Yarrell's *British Birds* (Vol II, p. 389, note), stated that although the arrival of the cuckoo has frequently been reported in March, or even earlier, such records must be treated with suspicion, if not with incredulity. And Mr J. E. Harting (*Handbook of British Birds*, p. 112) goes even further than this, stating that there is no authentic record of the arrival of the cuckoo in this country earlier than 6 April.

R. Lydekker

2

  A Hi. I've got one. It took ages.
  B Hi. Mind all that stuff.
  A You've got a lot done.
  B Colin's given us a hand.
  A Hi.
  C Hi.
  B Where'd you get it?
  A Holroyd's.
  B Give us it here.
  C Is this coming out?
  B What? Er, no, leave that. Thanks.
  A Is it right?
  B Yes.
  C What needs doing next?
  B Let's knock off for a brew.
  C Great idea.
  A Look I'm a bit pushed, I'll come back this aft. Gavin and Simon'll help.
  B Keep out of the boozer.
  A Skint anyway.
  C It's nearly off, this.
  B It'll plaster back in again. Don't make it worse.

3

Had we but world enough, and time
This coyness, Lady, were no crime.
We would sit down, and think which way
To walk, and pass our long love's day.
Thou by the Indian Ganges' side
Shoulds't rubies find: I by the tide
Of Humber would complain. I would
Love you ten years before the flood:
And you should, if you please, refuse
Till the conversion of the Jews.

4

Oris Big Crown Commandante. Model 640 7482 40 64.
Automatic movement. Small subsidiary seconds dial,
positioned at 9 o'clock. Pointer calendar. Stainless
steel case with screw down security crown, water
resistant to 50m. Stainless steel skeleton screw back
with mineral crystal. Dial with luminous numerals and
hands. Water resistant genuine calf skin leather strap.
Also available with stainless steel bracelet.

5 How to book

Call at the RNCM Box Office which is located in the College, through the Refectory and beside
the steps to the concourse. The opening hours are Monday to Saturday from 11.00am until
6.00pm. or until 8.30pm on performance days. It is also open for one hour before performances
on Sundays. Mastercard, Visa and Switch cards are accepted, so you can pay in whatever way
suits you best. If you wish to book by post just send off your request with a covering note,
enclosing payment and a stamped, self-addressed envelope for the tickets.

6

Wilcox welcomed our interest; we had bottles brought up from every bin, and it was during those tranquil evenings with Sebastian that I first made a serious acquaintance with wine and sowed the seed of that rich harvest which was to be my stay in many barren years. We would sit, he and I, in the Painted Parlour with three bottles open on the table and three glasses before each of us; Sebastian had found a book on wine-tasting, and we followed its instructions in detail. We warmed the glass slightly at a candle, filled it a third high, swirled the wine round, nursed it in our hands, held it to the light, breathed it, sipped it, filled our mouths with it, and rolled it over the tongue, ringing it on the palate like a coin on a counter, tilted our heads back and let it trickle down the throat. Then we talked of it and nibbled Bath Oliver biscuits, and passed on to another wine; then back to the first, then on to another, until all three were in circulation and the order of glasses got confused, and we fell out over which was which, and we passed the glasses to and fro between us until there were six glasses, some of them with mixed wines in them which we had filled from the wrong bottle, till we were obliged to start again with three clean glasses each, and the bottles were empty and our praise of them wilder and more exotic.

... It is a little, shy wine like a gazelle,'

'Like a leprechaun.'

'Dappled, in a tapestry meadow.'

7

GUS: Have you noticed the time that tank takes to fill?

BEN: What tank?

GUS: In the lavatory.

BEN: No. Does it?

GUS: Terrible.

BEN: Well, what about it?

GUS: What do you think's the matter with it?

BEN: Nothing.

GUS: Nothing?

BEN: It's got a deficient ballcock, that's all.

GUS: A deficient what?

BEN: Ballcock.

GUS: No? Really?

BEN: That's what I should say.

8

There's happiness and laughter
  and excitement in the air –
Gifts to give and friends to meet
  and special treats to share ...
May every day of Christmas
  and the year that follows, too
Hold such warm and happy times
  especially for you.

9 **gimlet,** *gim'lit, n.* a small tool for boring holes by turning it by hand: half a glass of whisky, gin or vodka, and lime-juice: to turn like a gimlet. – *adj.* **Gimlet-eyed,** very sharp-sighted.

10. **Step 2.** Since a wine's flavour molecules are given off only on the liquid's surface, they can be seriously encouraged by maximising the wine's surface area. Swirl the wine round in a glass, ideally one with a stem so that a graceful movement which has no effect on the wine's temperature can be achieved, and preferably no more than half-full so that no wine is spilled. The ideal wine glass goes in towards the rim so that the swirled wine tends to stay in the glass and so

does the heady vapour above it. Just one short sniff while you concentrate is enough. Notice whether the smell is clean and attractive, how intense the smell is, and what the smell reminds you of.

11

A Bird came down the Walk –
He did not know I saw –
He bit an Angleworm in halves
And ate the fellow, raw.

And then he drank a Dew
From a convenient Grass –
And then hopped sidewise to the Wall
To let a Beetle pass –

12

The quality of mercy is not strain'd,
It droppeth as the gentle rain from heaven
Upon the place beneath: it is twice blest,
It blesseth him that gives, and him that takes,
'Tis mightiest in the mightiest, it becomes
The throned monarch better than his crown.

13

In this factory in the north of England acid was essential. It was contained in large vats. Gangways were laid above them. Before these gangways were made completely safe a young man fell into a vat feet first. His screams of agony were heard all over the department. Except for one old fellow the large body of men was so horrified that for a time not one of them could move. In an instant this old fellow who was also the young man's father had clambered up and along the gangway carrying a big pole. Sorry Hughie, he said. And then ducked the young man below the surface. Obviously the old fellow had had to do this because only the head and shoulders – in fact, that which had been seen above the acid was all that remained of the young man.

COMMENTARY It's unlikely that you will have found much difficulty in assigning the texts into the two categories. Most of them will have fallen easily into one or the other, though perhaps numbers 7 and 8 caused problems. Was 7 a real or a scripted conversation? Could 8 *really* be counted as literature? Later in this chapter, we'll see that there may be more problems than these in deciding what is and is not literature, but, for the present, what we can say is that most people seem instinctively to recognise what may be called literature *at the present time*. The reasons that helped you decide may well have included:

the language of the extract
the purpose of the extract
the genre of the extract.

The next activity will examine these in more detail.

ACTIVITY 38

In the previous activity you placed each text into one of two categories: literary or non-literary. Here we are asking you to organise the texts in different ways.

1 Discuss the texts and place them in categories other than literary/non-literary. You can use any method of classifying them that you like, as there can be no right nor wrong answers here, but you should aim to have five groups. You should have at least two texts in each of your groups.

2 Complete the accompanying table as you work, making sure that you clearly explain the basis for your classification. What are the common factors linking your texts? You may find that a text may legitimately go into more than one group.

Group no.	Texts included	Reasons for inclusion

COMMENTARY There are many possible ways for you to have classified these texts, but we'll look here at some of the most important ones.

Purpose

In Chapter 2 (p. 50), we looked at the purposes writers (and speakers) could have in producing their texts and saw that identifying the purpose of a text, especially a literary one, was not always a simple task. A number of A level English specifications classify purpose under four main headings: texts that:

> entertain   advise/instruct
> inform   persuade

and you might find this a useful way of looking at texts. Of course, as we saw earlier, texts may have more than one purpose, so it can also be useful to think about the *primary* purpose of a text in your initial response to it.

Audience

The fact that texts are produced for different audiences will affect the ways writers or speakers present their material. Not only will the selection of what to say or to write be affected, so too will the order in which that material is presented. The type of audience will also be of the utmost importance in determining the language that a writer or speaker uses in her work. You wouldn't write for, or speak to, an audience of, say, specialist rose growers in the same way as you would to an audience of leisure gardeners even if the subject matter, such as plant propagation, were the same. You would tailor what you said and how you said it to the needs of the particular audience in front of you. Audiences can be differentiated, as in this example, not only by their level of knowledge of the subject, but also by their age, gender, social and ethnic background and, of course, by the period in which they are or were living. Whether you are producing a text for an audience that consists of a single person or of many is also important.

Mode

The basic distinction here is between those texts which are in the spoken mode and those which are in the written. Usually it is quite easy to distinguish between these two modes, but sometimes it can be a little more problematic. What about a text, for instance, that is written, but is intended to be spoken? Sermons, speeches and lectures are some such. Or even Texts 7 and 12 here, which are extracts from well-known plays?

Medium

We can encounter texts in a variety of media and this too can provide a method of classification. In the 13 texts you have been examining, there are examples of various media: magazines (4 and 10); books (3, 6, 9, 11 and 13); the theatre (7 and 12); impromptu conversation (2); newspapers (1); pamphlets (5) and cards (8). These are not the only media possible: television, radio, cinema and posters spring quickly to mind. You will be able to think of many others. We can sometimes even encounter the same text in more than one medium. Think, for example, of a television production of a Shakespeare play. The text, originally written for the theatre, appears in a much more modern medium. However, are television or radio adaptations of famous novels, such as *Pride and Prejudice* new texts or are they just the same text in a new medium?

Genre

A genre (or text type) is a grouping together of a number of texts that share some significant features. These 'significant features' can be seen as the conventions or rules of the particular genre. A traditional way of looking at genre in literature is to divide it up into poetry, prose and drama, but a moment's thought will tell you that this division, whilst useful, is rather too broad. For example, there are different types of poetry (narrative and lyric are just two) and of drama (comic and tragic are, again, two traditional genres) and, of course, there are many genres of prose, including novels. And there are many types of novel: popular novels can be subdivided into crime, horror, sci-fi, romance and so on.

But there are other genres not restricted to 'literature'. Think of letters, recipes, reports, newspaper articles . . . Again, you'll be able to think of many other genres yourself. The fact that we can instantly recognise a genre from even the slightest linguistic clues ('Dear Sir'; '300g. of self-raising flour'; 'Thank you for calling') demonstrates our familiarity with a huge number of different genres, both literary and non-literary. This knowledge forms an important part of our socio-cultural make-up. Very significant features (or conventions) of a particular genre will be its topic or subject matter, the structure and organisation of this subject matter and the style in which it is generally written or spoken.

Register

Register is the generally recognised and approved set of conventions for 'putting into words' ideas, thoughts and information about a particular field or subject. It can be compared with wearing the right type of clothes for a particular event or occasion: wedding, cricket match, funeral, cocktail party, club, hiking trip. Historians, for example, know what the rules are for writing history and the reader knows what to expect. Three different historians (Alan Bullock, A. J. P. Taylor, Hugh Trevor Roper) all use the same register for writing about the last days of Hitler, but there is still room for individual touches of style without breaking the history register conventions. As we have seen, the choice of a writer's topic, purpose and audience will affect the way he will write or speak. The topic and purpose are sometimes referred to as the *field* of the register and the writer's relationship with his audience is sometimes referred to as the *tenor* of the register. This relationship will be shown by the tone in which the audience is addressed and also by the level of formality (or informality) the writer choose to use. The third area of register we have already discussed on page 62 – *Mode*.

Date

Obviously, the date of a text or the period in which it was produced can be a justifiable basis for its classification and the texts you have been considering vary in date from 1999 (Text 5) to 1596 (Text 12).

Other factors

It is, of course, possible to have classified these 13 texts on other grounds, but to have done this confidently, you would have needed further information about them. For example, knowledge of the gender of the authors or their country of origin might have been useful. As you work through this book, you will come to see many other ways of looking at texts, but the ones we have just outlined here are arguably the most important.

Not surprisingly, you will have based many of your judgements about these texts principally on the ways in which their authors used language – the words they chose, the order and combination of these words and, to some extent, the way they are presented on the page. In fact, for this activity, there was little else that you could have based your decisions on. What resources other than the English Language do authors have? In Chapter 4, we take a close linguistic look at texts.

You might find it useful (or enlightening) to know the sources of the 13 texts you have been working on. We will be returning to some of them later in the chapter because they illustrate interesting issues.

1 A letter to *The Times* (1913). A few days later, a second letter from Mr Lydekker was published in which he admitted that he had been deceived about the cuckoo. The sound that he had heard was that of a bricklayer imitating the bird!

2 A conversation between friends, recorded as data for an A level student's project.

3 The opening ten lines of Andrew Marvell's poem *To His Coy Mistress*, first published in 1681.

4 The text of an advertisement for Oris watches.

5 Booking information from a Royal Northern College of Music brochure (1999).

6 An extract from Evelyn Waugh's 1945 novel *Brideshead Revisited*.

7 An extract from Harold Pinter's 1960 short play *The Dumb Waiter*.

8 A verse from a Christmas card.

9 A definition of *gimlet* from *Chambers 20th Century Dictionary* (1972 edition).

10 Part of Jancis Robinson's *Radio Times Wine Course*.

11 The first two stanzas of a poem by Emily Dickinson, an American writing in the late nineteenth century.

12 Part of Portia's famous speech to the court in *The Merchant of Venice* (1596).

13 A complete short story, *Acid*, by the Scottish writer, James Kelman (1983).

What *is* literature?

This, as no doubt you will have begun to realise, is no easy question to answer. Not only is it difficult because many people today, including readers, teachers and critics, are still arguing over its exact definition, but the meaning of the word *literature* has changed considerably over time. This, of course, is not unusual, for many words *do* change their meaning, as Chapter 6 will demonstrate. What, perhaps, sets the debate about *literature* apart is the passion with which the participants argue their case and hold to their views – and try to impose these views on others. One example of this which has directly affected you, whether you realised it or not, is in the choice of authors that you studied at Key Stage 4. The Government has its own ideas about which authors write texts deemed worthy to be called *literature* and therefore included these authors in its National Curriculum for English. That's why you read them!

We shall continue by examining a number of the ways in which *literature* has been defined.

1 Letters alone

The origin (or etymology) of the word *literature* shows its essential connection with writing. The Latin word *literatura* means *writings*, stemming from the word *litera*, a letter of the alphabet and the first definition in the Oxford English Dictionary (OED) stresses this connection: 'acquaintance with "letters" or books'. Perhaps the modern use of the word *literacy* (being able to read and write) comes close to this early definition of *literature*. This seems straightforward enough, but, as usual with what seems straightforward, it raises a number of questions. We'll deal with one of these questions here and with one in the next section. Does the emphasis on *writing* mean that there is no such thing as 'oral literature'? We've already seen (p. 54) how important a part oral performance plays and, of course, much that is written is written to be heard and never intended to be read.

ACTIVITY 39

In groups, discuss whether you think any of the following can be called literature:

the lyrics of a pop song
a rap
a traditional oral children's narrative
a speech, such as Martin Luther King's *I have a dream*

the routines of a stand up comedian
a film script, such as *Pulp Fiction* or *Four Weddings and a Funeral*
a radio play
stories, poems, chants, rituals from a non-literate society.

2 All writing?

ACTIVITY 40

Here are three quotations in which the word *literature* appears. Read them carefully and then write a definition of *literature* based on how the word is being used in these quotations.

1 I was well acquainted with the literature of the subject (1860).
2 It has accumulated a literature of its own which an ordinary lifetime is hardly enough to master (1873).
3 A voluminous scientific literature accumulates each year on the normal vibrational modes of molecules in liquids (1973).

Two further quotations follow. Again, write a definition of the word as it is used here.

4 Full details and literature from: Yugoslav National Tourist Office (1962).
5 I talked my throat dry, gave away sheaves of persuasive literature (1973).

COMMENTARY For the first set of quotations, you may well have arrived at a definition that suggests that literature consists of anything important written on a particular subject. For example, we could say that economics has a literature that includes the classic writings of J. M. Keynes, current research papers, learned journals, textbooks and so on. Every subject from astro-physics to zoology has its own literature. The final two quotations widen the definition somewhat and begin to include printed matter of any kind. For instance, you may well have heard someone casually remark that she's just going to pick up some literature about Spain from the travel agent's. You know very well she doesn't mean *Don Quixote* or Ernest Hemingway's novel about the Spanish Civil War *For Whom the Bell Tolls*, but some brochures about holidays on the Costa del Sol. Similarly, we use *literature* about estate agents' leaflets, about the material we receive from political parties at election times, about insurance documents and about a host of other things. With these two definitions of *literature*, we are still a long way from Shakespeare, Jane Austen and William Wordsworth! In fact, it is only since the late eighteenth and early nineteenth centuries that *literature* has narrowed in meaning to its current sense of imaginative or creative writing. Up till that time, the broader definitions that you have been working on in this activity were the dominant ones. *Literature*, in the sense of fine or imaginative writing, is a relatively recent use.

3 Fire the canon

George Keith, in his book *Language and Literature,* defines a canon as 'an authorised collection of writings, "great works" if you like, that has been accumulated over several centuries of literature. It forms a basis for the National Curriculum, GCSE, GCE syllabuses and university courses in English Literature'. The three authors, Shakespeare, Austen and Wordsworth, referred to in the previous section, are very important members of the canon. If you went up to someone in the street and asked them to name some of the great authors of English Literature, chances are that they would cite writers such as these. Other names that are likely to crop up would be Dickens, Keats and Hardy. But there are, of course, many others that could be included. Recently, there has been much dispute, however, over which authors and which types of work (genres) should be included in a canon. Or even whether there should be a canon at all. This next activity will enable you to take a critical look at 'canonical' authors.

ACTIVITY 41

The list that follows contains the set books for A level English Literature for 1969.

1 For each title on the list, fill in the accompanying chart. You may have to do some research in the library or from the Internet, if you do not immediately know some of the answers.

2 Then complete the chart for the set books for the current A level English Literature specification. You may have to ask your teacher to supply you with this information.

William Shakespeare	*Othello; The Tempest*
Geoffrey Chaucer	*The Pardoner's Tale* and *The Prioress's Tale*
Sir Philip Sidney	*The Defense of Poesy*
John Donne	*Songs and Sonets*
Ben Jonson	*Volpone*
John Milton	Selections from *Paradise Lost* (Books 1, 2, 3 and 4)
Alexander Pope	*An Essay on Man*
Henry Fielding	*Tom Jones*
James Boswell	*Journal of a Tour to the Hebrides*
William Wordsworth	*Selected Poems*

Jane Austen	*Emma*
Charles Dickens	*Hard Times*
Robert Browning	*Men and Women*
Thomas Hardy	*The Return of the Native*
Bernard Shaw	*Man and Superman*
James Joyce	*A Portrait of the Artist as a Young Man*
Wilfred Owen	*Selected Poems*
T. S. Eliot	*The Cocktail Party*
D. H. Lawrence	*Sons and Lovers*
Arthur Miller	*Death of a Salesman*

Chart

Author				
Male/Female	**Date of Birth**	**Nationality**	**Ethnic Background**	**Social Class**

Text		
Genre	**Standard English/Non-Standard English**	**Theme**

Genre Standard English/Non Standard Theme

1 Discuss, in groups or in class, the following questions:
   Are there any authors, titles or types of writing you would like to see included?
   Are there any authors, titles or types of writing you would like to see excluded?

2 Write a piece, in any genre you choose (newspaper article, essay, etc.) expressing your views on this canon. You might, for instance, agree with the often heard criticism that literature is mainly written and read by the middle class and that the canon represents white, male, middle-class taste. *Is* literature, in your view, merely a middle class hobby? This could form the basis of a piece of original writing for your coursework.

4 Organised violence?

Read the following short extract from the famous opening page of James Joyce's *A Portrait of the Artist as a Young Man*. Note down what seems to be unusual about the way that Joyce uses language here. You'll find our comments at the end of the chapter, but don't read them until you've tried the activity yourself.

Once upon a time and a very good time it was there was a moocow coming down the road and this moocow that was coming down the road met a nicens little boy named baby tuckoo . . .

His father told him that story: his father looked at him through a glass: he had a hairy face.
He was baby tuckoo. The moocow came down the road where Betty Byrne lived: she sold lemon platt.

> O, the wild rose blossoms
> On the little green place.

He sang that song. That was his song.
> O, the green wothe botheth.

You'll probably agree that there is some unusual language use in this extract and that it deviates from the 'normal'. Joyce is certainly drawing attention to his use of language in a way that this paragraph, for example, isn't. Because the sentence structure and vocabulary in Joyce is unusual, the reader is likely to pay close attention to it. In that sense, Joyce's language is demonstrating 'organised violence committed on ordinary speech'. This quotation is an attempt to define what literature and the literary is by focusing solely on the way language is used.

Another way of saying this is that 'literature transforms and intensifies ordinary language, deviates systematically from ordinary speech' (Terry Eagleton). So, according to this view, literature *is* literature because it uses language in peculiar or heightened ways. We should expect to find in literature language that, (though obviously English in its grammar, vocabulary, meaning and sounds) is an English that draws attention to itself by, for example, its repetition of certain sounds or grammatical patterns, by its use of figures of speech) such as simile and metaphor, and by its use of unusual vocabulary or word order. These by no means exhaust the ways that writers can commit organised violence on language. This purpose of making language strange, according to the Formalists, the name of the people who held to this view, is to enable readers to see the world in new and different ways, rather than in the dull and tired ones they have always done. It would certainly make you view very differently the person who came up to you in the student common room to remind you that you should have been in class five minutes ago with the words *Redeem thy mis-spent time that's past* or tried to chat you up by saying *O Mistress mine, where are you roaming?*

ACTIVITY 43

The following passages from novels or poems use language in ways that are deviant. Discuss each one with a partner and identify and describe these uses.

1 All of it is now   it is always now   there will never be a time when I am not crouching and watching others who are crouching too I am always crouching   the man on my face is dead   his face is not mine   his mouth smells sweet but his eyes are locked   some who eat nasty themselves   I do not eat   the men without skin bring us their morning water to drink   we have none   at night I cannot see the dead man on my face daylight comes through the crack and I can see his locked eyes

> from *Beloved* by Toni Morrison. (The extract is about the memories of a slave being transported to America from Africa)

2

        Buffalo Bill's
        defunct
                who used to
                ride a watersmooth-silver
                                        stallion
        and break onetwothreefourfive pigeonsjustlikethat
                                                Jesus
        he was a handsome man
                                and what I want to know is
        how do you like your blueeyed boy
        Mister Death

                                        e e cummings

3

Me Cyaan Believe It (extract)

me seh me cyaan believe it
me seh me cyaan believe it

room dem a rent
me apply widin
but as me go een
cockroach rat an scorpion
also come een

Waan good
nose haffi run
but me naw go siddung pon high wall
like Humpty Dumpty
me a face me reality

                                        Michael Smith

4 On my naming day when I come 12 I gone front spear and kilt a wild boar he parbly ben the las wyld pig on the Bundel Downs any how there hadnt ben none for a long time befor him nor I aint looking to see none agen. He dint make the groun shake nor nothing like that when he come on to my spear he wernt all that big plus he lookit poorly

> from *Riddley Walker* by Russell Hoban (set in the aftermath of a nuclear war)

ACTIVITY 44

Here are some further short extracts. Again, discuss them with a partner. Place them in a rank order from the one that seems to you to use language in the most unusual way to the least unusual.

  1 **Hat gets ahead**
    It was a simple case of 'many nappy returns' in yesterday's Champion stakes at Newmarket.
    Flying french filly Hatoof had reigned supreme over the Rowley Mile in last year's 1000 Guineas.

  2 Bartley Costello, eighty years old, sat in his silver-grey tweeds on a kitchen chair, at his door in Carraroe, the sea only yards away, smoking a pipe, with a pint of porter beside his boot.

  3 Smooooooooth.

  4 Fancy a top up luv? By 'eck, it's gorgeous, petal!

  5 'Scone or scone – which do you say?' he said, assertive, now, his face flushed. It was as if he was just looking for a fight.
    As ever, she rose to the bait. 'Scone, as

everyone knows, rhymes with gone. It's
more elegant.'
 'Ha!' he cried, triumphant. 'Bone! It rhymes
with bone! – look up the phonetics in the
dictionary.'
 'Either way!' she countered, 'you can say it
either way – I looked it up once.'

6 Complicated be The Internet can a
Macintosh Performa unless you buy.

7 We didn't have to scramble for a parking
place near the Apollo Theatre, since we live
less than five minutes walk away. I couldn't
believe my luck when I discovered this
development halfway through my first year
as a law student at Manchester University.

8 We could count the times we went for a
walk or the times we danced together in the
past months.

9 Want a chat, quiet word, tête-à-tête, natter,
parley, an interface *(interface?)*, confab,
gossip, chinwag, pow-wow, heart-to-heart,
rabbit, conversazione . . .?

10 Polished mahogany with red-gold lights.
This has a nose to eulogise over; blood-
orange juice, vanilla, assorted nuts,
cinnamon, ginger and nutmeg. The
experience begins with citrus freshness and
ends with an enticing soft-liquorice feel.

11 I met Jimmy a couple of years ago when I
came back to work this place. The hardest
thing about street work is gathering a
crowd.

12 It's boring. Get engaged. Probably work in
Safeways worst luck.

COMMENTARY

Only five of these twelve short pieces were from literary texts. These were
numbers 2, 8 and 12, which were extracts from poems (though without the
usual lineation) and 7 and 11, which were taken from two modern novels.
It would be quite surprising had you placed any of these near the top of
your list of unusual uses of language. 'I couldn't believe my luck' (7) or 'We
could count the times we went for a walk' (8) do not leap out and demand
your attention. They could easily be seen as unexceptionable everyday uses
of language. In fact, all the ones that seem to us to 'commit violence' on
everyday language are taken from sources that are not considered to be
literary. One (1) is from a tabloid newspaper, whilst the remainder are
extracts from advertisements. Each one, in its own way, draws attention to
the way language is being used. The language is not neutral in any of them.
We notice the sound in 3, the word-play in 1, the vocabulary in 9, the
syntax in 6, the use of figurative language in 10, dialect in 4. Arguably, only
5 does not draw attention to itself, though in context, an advertisement for
jam, it *is* an unusual use of language. 'Foregrounding' is the term linguists
use to refer to this attention-seeking aspect of language use.

What can we learn from this? Clearly unusual language use, or
defamiliarisation, is not confined to literature. Advertisements (as here),
jokes, headlines, word games, for instance, all use language flamboyantly,
whilst the language of some novels, plays and poems is low-key and
understated. So, systematic deviation from the ordinary is not a
pre-requisite for literature. If it were, then only the most way-out uses of
language would count as literature and this clearly is not the case.

There are two other problems with this view that are worth mentioning.

1 If literary language is supposed to be a language that deviates from the
ordinary, who is to decide what 'ordinary' is ? One person's 'ordinary'
might well be another's 'deviant'! For example, my middle-class standard

English might be ordinary for me, but 'deviant' for a fisherman in Stornoway or a street trader in the Portobello Road or Huddersfield markets. Dialects can vary across social classes as well as between them, so that the traders in London and Huddersfield, though likely to be from the same class, may still find each other's language strange.

2 Most language from an earlier age is deviant to us in some way. We no longer use some of the vocabulary or the grammar of Elizabethan English, so does that mean that everything written in 1590 is literary? An Elizabethan shopping list or laundry bill, for instance!

5 Be practical!

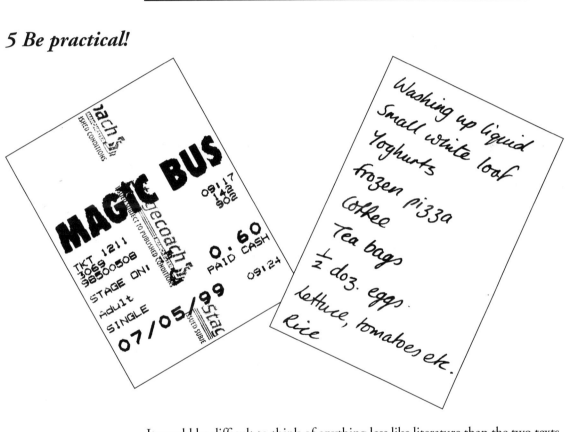

It would be difficult to think of anything less like literature than the two texts above. Bus tickets and shopping lists seem light years away from Shakespeare and Jane Austen. There are many other types of text, too, perhaps not such extreme examples as these, that also seem to have no connection at all with literature. Think of a handbook on fishing, a history book, a political speech or a popular magazine article on contemporary social behaviour. We wouldn't think a speech by the present Prime Minister or the history book we plough through at A level qualify as literature, would we? And certainly not a practical handbook on such a popular pastime as fishing. But, there are plenty of texts like these that are read as literature nowadays. We read Izaak Walton's *The Compleat Angler*, Gibbon's *Decline and Fall of the Roman Empire*, Abraham Lincoln's *Gettysburg Address* and Henry Mayhew's articles on the poor of Victorian London as literature today, though they were not originally written as such. Izaak Walton would have been amazed to find that this practical handbook on fishing was now regarded as a classic of English literature. And what about diaries (Pepys), sermons (John Donne), accounts of natural history (Gilbert White) and essays (Bacon)? Not to mention travel writing, journalism and sports writing? Admittedly all the examples we have cited have stood the test of time and there will be many handbooks on fishing and many political speeches that deserve never again to be read. But who is to say that in 400 years' time, your equivalents will not be reading a handbook on computer games or the sound bites of Tony Blair as classics of English literature?

The point here is that it is very difficult to restrict what we call 'literature' to the traditional genres of poetry, prose fiction and drama and refuse entry to any other genres. Events have a nasty habit of undermining certainties. If I, together with lots of other people, choose to read *Ancrene Wisse*, a handbook containing advice for medieval nuns, as literature, then nearly 800 years later literature has it become. As Terry Eagleton says 'some texts are born literary, some achieve literariness, and some have literariness thrust upon them'. But where does that leave the bus ticket and the shopping list? Still standing in the cold outside the house of literature, presumably? Well, perhaps not.

ACTIVITY 45

Read the following six short texts and identify what text type (or genre) you think each one is. Note down what it was about each text that lead you to your decision.

1
**Arson Suspected in
Penn Villas Blaze**

Out-of-Stater Perishes

West Brewer police are still collecting testimony from neighbors
in connection with the mysterious fire
that destroyed the handsome Penn
Villas residence of Mr and Mrs
Harold Angstrom.

2
The Unknown Citizen
To
JS/07/M/378
This Marble Monument is erected by the State

3
**Viper's Bugloss
Productions**

A Year in the Life:

'Clive's Seasons'

GENERIC TITLE SEQUENCE
TITLE ON SCREEN
'A YEAR IN THE LIFE'

EXT. DAY: DAWN CHORUS
WIDE SHOT TUMULUS WITH SUN
RISING BEHIND IT
LONG-SHOT ROOKS CIRCLING
TREES

4　A sudden shut-down of the arterio-venous anastomoses of the face floods the capillaries with the blood that produces the characteristically heightened colour.

5　Sparse juniper forests on dry lavender hills, down Ritter Butte to Pass Creek, a pot dream recounted: crossing Canada border with a tin can in the glove compartment, hip young border guards laughing – In meadow the skeleton of an old car settled: Look to Jesus painted on door.

6　The object similar in this respect to all other phonotypes previously unearthed and duly described in archeological catalogues is black of color, flat and circular in shape and its surface graven with countless barely perceptible anfractuosities.

COMMENTARY　You will have identified a variety of text types here. But all is not as it seems, for each of these texts is taken either from a novel (1, 3 and 4) or a poem (2, 5 and 6) and the writer is either deliberately imitating the style of another text or, in the case of 4, incorporating a direct quotation from another text into his own novel. So, not only can literature admit a host of other genres into its house, as we saw earlier, but it can also incorporate other types of writing into itself. A novelist can either imitate different styles in her novel when it suits her purpose or can directly use other texts. This practice of using texts or styles of texts from other genres in literary works is sometimes known as re-registration. A style that is 'non-literary' can be re-registered for use in a literary text. All types and styles of writing are fair game. This is where the bus ticket and shopping list come in. For, if any text is fair game, then you could expect to find a bus ticket or shopping list as part of some literary text!

ACTIVITY 46

Choose a 'non-literary' text. It might be the bus ticket or shopping list, but it could just as easily be a newspaper headline, an advertisement, a guarantee, a letter to a problem page, a horoscope, an e-mail or a recipe or . . . Write a short story or poem that incorporates your chosen text (or texts). Again, you could write this as part of your coursework submission.

6 Pulp fiction?

In the previous section we saw that the concept of 'literature' can be somewhat leaky and that many works of non-fiction are counted as literature. But there are still many works of fiction outside in the cold not allowed to call themselves 'literature'. Many of these works are enormously popular with many readers, whilst 'classics' of literature make do with far fewer readers. Writers like Catherine Cookson, Agatha Christie and Jilly Cooper command enormous sales, whilst others, much praised by literary critics, have to make do with far smaller scales. Why is this? Why are crime fiction, romantic novels, thrillers and Westerns, for instance, usually excluded from 'literature'? Does the 'canon' that we looked at in Section 3 extend not just to approved writers, but to approved genres as well? Of course, sometimes an occasional representative of one of these genres, like Raymond Chandler's crime fiction or Jack London's Westerns, is deemed worthy to be called 'literature', but, in the main, genres such as these are not valued highly. Perhaps the key lies in the word *valued* and the closest we can get to a definition of 'literature' is that it is the kind of writing that is valued highly. But valued by whom? And, of course, values change so that works that are considered classics of literature today might not be so tomorrow. There are some signs, however, that previously excluded genres, such as crime fiction, might be breaking down the barriers.

ACTIVITY 47

1 Each member of the group should choose a book that they have recently read and which they particularly enjoyed.

2 On your own, write down (a) a list of reasons why you read and enjoyed the book and (b) a list of the reasons why the book should be studied on an A level Literature (or Language and Literature) course. Some of the reasons in (a) and (b) may overlap.

3 Justify your choice of book to others in the group.

4 Now do the same for an acknowledged classic of English Literature. This could be a text you studied at GCSE.

5 Choose an acknowledged classic and list the reasons why it *shouldn't* be included on an A level Literature course. Warning: you are not allowed to use the word *boring* in this activity. Remember, boredom is just as likely to be the reader's fault as the writer's!

7 English, whose English?

So far in this chapter, we've explored some of the implications of the word *literature* and seen that once we begin to unpack it then things aren't quite as straightforward as they first might have appeared. We've looked at areas of controversy about *literature* that people are still discussing in the hope that you might reach some conclusions of your own about what is and is not *literature*. But the subject you are studying for A level is not simply *Language and Literature* but *English* Language and Literature, so we want to close this chapter by exploring the notion of *English*.

ACTIVITY 48

1 Working in small groups, brainstorm what the word *English* means to you in the term *English Literature*.

2 Discuss these ideas and formulate an agreed definition for *English* Literature.

3 Report back to the class and see if you can reach a class agreement about what the term means.

COMMENTARY You will probably have discovered that *English* Literature is, at best, a rather ambiguous term. It can be used in at least four ways:

- the literature of England (Chaucer, Shakespeare, Milton, Wordsworth, the Brontës, Hardy Larkin, Golding, Hughes ...).
- the literature of Great Britain (and Ireland) (all of the above plus Burns, Shaw, Wilde, Yeats, Heaney, Dylan Thomas ...). Of course, this definition would exclude those writers who wrote in Welsh, Irish and Scots. Nothing is ever clear-cut!
- all literature written in English, whatever the country of origin of the author (all of the above plus Arthur Miller, Chinua Achebe, Margaret Atwood, Vikram Seth, Mark Twain ...)
- a mixture of all of these.

And, of course, there's always literature in translation to consider! Few people in England read Ibsen in Norwegian, Chekhov in Russian or even Balzac or Proust in French.

Nor should you forget the work of dialect writers. William Barnes, a highly regarded English poet, wrote all of his work in Dorset dialect.

ACTIVITY 49

Below is a map of the world followed by a list of authors who write in English and appear on A level syllabuses. Link these authors with their country of origin on the map. This may well involve you in some research.

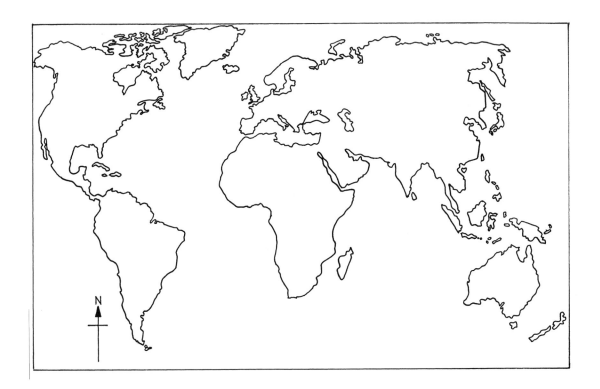

Salman Rushdie	Doris Lessing	Jean Rhys	James Kelman
Nadine Gordimer	Margaret Atwood	Timothy Mo	Brian Friel
Jonathan Swift	R. S. Thomas	Irvine Welsh	Derek Walcott
Kazuo Ishiguro	W. B. Yeats	Tennessee Williams	Peter Carey
Samuel Beckett	James Joyce	Kate Chopin	Katherine Mansfield
Robert Frost	Athol Fugard	Seamus Heaney	Stephen Crane
Ernest Hemingway	e e cummings	F. Scott Fitzgerald	Sylvia Plath
Patrick White	Tom Stoppard	V. S. Naipaul	Toni Morrison
Grace Nichols	Carol Shields	Emyr Humphries	Keri Hulme
Robert Burns	Louis MacNeice	Joseph Conrad	Emily Dickinson
Isaac Bashevis Singer	Vladimir Nabokov	Samuel Selvon	James Ngugi

If there are any glaring gaps on the map when you have finished, then you should do more research to enable you to fill these in.

ACTIVITY 50

Some of the same problems occur when we start to talk about the *English* language. This, too, is quite difficult to define, as the following questions will show. Discuss each of them in small groups.

1 What language does the President of the United States speak?
2 Does a person born, brought up and living in Kingston, Jamaica speak the same language as one born, brought up and living in Liverpool? Are the languages English?
3 Would they *write* the same language?
4 Is *The Queen's English* the model to which we should all aspire?
5 What does it mean to call English a world language?
6 Is someone who speaks with a broad Yorkshire (or Devon or Norfolk) accent and who uses dialect words speaking English? And what about Glasgow, Belfast, New York or Johannesburg?
7 What are Spanglish and Singlish?
8 Where do you think the best English is spoken and written? And by whom?

Neither a borrower nor a lender be. This might be good advice in domestic circles, but not in linguistic ones. We all know that the English (and American) export their words to almost every language in the world so that, for example, *jeans* are worn everywhere. We know that the French enjoy *le weekend* and go *camping* and that Germans can listen to *der Reporter* conducting *die Interviews*. Italian is a very good example of a market for our exported words. Since the 1960s the pace in which English words have been assimilated into Italian has accelerated rapidly. Recent borrowings (quoted by Tom McArthur in his excellent *Oxford Companion to the English Language*) include *baby, boom, boy, budget, cartoon, catering, ceiling, club, control system, deadline, dee-jay, designer, egghead, fifty–fifty, flash, girl, happiness, identikit, killer, lady, leader, life-saver, market* and that's got us only through half the alphabet! But it's not all one way traffic, of course. Perhaps we're just paying back the Italians for all our borrowings from their language. *Adagio, alfresco, alto, bimbo, bravo, cello, confetti, extravaganza, fiasco, fresco, ghetto, lasagne, mafia, minestrone, pasta, regatta, soprano, solo, stanza* are just a few of these. How many more can you think of?

ACTIVITY 51

English imports lots of words, many of which we may not even realise *are* of foreign origin. Using the same map you used in the earlier exercise, link these following words, now common in English, with their country of origin. You may need to use a good dictionary to help you in your search.

bungalow	yacht	slogan	juggernaut	commando	pundit
robot	muster	reservoir	basket	anorak	barbecue
potato	ukulele	hussar	bog	ketchup	tundra
sarong	chocolate	toboggan	budgerigar	shawl	walkabout
alcove	intelligentsia	tattoo	scoff	abattoir	husky
loofah	almanac	bagel	eisteddfod	typhoon	catamaran

Notes

These are some of the unusual ways that Joyce uses language in the passage on page 68:

childish vocabulary (moocow, nicens, tuckoo)
naive repetition of words and phrases (coming down the road, his father, song)
use of *wothe botheth* for *rose blossoms.*

All are unusual, yes, but Joyce's use of them is deliberate, as he is trying to imitate in his language the way a very young boy would think and speak.

4 Language Roundabout

You will all probably have been in a situation where someone asks you a question to which you don't know the answer or you don't want to give one. A possible way out of the situation is to counter the question with another question. For example:

What time is it?
Why do you want to know?

This is likely to throw the original questioner off balance, because the natural response to a question is to provide an answer. It's very difficult not to do so. Sometimes, of course, it can be quite natural to answer a question with a further question:

Has Percy been in touch with you?
Oh, does he need to?

However, most questions provoke answers as responses. *Question and answer* is a type of conversational structure or sequence known to linguists as an *adjacency pair* and such adjacency pairs are very common in conversations. Others include requests and responses, greetings and greetings (*Hello./Hello. How are you?*) and complaints and denials (or apologies).

ACTIVITY 52

With a partner, improvise a conversation that consists entirely of questions. Try to make it as fluent and realistic as possible and see how long you can keep the conversation going. You win if your partner fails to come up with a question or responds with an utterance other than a question. Suitable scenarios might include a teacher asking a student why her essay is late or a 'discussion' with your mother about your new hairstyle, (un)suitable clothing or state of your bedroom.

COMMENTARY

Now read this extract from *Rosencrantz and Guildenstern are Dead*, Tom Stoppard's comedy based on *Hamlet*. Rosencrantz and Guildenstern are bored and are trying to pass the time.

ROS: We could play at questions.
GUIL: What good would that do?
ROS: Practice!
GUIL: Statement! One–love.
ROS: Cheating!

GUIL: How?

ROS: I hadn't started yet.

GUIL: Statement. Two–love.

ROS: Are you counting that?

GUIL: What?

ROS: Are you counting that?

GUIL: Foul! No repetitions. Three–love. First game to . . . .

ROS: I'm not going to play if you're going to be like that.

GUIL: Whose serve?

ROS: Hah?

GUIL: Foul! No grunts. Love–one.

ROS: Whose go?

GUIL: Why?

ROS: Why not?

GUIL: What for?

ROS: Foul! No synonyms! One–all.

GUIL: What in God's name is going on?

ROS: Foul! No rhetoric. Two–one.

GUIL: What does it all add up to?

ROS: Can't you guess?

GUIL: Were you addressing me?

ROS: Is there anyone else?

GUIL: Who?

ROS: How would I know?

GUIL: Why do you ask?

ROS: Are you serious?

GUIL: Was that rhetoric?

ROS: No.

GUIL: Statement!. Two–all. Game point.

This is the same game as you have just been playing, though these two had the advantage of the fact that it wasn't an improvisation, as yours was. The point we want to stress is that both you and Rosencrantz and Guildenstern were engaged in the same activity, but one is called *literature* and the other isn't. It's important for you to realise that *literature* uses the same set of linguistic resources as *non-literature*. The same linguistic structures and the same linguistic functions form the basis of all writing and of all speech. Tom Stoppard wasn't inventing a new set of language rules just for the extract above; you and he were playing the same game. The range of structures and functions that we use and interact with in the normal course of our everyday lives is also found in those texts that we call literature. Think about jokes, adverts, conversations, letters and song lyrics and all the other texts you encounter every waking minute and you'll soon realise that the ways writers and speakers use language is replicated in those texts we call *literary*. Don't forget that the word *text* is used by linguists to mean any stretch or piece of language, whether it's spoken or written, long or short. To a linguist, the label on a baked beans tin is as much a *text* as is *Oliver Twist*. The transcript of a conversation in the common room is as much a *text* as is *Macbeth*. Not only are the same language structures used, but many of the same forms appear in literary texts as well as in non-literary ones. We've seen that already in the Stoppard extract, but think of the part letters play in some novels (think of *Tess of the d'Urbevilles*) and lawyers' cross-examinations in some plays (*The Winslow Boy*, for example). Diaries

(*Robinson Crusoe*), military instructions (*Naming of Parts*) and sermons (*A Portrait of the Artist as a Young Man*) are just three other genres that appear in literary texts. In fact, it is probably true to say that there are few, if any, non-literary genres that have not been used by literary writers at some time or other. We will be considering later what it is that makes literature special, what it is that sets it apart from non-literary texts, but for the moment we just need to stress that both literature and non-literature have their basis in the same set of language structures and functions. As this is, indeed, the case, it follows that some non-literary texts use many of the language features that we conventionally think of as the preserve of literature. The next activity will illustrate this.

ACTIVITY 53

Read the following text, which is part of an advertisement for Arniston Bay wines, and identify those features which you might also expect to find in a poem. Of course, taken out of context as this text is, you could also be forgiven for thinking that it was an extract from a holiday brochure.

I came across a sandy bay
 secluded from the world
  and as I sit, by the dancing fire

with the fish growing hot on the coals
I watch the gulls and the fishing boats
 sailing slowly over the sea
and I take a deep breath
 and smell the air
the salty, fresh, clean smell of the air
and as I sit, I can almost see time
 dancing idly on the waves
and as I sit, I somehow know
 I will not leave today.

One very useful way of thinking about literature is to consider it as a prime example of verbal art. In other words, we can see literature as a way of using the resources of language that springs primarily from an artistic or creative impulse. Writers of other texts may share this artistic or creative impulse, but not, perhaps, to the same extent as the writers of literary ones.

A useful distinction that can be made is between those texts (both spoken and written) that use language for practical or social purposes and those that use it for more artistic ones. Some linguists, notably Michael Halliday, have called the former *transactional* uses of language and the latter, *poetic* uses. Of course, some texts blur this distinction and the wine advertisement is a good illustration of this. You will have seen that it shares many features you might find in a poem (the use of figurative language is just one of these you should have noted) and thus the advertisement could well be seen as *poetic*, but clearly its main purpose or function is *transactional*, as it is intended to increase the sales of Arniston wines – a highly practical purpose. Many texts or text types fall into this rather grey area, using the resources of verbal art for transactional purposes. Let's, however, return briefly to the poetic or the artistic, literary, entertaining uses of language. Note that these terms live together quite comfortably.

1 In a small group, list as many of these artistic or entertaining uses of language as you can. Don't restrict yourself merely to written examples nor to the conventionally literary. Here are just a few to get you started.

Written

Newspaper headlines
Advertisements
Song lyrics
Greetings card messages

Spoken

Telling jokes
Deejaying
Performance poetry
Football chants

2 When you have a substantial number of examples, try to put them in a rank order, beginning with those that use verbal art mainly to fulfil practical or social purposes and ending with those that use it purely creatively. You might, for instance, put advertising at one end and poetry at the other. Or, you might not . . . .

Language frameworks

One thing that all the texts we have been discussing so far in this chapter have in common is that they are all examples of *verbal* art. As we have seen, all texts, including literary ones, use the same language resources. Thus, in order for us to be able to examine *how* it achieves the effects it does on its hearers or listeners, we need to be able to understand the ways in which language works. To do this, it is helpful to think of language as a series of interlocking systems.

To achieve their effects, writers and speakers make choices, sometimes consciously, often instinctively, from the many, many options available to them within each of these systems. For example, if you are writing an essay, say, or a short story, letter of apology or condolence, you have to think very carefully about your choice of words. It can be crucial. What you are, in effect, doing is selecting the most appropriate words for your purpose from one of the systems of the English language – the lexical. The lexical system is just one of the systems that go to make up a language. So what are these systems that constitute a language?

Phonology	The sound system. Phonology is the study of the sound patterns in a language and consists of both *phonemes* (the vowels and consonants) and *prosody* (stress, rhythm and intonation)
Graphology and Orthography	The writing or print system. Graphology is the study of how texts appear on the printed page, whilst orthography is the study of the spelling system of English.
Lexis	The vocabulary of English. All the words and their origins which constitute the total word stock.
Grammar	This can be seen as consisting of three parts: the structure of individual words (morphology or word-grammar), the way these words combine to form phrases, clauses and sentences (syntax or sentence-grammar). Most linguists nowadays would want to extend the study of grammar beyond the sentence to look at how a whole text is structured and linked (text–grammar).

There is another key framework in language study that is covered more fully in Chapter 7. This is pragmatics which can be defined as the study of what speakers mean when they speak.

You will sometimes see these systems described as language *levels* (or levels of language). We have avoided using this term because it seems to imply a hierarchy of systems. *Level* suggests that some things can be higher (or more important) or lower (less important) than others. This obviously cannot be the case where language is concerned. Lexis, for example, cannot be more important than grammar, as one cannot operate without the other and each will have a part to play in creating meaning. No, language is a series of interlocking systems. When we speak, we are uttering meaningful combinations of sounds (phonology) which our hearers interpret as words (lexis) which themselves combine (grammar) into a meaningful series of utterances. And, of course, *meaningful* implies semantics. For the purpose of studying texts we may isolate one of the systems, but we must never forget that this one system cannot operate on its own. A spoken or written text is the product of a combination of linguistic systems.

This close study of the ways in which the various linguistic systems operate within a text is known as *stylistics*. The purpose of stylistics is to observe how writers or speakers have used the resources of the language to create their effects and elicit a response from their readers.

In this chapter we are concentrating on literary texts and seeing how by taking a linguistic approach to them we can illuminate our understanding. There is, however, another important dimension to the study of texts, both literary and non-literary, that we will not be covering in this chapter, but which we examine in detail in Chapter 10 and that is the study of genre and form.

Linguistic lenses

In the next sections of this chapter, we are going to look at a number of literary texts and examine the ways in which the writers have used the different language systems to achieve their effects.

First, however, two words of warning. One: remember that although we will be looking at the systems separately that is not how readers normally respond to a literary text, or indeed a text of any kind. You don't read a text five times, once to study the phonology, once to study the lexis, once to study the grammar and so on. Of course you don't! Your response to any text is a response to the sum of its parts, not each part (or system) on its own. However, that's what we'll be doing here – but it's only a means to an end, the end being a fuller appreciation of how literary texts work. The second word of warning: though we are obviously going to choose texts that illustrate how writers effectively use the various language systems, not every text you encounter in the course of your reading will be like this. Some of the language systems will be sitting quietly in the background of the text, efficiently getting on with their jobs, but it won't always be necessary for you to comment on them. You only really need to comment on those parts of the language system that the writer has foregrounded.

So we're going to put a number of texts under different high definition language microscopes, or, in the case of phonology, a powerful ear-piece! Each is designed to focus on one of the different language systems; we begin with phonology.

Phonology ear-piece

ACTIVITY 55

Here are 19 'words' in alphabetical order that could possibly exist in English. As you will quickly realise, none of them do. Working in a small group, discuss and rank them beginning with the one that sounds the least pleasant and ending with the one that sounds the most pleasant.

beel	*bibble*	*denkst*	*gratch*	*laysome*	*leel*	*mitty*	*molo*	*palume*	*pib*
ramelon	*sklank*	*soase*	*spikky*	*thrib*	*threeb*	*threeve*	*vodge*	*yopbolk*	

COMMENTARY

We have, of course, no idea of the order you decided on, but it wouldn't surprise us to find that words like *sklank* and *yopbolk* were near the beginning of your list and *palume* and *ramelon* somewhere near the end. Why should this be the case? It's suggested that there is a gradient of sounds in English from 'hard' to 'soft'. The 'hardest' sounds (like /p/ /b/ /t/ /d/ /k/ /g/) all involve the blocking of breath coming from the mouth, followed by its sudden release; the 'softest' (the vowels, together with /w/ and /l/) have no blockage of the air flow, merely reshaping the sounds by changing your lip and tongue position. Writers sometimes use this perception of hard and soft sounds in their work.

We deliberately didn't use real words because we wanted you to concentrate on the sounds alone and not have the meanings of the words interfere with your decisions. For instance, only the initial sound distinguishes pairs like *tumour* and *rumour* or *vermin* and *ermine*, but the meaning of the words would probably have influenced you.

Sound symbolism

Individual sounds do not have meanings. We can't say that /b/ has a meaning or ask *What does /t/ mean?* Sometimes, however, people feel that a sound or a group of sounds may have a symbolic meaning or create expressive effects and the work in the previous activity indicated this. But, be warned! This is a very tricky and subjective area. **Phonaesthesia** is the linguistic term for the idea that certain sounds suggest meanings.

Each group of words in the following list contains a common sound. The words in each group are also linked in meaning in some way and it is suggested that the sound and meaning are connected. You should say the words aloud, perhaps slightly exaggerating the sound when you do so and listen carefully to what you say. You could also try the mirror and ear test! Watch what happens to your face when you say each word. For example, some people have suggested that when you say the /sn/ sound in group 1, an unpleasant expression appears on your face together with a slight tremor on the side of your nose. Is this true? For each group:

- identify the common sound
- identify what meaning each group has in common
- add further examples of words to the groups. Remember that not all words that share this same sound will convey this linked meaning.

1 sneeze   snore   snuffle   snag   snot   snide   snipe   snicker
2 clatter   clang   clump
3 bash   rush   gush   splash   whoosh
4 slash   slant   slope   slope
5 flash   flicker   flame
6 bump   thump   dump   clump

Onomatopoeia

There's a particular form of sound symbolism that you will probably have encountered already. In this, the sounds of the words are said to imitate the sound in the real world to which they refer. Obvious examples include 'tick-toc' for the sound of a clock or 'cuckoo', 'buzz' and 'murmur'. But onomatopoeia and, indeed, all forms of sound symbolism, are not usually as clear cut as these examples. Don't be one of those A level students who, when writing about literary texts, discovers significance in almost every sound or pattern of sounds. Often there isn't any over and above the pleasure we all take in such things as tongue twisters, nursery rhymes and jingles. Remember, sound symbolism is based on people's somewhat vague or subjective impressions, not on any systematic features of the language.

Patterns of sound

Many texts, both literary and non-literary, employ patterns of sound. These are, of course, most noticeable in poetry but, as we shall see, prose writers use them too. There is something essentially satisfying in regular repetition, whether it be in music, flower-beds, painting, wallpaper or fabrics, though prolonged repetition can turn to monotony. Phonological patterning is no exception. We all enjoy hearing and anticipating the regular repetition of rhyme, whether it be in a Shakespearean sonnet, a limerick or an advertising jingle.

These are the most common types of sound pattern found in literary (and non-literary) texts.

Alliteration: the repetition of sounds made by consonants or consonant clusters (e.g. /spl/ /tr/ /gl/) at the beginning of nearby words. Remember, it's the repetition of *sounds*, not *letters*, that counts. So *soap* and *ceiling* alliterate even though they begin with different letters, whereas *ceiling* and *carrot* do not.

Assonance: the repetition of the same vowel sound in nearby words. For example *strain* and *fake* or *plight*, *wide* and *fine*.

Consonance: the repetition of sounds made by consonants or consonant clusters at the end of nearby words. For example, *crab* and *web* or *pant*, *mint* and *evident*.

Rhyme: the repetition of the last vowel and consonant or consonant clusters in nearby words: *goat* and *stoat*; *crosses* and *losses*. Again, remember it's sounds that count, not spelling, so *tough* doesn't rhyme with *bough*, but *cough* rhymes with *scoff*.

Reverse rhyme: this is similar to alliteration, but occurs when the sounds of the initial consonant and vowel are repeated – *seep* and *ceiling* or *cash* and *carry*, for example.

Half (or para-) rhyme: the repetition of initial and final consonants sounds in nearby words, but without any repetition of any vowel sound. So *bait* and *bite* and *wound* and *wind* are half rhymes.

Repetitions of sounds, as long as the words that contain them are close enough together for the reader or listener to remember, can be used in a number of ways. We've already looked at sound symbolism, but writers can also use these repetitions to:

- bind the text together. This contributes to its cohesion.
- emphasise some particular aspect of the text. This emphasis is sometimes known as foregrounding and is not necessarily restricted to sound patterning.
- point out and emphasise links, parallels or contrasts in the meaning of texts.

Some patterns of sound, especially rhyme, are pre-ordained in that they are part of the form of a particular genre. Limericks and sonnets, for example, have to follow a given rhyme scheme.

Remember, though, that some patterns of sound within a text may be entirely random or accidental. There are only a limited number of meaningful sounds in English and it wouldn't be surprising if, for example, some alliteration arrived by accident. As here!

1 Read the following four short texts.

Text 1

Henry V is scornfully responding to the challenge from the heir to the French throne.

And tell the pleasant prince this mock of his
Hath turn'd his balls to gun-stones; and his soul
Shall stand sore charged for the wasteful vengeance
That shall fly with them: for many a thousand widows
Shall this his mock mock out of their dear husbands;
Mock mothers from their sons, mock castles down;
And some are yet ungotten and unborn
That shall have cause to curse the Dauphin's scorn.

Text 2

The opening three stanzas of Punishment *by Seamus Heaney*

I can feel the tug
of the halter at the nape
of her neck, the wind
on her naked front.

It blows her nipples
to amber beads,
it shakes the frail rigging
of her ribs.

I can see her drowned
body in the bog,
the weighing stone,
the floating rods and boughs.

Text 3

The first verse of a poem entitled 'Ballade Made in the Hot Weather'

Fountains that frisk and sprinkle
The moss they overspill;
Pools that the breezes crinkle;
The wheel beside the mill,
With its wet, weedy frill;
Wind-shadows in the wheat;
A water-cart in the street;
The fringe of foam that girds
An islet's ferneries;
A green sky's minor thirds –
To live, I think of these!

Text 4

The opening of 'Lolita' *by Vladimir Nabokov*

Lolita, light of my life, fire of my loins. My sin, my soul. Lo-lee-ta: the tip of the tongue taking a trip of three steps down the palate to tap, at three, on the teeth. Lo. Lee. Ta

She was Lo, plain Lo, in the morning, standing four feet ten in one sock. She was Lola in slacks. She was Dolly at school. She was Dolores on the dotted line, But in my arms she was always Lolita.

Did she have a precursor? She did, indeed she did. In point of fact, there might have been no Lolita at all had I not loved, one summer, a certain initial girl-child. In a princedom by the sea. Oh when? About as many years before Lolita was born as my age was that summer. You can always count on a murderer for a fancy prose style.

Ladies and gentlemen of the jury, exhibit number one is what the seraphs, the misinformed, simple, noble-winged seraphs, envied. Look at this tangle of thorns.

2 Fill in the chart below, giving examples of each type of sound patterning from each text (where appropriate).

3 Discuss your examples and try to say what is the effect (if any) of the sound patterns you have identified. Remember the warning given on page 84. You might want to think about what is sometimes called echo phonology. This is when you might hear 'echoes' in the texts of the way people speak in real life. This effect is more fully considered in Chapter 8.

	Text 1	Text 2	Text 3	Text 4
Alliteration				
Assonance				
Consonance				
Rhyme				
Reverse rhyme				
Half rhyme				

Graphology lens

Read the following four short extracts from novels. Discuss what is the effect of the way each of these texts is printed on the page.

1 *Two French nuns are trying to encourage two mules to move. The mules only respond to swearing.*

ABBESS}   Bou – -bou – - bou – -
MARGARITA} ——-ger, – - ger, – - ger.

MARGARITA} Fou – - fou – - fou – -
ABBESS}   ——-ter, – ter, – - ter.

The two mules acknowledged the notes by a mutual lash of their tails; but it went no further – ' 'Twill answer by an' by,' said the novice.

ABBESS }   Bou- bou- bou- bou- bou- bou-

MARGARITA} ——ger, ger, ger, ger, ger, ger.
  'Quicker still,' cried Margarita.
Fou, fou, fou, fou, fou, fou, fou, fou, fou.
  'Quicker still,' cried Margarita.
Bou, bou, bou, bou, bou, bou, bou, bou.
  'Quicker still – God preserve me!' said the Abbess
– 'they do not understand us,' cried Margarita.

> *The Life and Opinions of*
> *Tristram Shandy,* Laurence
> Sterne (1759)

2 *Part of a letter home from a young rookie baseball player*

But worse of all is the sun. Another ju. A 7 yr old boy who is a Gene Yuss. Izik. He duz not even go to skule he is that much of a Gene Yuss. His i cue is 424 same exack as Wee Willie Keeler hit in '97. Only it aint base hits but brains. Paw he trys to manig the team. A seven yr old. It just aint what we had in mind is it Paw. What shud I do now. Yr sun Slugger.

> *The Great American Novel,*
> Philip Roth (1973)

3 *An exchange between Renton and a psychiatrist.*

DR FORBES: You mentioned your brother, the one with the, eh, disability. The one that died. Can we talk about him?
(pause)

ME: Why?
(pause)

DR FORBES: You're reluctant to talk about your brother?

ME: Naw. It's just that ah dinnae see the relevance ay that tae me bein oan smack.

> *Trainspotting,* Irvine Welsh
> (1993)

4 `You had to have a car to get to`
`Grider Creek where the good`
`fishing was, and I didn't have a`
`car. The map was nice, though.`
`Drawn with a heavy dull pencil on`
`a piece of paper bag. With a`
`little square for a sawmill.`

> *Trout Fishing in America,*
> Richard Brautigan (1967)

Each of these extracts is using graphology, the visual medium of language, to make an impact on readers. For example, part of the graphological effect is owing to the diminishing size of the font in Text 1 which emphasises the speed at which the nuns speak; the choice of font in Text 4 is meant to demonstrate the casual nature of the writing. Of course, in reality, casual it isn't! So, even where you might not expect it, in prose fiction, writers sometimes use the features of the graphological system to enhance their meaning. Such features may well include: choice of font and font size, layout of the text, spelling and punctuation conventions and typography.

It is, of course, relatively unusual for novelists to foreground their use of the graphological system; most of the time they pay it no attention. This is not, however, the case with poetry. Line length, verse form, where the poets break their lines, the shape of the poem on the page and, again, in some case, typography, are all of vital importance in contributing to the overall effect of the poem. Clearly, we are not going to be able to cover all of these in this short chapter, so we'll concentrate on just one: line breaks.

ACTIVITY 59

In pairs, read the following poem.

Why bother where I went
for I went spinning on the

four wheels of my car
along the wet road until

I saw a girl with one leg

Discuss the impression left on you by the poem, concentrating particularly on the last line.

COMMENTARY

You probably found that the poem evokes feelings of pity (?) for the girl with one leg.

ACTIVITY 60

Now read this line, which completes the poem:

over the rail of a balcony

How are your impressions of the poem changed by the addition of the last line? Why do you think the writer (*William Carlos Williams*) split the final couplet after leg? Have your initial impressions of pity (revulsion? violence?) entirely disappeared? Did the writer intend you to hold both impressions in your mind at once?

ACTIVITY 61

Here are two short poems. Each has four verses, but we have printed the poems as prose. Working in pairs, write them out as poems, paying particular attention to where you put the line breaks. Discuss your versions with another pair and justify your choices.

1 I wait for your step. A jay on the cherry tree trembles the blossom. I name you *my love* and the gulls fly above us calling to the air. Our two pale bodies move in the late light, slowly as doves do, breathing. And then you are gone. A night-owl mourns in darkness for the moon's last phase.
   Lovebirds, Carol Ann Duffy (1985)

2 so much depends upon a red wheelbarrow glazed with rain water beside the white chickens
   XXII, William Carlos Williams (20th Century)

Lexical lenses

We're going to be putting the vocabulary chosen by writers under the microscope now, but before we do this we need to sort out some potential confusion of terminology. Because words (lexis) and meanings (semantics) are inseparable, almost as if they were the Siamese twins of language, many linguists sometimes use the term *lexical-semantic*. There's also a very useful term *lexico-grammatical* which indicates that lexis and grammar are also inseparable. That's not very surprising either, as it's words that form the basis of all grammatical structures, as we shall see. You can't have grammar without words. So we shall also find ourselves looking at texts through the grammatical lens from time to time.

The meaning of a text, whether it's a written or a spoken one, is constructed through a combination of lexis, grammar and phonology. In this book, we're going to use *lexis* to refer to the total word-stock of English, to the origin of these words (*etymology*) and to the company they habitually keep (*collocation*). We're going to reserve *semantics* for the total meaning of a text. Though it's sometimes tidier to separate them for study purposes, in practice they all work together to construct meaning. It's rather like a garage mechanic learning about the function of the gearbox, but knowing that without all the other engine parts, the car just wouldn't move.

It's your choice

When you are writing, you will know very well that sometimes the words flow easily onto the paper or screen and that at other times you have to struggle to find the right one to express your meaning. You know that this choice of word can be crucial and you may experiment with many alternatives before you hit upon the exact one that expresses what you want to say. All writers do this and it can sometimes be very daunting and difficult when faced with finding *the* word from the hundreds of thousands that form the lexicon (word stock) of English. It is these sort of choices that we will be looking at in this section.

ACTIVITY 62

Fill in the gaps in the following:

1 Humpty Dumpty sat on – wall.
2 I never really warmed to Clovis, – was far too stupid to inspire real affection *Brazzaville Beach*, William Boyd *(1990)*
3 Jack and Jill went – the hill.

COMMENTARY This probably didn't prove too difficult a task. Humpty Dumpty can only have sat on *a* or *the* wall. English provides you with no other possibilities. Nor are there other possibilities than *he* or *she* in 2; your problem is that you may be uncertain of Clovis' gender (it's *he*, actually). 3 offers more possibilities. Though you know very well that Jack and Jill first went *up* and then *down* the hill, they could have gone *by, alongside, over, across* and so on. But even here the possibilities are limited. The Clovis example continues ' – he always claimed a corner of my heart' and again there are only a few words open to you. What are they?

All the gaps you have been filling in can only have been completed by using words from *closed* or *grammatical* classes of words. They are closed because new entries to the class are unnecessary. English does not need any more determiners (Text 1), pronouns (Text 2), prepositions (Text 3) or conjunctions (the continuation of Text 2). Such choices, and they *do* remain choices for writers, are relatively easily made. This is not always so with words from the open classes – nouns, verbs, adjectives and adverbs. They are *open* because new words are forever being added to them as the English lexicon continually expands. It is these choices that we now go on to examine.

ACTIVITY 63

One word is missing from the following phrase.
In pairs, brainstorm as many words as you can
that could fit in the gap:

the – from the chimneys

COMMENTARY Our guess is that you will have come up with a list that will include such words as *smoke, soot, dirt, smell, fumes* and so on. Were we right? If we were, there are two possible reasons for this:

1 **Word class**: only one class of word can follow *the* – a noun. Sometimes the noun stands alone; sometimes it could be pre-modified with adjectives and adverbs. For example, *the black smoke* or *the exceedingly black smoke*, but nothing other than a noun or noun group could be in that position in the phrase.
2 **Collocation**: the word *chimneys* suggests a number of associated words, such as the ones we have already given. One linguist has said that 'you know a word by the company it keeps' and the company *chimneys* usually keeps is *smoke, soot*, etc. This principle is known as collocation. These then are the two reasons you should have found it relatively easy to fill in the gap. We can show this diagrammatically.

Choices and chains

	smoke	*Choice* (or paradigmatic axis)
	smell	↓
	soot	
	dirt	
	fumes	
The	_ _ _ _ _	from the chimneys
→	*Chain*	(*or syntagmatic axis*) →

The chain (sometimes known as the syntagm) is the grammatical framework into which we slot our choice (sometimes known as the paradigm) of words. There are more choices available to us in the open word classes, but the framework (syntagm) determines from what class (or classes) of word we can make our choice. For example, only the word class in the brackets would fit into these frames:

He smiled (adverb) at the girl.
She wore a blue (noun).
Her jeans were very (adjective).

Let's return to our original example. We know that the gap has to be filled by a noun, but we'd be very surprised if you'd chosen *tunes* to fill it. But that's what Dylan Thomas in his poem *Fern Hill* wrote. Like many writers he deliberately broke all the collocational expectations. We could say that he dislocated them to surprise us and perhaps make us view the world in a new way.

ACTIVITY 64

1 Discuss with a partner the effect of Dylan Thomas' dislocation. In what way might *chimneys* be said to have *tunes*?

2 Obtain a copy of *Fern Hill* and identify all the other unusual collocations in the poem. What is their effect?

ACTIVITY 65

1 Brainstorm as many words as you can that collocate with *subtraction* and *transaction*.
2 Now read the opening verse of this poem by John Crowe Ransome about the death of a young boy from one of Virginia's oldest families.

Dead Boy

The little cousin is dead, by foul subtraction,
A green bough from Virginia's aged tree,
And none of the county kin like the transaction,
Nor some of the world of outer dark, like me.

What is the effect of Ransome's use of the words *subtraction* and *transaction* to describe the boy's death?

COMMENTARY

We want to comment on only one aspect of these words. You will no doubt have discussed many others to do with the unusual collocation as well. However, we want to point out that *subtraction* and *transaction* are very formal words which add grandeur and dignity to the verse, because of this very formality.

ACTIVITY 66

Now read the remaining verses of the poem. Identify (a) words which also seem to be formal and dignified; (b) words which are very informal and colloquial and (c) words which seem to you fairly neutral. What is the effect of this mixture of formality and informality?

A boy not beautiful, nor good, nor clever,
A black cloud full of storms too hot for keeping,
A sword beneath his mother's heart – yet never
Woman bewept her babe as this is weeping.

A pig with a pasty face, so I had said,
Squealing for cookies, kinned by poor pretense

With a noble house. But the little man quite dead,
I see the forbears' antique lineaments.

The elder men have strode by the box of death
To the wide flag porch, and muttering low send round
The bruit of the day. O friendly waste of breath!
Their hearts are hurt with a deep dynastic wound.

He was pale and little, the foolish neighbors say;
The first-fruits, saith the Preacher, the Lord hath taken
But this was the old tree's late branch wrenched away,
Grieving the sapless limbs, the shorn and shaken.

COMMENTARY

We have already seen that writers make choices of words. In this poem, John Crowe Ransome mixes words that have different levels of formality: from the very formal (*antique, dynastic*) through the fairly neutral (*boy, good*) to the colloquially informal (*pasty*). Because of its history of borrowing words from other languages (see Chapter 9), English is unusually rich in synonyms, words which denote the same thing. On the every day level of formality are native English words, then moving up the scale of formality, there are words borrowed from French, then Latin and finally Greek. This abundant choice of synonyms at different levels of formality that English provides allows writers maximum freedom to write at a particular level or to mix levels, as John Crowe Ransome does in this poem and to create specific effects. You should always pay attention to the etymology of the words a writer chooses.

The variety of words we have at our disposal in English to denote just what we have been talking about illustrates this richness of choice available to writers. If we want to refer to the total number of words available in English, we can use the technical word *lexicon* (from the Greek) or the less formal *vocabulary* (from the Latin) or the down-to-earth and very effective *word-stock* (from Anglo-Saxon). The Anglo-Saxons themselves used, as we saw in Chapter 1, the vividly memorable *word-hoard*. All these words refer to the same thing, but choose one rather than another in your text and you send out very different signals to your reader or listener. This next activity illustrates just a very, very few of these choices. We could have extended the table almost ad infinitum (a very formal, untranslated piece of Latin that now adds formality to the word-hoard of English!)

Complete the table below, putting as many synonyms as you can in each gap.

Informal	Neutral	Formal
puke	be sick	vomit
shove		momentum
shiny	bright	
	steal	
	policeman	
		regal
		emolument
find out		
	spit	
	stupid	

Lexical fields

What do the following words have in common? *Toast, boil, grill, fry, bake, barbecue, simmer, braise*? It's fairly obvious that they are all terms to describe cooking processes. If we add to this list words like *kitchen, knife, sieve, pan, wok*, we are beginning to collect a set of words to do with cookery. It wouldn't be difficult for you to add other words to this list. Such a set of words is known by linguists as a lexical (or sometimes as a semantic) field: a group or set of related words that refers to a particular aspect of the world. So there are lexical fields for education, sport, colour, war, the weather, fashion and so on. Again, this provides writers with an immense choice of words. To choose the right word with the exact nuance of meaning for, say, a colour or a sound or a movement is part of a writer's skill.

Working in pairs, choose a particular topic and brainstorm as many words as possible that belong to the lexical field for this topic. Make sure that you include examples from all the different, relevant word classes – nouns, verbs and adjectives. Which words that you have come up with could belong to other lexical fields?

ACTIVITY 69

In this next text, an extract from a longer eighteenth century poem *Essay on Criticism*, Alexander Pope is writing about writing and seeks to demonstrate that a poem (or, indeed, any work of literature) is the result of hard work, craft and skill (*Art*) not just *Chance*. Here, Pope is writing about something we have already looked at – the way phonology can enhance the meaning of a text. In doing so, he uses six lexical fields:

Water/liquids sound air motion classical mythology action verbs

Identify the words which fall into each of these semantic fields. Remember that some words might be part of more than one field.

True Ease in Writing comes from Art, not Chance,
As those move easiest who have learn'd to dance.
'Tis not enough no Harshness gives Offence,
The *Sound* must seem an *Eccho* to the *Sense*.
Soft is the Strain when *Zephyr* gently blows,
And the *smooth Stream* in *smoother Numbers* flows;
But when loud *Surges* lash the sounding Shore,
The *hoarse, rough* Verse shou'd like the Torrent roar.
When *Ajax* strives, some Rocks' vast Weight to throw,
The Line too *labours*, and the Words move *slow*,
Not so, when swift *Camilla* scours the Plain,
Flies o'er th'unbending Corn, and skims along the Main.

COMMENTARY

One of the results of using these groups of words is to give unity to the poem. The lexical fields are acting as a device that ties the poem together and provides it with a firm structure. Linguists often describe this process of tying a text together as *cohesion* and the type of cohesion you have been looking at here is lexical cohesion. Of course, there are additional ways of giving cohesion to a text and Pope very obviously demonstrates one of these – he uses phonological cohesion, or patterns of sound to tie his text together.

What are (a) the sound patterns that Pope uses and
(b) how do they enhance the sense of what he is saying?

Grammatical lens

This, too, is a huge subject and one that we will only be able to touch on here. For a more in depth look, we recommend you read *Grammar* by Michael Jago in the 'Living Language' series. Remember, however, our distinction between word-grammar, sentence-grammar and text-grammar (p 81).

Here we are going to illuminate some grammatical features by looking at the opening sentence of the first eighteen stories in American writer, Tobias Wolff's collection.

ACTIVITY 70

Read the sentences from Tobias Wolff. With a partner, classify them according to any grammatical features that you notice. Aim to have five or six precisely defined categories. Ensure that there are at least two sentences in each category.

1 I woke up afraid.

2 Tub had been waiting for an hour in the falling snow.

3 Professor Brooke had no real quarrel with anyone in his department, but there was a Yeats scholar named Riley whom he could not bring himself to like.

4 I noticed Eugene before I actually met him.

5　She met him at a fireworks display.

6　Glen left Depoe Bay a couple of hours before sunup to beat the traffic and found himself in a heavy fog; he had to lean forward and keep the windshield wipers going to see the road at all.

7　Twice the horn had sounded, and twice Howard had waved and shouted dumb things at the people below; now he was tired and they still hadn't left the dock.

8　Davis and his dinner partner were waiting for a taxi one night when she saw a pinball arcade across the street.

9　When we arrived at the camp they pulled us off the buses and made us do push-ups in the parking lot.

10　When she was young, Mary saw a brilliant and original man lose his job because he had expressed ideas that were offensive to the trustees of the college where they both taught.

11　Wharton was a cartoonist, and a nervous man – 'highstrung', he would have said.

12　My mother read everything except books.

13　Jean was alone in the theatre.

14　Father Leo started out with the idea of becoming a missionary.

15　They were doing the dishes, his wife washing while he dried.

16　The trouble with owning a Porsche is that there is always some little thing wrong with it.

17　There was a park at the bottom of the hill.

18　On Friday Hooper was named driver of the guard for the third time that week.

COMMENTARY

How long are the sentences?

This might be a useful starting point, but it won't get you all that far, because you'd need to decide how *long* (or how *short*) a sentence has to be to qualify. More than 10 words? More than 20? Obviously there's a difference in length between sentences 1 and 6, but a more precise category is probably required. However, when you're looking at longer texts the way that a writer has contrasted or balanced long and short sentences can be very illuminating.

Notice the punctuation

The punctuation will often help you to see how a sentence is constructed. For instance, sentences 6 and 10 are approximately the same length (38 and 32 words), but 6 contains a semi-colon (;) to separate the two parts of the sentence, whereas 10 uses only a comma to mark off the clause about Mary's age. Would the effect of 6 have been different if Wolff had made two sentences out of it by substituting a full stop for the semi-colon? Paying close attention to the punctuation of sentences and texts will certainly help you to notice the clause structure used by the writer.

How many clauses?

To categorise the sentences on the basis of the number of clauses they contain is a more precise way. If we define a clause as a sentence or part of a sentence that contains a finite verb (one that signals de*finite*ly when the action occurs or occurred and de*finite*ly who or what performed the action) then this gives us a firmer basis on which to make our judgements. Take, for example, Sentence 5 *She met him at a fireworks display. Met* is a finite verb because it tells us definitely when the action occurred – in the past. *She meets him at a firework display* would definitely signal a different time – the present. *Meeting at a fireworks display* wouldn't tell you the time of the action at all – now, tomorrow, yesterday, last year . . . so the verb *meeting* is non-finite. Sentence 1 contains one clause (signalled by the one finite verb *wake up* together with the subject *I*), whereas Sentence 10 contains six clauses (signalled by the by the finite verbs *was, saw, lose, had expressed, were* and *taught* and their respective subjects *she, Mary, a brilliant and original man, he, (ideas) that* and *they*)

Sentence forms: what's the structure?

Counting the number of clauses allows us to say what forms of sentence are used by Wolff. Basically there are three. A simple sentence contains just one clause, whereas sentences that contain more than one can either be complex (in structure, not necessarily in meaning) or compound. Complex sentences have one or more subordinate clauses embedded within them, whereas compound sentences have two or more clauses of equal weight or power. So *she drinks tea* is a simple sentence, *she drinks tea, but I drink coffee* is compound and *She drinks tea when the weather is cold* is complex. In our sentences, 5 and 12, for example, are simple, whereas 4 and 9 are complex. Does Wolff use any compound sentences?

Sentence functions: what are they doing?

There are four functions of sentences. You can make a statement (declarative) *I am wearing jeans*; ask a question (interrogative) *Is she wearing jeans?*; issue a command (imperative) *Take those jeans off* or utter an exclamation *What awful jeans!* Even if a writer seems only to habitually use one of these sentence functions, you have still been able to say something valuable about his style.

Point of view: who's speaking?

You can categorise these sentences on the basis of the voice that appears to be speaking. There's a difference, for instance, between those in which Wolff adopts the first person singular (1 and 4), first person plural (9), third person (13, 14, and 15) and whether he uses pronouns (15) or names the character (14). Of course, if a text uses *I*, this doesn't mean it's the real voice of the writer, *I* is just another character or persona he's adopted for that particular text. But no one seems to be speaking in Sentence 17: *There was a park at the bottom of the hill.* This is known as an existential sentence, because if you want to say that something exists or if you want to mention the presence of something or someone you can't do so unless that thing or person has been introduced into the text. The way round this problem is to use *there* as the subject of the sentence, though it has very little meaning in such sentences. Sentence 17 just means *a park exists at the bottom of the hill.*

Collect as many existential sentences as you can in the course of your reading. What sorts of text do they most frequently occur in?

Tense: then or now? Once or frequently?

To look at how a writer signals time in her verbs is also useful and illuminating. Is the action taking place now? Did it take place in the near or recent past? Does the verb refer to an action (*I kissed him*) or a state of being (*I am happy*)? Does or did the action or state of being occur only once? For instance, Sentence 5 clearly refers to one single occasion in the past and 12 refers to frequently repeated actions in the past. But what about 1? Or 7?

Adverbs and adverbials: time and place?
Another way of classifying these sentences grammatically is to explore how
Wolff signals when (and where) the action happens/ed other than by
varying his tenses. How many indicate place (*at a fireworks display*) or time
(*when she was young*). How many indicate both? Usually writers signal such
things by using adverbs (*then, yesterday, here, outside*) or adverbial phrases
(*at a fireworks display, on Friday*) or adverbial clauses (*when she was young*).
Often it is simpler to name all of these adverbials, on the basis of the job
they are doing in the sentence. Where does Wolff place his adverbials in his
sentences – at the beginning to emphasise them or elsewhere?

Figurative language

If what we've looked at so far in this chapter (the phonological,
graphological, lexical and grammatical systems) are the moving parts of
the engine we call language – the ones we can actually see (and hear!),
then there is a further aspect of language that writers and speakers
sometimes use that you can't really see. But it's one, nevertheless, that
can have an important contribution to make to the meaning of a text.
This is figurative language. You can't see it, because, in figurative
language (often referred to as metaphorical language) words are not being
used to mean exactly what they say; they can be used to make
connections between things that are not normally linked. The opposite of
figurative usage is literal usage and we can illustrate the difference quite
simply. Let's take the word *blood*. A literal usage of the *blood* would be *he
cut his finger and before long his hand was covered in blood*. When,
however, we extend the idea of *blood* to draw on all the connotations that
the word possesses, we are likely to be moving into the area of figurative
meaning. Take, for example, the sentence *her blood is on your hands*. To
be used literally, this would have to refer to some real blood on the hands
of the person spoken to. The words might be addressed to a surgeon after
an operation *You still have some blood on your hands*. Imagine, however,
that the words are addressed to the surgeon by a nurse who feels that,
after a patient's death, the surgeon's faulty operating technique was to
blame. *Blood* would not then be used in its literal sense, as there would
be no real blood on the surgeon's hands. What is meant is *You are
responsible; you carry the guilt*. This is a figurative or metaphorical use of
the word.

Metaphor can do a number of things: it can clarify and enhance ideas and
meanings; it can make them more vivid; it can also create new meanings by
linking ideas that are not usually linked; it can also allow ideas to be
expressed much more succinctly and often much more memorably than a
literal usage. Metaphor is a very powerful lexical-semantic tool.

Most people think that figurative language is restricted to literature, but as
we've seen, this cannot be so, because 'literary' and 'non-literary' texts use
the same resources of language. As an example, look at these metaphorical

expressions taken from just *one* column of a newspaper article about the Government's plans to reform the Social Security services:

<u>Big Brother</u> Britain   <u>sweeping</u> new powers   an <u>invasion</u> of privacy   the Government is already <u>under fire</u> for <u>watering down</u> its commitment to <u>release</u> its own documents <u>fiddle</u> their tax returns   their <u>battle</u> to <u>combat</u> fraud

Notice how many military metaphors there are here!

ACTIVITY 71

Obtain a selection of newspapers (broadsheet and tabloid). Draw up a list of the metaphorical uses of language in some of the different sections (news, sport, financial, editorial, etc.) Is there a difference between the metaphors used (a) in the different sections of the same paper and (b) in the same sections of different newspapers? What are the most common semantic fields for the metaphorical language to draw on? (e.g., War? Health?) What does this metaphorical language tell us about how newspapers view the world?

Metaphor is not only part of the language of newspapers, it's part of everyday language, so much so that we might not even be aware of it. Our conversation is full of metaphorical, idiomatic expressions: *down in the dumps, down and out, on a high, up for it, up for grabs*. All these are variations on the same metaphorical theme.

Let's now turn to the use of metaphor in literature – a vast subject, whose surface we can only scratch here.

ACTIVITY 72

In the following passage, Nadine Gordimer uses a great many metaphors when writing about a locust. Identify each one and explain what the locust has in common with the thing with which Gordimer is comparing it.

There, absolutely stilled with fear beneath his glance, crouched a very big locust. What an amusing face the thing had! A lugubrious long face, that somehow suggested a bald head, and such a glum mouth. It looked like some little person out of a Disney cartoon. It moved slightly, still looking up fearfully at him. Strange body, encased in a sort of old-fashioned creaky armour. He had never realised before what ridiculous-looking insects locusts were! Well, naturally not, they occur to one collectively, as a pest – one doesn't go around looking at their faces. The face was certainly curiously human and even expressive, but looking at the body, he decided that the body couldn't really be called a body at all. With the face, the creature's kinship with humans ended. The body was flimsy paper stretched over a frame of matchstick, like a small boy's homemade aeroplane. And those could not be thought of as legs – the great saw-toothed back ones were like the parts of an old crane, and the front ones – like one of her hairpins, bent in two. At that moment the creature slowly lifted up one of the front legs, and passed it tremblingly over its head, stroking the left antenna down. Just as a man might take out a handkerchief and pass it over his brow.

COMMENTARY

We will introduce you to three linguistic terms here. Metaphors have two parts: *tenor* and *vehicle*. The tenor is the literal part of the metaphor, what is actually being talked about and the vehicle is what it is being compared to. So, to give you one example from the Gordimer extract, in *the front ones – like one of her hairpins, the front ones* is the tenor and *her hairpins* is the vehicle. The third technical term is one with which you may be familiar: *simile*. Simile is a specific form of metaphorical language in which the link between tenor and vehicle is signalled explicitly by the use of *like* or *as*.

Extended metaphor

When a writer uses variations on the same metaphor throughout a text (or section of a text) this is known as an extended metaphor. A more technical way of saying this is that a text 'uses several vehicles from the same area of thought'. Extended metaphor is very common in literary texts.

ACTIVITY 73

Trace the extended metaphor that George Herbert uses in his seventeenth century devotional poem, *Love (III)*.

What use does he make of it? How effective do you consider it to be?

> LOVE bade me welcome: yet my soul drew back,
>   Guiltie of dust and sinne.
> But quick-ey'd Love, observing me grow slack
>   From my first entrance in,
> Drew nearer to me, sweetly questioning,
>   If I lack'd any thing.
>
> A guest, I answer'd, worthy to be here:
>   Love said, You shall be he.
> I the unkinde, ungratefull? Ah my deare,
>   I cannot look on thee.
> Love took my hand, and smiling did reply,
>   Who made the eyes but I?
>
> Truth Lord, but I have marr'd them: let my shame
>   Go where it doth deserve.
> And know you not, sayes Love, who bore the blame?
>   My deare, then I will serve.
> You must sit down, sayes Love, and taste my meat:
>   So I did seat and eat.

Semantics

A final reminder about semantics. This can be defined as 'the study of meaning'. Traditionally, semantics has been seen as being closely related to lexis – hence the term *lexical semantics*. This has meant that the contribution the other language systems (grammar, phonology and graphology) make to the meaning of a text has tended to be pushed into the background. However, more recent linguistics stresses that the total meaning of a text comes about as a combination of *all* the language systems working together and though we have separated them out in this chapter for the purpose of study, we want to stress to you that we are using *semantics* in its modern sense – the way that meaning derives from phonology, lexis, grammar and graphology working together. Do keep in mind, as well, that the context in which a text is written or spoken (and received) has an important bearing on meaning, as does the function of the text. These issues are discussed further in Chapter 00.

In this chapter, we've begun to examine ways in which you can take a linguistic look at literary texts and we've begun to show you how you can apply systematic language frameworks to texts. The important word in the previous sentence is *begun* because, as you'll have realised, there's a lot more to say and explore than we've been able to cover in our short chapter. We've only just begun, for instance, to scratch the surface of the grammatical system. But we'd like to close by suggesting one final framework that may help you clearly to form your own responses to texts, both literary and non-literary that you encounter during your A level studies. It's in the form of a check-list of questions and suggestions. It begins with questions designed to help you frame an overall response to a text and then focuses on the frameworks we have been discussing in this chapter. Some of the issues that the initial questions ask you to consider are dealt with in chapters other than this one (see Chapter 10).

Remember, however, that this is only a check-list containing suggestions and that therefore:

- not every question will be equally relevant to each text
- there won't be as much to say in answer to some of the questions on one text as on others
- always support your answers by direct reference to, or quotation from, the text
- you don't have to follow the structure of the check-list slavishly, but it might be a good idea (at least initially) to be systematic in your responses, until your confidence grows
- the questions aren't designed to tell you what to think; they're designed to provide a sound linguistic basis for your opinions and responses to the text.

Questions

What's the text about?
More errors and misjudgements about texts are made because of careless, casual or superficial readings than for almost any other reason. Make sure, then, you've got the meaning clear. If a brief summary helps you clarify matters, then make one.

What type of text is it?
Is it spoken or written? If so, is it for public or private consumption? What genre of text is it? Does the text stick to one genre or use a variety of

genres? For instance, advertisements sometimes do this, as we saw earlier. What is the purpose (or purposes) of the text? Is it intended to instruct, persuade, amuse, argue, advise, frighten, sell . . .? Remember that we said earlier that the purpose of literary texts is very hard to define and you might just as well say 'this is a poem' or 'this is a short story'. Don't search for a moral everywhere!

Who seems to be addressing you? Who else is addressed in the text?
Who is/are 'speaking' in the text? What relationship is being constructed between the speaker/writer and you, the reader? How does the language do this? What assumptions does the text make about you, the reader? About your age, interests, gender, cultural background etc? How do the characters in the text speak to each other?

How is the text structured? How does it 'hang together'?
What is the overall organisation of the subject matter? Is it unified or loose? What are the links between the sections of the text? Are they clear and easy to follow? How are the paragraphs and sentences connected? What conjunctions or connectors are used? How do you know that one section, paragraph or sentence follows on from another? Has the writer chosen a pre-determined structure, such as a sonnet or haiku? Are there any obvious structural patterns in the text?

Are there any phonological or visual patterns in the text?
Does the writer make use of alliteration, assonance, consonance, rhyme/half rhyme? Phonaesthesia? Rhythm or stress patterns? Does she use particular visual patterns? Unconventional spelling or punctuation? Do any of these help the text to cohere or hang together?

What sorts of words does the writer use?
Simple or complex vocabulary? Formal or informal? Concrete or abstract? Everyday or specialised words? A mixture of these? Words from particular semantic fields? Literal or metaphorical language? Are there any unusual, unexpected or foregrounded collocations? Are there lots of adjectives or adverbials? Or is the text plain and unadorned?

What are the important grammatical features of the text?
Long or short sentences? Simple, compound or complex? Statements, questions, commands or exclamations? Any sentences without verbs? Does the writer use particular grammatical patterns and repeat them – parallelism of grammatical structures?
Are nouns used on their own or in combination with adjectives? Are the adjectives single, double or even triple? Lots of pronouns or few?
What tense are the verbs? Does the writer use lots of auxiliary verbs? Or modal auxiliaries (could, would, may, might, must, should etc)? Are the verbs dynamic (verbs of action) or stative (ones that describe a state of being, not an action)? Passive or active? Transitive or intransitive (those that take an object and those that don't)?

5 Roundabout Functions

In the previous chapter we saw how the four structural frameworks of phonology, graphology, lexis and grammar are used by the writers of literary texts to construct their meanings. We have also stressed throughout this book that there is no difference between the linguistic resources available to the writers of literary texts and to the writers of non-literary ones. You've seen that there is a clear relationship between the structures used in everyday language and the structures used in literature; you could therefore argue that what happens in literature is but an extension of what happens in everyday language. But to look at linguistic structures alone as we have done is to take only a one-sided look at texts. By structure, we mean the way the underlying building blocks of language are put together. So, for example, we can talk about the grammatical structure of a sentence or text and consider the order in which the words are put by the writer or speaker and additionally the way all the constituent parts of the sentence or text are linked. Or we could just talk about the morphological structure of an individual word or, if it is spoken, its phonological structure. Language, as we have already seen, is a combination of a number of structural systems. Think, as a comparison, of a building. Yes, we can observe it very closely, commenting on the materials that the builders have used in its construction: the bricks, the glass, the steel and so on. We could talk knowledgeably, if we were structural engineers ourselves, about the different types, shapes, sizes or names of the bricks and the overall part they play in the structure of the building and we could even comment on how all the parts inter-relate to create a satisfying (or unsatisfying) whole. In other words, we could comment solely on the structure of the building. Fine, but there'd be something missing in our comments, wouldn't there? We wouldn't have commented on what the building is used for. Is it a bus station, a block of flats, a mosque or a pub? To give a full account of the building, we'd need to talk about this aspect as well. What's its function? Is it to be used for practical purposes like catching a bus or recreational purposes such as meeting friends for a drink and so on? We need to talk about both the structure and the function of the building. To talk about one without the other would be to leave the job half finished.

To a certain extent, the same is true of the study of language. If our account of a spoken or written text focuses only on its structural features, then we are giving only half the story. We need also to comment on what the text is for, what its function is. And, of course, a successful or satisfying text is one that marries structure and function perfectly, as in a building.

So, for a full picture, we ought now to turn our attention, not to the forms and structures of language, but to its functions and purposes. Remember to distinguish between function and purpose. We looked at functions in Chapter 1 and saw that the function of a text, whether written or spoken, is what it does. So an income tax form has a particular function, as does a marriage certificate, a notice forbidding entry or even an examination paper. Some texts, of course, such as a newspaper article or an advertisement, may have more than one function. The purpose of a text is dependent on the writer's or speaker's intentions. It might be that a writer uses a particular resource of language, such as alliteration, strong rhythm, vivid metaphor or unusual collocation to make the text come alive in some striking way or to make what she has to say crystal clear. These would be the writer's intentions or purposes, and though they would not be the function(s) of the text, they should help it to perform them. You'll be familiar with functions already because in the first chapter, you looked at the ideas of a number of linguists, including Michael Halliday and Joan Tough, about how the different functions of language could be categorised. In Chapter 2, we reminded you of what the GCSE syllabuses said were the purposes of speaking and writing. These were, however, rather baldly expressed: 'writing to argue, persuade or instruct', for example. Expressed in this way, they give only a very limited picture of the varying purposes for which people use language.

Language functions: what is language for?

To most people the answer to the question 'what is language for?' would seem blindingly obvious. If pressed for an answer, they would probably come up with something close to one dictionary's definition of 'communicating ideas or feelings' (Longman). Language *is* a means of expressing or transmitting ideas, feelings and information, either face to face or in print or via some electronic form of communication. That, we suggest, for most people, would be that. But, as A level students of language and literature, you know that is certainly not that! We need to look in more depth at language functions. Yes, language helps us to transfer and transmit information, but it has other functions in addition, most of which have little to do with the transfer and transmission of information.

We want to focus then in this chapter on what is sometimes known as the interpersonal function of language. By this we are referring to the sharing of our ideas and feelings with others through interacting and communicating with them. Language allows us to interact with people in a wide variety of social situations. When we meet people, talk to them or even write to them, we are using language to establish a relationship. The words we choose, the way we express them can all signal how we relate to others. Are we members of the same group? Do we know each other well? Is this the first time we have met? Are you less confident, less powerful than others in the group? Are both (or all) members of the group the same sex?

The way we use language in social and interpersonal situations can provide an alert observer with answers to these questions and to many others like them. Language is also one of the most important factors in establishing who we are, of giving us our sense of identity. It is a powerful way of signalling that we belong. But belong to what?

ACTIVITY 74

Each of us can be said to belong to various 'groups'. The groups may be as large as a sex, race or nation or as small as one family, church congregation or part-time employees at one Burger King.

In pairs, brainstorm as many 'groups' as you can that you are part of. Compare your lists with those of another pair.

COMMENTARY

When linguists talk about groups and the sense of belonging, they usually define these under three broad headings: regional or national groups (where do you come from?); occupational groups (what do you do for a living?) and social groups (what class are you?). As we indicated earlier, you might want to add race, gender or even age to these.

ACTIVITY 75

1 Working together with another pair, classify the results of your brainstorming in the previous activity and place your groups into the broader categories outlined in the commentary above.
2 Choose any one group, either from your first lists or from the broader categories and discuss what you think are the characteristic features of language that are associated with or identify that particular group. You will find it helpful if you do this using the linguistic frameworks you are now familiar with – lexis, phonology and grammar. Graphology probably won't be very productive here.

COMMENTARY

As we have said, language is one of the most powerful ways we have of expressing our group identity. Accents (the way we pronounce words) can certainly identify not only where we were born and brought up or currently live, but they can also identify our social class. People can react very strongly (either favourably or unfavourably) to accents and there has been much linguistic research done in this field. For example, one experiment showed people's irrational dislike of accents associated with large industrial cities such as Birmingham, whilst other studies have shown approval of social accents such as Received Pronunciation. However, the picture is constantly changing as can be seen, for example, by the establishment of many telephone call centres in places like Glasgow, Liverpool and Newcastle: This is because recent research has shown that people consider such accents to be friendly and trustworthy.

Lexis can also express our identity. It, too, can reveal where we come from (regional words like *beck* and *burn* for a stream, for example), our occupation (words such as *report, examination, assessment, half-term* and *detention* would indicate the lexical field of teaching) and our social class.

Our grammatical choices can serve as markers of identity. *My hair needs washed* is a grammatical form that is commonly used in Scottish dialects of English and in standard Scottish English, whilst Welsh speakers of English often say things like *Going away tomorrow he is* where standard English would have *He's going away tomorrow. It was very ill he looked* is, of course, a grammatical construction that is characteristic of standard Irish English, but not found in other Englishes. It is very difficult to read these last two examples of Welsh and Irish English without 'hearing' a Welsh or Irish accent! This last point does allow us to underline the important distinction between accent and dialect. *Accent* is reserved for the way of speaking, the pronunciation that identifies your place of origin or social class, whereas *dialect* is the particular combination of lexis, grammar *and* pronunciation that you share with other people from your area and social background. Standard English is a particular social dialect (or *sociolect*) that can be pronounced with a variety of regional accents. One further term that is useful in this discussion is *idiolect*. This is sometimes known as 'personal dialect' and is your own personal style of language. Your idiolect is as personal and unique to you as are your face and fingerprints. You have an idiolect and a dialect no matter where you come from, no matter your occupation nor your social class.

Our linguistic identity thus is extremely important to us. It might be just that we are proud of our Lancashire accent because it demonstrates our pride in our area and solidarity with other Lancastrians or we might feel so strongly about our language that it causes us to campaign (think of the Welsh Nationalists and the Welsh Language Society) or even to fight. There have been language wars, for example, in India and in medieval Sicily, your accent could mark you out as an enemy to be killed.

'He talks like one of us' is equivalent to saying 'he is one of us'.

But what has all this to do with literature?

A great deal, actually. One of the great themes that literature deals with is exactly this idea of identity, whether it be individual, social, political, regional, national or racial identity. As we've seen that language is integral to our notion of identity, it won't be surprising to you that a study of the language of literature will show how these themes are presented by novelists, poets and playwrights. In the next part of this chapter, we're going to be looking at how some writers use different varieties of language to explore and express identity.

ACTIVITY 76

In a number of his poems, Tony Harrison writes about his memories of life as a grammar school boy in Leeds. In *Me Tarzan* he is remembering how he had to do his Latin homework whilst his friends went out enjoying themselves. The reference in the last line is to the famous Roman orator, Cicero.

Me Tarzan

Outside the whistled gang-call, *Twelfth Street Rag,*
then a Tarzan yodel for the kid who's bored,
whose hand's on his liana ... no, back
to Labienus and his flaming sword.

Off laikin', then to t'fish 'oil all the boys,
off tartin', off to t'flicks but on, on, on,
the foldaway card table, the green baize,
De Bello Gallico and lexicon.

It's only his jaw muscles that he's tensed
into an enraged *shit* that he can't go;
down with polysyllables, he's against
all pale-face Caesars, *for* Geronimo.

He shoves the frosted attic skylight, shouts:
Ah bloody can't ah've gorra Latin prose.
His bodiless head that's poking out's
like patriarchal Cissy-bleeding-ro's.

How does Tony Harrison use his representation
of Yorkshire dialect to express his feelings?

COMMENTARY The contrast between the Tony Harrison who would much rather be out with his friends and the Tony Harrison who feels he has to complete his Latin prose is forcefully shown through the contrast between the Yorkshire dialect speech and thoughts of the schoolboy and the more standard English of the poet who is ironically observing the schoolboy's dilemma. The dialect is represented by non-standard lexis (*laikin'* for *playing, tartin'* for *chasing girls*) and informal lexis (*flicks* for *the cinema* or *the pictures*), and by an attempt to portray the authentic Yorkshire accent (the omission of the /g/ sound and of the initial /h/ on *'oil,* the elision of *the flicks* into *t'flicks,* the representation of *I* as *ah,* the pronunciation of *hole* as *'oil,* the assimilation of *got to* into *gorra*) and the clipped grammar of informal speech. The contrast between the dialect lexis and the formal Latinate lexis of *lexicon, polysyllables* and *patriarchal* is marked, but it's also worth noticing that even the Standard English lexis of the poem is quite informal in places – *shoves, poking out* and the ambiguous *flaming* (a euphemism for *fucking*). The grammar also reinforces this informality with the ellipses of *who's, hand's, it's, can't* etc. Note, too, the non-standard morphology (word grammar) of *Cissy-bleeding-ro's* with its rare example of infixation – opening up a polysyllabic word (*Cicero*) to make room for another element, in this case, a swear word *bleeding.* Tony Harrison is using the contrast between the two varieties of English in *Me Tarzan* (three, if you count the title!) to define the two identities that lie at the heart of the poem.

ACTIVITY 77

In this second poem, Tony Harrison writes about the occasion when his father came to see him off at Leeds station as he began the first stage of a journey to New York. They had a meal together at the Queen's Hotel, at that time, the most exclusive in Leeds.

The Queen's English

Last meal together, Leeds, the Queen's Hotel,
that grandish pile of swank in City Square.

Too posh for me! he said (though he dressed well)
If you weren't wi' me now, ah'd nivver dare!

I knew that he'd decided that he'd die
not by the way he lingered in the bar,
nor by that look he'd give with one good eye,
nor the firmer handshake and the gruff ta-ra,
but when we browsed the station bookstall sales
he picked up *Poems from the Yorkshire Dales* –

'ere tek this un wi' yer to New York
to remind yer 'ow us gaffers used to talk.
It's up your street in't it? ah'll buy yer that!

The broken lines go through me speeding South –

As t'Doctor stopped to oppen woodland yat –

and
            wi' skill they putten wuds reet i' his mouth.

Discuss the following questions.

1 How many varieties of English are there in this poem?

2 What are their characteristics?

3 What do these different varieties of English tell readers about the sense of identity felt by the writer?

So far we have looked at the way that language can reflect an individual's identity and how, in Tony Harrison's two poems, this is closely tied up with a sense of class and regional identity. Harrison has shown himself very aware of his Yorkshire roots and also how the academic and literary paths he has followed are taking him away from these roots and from the social class of his father and friends.

We are now going to turn and look at how a sense of national identities reflected in the work of a Scottish writer.

ACTIVITY 78

In this extract from William McIlvanney's novel *Docherty*, a young boy, Conn Docherty, has been fighting in the playground of his primary school. The headmaster is about to punish him.

'Docherty!' Less a voice than an effulgence of sound falling across their suddenly stricken silence. Outwith its paralysing glare, others freeze. Conn stands up slowly, carefully doesn't look at anybody else, as if a glance might prove infectious. They all wait. 'Simpson! Would you two creatures come out here.'

They are allowed to stand on the floor for a moment, to become the relief of the others, a moral.

'You'll excuse us, Miss Carmichael. I wouldn't want to get blood on your floor.'

Some titters are gratefully offered, withdrawn. Silence is safest.

'Certainly, Mr Pirrie.'

They pass into the next room. Their small procession isn't a unique sight but they gain a brief attention here too. Beyond this room, a small cloakroom area, where they stop.

Conn almost swoons with the staleness of the place. It is a small passageway, foetid with forgotten children, a knackery for futures. He sees the drifting motes as clear as constellations. Two coats hang damp. Their quality of sadness haunts his inarticulacy. Mr Pirrie inflates, enormous in the silence, hovers like a Zeppelin.

'Well, well, well. Who started it?'

On one of the floorboards an accentuation in the grain makes a road. It runs winding, vanishes under Mr Pirrie's boot.

'It doesn't matter. You'll both be getting the same. What's wrong with your face, Docherty?'

'Skint ma nose, sur.'

'How?'

'Ah fell an' bumped ma heid in the sheuch, sur.'

'I beg your pardon?'

'Ah fell an' bumped ma heid in the sheuch, sur.'

'I beg your pardon?'

In the pause Conn understands the nature of the choice, tremblingly, compulsively, makes it.

'Ah fell an' bumped ma heid in the sheuch, sur.'

The blow is instant. His ear seems to enlarge, is muffed in numbness. But it's only the dread of tears that hurts. Mr Pirrie distends on a lozenge of light which mustn't be allowed to break. It doesn't. Conn hasn't cried.

'That, Docherty, is impertinence. You will translate, please, into the mother-tongue.'

The blow is a mistake, Conn knows. If he tells his father, he will come up to the school. 'Ye'll take whit ye get wi' the strap an' like it. But if onybody takes their hauns tae ye, ye'll let me ken.' He thinks about it. But the problem is his own. It frightens him more to imagine his father coming up.

'I'm waiting, Docherty. What happened?'

'I bumped my head, sir.'

'Where? Where did you bump it, Docherty?'

'In the gutter, sir.'

'Not an inappropriate setting for you, if I may say so.'

The words mean nothing. Only what happens counts.

'I'm disappointed in you, Docherty. You'll soon be coming up to the big school. And I'll be ready for you. I used to hear nice things about you. But not any more. You might've had the chance to go to the Academy. You still could. Do you know what that means? But what's the point? I wouldn't waste the time of highly qualified men. But while you're here you'll behave like civilised people. Brawling in the playground!' His voice shudders the wood around them. The words have worked, mystically invoke his anger. It possesses him. The veins in his nose suffuse. The strap snakes out from its nest under the shoulder of his jacket.

'Simpson first!' It is a ritual. He holds the strap in his right hand, drops it over his shoulder, reaches back with his left hand, flexes the leather, begins. 'I will not. Have. Violence. In my school.'

Four. Conn can prepare.

'Docherty!' One. Conn recites to himself: *Ah bumped ma held in the sheuch.* Two. *Sheuch.* 'You're getting as bad as your brother was.' Three. *Fat man.* 'I was glad to get rid of him.' Four. Conn's hands drop, stiff as plaster-casts. 'Up, Docherty, up! Two more for insolence.' Five. *Bastard.* He is watching- for signs of tears. Six. *Big, fat bastard.*

He has become his hands. His will huddles round them, containing the radiations of their pain, refusing them the salve of tears. The two of them are led back to the room.

Mr Pirrie says, 'I've just been tickling these two's hands. As a little warning. The next boys I catch behaving like savages won't be able to use their hands for a week.'

In pairs, or small groups, discuss the following questions. Remember always to justify your answers by close reference to the text.

1 What are the characteristic features of Conn's Scots language that distinguish it from the way Mr Pirrie speaks?
2 Is there anything in the extract to suggest why he uses Scots?
3 In what ways does the extract suggest that language can be a marker of social class divisions?

At the end of the chapter, Conn returns to his classroom after his punishment. The teacher, Miss Carmichael, 'gave him sympathetic exemptions from her questions' and allows him to sit quietly at his desk. Conn 'took a stub of pencil in his fingers'.

Slowly across a scuffed piece of paper a word moved clumsily. Opposite it another word was manoeuvred and settled, the way he had seen in a dictionary Miss Carmichael showed him. His hand shook as he did it. It was a painful and tremulous matter, like an ant trying to manipulate stones. He sat buried inside himself while the words spread themselves across the paper. Minutes later, he was stunned into stillness, looking at the big awkward shapes they made before him.

sheuch	*gutter*
speugh	*sparrow*
lum	*chimny*
brace	*mantalpiece*
bine	*tub*
coom	*soot*
coontie	*foolish man (Mr Pirrie)*
gomeril	*another foolish man*
spicket	*tap*
glaur	*muck what is in a puddle after the puddle goes away*
wabbit	*tired*
whaup	*curloo*
tumshie	*turnip*
breeks	*troosers*
chanty	*po*
preuch	*anything you can get*
I war taigled longer nor I ettled	*I was kept back for a more longer time than I desired.*

One side of the paper was filled. He didn't start on the other side because he now wanted to write things that he couldn't find any English for. When something sad had happened and his mother was meaning that there wasn't anything you could do about it, she would say 'ye maun dree yer weird'. When she was busy, she had said she was 'saund-papered tae a whuppet.' 'Pit a raker oan the fire.' 'Hand-cuffed to Mackindoe's ghost.' 'A face tae follow a flittin'.' If his father had to give him a row but wasn't really angry, he said 'Ah'll skelp yer bum wi' a tealeaf tae yer nose bluids.'

Conn despaired of English. Suddenly, with the desperation of a man trying to amputate his own infected arm, he savagely scored out all the English equivalents.

On his way out of school, he folded his grubby piece of paper very carefully and put it in his pocket. It was religiously preserved for weeks. By the time he lost it, he didn't need it.

It's quite clear from this that Conn is using language as a defiant assertion of his own identity, both as an individual and as someone who is Scots. By his writing out of what, to all intents and purposes, are the beginnings of his own dialect dictionary, Conn is championing the values of himself and his family. Note that both his mother and his father speak Scots, not English. It's no wonder, then, that with the treatment he received *Conn despaired of English*. English seems to him to be attacking all that he values most about himself.

ACTIVITY 79

Compile a dialect dictionary for your own area or region.

There are a number of ways you can set about doing this. Obviously, there may be dialect words that you, your friends or your parents use as part of everyday speech. Be careful, though, that you do not confuse dialect terms with everyday slang and casual speech. However, the dialect terms you use yourself are a start. But you are likely to find that older people use more dialect in their speech than the younger generation. A more systematic way of collecting dialect is to design a questionnaire or a series of interview questions that you can use to collect the data. But, be warned, it's not easy. You need to gain the confidence of the people you are asking. Some good topics to base your questions on that should yield interesting results include food and drink, terms of approval and disapproval (good and bad), terms for animals and insects, personal characteristics of people (lazy, stupid, mean, greedy, fat, etc), terms to do with children and terms to do with the temperature or the weather. There are also lots of books on local dialects, but one of the most fascinating is *An Atlas of English Dialects* by Clive Upton and J. D. A. Widdowson (Oxford) in which a series of word maps shows you how English lexis varies across the regions of the country.

So far, we have looked at language and regional, class and national identity. In this next example, we can see how the poet is using language to express her sense of racial identity. The writer, Merle Collins, is from Grenada and has worked as a performance poet. The poem, with its punning title, deals with attitudes towards Black English and also offers a potted history of its development. Try reading it aloud for the greatest impact.

No Dialects Please

In this competition
dey was lookin for poetry of worth
for a writin that could wrap up a feelin
an fling it back hard
with a captive power to choke de stars
so dey say
'Send them to us
but NO DIALECTS PLEASE'
We're British!

Ay!
Well ah laugh till me bouschet near drop
Is not only dat ah tink
of de dialect of de Normans and de Saxons
dat combine an reformulate
to create a language-elect
is not only dat ah tink
how dis British education mus really be narrow
if it leave dem wid no knowledge of what dey own history is about
is not only dat ah tink
bout de part of my story
dat come from Liverpool in a big dirty white ship mark
AFRICAN SLAVES PLEASE!
We're the British!

But as if dat nat enough pain
for a body to bear

ah tink bout de part on de plantations down dere
Wey dey so frighten o de power
in the deep spaces
behind our watching faces
dat dey shout
NO AFRICAN LANGUAGES PLEASE!
It's against the law!
Make me ha to go
an start up a language o me own
dat ah could share wid me people

Den when we start to shout
bout a culture o we own
a language o we own
dem an de others dey leave to control us say
STOP THAT NONSENSE NOW
We're all British!
Every time we lif we foot to do we own ting
to fight we own fight
dey tell us how British we British
an ah wonder if dey remember
dat in Trinidad in the thirties
dey jail Butler
who dey say is their british citizen
an accuse him of
Hampering the war effort
Then it was
FIGHT FOR YOUR COUNTRY, FOLKS!
You're British!

Ay! Ay!
Ah wonder when it change to
NO DIALECTS PLEASE!
WE'RE British!
Huh!
To tink how still dey so dunce
An so frighten o we power
dat dey have to hide behind a language
that we could wrap roun we little finger
in addition to we own!
Heavens o mercy!
Dat is dunceness oui!
Ah wonder where is de bright British?

ACTIVITY 80

In small groups, discuss the following questions.

1 How many different attitudes towards the language(s) spoken by Blacks can you identify in the poem?
2 How does Merle Collins demonstrate the foolishness of some (all?) of these attitudes?
3 What does the poem tell us about the development of Black English? You'll need to find out what pidgin and creole languages are to answer this question fully.

4 Is Merle Collins right to wonder *where is de bright British?*?
5 Basing your answer only on the language used in the poem, what are some of the characteristic features of contemporary Black English? Grammar and phonology will be fruitful areas to concentrate on here.

We've just looked at how poets and novelists have written about the way that language can reflect identity, but, of course, there have been many research projects that have covered the same ground. Obviously, we haven't time to look at them all here, but one of the most famous was undertaken in the 1970s by the American sociolinguist, William Labov, about the language used on Martha's Vineyard, an island about three miles off New England on the east coast of the United States. In this study he found that language was a very strong marker of regional identity. He noticed that the pronunciation of certain sounds in the speech of the islanders seemed to be changing, particularly the diphthongs found in words such as m*i*ce (/ay/) and m*ou*se (/aw/) and a number of diphthongs in other words. He wanted to know why this change was taking place. To find out, Labov interviewed a number of islanders from different ages, locations, occupations and ethnic groups. He found that the change in pronunciation of these diphthongs was most marked amongst the younger inhabitants and least marked in the oldest group. What seemed to be happening was that amongst these younger speakers, there was a movement away from the received pronunciations of the standard New England mainland speech which many had been using (remember Martha's Vineyard is only three miles off the coast and many islanders went to New England to study and work) and back towards a pronunciation associated with more traditional and characteristic island speech. The change was most common in the western part of the island where the traditional fishing industry was based, but it was spreading, particularly amongst young men. But why? To answer this question, Labov looked at what was happening to the social and economic structure of the island. Martha's Vineyard had, over the years, seen an influx of wealthy summer residents from the mainland who had bought up good property as holiday homes and the natives, especially the fishermen, resented this 'invasion' of people whose wealth and values they did not share. The fishermen wanted to assert their identity as Vineyarders and one way of doing this was subconsciously to exaggerate the speech features that made them different from the summer residents. Other native islanders, particularly the young, began to imitate the way the fishermen were speaking, because they admired (again, subconsciously) their traditional island values and character. Just as Conn in the extract from 'Docherty' we looked at earlier is asserting his Scots identity against the socially superior and invading English of the school, so the Martha's Vineyarders were reverting to their regional language as a protest against an invading 'foreign' culture that was destroying their identity.

As we said, Labov's work on Martha's Vineyard is but one of a large number of studies that are concerned with language as a marker of identity. If you are interested in the topic, these are a few of the other studies that you should find out about:

1 Labov's study of the language used by shoppers in three New York department stores (Labov, W. (1976) *The Social Stratification of English in New York City*, Washington DC: Centre for Applied Linguistics).
2 Peter Trudgill's work on the speech of men and women in Norwich (Trudgill, P. (1974) *The Social Differentiation of English in Norwich*, Cambridge University Press).
3 Lesley Milroy's study of the speech of working class communities in Belfast (Milroy, L. (1980) *Language and Social Networks*, Oxford, Basil Blackwell).
4 Jenny Cheshire's research into the language of teenagers in Reading. (In Trudgill, P. (ed) *Sociolinguistic Patterns in British English,* London, Edward Arnold).

We have seen, then, how language used both in everyday life and in literature can express an individual's identity and that this is one of language's most important functions. We are going to turn now and examine another of the functions of language.

Language can be a marker of our social relationships. The way in which we speak to each other can indicate, for example, the degree of closeness we feel towards the person we are addressing; it can indicate that we feel intimate with or distant from someone. It can indicate whether we consider ourselves inferior or superior to a particular person, whether we feel we have power over someone or that we feel intimidated by them. It can indicate solidarity, agreement, leadership, deference, aggression, dominance and so on. In Chapter 7 some of these aspects are explored in greater depth. Here, we'll look at just one way in which language can act as a marker or barometer of our social relationships.

ACTIVITY 81

Here is a list of terms that you might use to address people. In the main, they are all male address terms, though in some instances like *Dr Jones* or *Your honour*, the terms can be used to address either men or women.

1 Discuss them and try to rank them, beginning with the most formal and distant (*Your Majesty?*) down to the most intimate

and informal. You'll probably find that there will be some that you might want to rank as equals. You might also find yourselves discussing the degrees of politeness that are involved. How polite is *guv* compared with *pal*, for example?

2 Discuss the circumstances or context in which these address terms might be used.

darling	mate	Your Honour	Your Worship
Colonel Jones	son	my good man	Jonesie
Your Excellency	uncle	Jones	sir
guv	dad	Mr Jones	Sir Paul
father	old chap	squire	pal
Professor Jones	grandfather	chum	Your Grace
mister	mac	Dr Jones	Your Majesty
grandad	you	sunshine	Paul

ACTIVITY 82

Rank the following variations on a single name from formal to informal.

Katherine	Kat	Katy	K
Kath	Kathy	Katherina	Kate
Kati	Kathryn	Katie	

COMMENTARY

How we address people is an important marker of social relationships and English allows us a great number of choices in the matter. Do you address someone by his or her title (*Doctor, Professor*), by first name (*Michael, Anne*), by last name (*Jones*), by a nickname (*Fatso*) or diminutive (*Mick, Annie*) or by a combination of these options? Of course, you can avoid the problem altogether by calling them nothing at all. In a country such as Britain, which some would argue is still a very class-ridden society, such decisions can be fraught with difficulty. A study conducted by Brown and Ford in 1961 showed that inequality in social and power relationships was demonstrated by one participant in a conversation using the other's title and last name (*Mr Jones*) and the second participant using the other's first name (*Michael*). If each participant used the other's title and last name (*Mr Jones, Mrs Smith*) this indicated 'inequality and unfamiliarity' and that mutual use of first names (*Michael, Anne*) indicated 'equality and familiarity'. If there were a switch between using title and last name to first name, the switch is more often than not initiated by the more powerful participant in the conversation. The least intimate form of address is signalled by the use of title alone (*Doctor, Waiter, Sergeant*) because such titles usually indicate the occupation or social rank and nothing else. *Doctor Jones* is more intimate than *Doctor*. If you know and use someone's first name, you are signalling that you are quite intimate with that person (or would like to be!) and the greatest degree of intimacy is signalled by the use of pet names or nicknames. You need only to look in any newspaper on Valentine's Day to see the hundreds of pet names that lovers (or would-be lovers) use to address each other and which are generally meaningless to outsiders. *The Toad Prince, Mrs Mars Bar, Prickly Hedgehog Noodle* and *Dimply Dumpling* are examples from just one paper. It is hard to imagine, for instance, your teacher being addressed as *Dimply Dumpling*, but you never know!

Ronald Wardhough points out in his book *An Introduction to Sociolinguistics*, 'when someone uses your first name alone in addressing you, you may feel on occasion that that person is presuming an intimacy you do not recognise or, alternatively, is trying to assert some power over you.' If you are ever unfortunate enough to be a patient in a hospital or to be arrested in a police station, you will recognise the truth of this.

ACTIVITY 83

Design and carry out an investigation into the ways address terms are used in your particular school or college. Here are some of the issues you might consider:

- How do the students/pupils address the teachers in/out of the classroom?
- Are older students/pupils addressed differently by teachers?
- Do all teachers address students/pupils in the same way?
- How do teachers address each other?

- How do they refer to each other when talking to students/pupils?
- Is there any difference between the ways males and females are addressed?
- Is there a difference between the way more senior/older staff are addressed/address each other/address students/pupils?

You'll be able to think of other questions or areas of investigation for yourselves. This work could very easily form the basis for a substantial piece of coursework.

ACTIVITY 84

You could also carry out a similar inquiry into family address terms. For example, terms like *son, our kid, gramps, luv, my child,* may be used within families, though there are, of course, many, many more. This could be a very fruitful investigation for you to do.

So, you can see, even from this one small example how social relationships can be very clearly signalled by specific features of language use. Social relationships are, of course, one of the major concerns of literature and form the basis of most novels and drama, so it's not particularly surprising that writers signal these relationships in their works in many of the same ways that people do in 'real life'. To illustrate this, we are going to examine a complete short play by Harold Pinter, *Trouble in the Works*. One of the themes of this play is what we have just been looking at in our work on address terms above: power relationships and how this power can shift. The play is set in an office in a factory. Mr Fibbs, the manager is sitting at his desk when there is a knock at the door. Mr Wills, the shop steward, enters.

FIBBS: Ah, Wills. Good. Come in. Sit down will you?

WILLS: Thanks, Mr Fibbs.

FIBBS: You got my message?

WILLS: I just got it.

FIBBS: Good. Good.
(Pause.)
Good. Well now . . . Have a cigar?

WILLS: No, thanks, not for me, Mr Fibbs.

FIBBS: Well, now, Wills, I hear there's been a little trouble in the factory.

WILLS: Yes, I . . . I suppose you could call it that, Mr Fibbs.

FIBBS: Well, what in heaven's name is it all about?

WILLS: Well, I don't exactly know how to put it, Mr Fibbs.

FIBBS: Now come on, Wills. I've got to know what it is, before I can do anything about it.

WILLS: Well, Mr Fibbs, it's simply a matter that the men have . . . well, they seem to have taken a turn against some of the products.

FIBBS: Taken a turn?

WILLS: They just don't seem to like them much any more.

FIBBS: Don't like them? But we've got the reputation of having the finest machine part turnover in the country. They're the best paid men in the industry. We've got the cheapest canteen in Yorkshire. No two menus are alike. We've got a billiard hall, haven't we, on the premises, we've got a swimming pool for the use of staff. And what about the long-playing record room? And you tell me they're dissatisfied?

WILLS: Oh, the men are very grateful for all the amenities, sir.
They just don't like the products.

FIBBS: But they're beautiful products. I've been in the business a lifetime. I've never seen such beautiful products.

WILLS: There it is, sir.

FIBBS: Which ones don't they like?

WILLS: Well, there's the brass pet cock, for instance.

FIBBS: The brass pet cock? What's the matter with the brass pet cock?

WILLS: They just don't seem to like it any more.

FIBBS: But what exactly don't they like about it?

WILLS: Perhaps it's just the look of it.

FIBBS: That brass pet cock? But I tell you it's perfection.
Nothing short of perfection.

WILLS: They've just gone right off it.

FIBBS: Well, I'm flabbergasted.

WILLS: It's not only the brass pet cock, Mr Fibbs.

FIBBS: What else?

WILLS: There's the hemi unibal spherical rod end.

FIBBS: The hemi unibal spherical rod end? But where could you find a finer rod end?

WILLS: There are rod ends and rod ends, Mr Fibbs.

FIBBS: I know there are rod ends and rod ends. But where could you find a finer hemi unibal spherical rod end?

WILLS: They just don't want to have anything more to do with it.

FIBBS: This is shattering. Shattering. What else? Come on Wills. There's no point in hiding anything from me.

WILLS: Well, I hate to say it, but they've gone very vicious about the high speed taper shank spiral flute reamers.

FIBBS: The high speed taper shank spiral flute reamers! But that's absolutely ridiculous! What could they possibly have against the high speed taper shank spiral flute reamers?

WILLS: All I can say is they're in a state of very bad agitation about them. And then there's the gunmetal side outlet relief with handwheel.

FIBBS: What!

WILLS: There's the nippled connector and the nippled adapter and the vertical mechanical comparator.

FIBBS: No!

WILLS: And the one they can't speak about without trembling is the jaw for Jacob's chuck for use on portable drill.

FIBBS: My own Jacob's chuck? Not my very own Jacob's chuck?

WILLS: They've just taken a turn against the whole lot of them, I tell you. Male elbow adaptors, tubing nuts, grub screws, internal fan washers, dog points, half dog points, white metal bushes –

FIBBS: But not, surely not, my lovely parallel male stud couplings.

WILLS: They hate and detest your lovely parallel male stud couplings, and the straight flange pump connectors, and back nuts, and front nuts, and the bronze draw off cock with handwheel and the bronze draw off cock without handwheel!

FIBBS: Not the bronze draw off cock with handwheel?

WILLS: And without handwheel.

FIBBS: Without handwheel?

WILLS: And with handwheel.

FIBBS: Not with handwheel?

WILLS: And without handwheel.

FIBBS: Without handwheel?

WILLS: With handwheel and without handwheel.

FIBBS: With handwheel and without handwheel?

WILLS: With or without!
         (Pause.)

FIBBS: (Broken) Tell me. What do they want to make in its place?

WILLS: Brandy balls.

ACTIVITY 85

1 Read through the play carefully and slowly.
2 Divide into pairs (or groups of three, if you need a director) and prepare a reading or a staged reading of the play. This, of course, will involve you in making decisions about exactly how the lines are to be spoken, the tones of voice, variations in pace, loudness and any accompanying moves or gestures.

COMMENTARY

Your reading of the play will have indicated that the initially dominant Fibbs has, by the end, become a broken man and that all the power has shifted to Wills. How has the language signalled this change of relationship? To find out, let's look at the opening of the play from *Ah, Wills. Good. Come in. Sit down, will you?* to *They just don't seem to like them very much any more.* In this section, Fibbs is clearly the dominant participant in the exchanges. We can see this from:

■ the address terms used. Fibbs addresses Wills by using only his last name, whereas Wills always uses title and last name *Mr Fibbs*.

■ Fibbs opens the conversation and initiates all the subsequent topics.

- Fibbs uses the question form to command *Sit down will you?*, asks questions *Well, what in heaven's name is it all about?* and issues commands *Now, come on, Wills, I've got to know what it is.* These two types of speech act, commanding and questioning, are an assumption of authority and superiority on the speaker's part.
- Wills' responses in the early stages are exact answers to the questions (*You got my message? I just got it.*) and he is very hesitant in bringing up the reason for his being there at all *Well, I don't exactly know how to put it Mr Fibbs.*
- Wills uses a lot of hedges in his speech (*Well,*), hesitations (*Yes, I . . . I suppose you could call it that, Mr Fibbs*) and even is silent for a time (*Pause*). The first time he gives Fibbs any real information is when he says *well, they seem to have taken a turn against some of the products.* Even this information is hesitantly given: *well; they seem* isn't a definite statement of fact; *taken a turn against* is a euphemism for *dislike* and *some* allows for the possibility that the men might like others of the products. Note that we don't yet know what any of these products are!

Let's move on and concentrate on just one aspect of Fibbs' use of language to see how it signals the shift in power between the two men. In most everyday exchanges, questions are used to elicit information. For example: *What time is it? Three o'clock.* This is how Fibbs uses some questions in the early stages of the play (*Well, what in heaven's name is it all about?*) though we pointed out that he also uses them to issue commands and invitations (*Sit down will you?*). But look at how the functions of Fibbs' questions change as the scene develops.

- By echoing Wills' words, the questions echo Fibbs' disbelief and uncertainty (*Taken a turn? Don't like them? The brass pet cock? The hemi unibal spherical rod end?*).
- This uncertainty and disbelief begins to turn to desperation (*What could they possibly have against the high speed taper shank spiral flute reamers?*) and Wills does not bother to answer these specific questions.
- By the end of the play his questions have become almost resigned exclamations (*Not my very own Jacob's chuck?*) and as the stage direction indicates he is a broken man, reduced to repeating in question form what Wills says (*Without handwheel?*).

ACTIVITY 86

Divide into groups. Each group should take a short section of the text and discuss how in your chosen section the language of each man signals the relationship between them. You should consider the kind of ways of looking at a text that we have highlighted in our commentary above. You'll also need to consider what part the names of the products play in these shifting power relationships. Make sure that, as a class, you cover all of the play.

As a footnote, though we couldn't say what any of the products mentioned in the dialogue are (and we doubt whether you could!), apparently they all do exist, even the ones with names that have the most obvious sexual connotations. We'll leave you to work out which these are!

The power has clearly shifted to Wills by the end of the play because he has knowledge about the situation in the factory that Fibbs hasn't. Knowledge *is* power and this power shift based on knowledge is signalled through the linguistic changes we have noted.

Finally, we want to turn to the way novelists use a distinctive voice to signal the characteristics of social groups. The way that characters are made to speak and talk to each other can indicate to an alert reader some of the characteristics of a particular social group at a particular time. What they speak about, the way they address each other, the level of formality in their speech, the lexical fields they use are some of the ways that novelists signal membership of a social group.

ACTIVITY 87

Read the following short extracts from novels. Discuss, in small groups, the 'voice' of each extract. What can you learn from this 'voice' about the characteristics of the social group depicted? What are the linguistic features that enable you to do so?

1 I wasn't what you might call in a fever of impatience.
   Bingo Little is a chap I was at school with, and we see a lot of each other still. He's the nephew of old Mortimer Little, who retired from business recently with a goodish pile.
   (You've probably heard of Little's Liniment – It Limbers Up the Legs.) Bingo biffs about London on a pretty comfortable allowance given him by his uncle, and leads on the whole a fairly unclouded life. It wasn't likely that anything which he described as a matter of importance would turn out to be really so frightfully important. I took it that he had discovered some new brand of cigarette which he wanted me to try, or something like that, and didn't spoil my breakfast by worrying.

   from *The Inimitable Jeeves,*
   P. G. Wodehouse (1924)

2 Ah couldnae mention the Barrowland gig tae Lizzy. No fuckin chance ay that man, ah kin tell ye. Ah had bought ma ticket when ah got ma Giro. That wis me pure skint. It was also her birthday. It was the ticket or a present for her. Nae contest. This was Iggy Pop. Ah thought she'd understand.

   from *Trainspotting,*
   Irvine Welsh (1993)

3 'To think of Molly, as I have held in long-clothes, coming to have a lover! Well, to be sure! Sister Phoebe –' (she was just coming into the room), 'here's a piece of news! Molly Gibson has got a lover! One may almost say she's had an offer! Mr Gibson, may not one? – and she's but sixteen!'

   'Seventeen, sister,' said Miss Phoebe, who piqued herself on knowing all about dear Mr Gibson's domestic affairs. 'Seventeen, the 22nd of last June.'
   'Well, have it your own way. Seventeen, if you like to call her so!' said Miss Browning, impatiently. 'The fact is still the same – she's got a lover; and it seems to me she was in long-clothes only yesterday.'
   'I'm sure I hope her course of true love will run smooth,' said Miss Phoebe.

   from *Wives and Daughters,*
   Mrs Gaskell (1866)

4 He broke off, frowning into his sherry glass. I don't know why I'm telling you all this,' he said, shooting a slightly resentful look at Persse, who had been puzzled on the same score for several minutes. 'I don't even know who you are.' He bent forward to read Persse's lapel badge. 'University College, Limerick, eh?' he said, with a leer. '*There was a young lecturer from Limerick* . . . I suppose

everyone says that to you.' 'Nearly everyone,' Persse admitted. 'But, you know, they very seldom get further than the first line. There aren't many rhymes to Limerick'.'

'What about "dip his wick"!' said Dempsey, after a moment's reflection. 'That should have possibilities.'

'What does it mean!'

Dempsey looked surprised. 'Well, it means, you know, having it off. Screwing.'

Persse blushed. 'The metre's all wrong,' he said. '"Limerick" is a dactyl.'

'Oh? What's 'dip his wick', then!'

'I'd say it was a catalectic trochee.'

'Would you, indeed! Interested in prosody, are you!'

'Yes, I suppose I am.'

'I bet you write poetry yourself, don't you?'

'Well, yes, I do.'

'I thought so. You have that look about you. There's no money in it, you know.'

from *Small World,*
David Lodge (1984)

5 It was one of the mixed blocks over on Central Avenue, the blocks that are not yet all negro. I had just come out of a three-chair barber shop where an agency thought a relief barber named Dimitrios Aleidis might be working. It was a small matter. His wife said she was willing to spend a little money to have him come home.

I never found him, but Mrs Aleidis never paid me any money either. It was a warm day, almost the end of March, and I stood outside the barber shop looking up at the jutting neon sign of a second floor dine and dice emporium called Florian's. A man was looking up at the sign too. He was looking up at the dusty windows with a sort of ecstatic fixity of expression, like a hunky immigrant catching his first sight of the Statue of Liberty. He was a big man but not more than six feet five inches tall and not wider than a beer truck. He was about ten feet away from me. His arms hung loose at his sides and a forgotten cigar smoked behind his enormous fingers.

from *Farewell My Lovely,*
Raymond Chandler (1940)

ACTIVITY 88

Write a short fictional piece in which your main characters are drawn from a social group that is well known to you. Make sure that the language you use creates a distinct and authentic voice for your chosen group. This then could form the basis for a piece of original writing for your coursework folder and, naturally, you should have plenty to say about it in your commentary both from a linguistic and from a literary point of view.

6 The Craft of Writing

Strengths and weaknesses

Take any seven present day writers:
Simon Armitage (poet and essayist), David Banks (formerly Editor of the *Daily Mirror*), Colin Dexter (the Inspector Morse novels), U. A. Fanthorpe (poet), Liz Lochhead (poet and playwright), Jan Mark (children's novelist), Jim Park (Coronation Street scriptwriter).

All of them regularly talk to A level students, yet ask them to write a brief chapter on writing, and they would not readily welcome the task. This is partly to do with the intrinsic difficulty of writing about writing (you will discover this for yourself, if you haven't already done so, when you come to write a commentary on your own writing), and partly to do with the fact that professional writers prefer to let their writing speak for itself. After all, that is what they sweated over!

Why then, are we writing a chapter about writing? Are fools going where the angels fear to tread? We hope not. There is an immediate reason for this chapter, and that is that the syllabus you are studying requires you to produce original writing of your own. There is another direct reason: every answer you write on an examination paper is a piece of original writing too. You may not look at it in that light, but regardless of how much common content, vocabulary, purpose and audience there is, every exam script collected up after a single examination, will be different from the next and will show different degrees of skill in communicativeness, style and genre. Yes – even examination scripts are a genre! No piece of writing, if it is intelligible, can be genre free. An exam script is like a photograph of how a candidate's mind works.

QCA regulations also require candidates to comment on their own writing, a well established feature now of A level English Language coursework, though if anything, more difficult than the original writing itself.

Apart, though, from these necessities, there are some very positive reasons why you should produce writing of your own, and reflect upon the process you have gone through.

1 It teaches you a great deal about yourself as a language user (your habitual adjectives and verbs, the way you construct sentences, how you think, the stereotypes you didn't know were lurking in your mind).

2 It teaches you a great deal about language itself, along the lines of the well known adage, 'You learn best by doing', e.g. about genre, communication strategies, vocabulary, style, register, metaphor.

3 It can be enjoyable and useful in other walks of life (e.g. at work or writing geography essays) if approached in the right spirit. In many respects it can be compared to creative photography and keeping fit: the one makes you notice more about people, places, things and life in general; the other increases your capacity for enjoying life.

Throughout this book the term 'verbal art' has been used to describe other people's original writing which you have been studying. The title of this chapter however, uses the word 'craft'. We are not for one minute suggesting that what the professionals do is 'art', and what you do is 'craft'. Both have an identical dictionary meaning (= 'skill') but as with all English synonyms there is a subtle difference. When you explore the stylistics of a poem or a short story, you are frequently identifying and describing the craft that constructs the art.

One of these words, 'art' has a Latin origin, coming into English via Norman French, as so many Latin words did (and not to be confused with the middle English word 'ars', meaning 'what you sit upon'!). Its meaning is joined to another Latin word 'arma' meaning 'weapons', which gives an added dimension to phrases like 'take up arms' and 'the arts of war'. The word 'craft' has a Germanic origin ('kraft' = 'strength'). Both words now mean 'skill', but one points to the means, 'weapons', the other to a necessary quality, 'strength'. 'Kraftwerk' was the name of an avant garde German pop group that was very popular in the 1970s and 1980s.

When examiners assess candidates' writing and commentaries they look for strengths and weaknesses, hoping to find more strengths than weaknesses. This chapter looks at some of the strengths you could show in your own writing. It won't tell you what to write; a choice, or series of choices you must make for yourself if your writing is to have real conviction. It will suggest some strategies and some crafts that you could think about, especially in the re-reading/revision stage, some questions you might ask yourself. It will also offer advice on the business of writing a commentary.

Me, myself and I

The title of one of Billie Holiday's best songs focuses attention on the place where writing most often begins but where it shouldn't end. After all, the first line of the song goes: 'Me, myself and I are all in love with YOU'. There is at least one other member of the human race in there somewhere.

The first activity in this chapter will be concerned with three interconnected genres of writing: autobiography, biography and narrative fiction. The first two of these require a careful balance between two primary purposes in writing: informing and entertaining. Normally, readers expect rather more objective information in a biography, but enjoy being informed in an entertaining way. Entertainment here, doesn't, of course, mean a laugh a minute. An autobiography may be highly 'imaginative' and 'very entertaining' and full of subjective personality, but it must be reliably informative. Downright lies are not expected. With narrative fiction, the primary purpose will be artistic: to tell a story well. What the reader expects, is to enjoy that story. Again, enjoyment doesn't mean 'a loada laughs'; it can also be the kind of satisfaction you get from a film like *Forrest Gump* or *Saving Private Ryan*. Entertainment can be a great source of learning about life and human behaviour.

ACTIVITY 89

Storytelling: getting stuck in

If you go in any market up and down the country, you are likely to find a paperback book-stall; the kind that charges you a pound or so for a book and gives you half the amount back when you return. And two of the biggest selling names will be Barbara Cartland and Catherine Cookson. Overheard at one such stall, was the following remark: 'Oh Barbara Cartland's alright for a bit of escape. You can read 'em in five minutes. They're nothing really. But you can really get stuck into Catherine Cookson. I love her books.'

Certainly, both writers knew their business and their readers. A look on the back of Catherine Cookson's *Hamilton*, will tell you that 27 million copies of her books have been sold in Corgi editions alone, while the back of Barbara Cartland's *Mission to Monte Carlo* tells you that it is her three hundred and twenty first novel

and that she is the world's top selling 'authoress' (*Guinness Book Of Records*, 1982)

In both cases, somebody is doing something right!

We think that the homespun remarks above get it just right, and we want you to begin this activity by reading two excerpts by Catherine Cookson. We make no apology for starting you off on a writing activity by giving you something to read. Writng feeds as much off other people's writing as it does off a writer's experience. Genres have a life of their own in the imagination, and given the slightest chance they will write themselves without you noticing. So much for being 'original'!

First, a piece of autobiography. The setting is Northumberland and the author is being driven through wild moorland and high hills by her husband.

> But up here in the hills I know that I am in my own country, not soft like the downs nor flat like the fens. This countryside is raw, and it is with me and I feel it. Tom must be tired of the times we have brought the car from Hexham to Langley and I have said that it is the most beautiful sight that I have ever seen. I first became afraid of hills up here when Tom took me up Shap Fell and over Alston . . .

> Before, when visiting the North to seek out localities for my stories I had travelled by train, but this time there we were in the car and Tom, as always, took the longest way round in order that we could see the beautiful scenery of Northumberland. I found myself heading for what I didn't know then was the great, great expanse of Alston moors.

> At different times in my life I knew when I had been any place that had a deep fall to the side I had the most strange feeling, sometimes touching on terror. But what I experienced that day went past terror. Tom drove over the hills, up, up, into this space that went on for eternity, the heights and everything about it found me

crouched on the floor of the car beside the seat. I was shaking with terror from head to foot. All I could gasp was, 'Get out of this!' On and on he went, aiming to get out of it of course, by reaching the end of it. At one point he stopped the car and said, 'Look, try, try to sit up and look about you. It's the most magnificent sight.'

I couldn't answer, my heart was racing so fast. My pulse was racing so fast that it was a great wonder to me that I didn't have a heart attack.

'Just lift your head', he begged, 'or look through the windscreen. Just lift your head.'

I managed to raise my head from my huddled, crouch position and look through the windscreen, and there I was confronted by a fly moving slowly, slowly upwards. I followed it. I followed its progress until I realised it wasn't a fly, it was a car in the far, far distance, mounting the rise, and I let out a scream and once more my head was buried.

So on and on he drove until we ran down into some sort of a village and he dragged me out of my cramped position and I sat on the footboard and I was sick. 'I'll never forgive you,' I said, 'for doing this to me.'

He got the map out and he said, Well, we can't go back. We've got to go on. It isn't very far now. We've just got to go up that bank and then we'll be all right.'

We went up that bank and then I died another death because dropping straight down from the edge of the car was this great, great fall, studded with trees.

from *My Land of the North: Memories of a Northern Childhood* Catherine Cookson (1986, 1999)

Now read the following excerpt from one of Cookson's novels, *The Mallen Streak* (1973). The story is the first in a trilogy, telling of family fortunes, rivalries and hatreds. The Mallen streak refers to a distinctive flash of white hair running to the left temple of successive generations of Mallen males. It was said that anyone who bore the streak seldom reached old age or died in bed, and that nothing good ever came of a Mallen. The excerpt concerns two brothers, the frail Matthew and the ambitious Donald, possessor of the Mallen streak. Miss Brigmore is a governess. A family crisis has come to a head and Donald is driving his brother and Miss Brigmore up to the very spot Catherine Cookson describes in the autobiographical excerpt.

She shook her head before letting it fall forward, and like someone in whom all hope has died she went out of the kitchen, without a word to Jane, and across the yard to the brake.

Donald was standing by the side of it. He did not speak to her but pointed into the back of it, and it was left to Matthew to help her up.

Slowly she covered her ankles with her skirts and sat, for once in her life, without any signs of dignity while the cart rumbled out of the yard and began the journey over the hills.

As they drove higher Matthew's coughing became harsher, but only once did Donald turn his head and glance at him and noted there was more blood than usual staining the piece of linen. It would be odd, he thought, if he died on this journey. He wanted him to die, and yet he didn't want him to die. There were still grains of love left in him that at times would cry and ask, Why had he to do it to me? I could have suffered it from anybody else in the world except him. But such times were few and far between and his hate soon stamped on the grains.

They were nearing the narrow curve in the road where the guard or snow posts stuck up from the edge above the steep partly wooded hillside. It was the place where

Barbara had experienced the terrifying fierceness of the gale as it lifted the carrier's cart over the ditch. The line of posts curved upwards for some forty yards and it was at the beginning of them that Matthew, putting his hand tightly over his mouth, muttered, 'I'm ... I'm going to be sick.'

Donald made no comment but kept on driving.

A few seconds later he repeated, 'I'm going to be sick, stop, stop a minute. I'll ... I'll have to get down.' His body was bent almost double now.

The horse had taken a dozen or more steps before Donald brought it to a halt, and Matthew, the piece of linen held tightly across his mouth, got awkwardly down from the cart and hurried to the edge of the road, and there, gripping one of the posts, he leaned against the wire and heaved.

Miss Brigmore watched him for a moment from the side of the cart and as she slid along the seat with the intention of getting down, Donald's voice checked her, saying, 'Stay where you are.' Then he called to Matthew, 'Come on, come on.' But Matthew heaved again and bent further over the wire. After a short while he slowly turned around and, leaning against the post, he gasped, 'I'm ... I'm bad'.

Donald looked down at him. There was blood running from one corner of his mouth, his head was on his chest. He hooked the reins to the iron framework, then jumped down from the cart and went toward him, and as he did so he slipped slightly on the frosted rime of the road, which as yet the sun hadn't touched. When he reached Matthew's side he said sharply, 'Get into the back and lie down.'

'I ... I can't.' Matthew turned from him and again leant over the wire and heaved.

Donald, bending forward now, looked down. There was a sheer drop below them before the trees branched out. He said harshly, 'Come back from there, you'll be over in a minute.' It was at this moment that Matthew turned and with a swiftness and strength it was impossible to imagine in his weak state he threw both his arms around Donald's shoulders and pulled him forward. Almost too late Donald realised his intention, and now he tore at the arms as if trying to free himself from a wild cat while they both seemed to hang suspended in mid-air against the wire. Donald's side was pressed tight against it; he had one foot still on the top of the bank, the other was wedged sideways against the slope. With a desperate effort he thrust with one hand to grab the post, and as he did he heard the Brigmore woman scream. Then Matthew's body was jerked from him and he was free, but still leaning outwards at an extreme angle over the drop. As he went to heave himself upwards his foot on top of the bank slipped on the frost-rimed grass verge, and the weight of his body drew him between the wire and the top of the bank, and with a heart-chilling cry of protest he went hurtling through the air. When he hit the ground he rolled helplessly downwards, stotting like a child's ball from one tree trunk to another ...

They lay on the bank where they had fallen, Miss Brigmore, spread-eagled, one hand still gripping a spoke of the cart wheel, the other clutching the bottom of Matthew's overcoat.

When, getting to her knees, she pulled him away from the edge of the drop and turned him over she thought he was already dead, for the parts of his face that weren't covered in blood were ashen.

'Oh, Matthew! Matthew!' She lifted his head from the ground, and he opened his eyes and looked at her. Then his lips moving slowly, he said, 'You should have let me go.'

She pressed his head to her and rocked him for a moment, then murmured, 'Try to stand. Try to stand.' Half dragging him, half carrying him, she got him into the back of the brake and pulled him up, and he lay on the floor in a huddled heap.

> Before she got up into the driver's seat to take the reins she walked a few tentative steps towards the edge of the road and looked downwards. Far, far below a dark object was lying, but it could have been a tree stump, anything. If it was Donald he might still be alive.

There is nothing remarkable about writers using specific incidents in their lives to give authenticity to locations in their fiction. Insofar as novelists draw on their own experiences of life, there is a sense in which all fiction is biographical and autobiographical. What is lucky here is that we have such a clear example.

ACTIVITY 90

Autobiography

First, write a short autobiographical piece (about the same length as Cookson's) focusing on a place and incident you can recollect vividly. It need not have been a terrifying experience. Try to make it come alive again but this time for a reader. Don't think grandly about 'audience' in the vast, abstract sense; do what Cookson does. Imagine you are telling your story to one person, but don't slip into a casual speech style. Listeners expect a bit of storytelling craft in both fiction and 'lifestories'.

Remember that when you are writing autobiography you are inevitably writing bits of other people's biographies too. Even in a very personal and emotional recollection, Cookson is not trapped in the first person. She gives her husband too, a distinct identity.

ACTIVITY 91

Telling a story

When you have done this, think of a brief outline for a fictional story and one or two characters. Use your autobiographical details to create a key point in the story, and invent a scene that would hold a reader's attention. Your own attention to detail (look how Cookson does it) will be an important factor here.

Finally, write a paragraph or two of commentary on the differences and connections between autobiography and fiction. In particular, discuss the mixing of 'facts' (i.e. concrete details) and feelings in both pieces. Say something too, about how you crafted your writing. Examples of 'craft' in the Cookson excerpts are: repetitions (do you like them?); occasionally putting herself in the passive ('it found me crouched') (what's the effect of this?); use of speech; choice of verbs (e.g. 'Matthew's body was jerked from him' and 'stotting like a child's ball'); use of modals to create dread and suspense at the end of the Mallen passage ('it could have been a tree stump' and 'he might still be alive').

Don't think of craft as automatically a virtue. You may not like the way some prose is crafted. The important thing is that there is some craft somewhere, and the more you have to choose from, the better your writing will be. Coursework that writes itself is always difficult to comment upon, because the author's role is largely a passive one, and more often than not it makes dull reading. The more care you take over your writing, here and there, the more care you are taking over your reader's response.

ACTIVITY 92

'Hot breath'

At the start of this chapter we referred to the impressive sales figures of two popular writers but implied a qualitative difference between one kind of fiction that was 'escapist' and another kind you could 'get stuck into'. There are critics of a killjoy disposition who wouldn't allow Barbara Cartland's 'books' (they wouldn't dignify them with the name 'novels') houseroom, and may well express reservations about Catherine Cookson. These are qualitative judgements stemming from a point of view of what literary culture is or ought to be. We shall look more closely at this in the final chapter on critical approaches. For the moment we are considering ways in which language is used in successful narrative fiction. By success we mean enjoyed by lots of people who are not fools. It's not its money spinning power that interests us, so much as its word spinning power.

Barbara Cartland's 'books' are examples of 'romantic fiction'. One publisher, Mills and Boon, is renowned throughout the English speaking world as a veritable factory, its production line turning out daily, anonymously written pastime tales of love requited and unrequited. There may well be a teacher in your own school or college who secretly earns pocket money writing them. Mills and Boon even have different tiers of raunchiness so that writers know which formula to use when they are writing for frisky twenty-odd-year-olds or sentimental grannies. They even publish a 'how to do it' guide (see Chapter 10 on Genre).

But it's all in the imagination anyway, which is the whole point about fiction. Barbara Cartland's formulaic writing can be viewed as

Enid Blyton for adults. You probably read, and enjoyed, lots of Enid Blyton as a child – nothing wrong with that. It is also possible that you returned to them in your early teen years, though you may not care to admit it in case word got round. Researchers into this 'return to the Famous Five and the Secret Seven' see it not so much as infantilism or regression as such, but as a perfectly understandable escapist strategy for projecting very real teenage anxieties and awful imaginings onto familiar, unthreatening stereotypes. In other words, don't ask, 'What do they get out of that stuff at their age?' but 'What are they putting into it?'

It is also true that other studies have pointed out the persuasive power of competent storytelling in fluent standard English to reinforce class, gender and racial stereotypes, especially when read first time round in the primary school years and even on mother's knee. Underlying the humour of a book like *Politically Correct Bedtime Stories* (by J.F. Garner, 1994, Souvenir Press) is a serious recognition of how influential fiction is in shaping attitudes and values. The imagination is a dangerous place!

Below are some excerpts from Barbara Cartland's *Mission to Monte Carlo*. Read them and identify the formula or the recipe for this kind of writing. Then have a go yourself. Don't make fun (e.g. write a parody or a burlesque). Write as though you wanted to make some money out of it. Your editor will expect you to get the writing 'right' according to the formula. Put aside the real you.

You do not need to write a complete Barbara Cartland romance, some samples will do.

Excerpts from Cartland's *Mission to Monte Carlo*

Him

'The marquess sat down opposite him thinking that, as a great many women had thought before about him, it would be hard to find a better-looking, more attractive young man anywhere in the world.

It was not surprising. Craig Vandervelt's father came from Texas, and it was his astute and brilliant brain which had turned what had been the Vandervelt's misfortune into one of the greatest fortunes in America.

His mother, a daughter of the Duke of Newcastle, had been one of the great beauties of her generation. It was therefore not surprising that their only son would be not only extremely good-looking and irresistibly attractive, but also, although not many people were aware of it, had a brain which matched his father's. Because he had no inclination to add to the enormous wealth his family had already accumulated, Craig had, from the world's point of view, become a 'playboy'.

He travelled extensively, enjoyed himself not only in the great Capitals which catered for rich young men, but also in more obscure, unknown parts of the earth, where a man had to prove his manhood rather than rely entirely on his pocketbook.'

Her

'By Jove! There is something to look at!' and Craig thought he could have echoed his words.

She was, as he had noticed when he had seen her walking down the passage, very slim. She was taller than many other women in the room, and if she had dressed in order to cause a sensation she had certainly succeeded.

Every other woman was clothed in colours of the spring fashions; green, blue, pink, yellow, and a great deal of soft white chiffon or tulle.

The Countess Aloya was wearing black. It was quite a severe black and the bodice was plain and very tight, accentuating the soft curves of her breasts and her very slim waist.

Her skirts, billowing out, were not ornamented, and what at first glance seemed so extraordinary was that unlike every other woman in the room she was not glittering with jewels.

Craig, as a connoisseur of women, knew there was no need for them, for the whiteness of her skin was a jewel in itself, and her hair, so fair that it seemed almost silver in the light from the chandeliers, appeared to glitter without the aid of diamonds.'

Them, together at last!

As Craig was kissing her he undid her gown and lifted her onto the bed. She realised he had pulled back the curtains from the porthole and now there were not only the stars, but the light from a young moon climbing the sky.

She felt it was like the life they were starting together, with a light of such beauty and glory to guide them that it was impossible to express it except by love.

Then Craig came to her and she felt his body against hers, his heart beating on hers, and his hands touching her.

The moonlight not only covered them with its silver light, but vibrated within them, and it was the Power of Love that had been theirs in the past and would be theirs in the future and for all eternity.

....

It was three o'clock in the afternoon and the sun was very hot, when Craig, after swimming in the sea, climbed back onto the yacht to join Aloya who was resting under an awning.'

1 What stereotype do you find here?
2 How are the characters described? Do they have any character at all?

3 What do you make of the narrative gap at the end of the third script? It is Cartland's gap, not ours.

Hotter than loaded

One criticism of Cartland's writing, from readers expecting a 'good read' or a book to 'get stuck into', is that there is in fact nothing there. It's all stereotypes and the author's adjectives. In no way do Craig or Aloya come alive on the page. There are no details of gesture, expression, action or idiosyncrasy, only generalised adjectives and adverbs: better looking, more attractive, brilliant (brain), great (beauties), extremely good-looking and irresistibly attractive, enormous (wealth), obscure, unknown (parts).

The odd pen portrait of a minor character written in this way is alright, but the language texture of the whole book consists of this kind of vocabulary. It's a great money spinner because the reader does all the work, projecting onto the stereotypes whatever she wishes. Don't knock the therapeutic value, but don't write like this unless it makes you money. It is interesting to note that much pornographic writing works in the same way, relying on the reader's imagination rather than the writer's.

The continuing success of the James Bond movies is another example of how popular is the blending of escapism and stereotypes but there is also a rattling good yarn. Ian Fleming's original books, best sellers in their day, still sell well, and it is a pity that Fleming's terse, stylish writing has been overshadowed by the films. No one can grab a reader's attention quicker or better than he does in the very opening sentences:

The scent and smoke and sweat of a casino are nauseating at three in the morning. Then the soul-erosion produced by high gambling – a compost of greed and fear and nervous tension – becomes unbearable and the senses awake and revolt from it. James Bond suddenly knew that he was tired.

Casino Royale, 1953

I was running away. I was running away from England, from my childhood, from the winter, from a sequence of untidy, unattractive love-affairs, from the few sticks of furniture and jumble of overworn clothes that my London life had collected around me; and I was running away from drabness, fustiness, snobbery, the claustrophobia of close horizons and from my inability, although I am quite an attractive rat, to make headway in the rat-race. In fact I was running away from almost everything except the law.

The Spy Who Loved Me, 1962

[We particularly like the semi-colon above! What do you think its effect is?]

The two thirty-eights roared simultaneously.
The walls of the underground room took the crash of sound and batted it to and fro between them until there was silence. James Bond watched the smoke being sucked from each end of the room towards the central Ventaxia fan. The memory in his right hand of how he had drawn and fired with one sweep from the left made him confident.

Moonraker, 1955

You will find three longer, even more arresting openings together with some stylistic analysis, in one of the 'Living Language' series of books (*Language and Literature* by G. Keith, Hodder & Stoughton, 1999)

It is perfectly possible to appreciate and enjoy (and learn from!) writing craft of this quality, without worrying about whether it is 'great literature' or not. That's another issue altogether.

A more recent writer whose work has achieved some popularity is Robert Harris. Two of his novels explore 'what might have been' themes. *Fatherland* (made into a film), tells of a Europe that made peace with Hitler who continued to this day as Germany's Chancellor. *Archangel* tells of a plot to use Stalin's secret son as a figurehead to restore the repressive Soviet regime.

The activity below starts with an excerpt from a Harris novel based on historical reality rather than historical fantasy. The excerpt is from *Enigma*, (1995) a story of how British cryptoanalysts cracked the German Enigma code used by High Command to communicate secretly with submarines in the Atlantic.

Imagination and infotech

Enigma contains many traditional elements of English novels: male rivalries, a love story, danger and misfortune, ironic reflections on life. It also contains a lot of technology, and the skill and imagination with which Harris weaves technological language into the texture of conventional fiction has been praised by many writers and critics. It is a likely future addition to GCSE set book lists.

The excerpt comes late in the story. Feiler is the commander of a damaged U-boat who needs to send a message via Enigma. The British cryptoanalysts (a secret army of crossword and mathematical wizards who crack codes) are waiting for just such a transmission. Thomas Jericho is the man who actually cracks the code.

The narrative gap is Harris's own, not one we have inserted.

He (Feiler) waited two hours, then surfaced.
The convoy was already so far ahead as to be barely visible in the faint dawn light – just the masts of the ships and a few smudges of smoke on the horizon, and then, occasionally, when a high wave lifted the U-boat, the ironwork of bridges and funnels.
Feiler's task under standing orders was not to attack – impossible in any case, given his lack of torpedoes – but to keep his quarry in sight while drawing in every other U-boat within a radius of 100 miles.
'Convoy steering 070 degrees', said Feiler. 'Naval grid square BD 1491.'
The first officer made a scrawled note in pencil then dropped down the conning tower to collect the Short Signal Code Book. In his cubbyhole next to the captain's berth the radioman pressed his switches. The Enigma came on with a hum.

At 7 a.m., Logie had sent Pinker, Proudfoot and Kingscome back to their digs to get some decent rest. 'Sod's law will now proceed to operate', he predicted, as he watched them go, and sod's law duly did. Twenty-five minutes later, he was back in the Big Room with the queasy expression of guilty excitement which would characterise the whole of that day.
'It looks like it may have started.'

St Erith, Scarborough and Flowerden had all reported an E-bar signal followed by eight Morse letters, and within a minute one of the Wrens from the Registration

Room was bringing in the first copies. Jericho placed his carefully in the centre of his trestle table.

RGHC DMIG> His heart began to accelerate.

'Hubertus net,' said Logie. '4601 kilocycles.'

Cave was listening to someone on the telephone. He put his hand over the mouthpiece. 'Direction finders have a fix.' He clicked his fingers. 'Pencil. Quick.' Baxter threw him one. '49.4 degrees north,' he repeated. '38.8 degrees west. Got it. Well done.' He hung up.

Cave had spent all night plotting the convoys' courses on two large charts of the north Atlantic – one issued by the Admiralty, the other a captured German naval grid, on which the ocean was divided into thousands of tiny squares. The cryptoanalysts gathered round him. Cave's finger came down on the spot almost exactly midway between Newfoundland and the British Isles. 'There she is. She's shadowing HX-229.' He made a cross on the map and wrote 0725 beside it.

Jericho said : 'What grid square is that?'

'BD 1491'.

'And the convoy course?'

'070.'

Jericho went back to his desk and in less than two minutes, using the Short Signal Code Book and the current Kriegsmarine address book for encoding naval grid squares he had a five-letter crib to slide under the contact report.

> RGHCDMIG
> DDFGRX??

The first four letters announced that a convoy had been located steering 070 degrees, the next two gave the grid square, the final two represented the code name of the U-boat, which he didn't have. He circled R-D and D-R. A four-letter loop on the first signal.

'I get D-R/R-D,' said Puck a few seconds later.

'So do I.'

'Me too.' said Baxter.

Jericho nodded and doodled his initials on the pad. 'A good omen.'

After that, the pace began to quicken.'

The prose here communicates to the reader something of the excitement of a game of Battleship with the precision of what actually happened in the war years. Elsewhere in the book, Harris weaves the complexities of the workings of the Enigma code machine itself into the everyday lives of men and women brought together in secrecy because of a common knack for solving word and number puzzles.

ACTIVITY 93

Writing, 2000

Try your own hand at writing a short story (about 1500–2000 words) that focuses on details of the work people do as well as on the people themselves. You could choose somewhere you know from work experience, a part time job or anywhere in which doing a job is part of the 'action'. Make sure you integrate action and dialogue in a dramatic or at least interesting way.

If you prefer, write a scene from a novel, but make sure you have some idea of the genre and the barest of plot outline.

Remember, this is a stylistics exercise to give you an opportunity to practise a bit of writing craft; it is the attention to detail that will count. Note, for example, the dramatic effect of the narrative gap Harris leaves between, 'The Enigma came on with a hum' and 'At 7am, Logie had sent . . .'. Note also the cumulative effect of:

'I get D-R/R-D . . .
'So do I'
'Me too', said Baxter.

And it only takes a short sentence like, 'His heart began to accelerate' to get the reader's own adrenalin flowing.

So far you have explored some examples of narrative, mostly fiction, and written versions of your own. In the next activity you are going to look at a narrative, plus a commentary written by an A level student and then compare it with a re-written version and our own commentary. The original was intended as a piece of journalism written as part of a light hearted series on part time work.

ACTIVITY 94

Bar staff wanted

I decided I needed a part time job, it was the only way I ~~could get~~ was going to get any money to buy those little things that make life worthwhile, like booze, clothes, CDs, tickets for concerts and getting into clubs. My parents can't fork out, they keep me anyway.

Most of my friends have got jobs and showed me where to look for job adverts. I found an advert for bar staff in a pub not far from where I lived so I went for an interview, if you can call it that, one afternoon after College. The advert was in the newsagents window. The pub was called The Flying Horse, it was run by a couple in their forties.

The interview was very casual and after they had gone through the necessary questions and information they told me that the hourly rate was £3.00 an hour. Tips went into a large jar at the back of the bar to be shared out among bar staff and if anyone said 'have one yourself', I was to say 'Thankyou, I'll save it till later', and put the money in the bar.

I think they were as unsure about the interview as I was, except when it came to money!

Most of the work I did was pretty menial stuff – collecting glasses, washing up, making sandwiches, emptying ashtrays, warming up pies in the microwave, and forever re-filling shelves. I was a general dogsbody but when it was slack I sometimes got chance to serve drinks and even pull a pint which isn't very difficult because all I had to do was push a lever with one finger.

She turned out to be somewhat of a fusspot and bossy with it. She always had an eye on the till and made you feel all the time that you were standing around doing nothing. He didn't seem to do much except check the pumps and chat to regulars. He could be nasty if you made the slightest mistake, like when I gave someone a cheese sandwich when they had asked for ham. She didn't seem too bothered but he made a big issue of it. If anything went wrong he always looked at me. Once she put a crate near the top of the stairs and he banged his shin on it and blamed me. She took no notice and carried on wiping down.

(Three paragraphs of further anecdotes in similar vein)

I was glad when I finished the job as revision time for exams came round. I made bit of money [*sic*] but it was slave labour really and if you were a student (I was the only one out of five bar staff) you were made to feel the lowest of the low.

COMMENTARY

I wrote this to show people what it was really like working behind a bar, not glamorous at all. I have written in the first person to make it more convincing as one person's experience. (You can express your feelings better.) I have kept it informal. I put in lots of information so the reader wouldn't get bored with too much description or waffle.

At the beginning I changed 'could get' to 'was going to get' because it sounded better.

I structured my writing in a logical way so that the reader could follow it easily. I think it shows the reader what I experienced and is amusing. I could have put in more conversation and said something about the regulars but on the whole I think it is a quite successful piece of writing. I have noticed though that the 'she' in 'She didn't seem too bothered' is ambiguous because you don't know who she is.

Here's a friendly reader response to this piece: a clearly told, simple tale of an inoffensive student's efforts to earn some pocket money; could have historical documentary value in the year 3000; conveys an impression of two characters, albeit very sketchily; rather downbeat writing; too many comma splices; commentary not very interesting. (Comma splices separate clauses that are better written as two sentences, separated by a full stop, or better written as one sentence, separated by a semi-colon.) In the following example, the comma is a weaker option compared with the semi-colon or full stop: 'The pub was called The Flying Horse, it was run by a couple in their forties'.

Here's a harder response: dull, pedestrian writing; relentlessly chronological; no title (unheard of in the genre of newspaper articles); choice of first person a mistake – comes across as a 'poor me'; much more interesting detail must surely have been available; commentary contravenes Trade Description Act – the reader *does* get bored!, and it is not amusing; it's rubbish! Yes, the 'she' is ambiguous. Why couldn't the 'couple in their forties' have been given names? I've taken a perverse liking to them, though why they employed such a wimp is beyond me!

You may share one of these views, though quite possibly your own lies somewhere between the two.

There are some 'good bits': the detail of the tips jar, the eye on the till, the tone of 'pretty menial stuff' and the crate incident. The logical structure however, noted approvingly in the commentary, is nothing more than a relentless chronology with a chronological beginning, a chronological middle and a chronological ending.

The beginning concentrates too much on things better implied, especially in a short piece of writing. Novels, like films, have the room in which to turn mundane details to advantage, but in this instance, there's little to see – just a recital of humdrum information that is only too familiar. The great French photographer of everyday life, Robert Doisneau, whose pictures tell a story without recourse to words, once said: It is much better to suggest than to describe.

The piece we are looking at here, need not have begun at the literal or logical beginning. Here are two different possibilities:

When John discarded his bar apron for the last time, with exams looming, he had earned a bit of pocket money but he also had serious doubts about whether it had been worth answering that advertisement in the newsagent's window, seven months ago:

Bar Staff Wanted
£3.00 an hour
Apply The Flying Horse
(just down the road)

Here the story begins at the end, as it were. The next example begins in the middle.

More ashtrays to empty. Filthy things! More glasses to collect. And she still had another three hours to work before she had earned enough for a meal out or a full priced CD. Was it all worth it? Tonight, she wished she had never seen that ad in the newsagent's window:

Bar Staff Wanted

Etc.

Storytime chronology is much more flexible, and interesting, than real time chronology which readers have no difficulty working out anyway, providing you are consistent in your writing. The narrative has got off to a better start; the reader can assume a lot of mundane information, and the article is potentially more lively. Notice too, the shift from first to third person which removes the unsuitable personal element without being any the less focused on a believable individual. Now there is a chance to write about actors in a scene rather than about yourself in a situation. The choice of the first person narrator/addresser in writing other than autobiography, diaries and personal letters, is something you need to discuss at length, to discern its relative strengths and weaknesses over the third person.

One of the problems with a piece of this kind is that the effect must be entertaining if it is to succeed as a piece of journalism. This is a prerequisite of the genre. As pure autobiography, it is not strong enough for a straight, first person account. It needs to be angled, crafted into a story with a strong point of view. If it is to be an enjoyable read, it needs to be enlarged or enlivened in some way, using the kind of crafts a good storyteller would use. As it is at the moment, the piece sits a bit uncomfortably between the kind of autobiographical stories that you only ever write for English teachers and behind the scenes journalism on the life of everyday folk.

There's a good deal of potential in working behind a bar that seems not to have been realised. As in the Barbara Cartland excerpt, the reader has to go on the adjectives rather than see or feel verbs in action.

The 'landlady' is 'somewhat of a fusspot, and bossy with it'. This could have been a nice bit of comic realism for the reader to visualise and hear: 'There's a place for everything, and I like to see everything in its place', she said, adjusting the remaining packets of salted cashews so that they looked neat and tidy on their display card. The writer here supplies something that the reader can see and hear. The reader is the one who thinks, 'What a fusspot!' A phrase such as 'somewhat of a . . .' needs thinking about for another reason. It gets in the way of the person, who is made a 'what' a thing, rather than a 'who'. 'Bossy with it' is colloquial but alright in this context, but combined with 'somewhat of a fusspot' is too generalised.

Below is an alternative version. We are not saying it is better, but it is different, and gives an idea of what redrafting is all about. Too often redrafting is interpreted as editorial corrections and little else. Redrafting involves re-composing parts or the whole of what has been written in a first draft. It may mean restructuring sentences and paragraphs, or resequencing events or information. (You may have felt, for example, that a sentence in the first version, 'The advert was in the newsagent's window', needs re-locating earlier in the text.) It is also likely to mean changing a word here and there, for a better effect.

We are not advocating re-drafting for the sake of it, or to find something to write about in your commentary, but you should look on your course work as an opportunity for experiment as well as self expression.

Read the piece below and itemise the differences, e.g. The piece has a title. It may not be a great one, but it has the right journalistic ring to it. Could be revised.

When you have done this compare the strengths and weaknesses of the two versions. If you prefer one to the other, you should know exactly why.

The New Slave Trade! or £3.00 an Hour!
A Look At Life Through The Empties

'Who left this bloody crate here?', cursed Leslie, glowering at John, the useless lad. Sally, who had left it there, said nothing, and continued polishing finger marks off the Give Generously to Lifeboatmen collection box.
'It wasn't . . .'. began John.
'Get them empties downstairs, pronto', said Leslie. 'And take this crate as well', he added, kicking it.
It was a slack time. If there'd been punters, he'd have said nothing. Just glowered.

You have to be either very, very hard up or mad, or both, to take on a temporary job behind a bar. It seemed more like slave labour to John, for slave wages. You'll meet people, his parents had said. Do you good. Well, it had made him more philosophical about life, and he hadn't entirely lost his sense of humour. And it was wonderful to go home, even though it was nearly one o'clock in the morning and your clothes reeked of beer and cigarette smoke.
Leslie and Sally were the licensees of The Flying Horse. They had five bar staff, on and off, and had taken on John the slave, who was otherwise doing his A levels at the Tech. He collected empty glasses, wiped down tables, re-filled shelves, washed up, lugged crates up and down the narrow cellar stairs, emptied ashtrays, washed his hands and made sandwiches or microwaved pies in the cramped kitchen at the back. Oh, and always remembered to smile at the punters as Sally had told him to.
'Whatever you are doing', she had said, lining up all the slop mats in an exact sequence on the bar, 'Always have a cheerful smile for the customers'.
John once called them slop mats but Sally told him very firmly that they were bar towels. Leslie called them runners, which amazed the other bar staff who had never heard them called that before.
'We need some more orange', called out Sally, moving the fruit juices ever so slightly, so that all the labels faced the right way.
'And there's a lot of glasses want shifting over there', she added, flicking a rebellious slop mat (sorry, bar towel) into place.
'What's this meat pie doing down here?', came a neanderthal voice from the cellar, and John suddenly remembered the jovial man who had ordered it twenty minutes ago, between bringing up the crate of Pepsis and replenishing the cheese and onion crisps, or was it between bringing up the tomato juices and emptying the ashtrays?
'This bottle of gin's getting low, somebody', said Sally, shaking the little dishes of nuts so that they didn't look as if fingers had just scooped them. Whenever she said 'somebody' in a particular tone of voice she always meant John.
When he left, he wondered how the next victim to read that fatal notice in the newsagent's window, would get on.

Bar Staff Wanted
£3.00 an hour
Apply The Flying Horse
(just down the road)

Describe the different crafts that have been used in the second version, as though you were writing a commentary on coursework drafts. Remember, 'craft' isn't necessarily an evaluative term; it describes strategies and methods available to all writers, e.g. use of dialogue.

Give particular consideration to the different effects achieved by the use of the first and the third person pronoun. Does it matter?

Being persuasive

So far we have concentrated on varieties of narrative where the purpose is essentially entertainment, though with judicious use of information to achieve that purpose. The next activity looks at persuasive writing.

There is an important sense in which all language uses are persuasive insofar as every speaker and writer seeks the attention of listeners or readers. Getting attention and getting people on your wavelength are as important to persuasion as they are to storytelling, which is itself a very persuasive activity if done well.

There are three things worth remembering about persuasive writing. There may well be other things, but the following three deserve consideration if you wish to be reasonably effective:

1 don't go over the top or get too personal (it is usually counter productive)
2 choose carefully the sequence in which you put the key points of your argument
3 nothing persuades better than thoughtfully presented information.

For your coursework, choose a topic you know about and believe in yourself. Don't fake it. Keep it brief (you are likely to have used up a lot of your word allocation on an entertainment or information piece anyway).

ACTIVITY 95

Know more, give more

Below is a persuasive piece (together with a commentary) written for coursework by an A level student.

Read both, and then choose a topic of your own. You may find it appropriate to write a longer piece than the example here which has been kept deliberately brief by the student herself.

A picture of scarred hands was reproduced at the top of the text.

Eczema

Robert is reaching out for your help.
Imagine trying to tell him it's only eczema.
Imagine you had eczema.
Imagine waking up bleeding because you can't stop scratching, even in your sleep.
Imagine your skin is on fire.
Imagine your skin stretched so stiff and sore you couldn't smile even if you wanted to.

Like Robert, you would not be the only one facing these problems.
One in ten of the UK population has eczema.
Babies, children, teenagers and adults.
Some are lucky and only suffer mild symptoms.
Others have to learn to cope with almost unbearable pain and irritation.
Many become increasingly depressed and isolated.
There is as yet no cure.
But with your support there is hope.
Pleases give your help to raise funds.
Contact . . .

Writer's commentary

I wrote this because my brother suffers badly from eczema. It is not something as well advertised as multiple sclerosis and other illnesses, but it needs to be.

I have tried to make a direct appeal by concentrating on the symptoms. It has to be informative.

I hadn't realised it until I read it through, that I have used five imperatives. There is a request at the end.

I thought that a name – it's not a real one – would give the hands an identity. It's a real person.

I wanted to shock because there was no point in writing it otherwise.

I thought it could be a little strip – vertically printed – which could be slipped in library books. It could also be used in lots of other ways.

It doesn't ask for money but for help in getting a campaign underway. I need to make that clearer with something like, 'If you wish to find out more, or help a local organisation, contact . . .'

Different ones could put their phone number and address at the bottom.

I have noticed that other organisations have a very direct and brief style. I got the idea of using 'Imagine' from an NSPCC leaflet on neglected children.*

I know of no advertising campaign at all for eczema but there is a national association. I sent them a copy of my idea and they wrote back saying they liked it very much but had no funds for a national campaign via printed media.

Originally I wrote this as an essay but it was too wordy (see first draft). I think the list of short statements is better. I know line nine isn't a sentence but you see this in lots of adverts.

---

* The original NSPCC texts have been separated in a QCA booklet entitled 'Teaching Grammar: Not Whether but How' (1999) See Chapter 3. There should be a copy of the publication in all schools and possibly colleges.

It should be clear that between the two kinds of writing considered so far, there is a significant difference of intention. The prime purpose of the pub piece was to entertain. It might additionally inform readers, and indeed some may be persuaded never to take on a bar job, but these are incidental. In the eczema piece the primary purpose is to persuade. It is certainly informative too, and engaging but hardly entertaining. Persuasive writing (e.g. to eat more healthily) can of course be made very entertaining, and often is in leaflets aimed at young children. But at no point must the intention to persuade be lost.

So there are two very different kinds of writing here, differentiated by primary purpose or intention. Once you have two kinds of texts to compare, and have recognised a fundamental difference, however much overlap, you can begin to construct a useful model of different varieties of writing. Imagine surfing the Internet, where you will encounter many kinds of writing. It doesn't take long though, before you notice their primary purpose or intention: it may be simply no-strings-attached information about an American jet fighter from the Korean war that is being restored; it may be a persuasive invitation to join a group that can get in touch with dead pet cats; it may be a collection of jokes about French farmers; it may be instructions on how to meditate, or advice on helping a child to read. These all exemplify different primary purposes, two of which have been examined so far. Before turning to informative writing, we would like to give some consideration to different ways in which writing may be described and classified.

On the face of it writing and reading seem such a straightforward business. The writers say what they have to say simply and clearly, and readers read what the writing says. It's all a matter of decoding. Or is it?

In quite ordinary functional writing, it is surprising how often writers don't quite say what they mean, or mean what they say, and otherwise intelligent readers have an annoying habit of taking things the wrong way, or misreading 'quite simple' instructions. If this is true of plain sense, for want of a better phrase, how much more will it be true of verbal art where there can sometimes be as many interpretations as there are readers?

We have already referred to the Internet. Writing, that is to say the process of doing it, and all the products produced, can be thought of as the original (and still surviving) Internet – a worldwide web in many languages. One way of sorting it out its diversity is to think of it in terms of primary purposes (or intentions), genres, language functions, and forms. There are other ways of classifying types of writing but this is a useful one for covering all the texts you have to read for A level English Language and Literature, and all the texts you have to write.

Primary purposes may be thought of as intentions, in which the writer's mind is set toward a particular goal. There is a point to the writing, an overall intention. The word 'intention' is appropriate here because it refers to an overall purpose. It is more readily discernible in functional, 'non-literary' writing, but there are, nevertheless, serious primary artistic purposes behind the writing of novels, plays and poems. The important thing is not to assume that every linguistic effect is therefore intended. Comments such as, 'He uses the words "lonely and pensive" to make the reader feel sad' or, 'She uses long, Latinate words because she is writing for an educated audience' are at best trite, at worst, rubbish! There is an assumption here (it has traditionally been called the 'intentionalist fallacy') that writers consciously intend all the effects of their writing. Often it is the case that a writer writes something without thinking, looks at it and thinks, 'That's quite good. I'll leave it in.' Happy accidents occur often in writing, just as puns and slips of the tongue, and even wise remarks occur unitentionally in speech: 'This lamb's very tough', said the customer. 'I'll get you some more sir', said the waiter, rather sheepishly.

When you find yourself talking about writers' linguistic intentions, 'He uses a metaphor to . . .', what you should be writing about, more often than not, is its effect on you the reader. Good writing contains much more than could ever have been consciously intended.

The most familiar primary purposes (it's actually very difficult to think of any others) are:

— to entertain
— to persuade
— to inform
— to instruct/advise.

Genres (more fully explained in Chapter 10) are sets of rules, conventions, forms, mutual understandings, traditions and contextual factors in which primary writing purposes are communicated. They are what writers observe and what readers expect. In writing that fulfils social, legal, economic, educational purposes, for example, genres are usually stable and predictable. In verbal art, there is a good deal of genre tradition and stability, but the history of English Literature demonstrates a good deal of genre experimentation. There seems always to have been an avant garde to set against the traditionalists. From the point of view of your own original writing for A level, don't imagine that because you have got your primary purpose clearly in mind, you are nearly on the last lap. The first big fence, at which many fall, is choosing the right genre for what you want to do, and sustaining it. If, on the other hand, you are confident or reckless enough to go in for 'genre busting', make sure you know what you are doing!

Language functions (discussed in more detail in Chapter 10), lie behind ninety five per cent plus of everything you say and write. Whatever the primary function of a text ('basically' what the writer intends and the reader expects = two main features of genre) there will be a wide variety of language functions in the text. Because of this, texts are sometimes referred to as 'polysemic', that is to say, they can have many meanings. The point of view of the reader and differing contexts also contribute to this polysemy. A great many of the words used, for example, will have a range of associations and connotations that may vary considerably from reader to reader (remember that readers are people who switch texts on!).

At different points, a text may ask a question, make an explicit statement, make a comparison, slip into a metaphor, explain a process, offer a definition, argue a point, create suspense, insult someone, crack a joke, explore an example, get passionate, and so on. Because there are so many possibilities, it is important to make sure, especially in a shortish text (e.g. 1500 words) that the primary purpose is assisted by the language functions, not buried under them, or lost altogether.

Here are the kinds of comments examiners frequently make:

— gets sidetracked into information that loses sight of the argument (of a persuasive piece)
— too much opinion ('In my view.') not enough information (of an informative piece)
— sometimes the information gets in the way of the instructions,

sometimes there isn't any information when it's needed (an instructional piece)
- lots of facts but doesn't explain the point of any of them (an informative piece)
- too many negatives, not reassuring enough (of an advisory piece)
- there just isn't anything entertaining in it (of a story)
- too many generalisations to be convincing; it puts you off (a persuasive piece).

The word 'form' is never very far away from linguistics or literary criticism. 'A sense of form' usually refers to a satisfying internal structure that holds together the elements of a short story, for example. It is the 'form' that matters most of all; plots, jokes, fairy stories, arguments, scientific theories, examination essays are all at their best when there is a strong internal 'logic', pattern or shape to them. This is what you should concentrate on in your own writing. Katherine Mansfield's *Miss Brill* (see complete story in *Language and Literature*, by G. Keith in the 'Living Language' Series, Hodder & Stoughton, 1999), is a wonderful example of internal form and structure.

The word also refers to external structures: e.g. the 14 lines of a sonnet; the division of a play into acts and scenes; the chapters of novels; the paragraphing of essays; subtitled sections; the alphabetical arrangement of a directory.

These then, are four significant choices you need to make in your own writing: purpose, genre (which includes audience), different language purposes as you begin to write (weave) your text, and form in both the internal and the external senses.

If you have given thought to these factors you should have no difficulty when it comes to writing your commentary. Remember that a commentary can take many forms, it doesn't have to be an extra essay tacked on. There will be pre-writing comments about purpose and choice of genre; there will be comments made during the process of writing and revising; and there will be summary and evaluative comment at the end. It is essential that you comment on the details of language functions and forms as well as on the origins and intentions of your writing. Once you start asking questions like, 'What are these sentences supposed to be doing?', 'Why have I put that there?', 'Is this the right word?' 'Am I losing my sense of direction?' 'Does that sentence really say what I think it's saying?' – you are earning marks!

ACTIVITY 96

'I HAVE A PLAN', Michele of the Resistance in the TV series, *Allo 'Allo*.

The important thing about real writing for A level English Language and Literature is that you should have a purpose of your own for doing it. You should want to do it.

In this activity however, we want you to practise planning in order to get an overview of the writing process.

Think about the following purposes:

entertaining, informing, persuading, instructing, advising. Each puts you in a different relationship with readers.

Think of a topic for each one and sketch, for each, a plan or outline for an appropriate text. Make it clear what the genre is, what kinds of language functions you would expect to employ and what form(s) the writing would take.

Whilst doing this activity you may well discover a piece you actually want to write.

Now let's turn to informative writing.

What's the point?

There is a sense in which the purpose of entertaining, instructing, advising or persuading is straightforward once you know your audience. 'Being informative' is an oddly neutral writing role at first sight. Do remember that part of writing effectively is understanding the role you have to adopt when writing in a particular genre. You can't just be yourself, however right that advice is in many other contexts. If you know the audience that you are to inform, that of course helps, but the actual business of informing is full of sub purposes you need to choose from.

Many kinds of information do not require 'writing' in the continuous sense of that word: telephone directories; the specifications of British Second World War fighter planes; dictionaries; Ian Allan LocoShed books; calorie charts, etc.

ACTIVITY 97

With a partner, identify and classify different forms of published information according to the use, non-use, part-use of continuous writing.

When is continuous writing necessary or preferable, when not?

In students' commentaries on informative writing, there are three recurring anxieties. One: getting information in the right sequence. Two: keeping it simple. Three: avoiding the most dreaded thing of all – being boring!

There is much good sense in the first, though it is usually a problem easier to solve than the other two. The trouble with the second concern is that too often it leads to a form of expression that seems to assume that readers are not very bright – not quite patronising, but a bit too obvious. The third fear often comes from a recognition that the writing is in fact boring. Sometimes this is rationalisd in commentaries by such remarks as: 'I have kept it short and simple because the reader doesn't want to be wading through lots of irrelevant stuff or spend too long on it.' The general impression can be one of readers who need to be spoon fed warm milk, but only a little, their intelligence extending to words of only one or two syllables and their attention span capable of only seven word sentences!

The problem of boredom has to be tackled. Examiners and moderators use euphemisms for it in their assessments: 'dull', 'pedestrian', 'rather basic', 'lacks sparkle', 'elementary', 'sleep inducing', 'low on adrenalin', 'zombie-like', 'flat', 'uninteresting', 'rudimentary'.

It is even sadder to see attempts to brighten up a boring text by recourse to such tactics as: 'Hiya folks' or 'Now this bit's really interesting' or 'Don't start yawning yet' or 'What's the point of all this, I hear you say?'

The last remark here (frequently used, by the way) gets to the point as we see it. If 'to infom' is not sufficient of a purpose in itself, often leading to inbuilt 'boringness', then you need to ask yourself from time to time as you write, 'Why am I telling them this?' and 'Have I created an interesting context for this information?' and 'Who am I anyway, to be telling them this?'

Let's put these three questions in reverse order and write them as answers:

Understand the role you have adopted in your writing, and make sure you have adopted one.

Create a context for the reader that makes the information interesting.

Know why you have chosen the bits of information you are writing about and what you are doing with them, i.e. not just stating the facts, but explaining a cause, comparing two things, setting out a sequence, indicating how important a particular piece of information is, listing effects, describing consequences, and so on.

Roles you might adopt are: teacher, guide, presenter, editor, fellow enthusiast, relative beginner a bit further on than absolute beginners, detached observer, hard nosed reporter, news commentator. These are all teaching roles (in the best sense of that word).

Creating a lively, interesting context will depend on the kind of information, but here is an example:

Task: to write a short booklet on medieval castles for 10 to 13-year-olds to be given away by a petrol company during the holiday season.

There are all manner of staggeringly boring ways of making this topic even more boring than the kids expect it's going to be yet faintly hope it might be fun. One student tackled it this way (we have summarised): you are one of Robin Hood's men; Robin has been imprisoned in the castle; here is a map of the castle showing a secret way in and the route to the dungeons; now we'll make the journey stealthily, following the map, and taking note of the many interesting architectural features on the way: the kitchens, bed chambers, privies, banqueting hall, armoury, etc.

The business of knowing why you have selected your information and how you have treated it is almost wholly dealt with in the above example by the writer's choice of context.

Here is a section from *A Century of Pop: A Hundred Years of Music that Changed the World* (Hamlyn, 1999).

Techno

The usual images conjured up by the term Techno are the frantic beats per minute issued through mega-watt stacks to hoards of sweaty dancers in some iniquitous den on the edge of nowhere.

Certainly that may well be a piece of the story, but it is a very small piece. For the roots of Techno can be traced back to the early 1970s when German Progressive Rock bands such as Can and Tangerine Dream began to substitute traditional instrumentation – guitar, bass and drums – with synthesisers and drum machines. At first, these items of new technology were considered too sophisticated for anyone other than an electronics engineer, but gradually, through groups like Yes and Motown star Stevie Wonder, they acquired a wider currency. The advent of the 12-inch single, *Love To Love You Baby*, by disco queen Donna Summer in 1975, with its hypnotic, rhythmic pulse, showed the potential of the synthesiser and the drum machine.

Producer Brian Eno, formerly of Roxy Music, oversaw a trilogy of albums, *Low* (1977), *Heroes* and *The Lodger* (1978), by David Bowie that evoked a bleak post-industrial landscape. For it Brian Eno with his own solo albums such as *Music For Airports* and *Another Green World* had invoked the minimalism of avant garde composer John Cage. Bowie's fragile vocals and gift for a strong melody, overlaying a hypnotic pulse, combined to create an effect that was desolate and unsettling in the extreme. The notion of a post-apocalyptic society . . . .

[The text goes on to describe developments through the 1980s and 1990s. It ends with a paragraph beginning . . .]

By the late 1990s, Techno had become fully integrated into the mainstream as artists such as Ultra Nate and Sash dominated the charts throughout Europe.

This article could have been a chronology from first to last, but it creates a context first by characterising the music. Notice how it contrasts a popular conception with what the writer considers to be a more informed perspective. Throughout, the 'plain facts', e.g. names and dates (potentially boring bits) are presented with a little comment or pen-portait from the author: 'disco queen Donna Summer' and 'gift for a strong melody'.

ACTIVITY 98

Working with a partner, collect two or three reference books and/or encyclopedias likely to cover an identical topic, and compare how the information is presented.

When you have done this, choose a topic upon which you could write informatively to two different audiences, e.g. 'The best in Modern Pop'. Allow yourself only three artists/groups and write:

– to inform readers in their sixties who would like to know more but are not familiar with the context you take for granted
– an entry for an encyclopedia likely to be consulted by fellow students

Think about the role you might adopt (will it irritate/attract/be taken on trust?).

Think about the context, the angle, the slant (though not the spin!) with which you are going to present the information.

Think about what else you will do other than state facts.

The Pop Music idea is just an example. When you come to chose your topic, make sure you have access to the information you need so that your writing is reliably informative, and make sure that you know what you are talking about so that your perspective will be a worthwhile one.

Instruction and advice

ACTIVITY 99

Writing for examinations

The following task will give you an opportunity to find out just what your values, attitudes and expertise are in the business of writing. Your school or college is producing a set of booklets to guide students re-sitting GCSE examinations. Some of the readers will be 16–17, others may be older. It is the view of teachers and examiners in all subjects requiring answers in continuous writing, that many candidates fail or do badly because they are unable to show themselves at their best when it comes to writing.

Write a leaflet of no more than a thousand words offering, not just encouragement, but some really useful advice on writing. Get a partner to read your first draft in return for reading theirs. Offer each other suggestions where appropriate. Treat the matter as very serious business, for there is no doubt that the inability to write adequately results in much unnecessary educational failure. The Government has already initiated a literacy drive in the primary years which for the year 2000 and onwards has been extended into the secondary years. Even undergraduates frequently do not justify themselves sufficiently in their writing.

We do not wish to end the chapter on a depressing note, but writing is not easy, and is most usually learned through a long and hard apprenticeship. But the crafts can be learned! Only one person in two thousand writes spontaneously and just right on a first draft, and whilst you may admire them, don't they make you sick!

7 Everyday Talk

We have called this chapter 'Everyday Talk' to distinguish its content from that of the next chapter, 'Literary Talk'. By 'everyday' we do not just mean casual talk, but all the varieties of talk used in life to pass the time and to get things done. It is evident from examination scripts that many students tend to polarise types of talk into the 'formal' and the 'informal'. This is not adequate; you need to think of a spectrum of everyday talk ranging between the very formal and the very informal. Between these lie all kinds of talk that are best described as 'semi-formal'. Much talk in your own educational and employment experience will be semi-formal in varying degrees: classroom discussions, post mortems with a tutor on your last essay, enquiring at the library for a book that is difficult to find, negotiations at work, discussing a bank loan, buying a car.

Very formal kinds of talk would be the marriage ceremony, being a witness in court, presentations and some job interviews. Very informal talk would be gossiping (which is good for you and doesn't have to be malicious), observations about the weather while in a bus queue, and all those ums and ers that go on between friends who do not need a lot of words.

Much academic study of talk and psycho-sociological research into how we do it, does in fact look at very familiar aspects of conversation: there is normally more than one participant; there has to be something to talk about (topic); the speakers try to not to speak at once (turn-taking); and there are usually some implied limits to how much you should say (turn length). The table below shows these factors at work in forms of talk with different levels of formality:

Form and Level of Formality

	Formal debate	Religious ceremony	Meeting	Ordinary conversation
Number of participants	Two principals	Varies	Varies	Varies
Topic	Fixed	Fixed	Varies	Varies
Turn-taking	Fixed	Fixed	Varies	Varies
Length of turn	Fixed	Varies	Varies	Varies

ACTIVITY 100

Look at the table on page 146 and think of specific examples of each of the four kinds of talk.

Think about each one in turn, concentrating on the different degrees of fixity and variation.

Think of a wedding, for example, or the kind of meeting you have experienced. Do you agree with the above generalisations?

For a number of historical and cultural reasons, it is very easy to take talk for granted and to underestimate its value and importance compared with writing. So often it is regarded as inferior to writing because 'people don't speak in proper sentences' or 'it's full of slang and dialect'. The truth of the matter is that it is in many, significant ways, different from writing and the emotion it really deserves is not pity, tolerance or a personal lack of self assurance, but amazement that humans do it so brilliantly, achieve so much and understand each other so well. Talk is remarkably subtle and sophisticated.

Think for a moment about the range of words and phrases used to describe varieties of talk:

Natter, chinwag, He's in conference, tete-a-tete, chat, We shall end up having words, interrogation, frank exchange of views, man-to-man, parley, dialogue, a good talk, discussion, interview, confab, brainstorming session, talk about it, putting the world to rights, girltalk, Don't listen to his spiel, lecture, seminar, all talk, blarney, patter, sweet talk, bad mouthing, slagging off, slandering, telling off, chatting up, smalltalk.

Each of these has a subtly different meaning; each encodes a particular relationship and context for the speakers. If you have in your mind only two kinds of codes, the 'restricted' and the 'elaborated' for example (whatever those terms may mean now, since they have become bankrupt), you will not be able to describe adequately the varieties of talk encoded in ordinary words and phrases which reflect everyday experience. Remember too, that we slip in and out of codes and levels of formality all the time.

To cope with describing the sheer varieties of talk and the variations within conversations, it is not a matter of having a long list of types and deciding which label fits which kind of talk. Nor is it a matter of spotting and counting all the features evident in a stretch of conversation. Numbers of participants, turn-taking and length of turn or utterance are some quantifiable features introduced so far. Topic, levels of formality and forms of talk provide some useful labels. But to come to grips with the functions and structures (the stylistics) of a particular stretch of talk (say, a short transcript you have made or are faced with in an examination) there are four determining factors you need to take into account.

1 **Social Context**. Talk is social, functional, interactive human behaviour that takes place in social settings.
2 **Discourse**. The style of talk is governed by rules and conventions that have accumulated around particular topics, genres and fields of knowledge and expertise. Doctors talk like doctors, lawyers like lawyers

and market traders like market traders. Each group has its own vocabulary and often special meanings for common words.

3 **Pragmatics**. The words spoken are accompanied by, and embedded in, all kinds of non-verbal signals, assumptions and implied meanings. Shrugs, hints, evasions, hedging are some examples.

4 **Phonology**. Not just the phoneme system by which the words themselves are constructed, but also the prosodic features of speech, e.g. intonation patterns and pauses. The sound patterns of an auctioneer are very different from a lecturer's, a newsreader's or a doctor in surgery.

Social context

Every modern linguist stresses the influence of social context on the production of speech. It is not just one influence among many but a climate in which language activity takes place: language variation, language change, language acquisition and any kind of language development. When you look at a transcript of a conversation, it is always necessary to have some contextual cues or guidance at the start, but it is also remarkable how much else of the social context can be inferred once you have started reading, and listening in your imagination.

Look at the following transcript, first, without any contextual clues whatever.

JAMES: there
HANNAH: uh?
JAMES: mm
HANNAH: hm ... er ...
JAMES: yep
HANNAH: ah!
JAMES: (laughs)
HANNAH: bingo!
JAMES: that's the only one it could be

There's not a lot to go on, yet it is an accurate report of what two people said. Here are some clues to how they said it:

J: there (heavy emphasis)
H: uh? (very puzzled, questioning tone)
J: mm (affirmative tone, implying 'right, go on')
H: hm ... er ... (thoughtful tone, then beginning to think aloud)
J: yep (affirmative again, meaning 'go on, you're on the right lines')
H: ah! (tone of sudden realisation)
J: (laughs) (pleasure that the penny has finally dropped)
H: bingo! (shout of pleasure, meaning 'I've got it')
J: that's the only one it could be (confirmatory tone, rounding off this part of the exchange)

The explanatory comments no doubt help you to guess that some kind of game is in progress, and possibly you may have recognised from your own experience that the game is in fact Mastermind, the pegs-on-a-board version, not the TV quiz with Magnus Magnussen.

Once you know the context you can see how expressive and quite comprehensible the conversation is. More important however, is that James and Hannah knew exactly what they meant. Hannah was trying to guess the correct sequence for a row of different coloured pegs. James' role was to say whether or not Hannah's guesses were correct. Notice how he is in charge of the conversation because only he knows the answer.

ACTIVITY 101

Twenty questions

This is a game for pairs. You will need beforehand to have prepared a short piece of transcript of spontaneous talk. Choose a section where the words on the page are not at all self explanatory because they are dependent upon other factors, e.g. body language, intonation, context. Leave in any ums and ers and indicate pauses. Don't supply any other information. Try to find a sequence that would be fairly incomprehensible to a reader but which you know worked perfectly well in real life. Refer to the speakers by number.

When your transcript is ready (about half a page) show it to your partner and allow him or her twenty questions to discover just what the conversation was about. They can ask anything they like. Bit by bit, they will begin to supply details of phonology and context which you will be able to confirm or not.

There is a variant of this game in which you write an invented conversation containing a number of phatic expressions and including an unexplained 'it' or two, e.g. 'It's a very funny shape'. You must be absolutely clear about the context and not deviate from it as your partner uses up twenty questions trying to guess what is being talked about by whom.

Social context can be looked upon in two dimensions. First, there is the immediate physical environment (e.g. office, college, home, disco, bus queue) and the activities and purposes going on at the time. Then there are less tangible but no less influential social factors such as class, status, age, gender, ethnic origin, perceived appearance, accumulated experience, shared or alien interests, and the attitudes engendered by these factors. When we participate in conversations we are intuitively guided by social experience and implicit codes learned through that experience. In the same way that we construct sentences without thinking where to put the grammatical subject and its verb, so we talk to each other following unwritten 'rules'.

ACTIVITY 102

Where computers cannot boldly go

Look at the following conversation.

A: you goin' to the gym today to work out?
B: well, I am flabby but only if I can hook a ride with Jim
A: I heard his transmission's conked out, and it's at the shop
B: oh (pause) then I guess it won't work out
    [source: Bernstein, Roy, Srull and Wickens, *Psychology* (1988), Houghton Mifflin.]

Comment on any implicit features of this conversation that you have detected.
Compare your observations with our commentary.

COMMENTARY You probably guessed that A and B are students or youngish adults. There use of such words as 'work out', 'transmission', 'shop' and 'I guess', in this context, also signals that they are American students.

Notice the remarkable number of ambiguities ('gym' and 'Jim' and the two meanings of the words 'work out'). The participants intuitively know which is which. Notice too, that there is only an implied reference to Jim's car. B is in no doubt about whose transmission they are talking about.

The opening remark is in the form of a statement but you are likely to have 'heard' it, quite correctly, as a question. Interestingly, B seems to have heard an implied criticism, 'well, I am flabby', or at any rate chooses to think aloud at this point. Notice too, the word 'hook', an idiom not to be taken literally. Indeed the literal meaning of the word is hardly likely to enter the speakers' minds.

A technical term for describing the process whereby speakers automatically reject unlikely meanings in favour of likely meanings is 'disambiguation'. We do it all the time. Just listen for it, next time you are people watching. With their literality of meaning and logical processes, computers cannot (yet!) cope with the highly accurate guesswork and disambiguation necessary for the most ordinary of conversations.

Phonology, discourse and pragmatics

We considered Context separately because of its all pervasive influence on meaning making in conversations. Phonology, Discourse and Pragmatics are interacting factors that influence conversations, and for that reason are dealt with here together.

Phonology

If you are recording real-life or television talk, then a major source of data will be the speech sounds themselves. Unless you are specifically doing a project on or a study of pronunciation features (not especially difficult if you have a good ear, a copy of IPA and don't try to do too much) you are less likely to be concerned with phonetic features than with prosody. Remember that Phonology is the study of the phonetic and the prosodic features that make up the sound/meaning system of one particular language. Phonetics is concerned with the ways in which humans articulate and hear the individual phonemes of the language (the smallest sound segments of meaning); prosody is concerned with larger sound units such as intonation patterns in which whole words, phrases and sentences are uttered. It is also concerned with pauses, stress, pace and volume, since these are all important communicators of meaning in that they modify or give a particular emphasis to the literal meanings of words.

Most of the work you do on speech and conversations will, however, be dependent on transcripts where you may not have the original tape recorded source. The trouble with transcripts are that they are a pale reflection of the real conversation they represent. They are rather like a black and white photograph of an Impressionist painting, of a Monet for example, which means that you have to exercise some imagination and not forget the phonological dimension. There's a big difference however, between unjustified speculation and showing a reasonable, educated awareness of likely phonological factors. Hence, the term 'echo phonology' which refers to our ability to imagine from experience, some likely prosodic features. The essential thing is not to read a transcript too quickly. Try to get a feel for the real time the conversation would have taken and the likely tones of voice. Often, the transcriber will give some indications of time taken (e.g. the length of a particularly long pause) and of tonal qualities (e.g. spoken with annoyance). Normally punctuation such as capitals and full stops is not used by professional transcribers, but some transcribers use question marks, dashes, rows of dots, and underlining (e.g. to show stress on a particular part of a word). The important thing is to provide the reader with a key.

ACTIVITY 103

Listening with the inner ear

With a partner, study carefully the two short conversations given earlier and practice how they might have sounded. Think of them as dialogue in a radio script.

As a follow up, though it will need a little forethought, record a snatch of conversation from a TV chat show (the easy option) or from real life (slightly less easy, but much better data) and transcribe it. Don't do any more than the samples you have just been considering. Then ask a partner to guess from the transcript how the conversation might have sounded. Finally, play the recording and see if there are any surprises.

Discourse

Formal kinds of conversations have very recognisable, explicit rules and procedures. Their effectiveness depends upon the strict observance of a code. Obvious examples are law court proceedings, religious ceremonies, air traffic control, very structured job interviews, shipping forecasts, public opinion surveys by spoken questionnaire. Semi-formal conversations are also governed by implicit codes. There is a tendency however, probably in all of us, to think of casual, informal conversations as freewheeling and absolutely spontaneous. Undoubtedly, there is a degree of freedom and unpredictability; things can turn unexpectedly nasty, or suddenly become interesting and delightful. You can decide what you want to say and get on with it, though you can also come away feeling that a conversation didn't quite go the way you wanted, wondering why. Managing people by managing talk is quite a profitable consultancy career nowadays. Some of it is intelligent, realistic and sincere; some of it is hard-nosed charlatanism in which conversation is treated as a game to be played and, above all, won.

Counsellors and psychotherapists on the other hand know only too well how a conversation can go wrong. Only in literature and soap operas does conversation go tidily according to plan.

The word 'discourse' can be used in two ways, but either way it is best treated as a verb, something that people do, rather than as a noun, an abstract 'thingy'.

One meaning of the word is that of a topic or topics being passed between two people or around a group. The idea of passing a ball round, sometimes consecutively, sometimes erratically, is not an inappropriate image. Imagine a party at which different kinds of discoursing are going on: the couple in the corner are talking of love; the group in the hall are arguing politics; two bores by the fireplace are 'going on about' fly fishing; another group is discussing Saturday's match, while somebody on the phone is dealing with a neighbour's complaint about the music being too loud. An A level Language and Literature student, grabbing the opportunity to do a bit of research, would notice vocabulary differences between these discourses and different ways of making a point and participating. To join in you need to be tuned in, or be prepared to pick up the style and the conventions. If it bores you or turns you off, you walk away. Switching from one kind of discourse to another involves making language and style adjustments.

The more closely you examine the differences, the more you become aware of another meaning of the word 'discourse' as mental and social traditions that have accumulated around the way we talk about particular topics and different fields of knowledge. It is a distinctive feature of the professions, for example, law, medicine, education, and of sports and recreations, football, motor racing, angling and pigeon fancying. Academic disciplines (History, Geography, Psychology, Economics, Physics) impart their style of discourse to A level students; you have to learn the 'lingo', i.e. use the right kind of discourse if you want to convince examiners that you have at least half an idea of what you are talking about.

The following examples show different kinds of discourse in action. You will be able to tell a great deal from quite short segments of talk.

(a) Two laboratory scientists

Sc 1: normally you get a slope error if the measured slope has fluctuated from the compensate level that has been put in the machine ... and just looking at it it looks as though the standards are the wrong way round ... yes they are ... the low is in the high position and vice versa.
Sc 2: so I'll have to recalibrate those then?
Sc 1: yes I'm afraid so ... you will have to ...
Sc 2: will it not take the previous calibration?
Sc 1: well ... it will take the last calibration and keep that in memory and use it ...

(b) Two administrators

M: actually there are a couple of things that I think we need to discuss ... first the quality on budgetary control information reports coming out of BRIBUD
W: right ... you mean the lower level reports from GLM and GT 1
M: yes that's right ... I think the source of the problem is our feeder system where potentially we're in a GIGO situation

w: we are going to have to watch that especially when we have live contracting information coming down through centre link from PAS

(c) Two surgeons attended by nurse in an operating theatre

The excerpts below have been selected from a continuous conversation to show the surgeons mixing medical discourse with everyday chat.

s 1: thank you a big one or even a holey one would do fine . . . a big one or a holey one . . . don't matter which

s 1: it's a small lump under the skin called a lymphoma it's a rather unusual place to get it but that's what it is

s 1: do you always operate like this
s 2: I think a man who's had his football team so heavily and badly defeated shouldn't have a chance to talk like this
s 1: I don't see why you should bring that up again I mean the real tragedy is getting beaten by Sunderland

s 3: four five now . . . one two three four five
s 4: do you want me to save all these bits?
s 2: no I don't think so thank you
s 1: take them home for your tea George
s 4: I'm a vegetarian
s 1: vegetarian!
s 2: after this operation so am I
s 1: it's alright he's always like this on a Friday

(d) Some students are discussing a famous painting with their teacher

The painting is *The Scream* by Edvard Munch.

TEACHER: what do you like about it?
PUPIL 1: there's . . . I don't like heights and that to me looks like a bridge and I don't like going across bridges . . . and that's just how I feel when I go across a bridge . . . it's really like the effect I really like it . . . I'd put it on my wall
P 2: you'd put it on your wall.
P 1: yes (laughs)
P 5: trying to take her back . . .
P 3: everything in this picture though . . . is just . . . like means something to me about death
P 4: yeah I saw it in the lines too . . . it's like no straight lines
P 1: it's called The Scream and you can really feel him screaming I can
P 3: yeah
P 1: it's really . . . the whole picture's like really . . . jagged and screamish
P 3: yeah It's a really rough picture
P 4: do you think it's a he?
P 3: I think it's a she (laughs and muttering)
TEACHER: does it make a difference whether it's a he or a she?
ALL: yeah (or nodding)
P 1: I bet it does
TEACHER: why?

ACTIVITY 104

1 Look at the four conversations on pages 152–153 and identify similarities of discourse and differences.

2 You have been given a little contextual information. What bearing does context have on each of these discourses?

3 Remind yourself of what we said about discourse (page 147) and explore the aspects of discourse in each of the conversations. You could, for example, compare task-oriented talk with more reflective talk.

4 Look at the prosodic aspects of phonology (see page 148), and identify some examples in the conversations, e.g. you might look at non-fluency (though the level of fluency in these examples is very high) or you might suggest likely falling or rising intonations.

5 Finally, show, by reference to some examples, how context and the type of discourse accounts for particular words used and the use of specific grammatical features, e.g. questions.

COMMENTARY

1 There are no hard and fast methods of classifying different kinds of discourse, but there are some sensible distinctions to be made. The important thing is to recognise essential characteristics. You could describe the examples here as:

(a) Experimental science – the talk is oriented toward a specific task of scientific measurement.

(b) Management and administration – don't scoff at the obvious jargon. The participants probably don't even know they are doing it; to them it's a job. Describe the features of the discourse objectively, e.g. it uses abbreviations and abstract noun phrases.

(c) Medical discourse in general but might be more accurately defined as 'operating theatre talk'. (Note, however, that modern hospital practice seems to have changed its discourse preferring nowadays, for example, the word 'procedure' to 'operation'. What is the significance of this word change do you think?) What is particularly interesting in these samples is the switching from one discourse into another. Note that it is a combination of task oriented talk and a kind of phatic communion. Humour has a generally subversive effect on discourse formality. There is no explicit humour in (a), nor in (b) on the face of it. If, however, you know that GIGO is an abbreviation of 'Garbage in, garbage out', then you are likely to detect a note of slightly sardonic humour, befitting the situation.

(d) This may be baldly described as the discourse of art, directed toward the appreciation of a well-known painting. It is clearly not as directly task oriented as (a) experimental science, (b) an administrative review, or (c) hospital theatre procedure. There is however more than meets the eye (or the ear) in (d) and to find it we need to consider context more closely.

2 The immediate, situational contexts of (a), (b) and (c) are self-evidently occupational with some passing of the time of day in (c), to relieve tension or tedium perhaps. Conversation (d) however, has a context within a context. Yes, they are talking about art but they are doing so within a strong educational context, driven, if that is the right word, by a teacher who knows where she wants the conversation to go. She is by no means a tyrant and is in fact creating opportunities for self-

expression. But notice that in this segment of a whole lesson she asks three questions which have a direct effect on the conversation. She is clearly more in charge of the discourse than the pupils, in the sense that they are discoursing, not just in relation to the painting but also in relation to their teacher's agenda. First and foremost, this is an example of classroom or educational discourse; the topic itself, unlike the topics in (a), (b) and (c) takes second place. The context makes all the difference.

3 We have already noted a significant difference in the status of the topic in these conversations. You may also have noticed that there are elements of specialist vocabulary in (a), (b) and (c) signifying expertise and shared knowledge, whereas in (d) the vocabulary contains no specialist vocabulary, notwithstanding the delightful invention, 'screamish' [compare it with 'holey' in (c)]. The lexical consistency of (a) and (b) make it easy to recognise the registers of experimental science and modern management. The talk in (c) however switches from a medical, operational register (the pun is intended!) to the register of friendly banter. The register in (d) is informal but when you have said that, you haven't really said anything very perceptive. The students here are in fact relaxed enough to express their feelings and risk thinking aloud. In conversations of this kind laughter is never far away, partly to relieve the tension and seriousness of this kind of talk. The laughter, like the jokes in (c), comes essentially from good humour.

Features of discourse also noticeable in these transcripts are the different degrees of authority and knowledge. In (a) and (b) one speaker takes the initiative in each case while the other co-operates, demonstrating shared knowledge. Both sets of speakers have learned a specific terminology. Transcript (c) needs caution because it is fragmentary, but there is no doubt that the surgeons share a good deal of specialist knowledge, though possibly at different levels of expertise. It is possible that S 4 is junior to S 1 and S 2 since he defers to S 1 by asking a question and gets a reply from both, one a serious reply, the other a jokey reply.

You may feel that there are long traditions of scientific and medical practice behind the discourse in (a) and (c) whereas (b) represents a more recent kind of knowledge and authority. In conversations of the kind represented by transcript (d) authority usually resides with the teacher who usually is the source of knowledge. In (d) however, the kind of knowledge here is owned by the students who are relating their own responses. The authority of the teacher, in this instance, lies in her ability to direct the conversation of a group of people. She may be very knowledgeable about art, she may not, but her main task is to get other people to talk, and is quite different from the tasks in the other three transcripts. There is an important point here about discourse that needs explaining. Ability to participate in a particular kind of discourse can be seen as a staged process along the following lines:

(i) **Initiation** – by, for example, education and training, life experience, employment. All of these socialise people into approved or appropriate ways of behaviour – language use being a prime kind of behaviour.

   (ii) **Practice** – including error, correction, guessing and reflection on experience.

   (iii) **Competence** – reaching a degree of proficiency that shows you know what you are about.

   (iv) **Expertise** – the acquisition of recognised authority in a field of knowledge.

Everybody goes through a process much like this in learning to handle different genres of spoken discourse. Some genres you are not likely to practise sufficiently in order to acquire them, nor may you wish to. In general we leave lawyers to speak on our behalf, GPs to speak to consultants, experts to discuss why our computer keeps on crashing and experts again to talk about how to deal with rising damp in a corner of the house. Education, recreation and employment are the genres of discourse essential to everybody. Genre here means a variety of discourse and the form it takes. In the chapters on written language you will be looking at genre in more detail. The kind of talk in which most people, throughout their lives, will have the greatest successes and the most abysmal failures is the everyday kind: family talk, talk between friends and lovers and talk between adults and children or between different generations.

Finally, there is the question of functions. We said earlier that it is more helpful to think of discourse as something that people do; what then, does language do in discourses? On the evidence of these transcripts we can say that it is used to solve problems (a), to accompany and facilitate specific activities (a) and (b), to share information or a viewpoint (all four). You can also detect elements of instruction in (c), entertainment, (c) again, and exploration in (d), a particularly good example of what Halliday means by 'heuristic' (see page 34). The overall, primary functions of the first three transcripts are not difficult to see but do remember that in a conversation of any length, secondary functions will shift from time to time and you may well have had the experience of taking part in a discussion that has completely lost track of its original purpose. A word that might be used to describe the fourth conversation is 'discursive' (note the family resemblance to 'discourse'). The trouble with this word is that it has two entirely opposite meanings in any dictionary. On the one hand it means, 'proceeding unmethodically from one topic to another'. On the other hand it means 'proceeding by logical steps'. In (d), the students appear free to be discursive in the unrestricted sense (so long as they refer to the picture) while the teacher's questions have a methodical purpose in asking statements to be followed up by reasons. Note though that the questioning role is also taken up by P 4, but more about that when we move on to pragmatics.

4 So far, we have considered similarities and differences in the four transcripts looking in particular at the influence of context on the talk; and at aspects of discourse such as topic, register, knowledge and authority, and language functions within the conversations and overall. The evidence for these observations lies in the lexico-grammatical content, that is to say, in the words used and in the ways they are used. Lexis and grammar work together.

5 We have already noted the use of technical terms (lexis) and the use of

questions (grammar). Given that none of the transcripts are supplied with phonetic and prosodic symbols (we can only make educated guesses at the phonology), the best data we have to go on is the lexico-grammatical. One issue worth exploring is that of grammatical fluency.

Speech cannot be as grammatically fluent as educated writing for a number of reasons that should be well known to you. This does not mean that speech is an inferior form of language to writing, just that the two are very different. Speech is characterised by degrees of non-fluency ranging from acceptable to incomprehensible, sense to nonsense, eloquence to jibberish. Transcripts (a) and (b) record purposeful and very fluent talk. There is a moment of simultaneous speech in (a) at a point where one scientist interrupts the other. Transcript (b) shows an even greater degree of fluency and cohesion (i.e. linking the bits). The speaker M even begins by enumerating the topics to be discussed.

Transcript (c) is fragmentary, to show how the conversation shifts between registers, but fluency and cohesion are nevertheless clear to see. Lexical knowledge and grammatical cohesion are clearly in evidence in the first three transcripts. Grammatical fluency is not so obvious in the last transcript but it would be quite wrong to regard this conversation as in any way inferior to the others. The participants, excluding the teacher, are not as practised in the discourse as are the others, nor are they task oriented. The teacher may well have a clear purpose and know exactly what her task is, but the students are thinking aloud, searching for the right words and phrases not because they don't know them but because they are trying to put into words immediate responses, not go through familiar occupational routines. It is doubtful that any of the other speakers would be any more fluent if placed in a similar situation. Notice how the non-fluency features indicate quick thinking and changes of strategy:

There's . . . I don't like heights
. . . is just . . . like means something
It's really . . . the whole picture's like really . . .

Notice too, how P 5 seems to be thinking aloud a completely different topic:

. . . trying to take her back . . .

The linguistic drive here is above all to make sense of the picture and their own thoughts and to communicate them to an apparently co-operative and friendly peer group. Teacher intervention on the issue of gender makes them all, predictably, focus their grammar on the affirmative: 'yeah'.

Pragmatics

If semantics is the general study of meaning, pragmatics is concerned with how speakers communicate their intentions and assumptions implicitly as well as explicitly. We introduced pragmatics in the first chapter by referring to the little girl who answered telephone messages literally (e.g. 'Is your father in?') because she hadn't yet learned the code or the context. The influence of context is an important feature of pragmatics since, in its unspoken way, it has as much effect on the way in which meanings are understood as the words themselves. We can detect such things as sarcasm, sincerity, uncertainty, implied threat, authority or duplicity even when the words in their literal meaning do not include any of these things. Sometimes the word 'sub text' is used to describe what a meeting is 'really about' or what somebody 'really means' as distinct from what is being said explicitly. A comment from a teacher that an essay is 'interesting' can sometimes mean, 'It is completely nondescript and I am at a loss where to begin'. At an audition, the words, 'We'll let you know', usually mean, 'We're not impressed'. Another familiar pragmatic feature is the use of euphemisms such as, 'I am just going to the bathroom' meaning, 'I am going to the lavatory'. The modern preoccupation in official minds with politically correct words and phrases is another aspect of pragmatics, as are strategies for communicating politeness, offence, co-operativeness, for being persuasive and for gaining power in a conversation.

Pragmatics is also concerned with the practical aspects of how speakers behave toward each other and how a conversation is sustained. Turn-taking and interruptions, agenda setting, topic changes, co-operativeness, the roles adopted and assigned in any given conversation are all to a large extent guided by codes and conventions.

ACTIVITY 105

Look for examples of pragmatics in the transcripts that follow. Don't just settle for feature spotting and leave it at that; show how context and the nature of the discourse make people behave the way they do. Don't just observe that the teacher asks three questions and the whole group of students, only one. It is one of the roles of teachers to ask questions, thereby setting the agenda for a discussion and even changing that agenda by asking another question later. Note though, that P4 initiates a new development by being the first to raise the question of gender. One criterion of a good leadership in discussions is the willingness of participants to adopt the questioning role rather than just respond all the time.

It is important when observing a pragmatic feature of a conversation to trace through its effects and consequences. It is important that you write your own detailed observations and only then look at our comments at the end of this chapter on page 174.

Writing about talk

Exploration of the four transcripts on pages 152–153 reveals how easy conversations are to take part in, yet how complex they are beneath the skin. Linguistically, it is important not to reduce this complexity to one or two of your favourite features, but to try to give a more rounded picture of what is going on, whether working from a tape recording as part of a project or reading a transcript in a textbook or an examination paper. It helps to keep in mind a menu or a catalogue of possible lines of enquiry, not to be followed slavishly but to jog the memory about other possible avenues. This chapter ends with some more transcripts for you to investigate, but first by way of summarising the chapter so far, here is a listing of features and aspects of everyday conversation that are central to, or not very far away from, the nature and functions of everyday talk.

1 Lexico-grammatical content

The core text of any kind of talk consists of the words used and their underlying grammar. This is an important component of meaning and is the easiest to transcribe. It is not by any means the only component. The choice of words and their grammatical function may take various forms, e.g. standard/non-standard, dialectal, formal/informal according to other significant factors influencing a conversation. But we need to consider phonology before looking at these factors.

2 Phonology

Whereas a transcript records the substance of a conversation – the lexico-grammatical content, the physical reality of a conversation is its phonological content, which is not quite so easy to transcribe yet it is nevertheless as much the text of the conversation as the lexico-grammar. Some linguist would say it is the real text. Phonology consists of phonetic components: pronunciation (and accent), pauses, fillers (ums and ers), simultaneous speech and syllable stress. It also consists of more extended features such as rhythm, tempo (or pace), intonation (rising and falling pitch) and volume (from whispering to shouting). The text of a conversation then, is the blending of words, grammar and phonology. Devising a way to represent phonological features in a transcript *when you feel it is necessary to do so* in order to explain a point, makes for a good project. Simple underlining will do very well for syllable stress, opening and closing hairpins for volume, and an upward or downward single line adequately represents rising and falling tones.

3 Context

If lexis, grammar and phonology are the core, the central part of a conversation, context may be viewed, as an outer ring, exerting considerable influence on a conversation, even to the extent of holding it together. Context may consist of relatively distant and historical influences (e.g. social class, education, nationality, cultural identity) and it may be relatively close (e.g. situation and immediate environment). Professional linguistic researchers, writers of examination papers and students doing projects are duty bound to give brief but sufficient details of the situational kind, since these are very helpful. Great care needs to be taken however with more distant influences, however influential you feel they may be. Social class is the contextual factor with the greatest pitfalls. It may seem unnecessary, silly even, to point out that the surgeon in transcript (c) who says 'don't matter' is not necessarily of working-class origin, yet it is the kind of wild assumption examination candidates do make under pressure.

Some questions you could ask yourself about context are set out below. You could run a quick check on their relevance by applying them to any of the previous four transcripts.

(i)   Where are the participants, and why are they there? What are they doing? If your answer is, 'Just talking', as in transcript (d), you need to look a bit further into, for example, the sort of context created by classrooms and the role of talk in learning.

(ii) Is the talk task oriented or at least an integral part of a specific activity?

(iii) Are there social-psychological factors to take into account, e.g. age? gender? legal implications (e.g. under arrest)?

(iv) Is the conversation you are studying, so far as you know, complete or an excerpt? More than likely it will be an excerpt so bear this in mind when you are commenting on how it begins and ends.

(v) Is there a marked difference in status between the participants that creates the major contextual influence on the talk that takes place?

Remember, the answers to these questions will lie in the lexico-grammatical and phonological features of the text, though sometimes this works the other way round and it is a word or a type of sentence that leads you to think about context.

4 Discourse

If contextual factors may be regarded as chiefly external influences on the ways in which people talk to each other, discourse may be thought of as the choice of topic in the appropriate language for the topic. Some discourses are intimately bound up with particular contexts, e.g. legal discourse in a courtroom setting, or the discourse of literary criticism in a seminar on the poetry of William Blake or preaching a sermon in church. Use any one of these discourses in the wrong context and the effect would seem odd possibly amusing.

Questions you need to ask are:

(i) What is the topic (or topics)? Does a topic change occur at all?

(ii) What level of formality/semi-formality/informality is evident?

(iii) What words, phrases and grammatical constructions contribute to the register?

(iv) What shared knowledge and assumptions underlie the discourse?

(v) Are there any particular rules or conventions of language use discernible? E.g. method of explanation, instruction or argument? Mode of address?

(vi) Is there any mixing of everyday terms and specialist ones?

(vii) What is the prime function of the discourse? Collaborative problem solving? Diagnosis by questioning? Discursive exploration of personal response?

(viii) What counts as authority in the discourse? What backs it up?

5 Pragmatics

Some writers use the terms text, context and subtext to describe the interacting features of a conversation. Text consists of lexis, grammar and phonology as we have described them here, and context also means exactly the same as here. Sub text refers to the parts of a conversation that are going on in an unseen, implicit way and consists of both discourse conventions and pragmatics. Pragmatics is especially concerned with implied meanings and how speakers understand what is going on. It is also concerned with the strategies used by speakers to achieve intended ends and with the ways in which unintended effects are created. Some linguists think of texts as the products of language (the lexico-grammatical and phonological bits) and the combination of discourse and pragmatics as the active processes by which texts are constructed. Remember that in conversation, it takes at least two to make a text. Some questions you need to ask are:

(i) Who decides the topic and agenda, or initiates topic or agenda change?

(ii) What roles are assigned and adopted by participants? Who is active/passive/reactive?

(iii) How are questions/commands/statements/exclamations distributed?

(iv) Who speaks most/least?

(v) If there are more than two speakers, who addresses whom?

(vi) What kinds of turn-taking take place? Adjacent questions and answers? Follow-ons (e.g. amplifying the previous point)?

(vii) Are there any interruptions? simultaneous utterances? pauses?

(viii) What implied meanings do you detect?

(ix) Are there any examples of phatic communion (see reference to Malinowski in Chapter 1)?

(x) Do you detect elements of positivity? Negativity? Anywhere?

(xi) What degree of co-operativeness or conflict do you detect? You could apply H. P. Grice's maxims of co-operativeness here. These are general principles that underlie a conversation that is going well but do not preclude other factors. They are: quantity (don't say too much or too little); quality (be truthful; and reliable); relevance (this should need no gloss); manner (don't be obscure or ambiguous).

(xii) If humour is introduced, what kind? and what effect does it have?

(xiii) If you have data for the start and finish of a conversation, what strategies or conventions are used to signal the start and finish?

Sorting out and communicating linguistic observations and your own thoughts about a transcribed conversation is not an easy kind of writing. Much of it will consist of fairly short, nitty-gritty sentences making a series of points. These will all earn you some marks, and if there are enough of them, they will rescue you from failure, but there are many more marks to be gained by showing an overall understanding of spoken language in action. It is, however, unlikely that you will show that understanding by working your way piecemeal through the questions above. This is true for any kind of stylistics writing: you can spend too much time looking at your shopping list at the expense of what is actually on display.

You need a starting point and you need some kind of concluding remarks. A good starting point will be the contextual information provided at the beginning of a transcript. That will show your awareness of the importance of context and provided you don't just repeat the information but develop it, you should be on your way to asking yourself questions. By the time you have explored the text, some sort of conclusion will already be forming in your mind.

Below is a brief transcript, much briefer than anything you will encounter in an examination. We have deliberately chosen a very short one in order to demonstrate that virtually all the questions above can be asked about it. In our discussion, we haven't followed the order of the questions as given above, and indeed, if we did it again we should most likely write our observations in quite a different order. We have, however, started from the prompts given in the introduction to the transcript, but we haven't slavishly followed the sequence of lexis, grammar, phonology, context, discourse and pragmatics.

Transcript

Interview with the Prime Minister on the BBC Radio 4 programme, *Today* (1998). He is being questioned about measures to reduce hospital waiting lists.

Interviewer (JH): yes but will it cut waiting lists?
Prime Minister (TB): what I would say to you is this ...

COMMENTARY

This is the sort of adjacency pair (question/answer) you would expect in an interview, since it is an interviewer's job to ask questions. The context, however, is much larger than two participants in a studio, on the phone or doing an outside broadcast, we don't know which. Because it is a broadcast interview it means that there are millions of non-participating listeners who are nevertheless a very real audience for both the interviewer and the PM. In media talk, it is always necessary to take account of the invisible audience. It is also quite likely, though again, we do not know from the data, that there was a 'script' in mind and probably a tight time limit. The script may have been no more than an agreed sequence of questions. Both speakers are practised public speakers and we would expect fluency.

The interviewer's opening 'yes but' is a familiar gambit. It indicates that the interviewer is not merely asking 'straight' questions but adopting an adversarial stance, voicing objections that listeners might wish to make. He has adopted the role of sceptical spokesperson. The lexico-grammatical form is a straight question, the tone of voice in which it is asked may well be controversial. Some modern interviewers have acquired a reputation for controversial interviewing, which can make entertaining listening.

Interestingly, the transcript doesn't gives us the PM's actual reply, only the preface to it. From a pragmatic point of view, his words are a remarkable mixture of defensive hedging and a sense of personal authority. The hedging (evasiveness) is expressed in the modal form of the verb, i.e. 'would say'. It is one of those 'would if I could' 'would that it were so' remarks, leaving the listener unsure as to whether he has actually answered the question or not. It is an answer that confirms a general assumption that all political discourse at the level of on the spot public interviews is bound to be evasive anyway. But it is a form of evasiveness that only a person in authority can practise. The interviewer couldn't begin a question in this way, 'What I would ask you is this . . .' and the ordinary citizen would be thought very presumptuous or awkward if he used it to a magistrate, a cross examiner, a doctor or to anybody who expected a straight answer. In this transcript, the agenda agreed between interviewer and the PM is an agenda on which the PM is, with these words, addressing not so much the interviewer as the nation. But he is addressing the nation through a medium over which he has limited control, hence the caution. All interviews are framed by the medium, and the sound bites that are broadcast can rebound disastrously. The most frequent defence of politicians is that their words have been taken out of context.

The shift into the first person singular is worth noting. Certainly it presents a personal touch, quite different from, say, 'What the government would like to do is . . .' Is it friendly/reassuring? trustworthy? smarmy?

It is interesting to apply Grice's maxims to this exchange. Certainly it satisfies the maxim of quantity, but then it has already been pointed out that both are practised speakers. It could be argued however, that political talk of this kind would have difficulty satisfying the other three maxims. A degree of relevance is likely to be evident, but there is a general scepticism today about the truthfulness and the non-ambiguity of political statements in the media.

There are two remaining issues. One is about the kind of discourse represented by this transcript; the other is about its wider context.

Politics and argument are never far apart, whether in the form of a news interview, in public debate, Prime Minister's question time in the house or in the text of election pamphlets and publicity hoardings. There is inevitably something of warfare and even gamesplay about political discourse in which the authority and knowledge cannot be objectively checked in the manner of academic history discourse, or physics or natural history. Political authority is an authority of office and the knowledge that goes with that office is often confidential, even secret. In recent times the term 'spin doctor' has come into being – a reference to someone who spins the news or a situation or a problem in the way that government want the public to view it. The remark, 'what I would say to you is this . . .' sounds like a politician doing his own on-the-spot spinning, pressed by a determined interviewer. Regularly listening to this kind of interviewing creates a model (not necessarily bad or good) of what political discourse is like – at its worst, a kind of blood sport. Only the tiniest minority of listeners will ever meet the interviewer or the Prime Minister, yet their voices and their style of talking are known almost as well as those of members of the family. We carry in our minds, disembodied yet very influential voices, which brings me to my second point, the wider context.

Media talk has considerable influence on the discussions people have at home, in the pub or passing the time of day at a bus stop. It is a major source of news, though news mixed with opinion – 'so-and-so said on telly the other day . . . right load of rubbish!' Any discourse, whatever kind, seems to be converted into something else by media presentation. The prevailing discourse in news programmes is that of a light, gossipy magazine in which an interview with a politician may well be followed by a story about a dog that sings opera. The interviewer in this transcript, John Humphrys, has himself criticised the BBC for 'dumbing down' news and information into palatable sound bites.

The following activities will give you an opportunity to explore different kinds of talk. In each activity a specific question will be asked, and the first thing you should do is discuss it before you write an answer to it. Do not read the commentary until you have written your own comments. The commentaries consist of excerpts from linguistic researchers' own observations on the transcripts.

When you have read the commentary, see what else there is in the transcript to comment on.

ACTIVITY 106

Taking a break

The conversation below took place between two office workers. What pragmatic features do you observe in the opening question and the reply?

A: are you gonna be here for ten minutes?
B: go ahead and take your break ( ) take longer if you want to
A: I'll just be outside on the porch ( ) call me if you need me
A: OK don't worry.

COMMENTARY

Since there are no overt linguistic cues, it seems reasonable to assume that both A and B rely on a shared understanding ... and their expectations of what normally goes on in offices. That is, it is taken for granted that both participants are office workers, that it is customary to take brief breaks in the course of a working day, and that staff members should co-operate in seeing that someone is present at all times

Conversationalists thus rely on indirect inferences which build on background assumptions about context, interactive goals and interpersonal relations to derive frames in terms of which they can interpret what is going on.

J J Gumperz in *Discourse Strategies* (CUP, 1982)

By 'frames', Gumperz means an intuitive understanding of limits. It is partly to do with the meaning of 'picture frame' but closer to the familiar saying, 'Well, there are limits!', implying an acceptance of how a person should behave in a given situation.

ACTIVITY 107

Don't talk when I am interrupting

Look at the two transcripts below, in which a doctor is examining a patient. Comment on the interruptions and their likely effect.

When you have written your comments, and read those of the researcher, look at the transcript again for other conversational features.

(i)

DOCTOR: somehow they got the impression that you were going to have a conization biopsy of your cervix ( ) that what you told your mother?
PATIENT: no ( ) when I talked to her yesterday she got upset but when I told her that you were just going to look at it today colpo
DOCTOR: colposcope
PATIENT: and uhm if a biopsy was necessary it was just a small pinch from the tissue of the cervix she got upset but I told her it would be okay

(ii)
PATIENT: what's to prevent me going through all this again?
DOCTOR: all we know is that
PATIENT: yeah didn't know
DOCTOR: if we cure it by freezing the cervix ( ) uh ( ) it doesn't seem to come back very often

(iii) A different doctor, a different patient.
PATIENT: it usually be (she reaches down to touch her calf with her left hand) in here ( ) You know it just be a lil
DOCTOR: can you pull up your cuff there for me? did you have the pain right now?
PATIENT: um ( ) um ( ) no it happens
DOCTOR: it's not happening now?
PATIENT: s-s some only one time when I was here
DOCTOR: can you take your shoe off for me please?
PATIENT: but I
DOCTOR: what are you doing when you notice the pain?

COMMENTARY   The first two transcripts were made by Sue Fisher and reported in a paper entitled, 'Institutional Authority and the Structure of Discourse' (*Discourse Processes, Vol 7*, 1984). She remarks:

Talk in the surgery is asymmetrical ... control resides with the institutional authority – the doctor. ['Asymmetrical' simply means that one person exercises authority or power over the other.] While patients identify medical problems, make medical appointments, stand to be helped by them and pay for them, it is doctors who ask most of the questions, establish most of the topics and most often control the floor.

By controlling the floor she means being in charge of the conversation.

Doctors ... correct patients' pronunciation of medical terms, correct their understanding of their medical problems and have the last word in the definition of the problem.

Her research shows that doctors are inclined to talk over patients' interruptions to maintain control of the floor, and that patients tend to give up the floor immediately they are interrupted by doctors.

The third transcript was made by another researcher, Candace West (see 'When the "doctor is a lady": power, status and gender in physician–patient encounters' in *Symbolic Interaction, No 7*, 1984).

She comments:

... each of the physician's intrusions into the patient's turn at talk is patently reasonable and warranted by the external constraints of medical examination ... To ask where a patient is feeling pain ... is justified by, even required for, precise diagnosis ... However, when these enquiries cut off what the patient is in the process of saying, particularly when what she is saying is presumably necessary ... then the physician is not only violating the patient's rights to speak, but he is also systematically cutting off potentially valuable information on which he must himself rely to achieve a diagnosis.

Notice, incidentally, how the title of West's paper contains three important aspects of conversation.

ACTIVITY 108

Playing at doctors

The following transcripts were made by Geoffrey Beattie, and are discussed in his book, *All Talk* (Weidenfield and Nicolson, 1988). Two children, Zoe (aged seven) and Ben (aged five) are playing at doctors. Joseph is a toy rabbit; 'Me' is the author.

The capitalisation indicates a loud voice. Read the transcripts and write down what the two children have learned about doctors and the way they talk. What kind of role has their experience of doctors modelled for them?

ZOE: are you all right Joseph? now I'd better examine you so LIE DOWN! Open your mouth ( ) I'm going to look down your throat ( ) let me put the torch on and I'll look down your throat ( ) you're ALL RIGHT now have some Calpol now go home ( ) you're a very naughty patient

BEN: (wearing a white coat) I'M A DOCTOR Is your throat okay? What? What? speak up I have to put a light up your ear to see if there's any wax up it ( ) there is some wax I'll have to take it out with a big digger

ME: what?

BEN: a big digger

ME: you want to take the wax out of his ear with a big digger

BEN: no I mean a spade

ME: a spade?

BEN: yes a SPADE

COMMENTARY

'Doctors ... speak with very deep voices ... and more dignified pronunciation than fathers ... and use less polite directives ... Doctors are dignified, no-nonsense individuals who, it seems, have to be quite direct in their speech to get things done ... Doctors talk in loud voices and leave few gaps for any potential answers; they also interrupt you when you are trying to talk. And they speak with great authority – even when they are apparently talking nonsense ('Yes, a spade'). That's at least what some children aged seven and under think.

I just wonder where they got these ideas from.'

ACTIVITY 109

Talking sense

Read first of all a brief description of cohesion from Halliday and Hasan's, *Cohesion in English* (Longman, 1976). Cohesion in linguistics refers to the means whereby the next thing a speaker is going to say (e.g. the next sentence) is linked to what has just been said. It's a thread of continuity. Halliday and Hasan suggest four ways in which cohesion is achieved. Below is an explanation with examples:

Reference e.g. We met Sarah last week and had tea with her. She said that ...' ('her' and 'She' refer back to 'Sarah'

Ellipsis e.g. He's got energy. He's got a lot more than me' ('energy' has been deleted from the second part because it's understood. The understood sentence would be something like, 'He's got a lot more energy than I have'

Conjunction e.g. It was a beautiful tree so I left it alone. (the 'so' makes the link, it tells you a consequence). Common conjunctions are 'and' 'but' 'then' 'if' 'although' 'when' 'because'.

Lexical e.g. I love fishing. I caught a bass last time. ('bass' is understood not as a singer with a deep voice or as a bottled beer; it picks up from 'fishing').

Now look at the following transcript which is the response of a thought-disordered schizophrenic to an interviewer's question, 'A stitch in time saves nine. What does that mean?'. Comment on both the cohesion evident here, and any lack of cohesion.

Oh! That's because all women have a little bit of magic to them – I found that out and it's called it's sort of good magic and nine is sort of magic number like I've got nine colours here you will notice – I've got yellow green blue grey orange blue and navy and I've got black and I've got a sort of clear white – the nine colours to me they are the whole universe and they symbolise every man woman and child in the world

COMMENTARY

The speaker appears to be making an effort at answering the question with the use of the word 'that' in the first two sentences but quickly gets sidetracked. Yet the successive statements are lexically related to one another. The connections are first made through the word 'magic', then 'nine', and still later 'colour'. These relations are achieved, however, only at a superficial level, since most people would regard a shift from nine as a magic number to nine colours as an abrupt change of topic. Thus, although there are some links between adjacent utterances, the overall answer is an incoherent response to the question.

See *Crazy Talk: a Study of the Discourse of Schizophrenic Speakers*, (Plenum Books, New York, 1979)

ACTIVITY 110

Domestic talk

In the sixties, Harold Garfinkel, along with J. J. Gumperz, carried out a number of investigations into what lies behind everyday talk. His students made tape recordings of various conversations for later analysis. Here is an example. Read it, and explain how, once again, background knowledge and implicit meanings underpin the words actually spoken. Each utterance has been numbered to correspond with Garfinkel's commentary on the implied meanings.

1 Husband: Dana succeeded in putting a penny in a parking meter today without being picked up
2 Wife: did you take him to the record store?
3 H: no to the shoe repair shop
4 W: what for?
5 H: I got some new shoe laces for my shoes
6 W: your loafers need new heels badly

COMMENTARY

1 'This afternoon as I was bringing Dana home from the nursery, he succeeded in reaching high enough to put a penny in a parking meter when we parked in a meter zone, whereas before he always had to be picked up.'
2 'Since you put a penny in the meter that means you stopped while he was with you. I know that you stopped at the record store either on the way to get him or on the way back. Was it on the way back, so that he was with you or did you stop there on the way to get him and somewhere else on the way back?'
3 'No, I stopped at the record shop on the way to get him and stopped at the shoe repair shop on the way home when he was with me.'
4 'I know of one reason why you might have stopped at the shoe repair shop. Why did you in fact?'
5 'As you will remember, I broke a shoelace on one of my brown oxfords the other day so I stopped to get some laces.'
6 'Something else you could have gotten that I was thinking of. You could have taken in your black loafers which need heels badly. You'd better get them taken care of pretty soon.'

It is clear from this example that:

(a) many things that the participants understood they were talking about were not specifically mentioned
(b) many things were understood on the basis not only of what was actually said, but what was left unsaid
(c) references were made to . . . a common scheme of interpretation and expression
(d) both participants waited for something more to be said in order to interpret what had previously been talked about, and were willing to wait.

See Harold Garfinkel's *Studies in Ethnomethodology*
(Prentice Hall, 1967)

Note. All 'ethnomethodology' means is 'how speakers behave when they interact'. Garfinkel's 'common scheme' has more or less the same meaning as 'frame' as used by Gumperz.

ACTIVITY 111

Talk therapy

The following transcripts record talk in a hairdressers' salon in Sheffield. Different people are involved in each one. What do you think is the function of such talk, and are there any differences between the two excerpts?

(i)
CLIENT: I thought it was time I had something done to my hair because I've been getting a bit depressed
RUTH: oh
CLIENT: well spring always depresses me all these young people out jogging my brother's just bought me a pair of trainers for my birthday but I can't go out in them – I'm too fat – people would stare at me I'd feel stupid
RUTH: I'm sure they wouldn't you know
CLIENT: there are all sorts doing it these days when I think about it aren't there?
RUTH: of course

(ii)
CLIENT: . . . and my husband just rang up this morning and said we're going away again ( ) another holiday – third this year – we're going to Marbella
ANGIE: Marbella's nice
CLIENT: have you been there then?
ANGIE: no
CLIENT: oh have you just heard about it then?
ANGIE: yes
CLIENT: yes it's a lovely place we've got an apartment there we bought with my brother in law . . .

COMMENTARY

When I listened to the tape, the first thing that surprised me (apart from how universal really was the 'holiday' as a conversational opener) was how willing clients were to discuss personal problems, and how discussion of these problems wasn't so much elicited by the hairdresser as unleashed.

In the first transcript 'the hairdresser provides the kind of support and sympathy identified in a sample of hairdressers in New York. The hairdresser acts very much as a professional friend – providing, on demand, a friendship which the client pays for. But hairdressers aren't just poor substitutes for real friends sought by lonely people.' In the second kind of conversation 'you get support and sympathy from your hairdresser, and in return you get to put them down! It makes you feel better in every way, and you couldn't get this service from a friend, a doctor or a psychoanalyst! And for £7.95 a session – you even get a haircut thrown in.'

See *All Talk* by Geoffrey Beattie (op cit)

ACTIVITY 112

In the 1960s there was a view on both sides of the Atlantic that non-standard English was inadequate for educational achievement. The view is still held by many people today. So called Black English is one example of non-standard English that has come in for much discussion though less actual investigation. One influential American investigator, William Labov, came to the view that despite its unusual syntax (e.g. 'Don't nobody know' and 'If you bad . . .') Black English was capable of expresing logical and complex thoughts. He also pointed out, as every linguist knows, that context makes all the difference to meanings. In this activity you will have an opportunity to look at some of Labov's data and to follow his line of thought. First of all, context, and in particular the situation in which talk takes place.

Compare the two transcripts below and explain the differences in C's language behaviour.

A = white, adult interviewer; c = black, eight year old boy.
A: tell me everything you can about this (12 second silence)
A: what would you say it looks like? (8 seconds of silence)
C: a space ship
A: hmmmm (13 seconds silence)
C: like a je-et (12 seconds of silence)
C: like a plane (20 seconds of silence)

Second interview
A = black adult; c = same child as above; F = the child's friend
C: I ain't had no fight
F: yes you did
A: you said you had one you had a fight with Butchie
F: and he say Garland ( ) an Michael
A: an Barry
C: I di'n you said that Gregory
F: you did
C: you know you said that
F: you said Garland remember that?

COMMENTARY

The same child who engaged in monosyllabic answers after long pauses now is actively competing for the floor with his friend, almost ignoring the adult.

Labov records a number of changes he introduced between these interviews. Here is a summary of what he reports:

– brought along some potatochips to make the interview more like a party
– brought along the boy's best friend
– reduced height imbalance by sitting interviewer on the floor

– introduced taboo words and topics
– introduced a black interviewer.

See Labov, *The Logic of Non-standard English* (1969)

ACTIVITY 113

Language and logic

Read the following transcript, unravelling the logic of Larry's argument. It comes from the same study by Labov as the one in the previous activity. Larry has been asked by the interviewer, 'What happens when you die?' In the commentary that follows we have supplied Labov's standard English version of Larry's non-standard English. Don't look at this until you have worked out your own version.

INTERVIEWER: what happens to you after you die? do you know?
LARRY: yeah I know
I: what?
L: after they put you in the ground your body turns into ( ) ah ( ) bones an' shit
I: what happens to your spirit?
L: your spirit ( ) soon as you die your spirit leaves you
I: and where does the spirit go?
L: well it all depends
I: on what?
L: you know like some people say if you're good an' shit your spirit goin' t'heaven ( ) 'n if you bad your spirit goin' to hell well bullshit your spirit goin' to hell anyway good or bad
I: why?
L: why? I'll tell you why 'cause you see doesn' nobody really knows that it's a God y'know 'cause I mean I have seen black gods pink gods white gods all color gods and don't nobody know it's really a God an' when they be saying if you good you goin' t'heaven tha's bullshit 'cause you ain't goin' to no heaven 'cause it ain't no heaven to go to

COMMENTARY

Larry's argument may be outlined as follows:

(i)   Everyone has a different idea of what God is like.
(ii)   Therefore nobody really knows that God exists.
(iii)   If there is a heaven, it was made by God.
(iv)   If God doesn't exist, he couldn't have made heaven.
(v)   Therefore heaven does not exist.
(vi)   You can't go somewhere that doesn't exist.
(vii)   Therefore you can't go to heaven.
(viii) Therefore you are going to hell.

Summing up Labov's work in this particular area, Andrew Ellis and Geoffrey Beattie in *The Psychology of Language and Communication* (1986) comment:

Larry is an excellent reminder that linguistic difference need not necessarily imply linguistic deficit. A point constantly worth bearing in mind.

ACTIVITY 114

Telephone talk

The last transcript records part of a telephone call between a customer and an operative at Directory Enquiries. Read the transcript and note the conversational strategies that take place, particularly in the handling of information. What differences do you detect between face-to-face conversations and telephone talk? The caller is having difficulty getting a number.

Remember, read the text slowly so that you can imagine the nuances of voice and 'hear' what is going on behind the words.

OPERATOR: it's Woburn Sands 9999
CALLER: 9999 er now um is there's not been any change of coding or anything like that about that number
O: just checking for you I've got a list of changed numbers but I don't think that's one of them ( ) no that's not on the changed numbers list it should be alright
C: well I can't get it I've just tried it
O: have you? ( ) well I should dial 100 and ask the operator to help you
C: yeah ( ) er well I see who will know if there is any change of ( ) ah exchange um and all the rest of it?
O: well you know I've got the changed numbers list for Woburn Sands so it ( ) um
C: and it's definitely not one of them?
O: no it isn't ( ) no
C: ah the thing is this is a bit of a mystery I've been trying this number for two days ( ) um yesterday somebody told me to put 58 in front of it ( ) which got me a very unusual dialling ( ) situation ( ) I haven't been able to get through and I'm you know I have a letter from a large company saying he's there waiting for me to phone and I CAN'T GET THROUGH
O: yes ( ) well 58 should be put in front of some numbers but these um ( ) let me just read this ( ) you've tried it with 58 in front?
C: yes
O: oh I should dial 100 and ask the operator to help you then because um ( ) you know if you dial it with 58 in front it should certainly be alright
C: but I should be able to dial it without the 58 in front?
O: just a moment let me read this list here properly no you should have the 58 in front of it
C: I should have a 58 in front
O: yes yes and I'll just check the code for you while you're on the line perhaps it's the code you see ( ) your code should be 0908
C: yes that's what I've been dialling
O: and then 58 and then the number ( ) that should definitely be alright
C: yes I I've got a feeling there's something going on on the exchange there because it gives a very funny very sort of you know it dials then stops

The call continues and ends with the caller referred to Fault Enquiries.

From unscripted conversations to scripted dialogue

In this chapter you have explored a wide variety of everyday talk, some of it recorded as it happened and later transcribed. All of it occurred in living contexts and then evaporated into the air. That is the nature of talk, though things that people say can live on for a long time in the memory. They can also have a powerful effect on actions and attitudes, as politicians and commercial advertisers well know. Song lyrics can also linger in the mind for many years, a lifetime even, yet most people learn them through repeated listening, not from reading.

When is real life talk ever written down? And why?

Audio typists record what people say in courts of law; Hansard is a record of parliamentary debate; newspaper reporters used to write down as fast as they could what people said.

The advent of audio recording has brought about a revolution since the 1950s. The police now record what goes on in Interview Rooms, Television companies record Parliamentary debates, and hand held tape recorders are to be seen in all walks of life. These are legal and legitimate uses, but of course the technology has also made possible illicit recording via bugging devices eavesdropping on private or supposedly secret conversations.

Modern recording apparatus also provides recordings of live events, e.g. radio broadcasts and even where the talk has been scripted as in a comedy programme, there is still much of the vitality of something as it really happened. Once of course, it is converted to words and symbols on a page, then much more has been lost. However useful transcripts are for studying language, they are very inadequate representations of life. They are not even as good as a black and white photograph of an Impressionist painting, all colour and light.

In the next chapter you will explore how and why the craft of writing imaginary dialogue is an important kind of verbal art. Before turning to that chapter, do the following activities as a preparation.

ACTIVITY 115

Writing talk

Using the examples cited above as a start, note down all the occasions you can think of, where what is being said is being written down in some form, either directly from life or via a recording. You should include, for example, your experiences taking notes at a lecture or seminar. There may have been an occasion in group work when you were asked, or volunteered, to make notes of what people said.

How difficult is this, and what exactly are the problems?

List some reasons for writing down what people say, and some of the difficulties. Be specific, e.g. legality, debriefing?

Finally, write a short series of instructions and advice to either note takers at a lecture, or to note takers of a working group's discussion.

ACTIVITY 116

Giving a talk

Notice how different the meaning of 'giving a talk' is from simply 'talking'.

Imagine that you have been invited to give a talk to one of the following groups: eleven-year-olds shortly due to leave primary school to attend your own school, or new entrants to your college about to start A levels.

Your brief is to introduce your audience to the building, the organisation and the daily life of the institution. What you say should be welcoming, friendly and reassuring, but also practical, useful and realistic. You have fifteen minutes, no more! You can use visual aids and one handout.

Prepare your talk, bearing in mind the following questions:

– should I write everything out word-for-word?
– should I rely on headings?
– what would be a good starter?
– what is best looked at and best listened to?
– how should I finish?
– if I am only allowed fifteen minutes, how much time should I allow for question?

Try out your talk on a friend.

ACTIVITY 117

'Please speak after the tone'

In the 1920s, a BBC motto was 'Nation Shall Speak unto Nation'. A motto for the turn of the twentieth century could well be 'answerphone shall speak unto answerphone'.

In this last activity we would like you to consider what answerphones do to the way people speak their messages.

Such messages live in a twilight world between speech and writing. There's none of the feedback you get from an immediate listener and once the message is spoken, it becomes an electronic form of writing – voice mail. But is what you want to say always a message as such? You may have wanted to natter. You may not even be sure why you rang.

You could do this activity in one of three ways:

1 Discuss your experiences of answerphones with a partner and each write a lighthearted piece (700 words at most) on why they should be banned, or why they are your best friend. Be a bit excessive in arguing your case. If you are pro-answerphones, write advertising copy for BT. If you are taking up an anti-answerphone position, write for a local newspaper competition for the funniest grumble of the year.
2 Tape record some answerphone messages and analyse how people actually talk to a machine, and how they try (or are unable) to establish some kind of personal contact. A very easy way to record answerphone recordings is simply to do it live, when the house is quiet, using the built-in microphone that many radio-cassette and cassette recorders possess. The results should be good enough for you and a partner to listen to and discuss. If it is the content, structure and vocabulary you are interested in, then you can of course transcribe directly from the answerphone. Often though, it is the tone of voice, the hesitations and the non-verbal sounds that are most interesting!
3 Working with a partner, write a short story or short radio script in which two answerphones relay messages between two lovers/friends/relatives/strangers/others who never actually talk to each other directly. A customer and a help line that is never in when you call is another possibility, or a psychoanalyst and her client.
   Your story is likely to get off to at least an intriguing start, but you must make sure you have a good ending. Don't start until you have decided how it will end. You will find that this will help you to shape the messages and put in little clues and/or suspense for the reader.

COMMENTARY TO ACTIVITY 105

In the first conversation (page 152), one scientist appears to be the junior, Sc 2. Note that both of Sc 2's utterances are questions, but they are questions seeking and clarifying instruction, not explicitly directing the conversation, as are the teacher's in (d). The seniority of Sc 1 is suggested by the instructive/informative mode of her utterances and the decisiveness about what must be done. There is, however, an easy co-operativeness between the two. Note how the instruction, 'you will have to' is a polite form of 'you must' and is preceded by a sympathetic 'I'm afraid . . .' Note also the use of the adverb 'well', a word that is frequently used at the beginning of an answer. It has a number of pragmatic functions: it makes a link with the question and signifies a welcoming response, it gives time to construct an answer and it often signals as here, some disagreement or modification. You can almost hear the 'but' coming up. Compare this with a another familiar strategy used in response to a statement or a question, 'Yes, but . . .' Which virtually means, 'No'. A more brutal paraphrase of Sc 1's remarks would be, 'You've cocked this up, and you're going to have to do it again'. Note that even when Sc 1 has given an instruction what to do, Sc 2 has the confidence to propose an alternative, while Sc 1 has the patience to listen but also the insistence to say, 'do another calibration'.

That's exactly what pragmatics is all about: the meanings that are going on behind what is being said.

The second conversation is another asymmetrical one. M's opening remark establishes his role and status: 'things I think we need to discuss'. He also sets out the conversational agenda. W signals understanding and co-operativeness by another of those familiar sentence opening adverbs; 'right'. M uses the same word later, but to confirm W's assumption. Note that M uses the inclusive 'we' pronoun twice whereas W uses the pronoun 'you'. Sometimes managers use the pronoun 'we' when they really mean 'you', but here it seems clear that there is a job they have to do together. Interestingly, later in the conversation (not reproduced here) W starts to use the pronoun 'we' as in 'we're going to have to watch that'.

Once again, there is a strand of pragmatic meanings woven (or encoded) into the conversation, not explicitly stated but implied and inferred.

The third transcript records a more symmetrical conversation than either (a) or (b). There is likely to be a senior surgeon among them, but all the signs are that they are working co-operatively on a specific task that requires discussion as well as action. The use of everyday language by s 2 right at the start could indicate a mind already focused on essentials, the job in hand. It might also indicate that the speaker cannot be bothered with trivial terminology. Certainly the effect is to introduce a light, easy going note into the procedings. Note that his later comment on the lymphoma is different in tone, authoritative thinking aloud as opposed to instructing an attendant nurse. (Note too the use of a non standard grammatical form in the first remark, 'don't matter which'. You should not be surprised at this, assuming that 'lower class' folk might do it, but surely not surgeons! People who normally speak standard English grammar, do from time to time, slip into non standard forms either deliberately or with an instinct for 'informalising' or relaxing a situation requiring considerable concentration and mutual trust.)

The remaining excerpts are evidence of the grim humour sometimes adopted by surgeons (for instance the American TV series, M*A*S*H). There is one quite specific language function in evidence when one surgeon counts out the 'bits' and double checks the number. Otherwise there is a code of humour at work, which you might want to argue has a kind of bonding function.

The last transcript records what is essentially a 'thinking aloud' conversation. Note however that the conversation 'monitor', the teacher, proffers no opinion and that her questions are very brief and direct, indicating a confidence that they will be attended to. Who listens to whom is an important aspect of pragmatics. Some people command attention the moment they open their mouths, others are ignored or have to work hard at getting attention. What do you think causes this? Perceived status? Bearing? Tone? Agenda relevance? Magnetism? The teacher nevertheless has a catalytic action on the conversation; she gets them going. One aspect of the conversation you could map out is who listens and talks to whom. Within the overall flow of the conversation, P 1 and P 5 listen and talk to each other, as do S 3 and S 4.

Conversations (b), (c) and (d) all contain an element of humour, an interesting pragmatic issue in its own right. You could explore this by identifying where it occurs, describing its observable effects and explaining its likely causes. Sardonic, self-realisation? Professional defence mechanism? Embarrassment?

8 Talking Books

A good listen

For more than fifty years the BBC has known and used the power of speaking voices to enchant, amuse, intrigue and terrify radio listeners. Even the advent of television has not displaced the pleasure of being told a story. The continuing popularity of storytime programmes for young children, the success of Alan Bennet's *Talking Heads*, and the steady demand for 'Books at Bedtime' and the performance of plays on both radio and TV all bear witness to a deep-seated need for traditional storytelling and dramatisations, alongside modern entertainments such as video games and virtual realities (see Chapter 11 on text transformations for more detailed exploration of TV and radio adaptations).

According to marketing figures for 1997, so-called 'Talking Books' (pre-recorded audio cassettes or CDs) have never been so popular or sold so well in supermarkets. It is highly unlikely nowadays that a GCSE or A level student will not have seen at least one video performance of a Shakespeare 'set book', and in addition, many students will have had some experience of listening to an audio recording of a play or a novel, in either excerpted or abridged form, if not complete.

We have called this chapter *Talking Books* not just to echo a trend, but to draw attention to the central importance of voices and listening to the spoken word for the appreciation and enjoyment of literature. The poet, Liz Lochhead, contends that poems have voices of their own, and once written, go on speaking if the reader has an ear to hear them. This chapter is mainly concerned with voices that speak in plays and prose fiction. Poetry has not been excluded, but the question of poetic voices is dealt with more fully in Chapters 3, 6 and 9.

The practice of silent, private reading together with the mass production of books, are relatively recent phenomena – the last hundred years or so. The practice of reading aloud and being read to is much older.

In fact, English literature (the bookish subject par excellence) has its origins in the oral traditions of Anglo-Saxon (or Old English) alliterative poetry, which in turn has its origins in older Germanic traditions. Literature of the later Middle Ages has many of its origins in French oral traditions of romantic tales and moral fables. Chaucer read his works aloud to audiences gathered specially to be entertained, and the construction of *The Canterbury Tales* as a series of stories told by travellers to amuse each other, is not just a literary device. If we move on nearly five hundred years to the time of Dickens, we find audiences in both Britain and America, eager to attend the novelist's theatrical readings from his works. In recent years, grants from the Arts Council have made it possible for many writers to travel the country, giving readings to the public, especially in schools and colleges. Some city bookshops and publishers also sponsor public readings by authors, which are almost invariably well received.

Our main point here is not to turn back the clock on universal literacy, far from it, but to emphasise the importance of reading with a listening ear as well as an observant eye. Linguistic investigation and literary criticism are both dependent upon a good ear, not only for dialogue between the characters, but also for the more subtly communicated voice of their author.

In the last chapter we explored real-life talk, noting a range of phonological, discourse, pragmatic and contextual factors all of which are relevant in one way or another to literary talk. We took one brief exchange between a BBC interviewer and an eminent politician to show how conversations took place in a network of influential factors. In the activity below, you will have an opportunity to carry out the same kind of analysis on literary talk, but also an opportunity to notice a very significant difference from real-life talk.

ACTIVITY 118

Two schools of thought

In this activity you are going to explore some excerpts from Dickens' novel, *Hard Times* (1854). The story is set in a northern industrial town in which Thomas Gradgrind, who has made his fortune in 'the hardware trade', has endowed a school for the education of workers' children. The very opening scene is set in a classroom where Gradgrind is addressing the teacher in front of the children who are sitting in orderly rows. The reader's first encounter with both Gradgrind and the novel is made through the following words.

Read them, and explore as many aspects of the speech as you can (lexis, grammar, phonology, discourse, pragmatics, context).

Referring to the observations you have made of Gradgrind's style or manner of speaking, write an account of how impressions of Gradgrind's character are conveyed in this passage. Do not read on until you have done this.

'Now, what I want is, Facts. Teach these boys and girls nothing but Facts. Facts alone are wanted in life. Plant nothing else, and root out everything else. You can only form the minds of reasoning animals upon Facts: nothing else will ever be of any service to them. This is the principle on which I bring up my own children, and this is the principle on which I bring up these children. Stick to Facts, sir!'

Now read the passage immediately following Gradgrind's words. How much does it confirm your impressions and expectations?
Since the passage is descriptive, it expresses the author's own voice. Write down your impressions of how Dickens speaks to his readers about the character he has created.

'The scene was a plain, bare, monotonous vault of a schoolroom, and the speaker's square forefinger emphasised his observations by underscoring every sentence with a line on the schoolmaster's sleeve. The emphasis was helped by the speaker's square wall of a forehead, which had his eyebrows for its base, while his eyes found commodious cellarage in two dark caves, overshadowed by the wall. The emphasis was helped by the speaker's hair, which bristled on the skirts of his bald head, a plantation of firs to keep the wind from its shining surface, all covered with knobs, like the crust of a plum pie, as if the head had scarcely warehouse-room for the hard facts stored inside. The speaker's obstinate carriage, square cat, square legs, square shoulders – nay, his very neckcloth, trained to take him by the throat with an unaccommodating grasp, like a stubborn fact, as it was – all helped the emphasis.
'In this life, we want nothing but Facts, sir; nothing but Facts!'

What, for example, do you think is the significance of so much repetition?
A commentary on this passage will be found at the end of the chapter.

The next excerpt you are going to consider comes from Chapter 6 of the novel and is spoken by Mr Sleary, the circus owner and horse trainer. Mr Gradgrind has offered to foster a young girl, Sissy Jupe, daughter of one of Sleary's employees and a pupil at the school.

Sleary is anxious about her happiness and offers some advice as he bids them farewell. Read what he says and write down the impressions you gain of his character. When you have done this, write a comparison of the two 'philosophies' propounded by Gradgrind and Sleary. Make sure first, though, that you explore as fully as possible different aspects of Sleary's spech (lexis, grammar, phonology, discourse, pragmatics, context).

'Tho' be it, my dear. (You thee how it ith', Thquire!) Farewell Thethilia! My latht wordth to you ith thirth, thtick to the termth of your engagement, be obedient to the Thquire, and forget uth. But if, when you're grown up and married and well off, you come upon any horthe-riding ever, don't be too hard upon it, don't be croth with it, give it a Bethpeak if you can, and think you might do wurth. People muth be amuthed, Thquire, thomehow,' continued Sleary, rendered more pursy than ever, by so much talking; 'they can't be alwayth a-working, nor yet can't be alwayth a-learning. Make the betht of uth; not the wuetht. I've got my living out of horthe-riding all my life, I know; but I conthider that I lay down the philothophy of the thubject when I thay to you, Thquire, make the betht of uth; not the wurtht!'

A commentary on this passage will be found at the end of this chapter.

Finally, look at a conversation between Gradgrind and Sissy, which takes place in the classroom. So far you have looked at single utterances as indicators of character and attitude.

Analyse the following conversation, looking at as many features as possible, noting also the voice of the author himself woven between what the characters say.

The excerpt comes from Chapter 2 and is Gradgrind's first encounter with Sissy.

'Girl number twenty,' said Mr Gradgrind, squarely pointing with his square forefinger, 'I don't know that girl. Who is that girl?'
'Sissy Jupe, sir', explained number twenty, blushing, standing up, and curtseying.
'Sissy is not a name,' said Mr Gradgrind. 'Don't call yourself Sissy. Call yourself Cecilia.'
'It's father as calls me Sissy, sir,' returned the young girl in a trembling voice, and with another curtsey.
'Then he has no business to do it,' said Mr Gradgrind. 'Tell him he mustn't. Cecilia Jupe. Let me see. What is your father?'

'He belongs to the horse-riding, if you please sir.'

Mr Gradgrind frowned, and waved off the objectionable calling with his hand.

'We don't want to know anything about that, here. You mustn't tell us about that, here. Your father breaks horses, don't he?'

'If you please, sir, when they can get any to break, they do break horses in the ring, sir.'

' You mustn't tell us about the ring, here. Very well, then. Describe your father as a horsebreaker. He doctors sick horses, I dare say?'

'Oh yes, sir.'

'Very well, then. He is a veterinary surgeon, a farrier and horsebreaker. Give me your definition of a horse.'

(Sissy Jupe thrown into the greatest alarm by this demand.)

'Girl number twenty unable to define a horse!' said Mr Gradgrind, for the general behoof of all the little pitchers. 'Girl number twenty possessed of no facts, in reference to one of the commonest of animals! Some boy's definition of a horse. Bitzer, yours.'

'Quadruped. Omniverous. Forty teeth, namely twenty-four grinders, four eye teeth, and twelve incisive. Sheds coat in the spring; in marshy countries, sheds hoofs too. Hoofs hard, but requiring to be shod with iron. Age known by marks in mouth.' Thus (and much more) Bitzer.

'Now girl number twenty,' said Mr Gradgrind. 'You know what a horse is.'

A commentary on this passage will be found at the end of this chapter.

Naturalistic speech

The special characteristics of much of Dickens' dialogue are not just due to a timespan of nearly one hundred and fifty years between the spoken English of his day and of our own times. His dialogue is more stylised than it is naturalistic. There are exaggerations, little twists, deliberate repetitions in order to achieve theatrical, melodramatic and comic effects. Dickens' purpose in the excerpts from *Hard Times* is satirical. There is much art in the way he makes Gradgrindism seem powerful yet absurd, and in the way he makes Sleary's philosophy seem, in contrast, weaker yet more amiable. Imagination, the very element absent from Gradgrind's philosophy is what transforms the natural elements of his speech into something larger than life. Elsewhere in the novel, dialogue is less stage managed, less stylised, and closer to what we may take as the natural style of the times. Gradgrind's daughter, Louisa, for example, talks very simply to Tom, a friend:

'You are tired.' She whispered presently, more in her usual way.

'Yes, I am quite tired out.'

'You have been so hurried and disturbed today. Have any fresh discoveries been made?'

'Only those you have heard of, from – him.'

'Tom, have you said to any one that we made a visit to those people, and that we saw those three together?

'No. Didn't you yourself particularly ask me to keep it quiet, when you asked me to go there with you?'

'Yes. But I did not know then what was going to happen.'
'Nor I neither. How could I?'
He was very quick upon her with this retort.

This has the interactive characteristic of everyday conversation, lots of questions and even a hesitation. Dickens' own voice makes only a brief comment in the last line of the excerpt.

Striking a balance between natural speech and literary style is a major artistic concern of many writers.

Getting it right mattered very much to Joseph Conrad, for example, who wrote: 'my task is to make you hear, to make you feel . . . to make you see; to show a moment of life in all its vibration, its colour, its form . . . its stress and passion'. Notice how he places hearing and feeling before seeing.

In his study of the novels of Joseph Conrad, Neville Newhouse mixes both linguistic observations and literary comment, especially in his criticism of the strengths and weaknesses of Conrad as a writer of dialogue. Don't worry if you haven't read any Conrad, the quotations below from Newhouse's book are given to show you how attention to quite ordinary linguistic features can throw light on the novelist's art.

Conrad's dialogue is vigorously idiomatic. It is characterised by question and exclamation marks, by 'eh's' and 'By Joves'. He often speaks directly to his reader in the same tone. Here is an example from the start of *Victory*:

> On most evenings of the year Heyst could have sat outside with a naked candle to read one of the books left him by his late father. It was not a mean store. But he never did that. Afraid of mosquitoes very likely. Neither was he ever tempted by the silence to address any casual remarks to the companion glow of the volcano. He was not mad. Queer chap – yes, that may have been said, and in fact was said; but there is a tremendous difference between the two, you will allow.

The clipped sentences (one is verbless) and the appeal at the end ('you will allow') seem to involve the reader in an exchange of views.

Conrad is an uneven writer. At his best he gives his characters a clearly individual tone – Captain Mitchell is fussy and pompous in speech, Dr Monygham suspicious and truculent, Giorgio slow and dignified, Nostromo vigorous and practical, Decoud mocking and sophisticated. But Conrad is not always so successful.
He finds it difficult to give Lena in *Victory* the right words and rhythms. We first hear her when Heyst addresses her during the break in the music provided by the Zangiacomo orchestra. 'I am sure she pinched your arm most cruelly', he says. She replies:

> 'It wouldn't have been the first time. And suppose she die – what are you going to do about it?'

A little later he asks her if she sings in addition to playing the violin. 'Never sang a note in my life', comes the answer. The tone is forceful; its abruptness suggests vigorous action. But Lena is not at all like that. When she has a long exchange with Heyst after their flight to the island, she uses languorous, falling rhythms:

> 'Too big?' he enquired.
> 'Too lonely. It makes my heart sink, too.'

The mood is different, it may be argued. True, but it is her normal mood, and the first words remain oddly misleading, more suited to Mrs Verloc in *The Secret Agent* than to Lena.

The point partly explains Conrad's weakness in depicting women; in giving them a largely passive role he is unable to find the right tone for their speaking voices. Laconic command and scandalised astonishment are exactly right for Mrs Verloc, e.g. 'Shop, Adolf. You go' and 'Whatever did you want to do that for?'

Conrad matches her decision of character with the terse decisive dialogue that always came easily to him. When he gives the same tone to the very different Lena, the result is unsatisfactory.

Conrad may have been aware of this danger, for many of his heroines speak relatively little. Jewel, in Lord Jim's absence makes a 'warlike and impassioned speech'. It is accorded two lines of text, introduced by Marlow's 'I am told that . . .' For the rest of the book, apart from her despairing outcries at the end, she flits wraith-like in and out of the edges of the reader's consciousness. 'I need not tell you what she is to me,' Jim says to Marlow. 'You've seen'. Marlow may have seen, but the reader has not. Or, more correctly, he has not heard her, and therefore has to take her on trust.

Those of Conrad's novels which have little or poor dialogue are his weakest.

All serious novelists use dialogue for a variety of purposes – to reveal character and motive, to slacken or quicken the action, to provide contrast or humour, or to pin-point a moment.

from *Joseph Conrad* by Neville Newhouse, Evans Brothers, 1966

We are not expecting you to take at face value one critic's evaluations of novels you may not even have heard of, let alone read, but we are drawing attention to his method of observing significant features of speech in prose fiction. Notice the references to 'tone', 'rhythm' grammar, the idiomatic, and the narrator's direct engagement with the reader in an exchange of views (pragmatics). Notice too, the emphasis on the reader's ability to hear a character, and the extensive vocabulary for describing vocal effects: e.g. laconic command, truculent, mocking and sophisticated.

ACTIVITY 119

The secret sharer

Here is a chance for you to examine Conrad's dialogue for yourself. The excerpt below comes from his short novel, *The Secret Sharer*. The excerpt comes from early in the novel and is set on the deck of Captain Archbold's ship. Archbold is smoking a cigar and looking idly over the side of the ship.

> The side of the ship made an opaque belt of shadow on the darkling glassy shimmer of the sea. But I saw at once something elongated and pale floating very close to the ladder. Before I could form a guess a faint flash of phosphorescent light, which seemed to issue suddenly from the naked body of a man, flickered in the sleeping water with the elusive, silent play of summer lightning in a night sky. With a gasp I saw revealed to my stare a pair of feet, the long legs, a broad livid back immersed right up to the neck in a greenish cadaverous glow. One hand, awash, clutched the bottom rung of the ladder. He was complete but for the head. A headless corpse! The cigar dropped out of my gaping mouth with a tiny plop and a short hiss quite audible in the absolute stillness of all things under heaven. At that I suppose he raised up his face, a dimly pale oval in the shadow of the ship's side. But even then I could only barely make out down there the shape of his black-haired head. However, it was enough for the horrid, frost-bound sensation which had gripped me about the chest to pass off. The moment of vain exclamations was past, too. I only climbed on

the spare spar and leaned over the rail as far as I could to bring my eyes nearer to that mystery floating alongside.

As he hung by the ladder, like a resting swimmer, the sea lightning played about his limbs at every stir; and he appeared in it ghastly, silvery, fishlike. He remained as mute as a fish, too. He made no motion to get out of the water, either. It was inconceivable that he should not attempt to come on board, and strangely troubling to suspect that perhaps he did not want to. And my first words were prompted by just that troubled incertitude.

'What's the matter?' I asked in my ordinary tone, speaking down to the face upturned exactly under mine.

'Cramp,' it answered, no louder. Then slightly anxious, 'I say, no need to call anyone.'

'I was not going to,' I said.

'Are you alone on deck?'

'Yes.'

I had somehow the impression that he was on the point of letting go the ladder to swim away beyond my ken — mysterious as he came. But, for the moment, this being appearing as if he had risen from the bottom of the sea (it was certainly the nearest land to the ship) wanted only to know the time. I told him. And he, down there, tentatively:

'I suppose your captain's turned in?'

'I am sure he isn't,' I said.

He seemed to struggle with himself, for I heard something like the low, bitter murmur of doubt. 'What's the good?' His next words came out with a hesitating effort.

'Look here, my man. Could you call him out quietly?'

I thought the time had come to declare myself — 'I am the captain.'

I heard a 'By Jove!' whispered at the level of the water. The phosphorescence flashed in the swirl of the water all about his limbs, his other hand seized the ladder.

'My name's Leggatt.'

The voice was calm and resolute. A good voice. The self-possession of that man had somehow induced a corresponding state in myself. It was very quietly that I remarked:

'You must be a good swimmer.'

'Yes. I've been in the water practically since nine o'clock. The question for me now is whether I am to let go this ladder and go on swimming till I sink from exhaustion, or — to come on board here.'

I felt this was no mere formula of desperate speech, but a real alternative in the view of a strong soul. I should have gathered from this that he was young; indeed, it is only the young who are ever confronted by such clear issues. But at the time it was pure intuition on my part. A mysterious communication was established already between us two — in the face of that silent, darkened tropical sea. I was young, too; young enough to make no comment. The man in the water began suddenly to climb up the ladder, and I hastened away from the rail to fetch some clothes.

'What is it?' I asked in a deadened voice, taking the lighted lamp out of the binnacle, and raising it to his face.

'An ugly business.'

He had rather regular features; a good mouth; light eyes under somewhat heavy, dark eyebrows; a smooth, square forehead; no growth on his cheeks; a small, brown mustache, and a well-shaped, round chin. His expression was concentrated, meditative, under the inspecting light of the lamp I held up to his face; such as a man thinking hard in solitude might wear. My sleeping suit was just right for his size. A well-knit young fellow of twenty-five at most. He caught his lower lip with the edge of white, even teeth.

'Yes,' I said, replacing the lamp in the binnacle. The warm, heavy tropical night closed upon his head again.

'There's a ship over there,' he murmured.

'Yes, I know. The *Sephora*. Did you know of us?'

'Hadn't the slightest idea. I am the mate of her –' He paused and corrected himself. 'I should say I was.'

'Aha! Something wrong?'

'Yes. Very wrong indeed. I've killed a man.'

'What do you mean? Just now?'

'No, on the passage. Weeks ago. Thirty-nine south. When I say a man –'

'Fit of temper,' I suggested, confidently.

The man in the water, Leggatt, has in fact murdered someone on another ship and then jumped overboard. The lives of the two men become strangely entwined as Archbold begins to see Leggatt as a symbol of his own darker self.

1 How convincing do you find the dialogue?
2 How appropriate is the dialogue to what turns out to be a very strange tale?

3 Notice that Conrad actually makes specific references to the act of speaking at the beginning and at the end of the excerpt. Do you see any significance in this? After all, he didn't need to.
4 You might have expected Archbold to reply. 'I'm sure he hasn't' rather than 'isn't'. How would you explain this variation.

Any attempt to write fiction for Original Writing coursework deserves close attention to the writing of dialogue, and an assessment of the strengths and/or weaknesses of the style you have adopted would make interesting reading if detailed in your commentary. Equally, the possession of a wide range of precise descriptions for tones of voice will add interest to your stylistic analyses of other people's writing.

The following activities will give you opportunities to explore various kinds of, mostly naturalistic, dialogue in prose fiction. Use the approaches introduced in the previous chapter but also address the single big difference between real-life conversation and literary dialogue, namely the all controlling authorial voice that is always present. 'Authorial voice' is another term for the narrator's voice, or the voice of the person telling you the story. In *The Secret Sharer*, for example, the authorial voice comes through the first person narrator, Archbold. In the *Hard Times* excerpts, written in the third person, Dickens' authorial voice comes through independently.

The authorial voice also has the power to affect context by creating a mood or expressing an attitude. It can very effectively 'spin' a dialogue – a word here, a phrase there – so that the speakers will appear silly, tragic, sinister, or whatever, despite the words they have been given to speak. Here are three examples:

'Help me', she whined, feebly.
'Help me', she demanded, imperiously.
'Help me', she begged, unashamedly.

You should have very little difficulty 'hearing' the differences here, guided by the authorial choices of verbs and adverbs. Authors are powerful people over the world of their creations. You could compare it to some extent with the power you feel while watching a soap opera: you know what is going on, who is stupid, who is innocent, who isn't, who loves who but won't tell, who deserves all she gets but probably won't get it!

Each activity is followed by a suggested follow-up activity which you do not need to do straightaway, but which will help you build up a repertoire of literary examples you have investigated in some detail. It may also suggest a piece of Original Writing, such as an interesting article or radio programme on how people talk to each other in fiction.

ACTIVITY 120

The following excerpt comes from a novel by Jim Eldridge about life in a modern primary school (*King Street Junior*, BBC Books, 1988). It describes a scene that is familiar enough. How natural and realistic do you find the dialogue? Show with reference to 'the usual factors' in everyday speech (e.g. context, pragmatics) what makes the conversation the way it is, and identify the strategies or techniques used by the storyteller to give literary effect to the raw material. Notice, for example, choices of verbs and adjectives.

Our detailed commentary will be found at the end of this chapter.

In Mr Sims's class the bell for morning break came as a merciful relief. The noise of the drilling, although distant, had been ever-present throughout the whole early part of the morning, making it almost impossible for either Sims or his class to concentrate. As the children scampered out of the room to the playground, and Sims gathered up his books, he became aware of tiny Chandra hovering by his elbow. 'Yes, Chandra?' he asked.

'Please, sir, Mr Sims,' said Chandra mournfully, 'Can I stay in? My leg hurts.'

A smile almost came to Sims's lips, but he held it back. Not again, he thought. 'Oh?' said Sims. 'What have you done to it?'

'I don't know, sir,' said Chandra. 'It just hurts. I must have hurt it coming to school.'

'And how did you hurt it?'

Chandra shook his head unhappily. 'I don't know, sir.' he said.

Sims sighed. This whole game had really gone on for long enough, it was really about time he put a stop to it. 'Look, Chandra,' he said, 'I might feel more inclined to believe that your leg hurts ...'

'It does, sir.'

'... if you hadn't come to me yesterday at break time asking to stay in because you had a cold.'

'I did have a cold,' protested Chandra righteously.

'And the day before,' continued Sims, 'saying that you didn't feel well because of your head? Frankly, Chandra, it does look to me like you just don't want to go out.'

Chandra shook his head in vehement denial. 'No, sir ...'

Sims held up his hand to stop Chandra's protestations, which he knew would be long and full of deep conviction. 'Go on,' he said, 'get your coat on and out you go. The fresh air will do you good.'

'But, sir ...' said Chandra, and this time a note of desperation seemed to be creeping into his voice.

Sims pointed at the door. 'Out,' he said.

Chandra's face dropped, and for a second, seeing the misery on the boy's face, Sims was tempted to change his mind and let him stay in. But then what? The next break all his class would want to stay in.

'Yes, sir,' said Chandra in a voice low with misery. And he went.

ACTIVITY 121

The following two excerpts look like scenes from a play but they are in fact from a novel by Jerome K. Jerome called *Three Men In A Boat* (1889).

The three men are taking a boating holiday on the river Thames. One of them, Harris, is given to singing comic songs, which he does in the second excerpt. The men are accompanied by a little dog, Montmorency, who appears in the first excerpt.

Read the passages and consider the questions that follow.

(i)

We were, as I have said, returning from a dip, and half-way up the High Street a cat darted out from one of the houses in front of us, and began to trot across the road. Montmorency gave a cry of joy – the cry of a stern warrior who sees his enemy given over to his hands–the sort of cry Cromwell might have uttered when the Scots came down the hill – and flew after his prey.

His victim was a large black Tom. I never saw a larger cat, nor a more disreputable-looking cat. It had lost half its tail, one of its ears, and a fairly appreciable proportion of its nose. It was a long, sinewy-looking animal. It had a calm, contented air about it.

Montmorency went for that poor cat at the rate of twenty miles an hour; but the cat did not hurry up – did not seem to have grasped the idea that its life was in danger. It trotted quietly on until its would-be assassin was within a yard of it, and then it turned round and sat down in the middle of the road, and looked at Montmorency with a gentle, inquiring expression, that said:

'Yes! You want me?'

Montmorency does not lack pluck; but there was something about the look of that cat that might have chilled the heart of the boldest dog. He stopped abruptly, and looked back at Tom.

Neither spoke; but the conversation that one could imagine was clearly as follows:

THE CAT: 'Can I do anything for you?'
MONTMORENCY: 'No – no, thanks.'
THE CAT: 'Don't you mind speaking, if you really want anything, you know.'
MONTMORENCY (*backing down the High Street*): 'Oh, no – not at all – certainly – don't
    trouble. I – I am afraid I've made a mistake. I thought I knew you. Sorry I disturbed you.'
THE CAT: 'Not at all – quite a pleasure. Sure you don't want anything, now?'
MONTMORENCY (*still backing*): 'Not at all, thanks – not at all – very kind of you. Good
    morning.'
THE CAT: 'Good morning.'

Then the cat rose, and continued his trot; and Montmorency, fitting what he calls his tail carefully into its groove, came back to us, and took up an unimportant position in the rear.

To this day, if you say the word 'Cats!' to Montmorency, he will visibly shrink and look up piteously at you, as if to say:

'Please don't.'

(ii)

Well, you don't look for much of a voice in a comic song. You don't expect correct phrasing or vocalization. You don't mind if a man does find out, when in the middle of a note, that he is too high, and comes down with a jerk. You don't bother about time. You don't mind a man being two bars in front of the accompaniment, and easing up in the middle of a line to argue it out with the pianist, and then starting the verse afresh. But you do expect the words.

You don't expect a man to never remember more than the first three lines of the first verse, and to keep on repeating these until it is time to begin the chorus. You don't expect a man to break off in the middle of a line, and snigger, and say, it's very funny, but he's blest if he can think of the rest of it, and then try and make it up for himself, and, afterwards, suddenly recollect it, when he has got to an entirely different part of the song, and break off without a word of warning, to go back and let you have it then and there. You don't – well, I will just give you an idea of Harris's comic singing, and then you can judge for yourself.

HARRIS (*standing up in front of piano and addressing the expectant mob*): I'm afraid it's a very old thing, you know. I expect you all know it, you know. But it's the only thing I know. It's the Judge's song out of *Pinafore* – no, I don't mean *Pinafore* – I mean – you know what I mean – the other thing, you know. You must all join in the chorus, you know.

Murmurs of delight and anxiety to join in the chorus. Brilliant performance of prelude to the Judge's song in 'Trial by Jury' by nervous pianist. Moment arrives for Harris to join in. Harris takes no notice of it. Nervous pianist commences prelude over again, and Harris, commencing singing at the same time, dashes off the first two lines of the First Lord's song out of 'Pinafore'. Nervous pianist tries to push on with prelude, gives it up, and tries to follow Harris with accompaniment to Judge's song out of 'Trial by Jury', finds that doesn't answer, and tries to recollect what he is doing, and where he is, feels his mind giving way, and stops short.

HARRIS (*with kindly encouragement*): It's all right. You're doing it very well, indeed – go on.
NERVOUS PIANIST: I'm afraid there's a mistake somewhere. What are you singing?
HARRIS (*promptly*): Why the Judge's song out of *Trial by Jury*. Don't you know it?
SOME FRIEND OF HARRIS'S (*from the back of the room*): No, you're not, you chuckle-head, you're singing the Admiral's song from *Pinafore*.

Long argument between Harris and Harris's friend as to what Harris is really singing. Friend finally suggests that it doesn't matter what Harris is singing so long as Harris gets on and sings it, and Harris with an evident sense of injustice rankling inside him, requests the pianist to begin again. Pianist, thereupon, starts prelude to the Admiral's song, and Harris, seizing what he considers to be a favourable opening in the music, begins.

HARRIS:
> When I was young and called to the Bar.

General roar of laughter, taken by Harris as a compliment. Pianist, thinking of his wife and family, gives up the unequal contest and retires; his place being taken by a stronger-nerved man.

THE NEW PIANIST (*cheerily*): Now then, old man, you start off, and I'll follow. We won't bother about any prelude.
HARRIS (*upon whom the explanation of matters has slowly dawned – laughing*): By Jove! I beg your pardon. Of course – I've been mixing up the two songs. It was Jenkins who confused me, you know. Now then.

Singing; his voice appearing to come from the cellar, and suggesting the first low warnings of an approaching earthquake.

> When I was young I served a term
> As office-boy to an attorney's firm.

(*Aside to pianist*): It is too low, old man; we'll have that over again, if you don't mind. *Sings first two lines over again, in a high falsetto this time. Great surprise on the part of the audience. Nervous old lady near the fire begins to cry, and has to be led out.*

HARRIS (*continuing*):
> I swept the windows and I swept the door,

And I –
No – no, I cleaned the windows of the big front door. And I polished up the floor –
no, dash it – I beg your pardon – funny thing, I can't think of that line. And I – and I –
Oh, well, we'll get on to the chorus, and chance it (*sings*):
And I diddle-diddle-diddle-diddle-diddle-diddle-de,
Till now I am ruler of the Queen's navee.
Now then, chorus – it's the last two lines repeated, you know.
GENERAL CHORUS:
And he diddle-diddle-diddle-diddle-diddle-diddle-dee'd,
Till now he is ruler of the Queen's navee.
And Harris never sees what an ass he is making of himself, and how he is annoying a
lot of people who never did him any harm. He honestly imagines that he has given
them a treat, and says he will sing another comic song after supper.

1 What is gained by slipping out of conventional narrative into a playscript format? (You could re-write one of the passages as conventional narrative with conversation in order to see the different effect.)

2 How does the author use language to bring humour into his storytelling? Many of the effects are quite subtly done. How naturalistic do you find the conversations, and how much art do you detect?

3 When you have considered these questions, and any other matters that interest you, identify linguistic evidence that tells you the text was written over one hundred years ago. You could look at words, phrases, overall style, attitudes.

Our detailed comments will be found at the end of this chapter.

ACTIVITY 122

The following excerpt comes from L. P. Hartley's novel, *The Go-Between*.

Leo, a young boy, is staying with the well-to-do family of a schoolfriend. He becomes the go-between in an affair between his friend's older sister, Marian, and a local worker, Ted Burgess. In the excerpt, Ted is sounding out the possibility of Leo taking secret messages to Marian.

Read the passage through a couple of times, noting significant features of real life talk. It is likely that you will find the dialogue very naturalistic.

When you have done this, look in detail at the way Hartley writes the dialogue. Read it aloud, with a partner, to get a feeling for the pace, the pauses and the insinuations. From whose point of view is the dialogue written, and what difference does that make?

As a stylistic exercise that would focus very closely on details, you could re-write the passage, or part of it, making Ted Burgess, the first person narrator.

Our own comments will be found at the end of the chapter.

The boy, young Leo, has grazed his knee sliding down a haystack. Ted Burgess, a farm labourer, tends his knee and persuades him to act as a go-between delivering love letters.

'Does that mean that you are alone with her sometimes? I mean, just the two of you in a room, with no one else?'
He spoke with great intensity, as if he was envisaging the scene.
'Well, sometimes,' I said. 'Sometimes we sit together on a sofa.'
'You sit together on the sofa?' he repeated.
I had to enlighten him. At home there were two sofas; here there appeared to be none; at Brandham Hall –

'You see,' I said, 'there are so many sofas.'

He took the point. 'But when you are together, chatting –?'

I nodded. We were together, chatting.

'You are near enough to her –?'

'Near enough?' I repeated. 'Well of course, her dress –'

'Yes, yes,' said he, taking that point too. 'These dresses spread out quite a long way. But near enough – to give her something?'

'Give her something?' I said. 'Oh yes, I could give her something.' It sounded like a disease; my mind was still slightly preoccupied by measles. He said impatiently:

'Give her a letter. I mean without anybody seeing.'

I almost laughed – it seemed such a small thing for him to have got so worked up about. 'Oh yes,' I said. 'Quite near enough for that.'

'Then I'll write it,' he said, 'if you can wait.'

As he was moving away a thought struck me. 'But how can you write to her when you don't know her?' I asked.

'Who said I didn't know her?' he countered almost truculently.

'Well, you did. You said you didn't know them at the Hall. And she told me she didn't know you, because I asked her.'

He thought for a moment, with the strained look in his eyes that he had when he was swimming.

'Did she say she didn't know me?' he asked.

'Well, she said she might have met you, but she didn't remember.'

He drew a long breath.

'She does know me, in a way,' he said. 'I'm a kind of friend of hers, but not the sort she goes about with. That's what she meant, I expect. . . .' He paused. 'We do some business together.'

'Is it a secret?' I asked eagerly.

'It's more than that,' he said.

All at once I felt rather faint, as if the Psalms had exceeded fifty verses: to my surprise (for grown-ups could be very dense about this) he noticed it, and said: 'You look all in. Sit down and put your feet up. Here's a stool. I haven't any sofas, I'm afraid.' He established me in the one easy chair. 'I won't be long,' he said.

But he was. He got out a bottle of Stephens' blue-black ink (I was rather shocked that it was not a proper inkstand), and a sheet of blue-lined writing paper, and wrote laboriously. His fingers seemed too large to hold the pen.

'Should I just give her a message?' I said.

He looked up with narrowed eyes.

'You wouldn't understand it,' he said.

At last the letter was done. He put it in an envelope, licked the flap, and laid his fist on it like a hammer. I stretched out my hand: but he didn't give it to me.

'If you can't get her alone,' he said, 'don't give it to her.'

'What shall I do with it?'

'Put it in the place where you pull the chain.'

One part of me wished he hadn't said this, for I was beginning to see my mission in romantic colours; but the other appreciated the practical side of the precaution; I was a born intriguer.

'You can be sure I will,' I said.

Now, I thought, he will really let me have the letter, but still he kept it under his clenched fist, like a lion guarding something with its paw.

'Look here,' he said, 'are you really on the square?'

'Of course I am,' I answered, hurt.

'Because,' he said slowly, 'if anyone else gets hold of that letter it will be a bad look-out for her and me and perhaps for you, too.'

He couldn't have said anything more calculated to put me on my mettle.

'I shall defend it with my life.' I said.

At that he smiled, lifted his hand, and pushed the letter towards me.

'But you haven't addressed it!' I exclaimed.

'No,' he said, and added with a rush of confidence that excited me, 'and I haven't signed it either.'

'Will she be glad to get it?' I asked.

'I think so,' he said briefly.

I wanted to have it all cut and dried.

'And will there be an answer?'

'That depends,' he said. 'Don't ask too many questions. You don't want to know too much.'

With that I had to be content. Suddenly there was a lull in my mind, like the *détente* after a retreating thunderstorm, and I realized it must be late. Looking at my watch, 'Golly!' I exclaimed, 'I must be off.'

'How are you feeling?' he asked solicitously. 'How's the knee, eh?'

'A.I,' I said, bending it up and down. 'The blood hasn't come through the handkerchief,' I added, half regretfully.

'It will do, when you walk.' He gave me his hard, searching stare. 'You're looking a bit peaked,' he said, 'Sure you wouldn't like me to drive you some of the way? The trap's there and I can put the horse to in a jiffy.'

'Thank you,' I said, 'I'll walk.' I should have liked to drive, but suddenly felt the need of being alone. Being too young to know how to take my leave, I lingered awkwardly: besides, there was something I wanted to say.

'Here, you've forgotten the letter,' he said. 'Where shall you put it?'

'In my knickers pocket,' I said, suiting the action to the word. 'This suit has several pockets' – I indicated them – 'but a man who knew a policeman once told me that your trousers pocket is safest.'

He looked at me approvingly and I noticed for the first time that he was sweating: his shirt was sticking in dark patches to his chest.

'You're a good boy,' he said, shaking hands with me. 'Hop off, and be kind to yourself.'

I laughed at this, it seemed so funny to be told to be kind to yourself, and then I remembered what I wanted to say. 'May I come and slide down your straw-stack again?'

'I'll have it combed and brushed for you,' he said. 'And now you must scoot.'

ACTIVITY 123

The next pair of excerpts come from a novel with very strong autobiographical elements, *One Small Boy* by Bill Naughton (1957). Set in Bolton in the 1920s, it tells of the childhood and schooldays of two boys, Mike and Charlie. Their school is a tough one but their imaginations, cheerful spirits and willingness to learn are not entirely crushed. The excerpts tell of an English composition lesson, and, later, of a poem by Keats that the boys have to learn (*La Belle Dame Sans Merci*).

Read the passages and comment on how the contribution dialect (words, grammar, and accent) adds to your understanding and enjoyment. When you have done this, write a short scene based on your own experience of school, paying particular attention to authenticity in dialect and children's ways of talking. Don't overdo the dialect; it is very easy to write stereotypes instead of real people.

(i)

He glanced sideways as he heard the rapid scratch of Charlie's pen beside him. He was able to make out the top line of Charlie's composition: '*When the manks cam they fun Heerward unconcon.*' He felt gingerly about with his clog-toe for Charlie's foot.

'Get off mi flappin' toe – can't you?' said Charlie.

He took his foot away at once and the violent scratching of Charlie's pen went on. If she sees it she'll clout him, and he's that near that I feel it.

'Who the 'eck art nudgin'?' asked Charlie loudly.

He bent his head, listened, waiting for Miss Skegham to go out. At last the door closed behind her. The buzz of talk began. He turned to Charlie.

'Stop!' he said. 'What's that?'

'What's what?'

"When the manks cam they fun Heerward unconcon.'

'What art talkin' about, M'Cloud? There are times when I think tha must be goin' off thy nut.'

'Read that top line of thine, Crid. Just read it.'

'I can see nowt wrong with it.'

'What's a *mank*?'

'Mank? Mank? Oh, tha means *monk*!'

'Then why not write monk, Chey?'

'Oh – flappin' Nora! Thanks, Mike.'

'Who's Heerward, Chey?'

'What the 'ell art talkin' about?'

'I said who's Heerward?'

'Heerward? Oh, Hereward – you piecan.'

'Then put *Hereward* – if it's Hereward the Wake. Chey, what's *fun*?'

'"Fun"? "Fun's" fun. I fun a penny in the street.'

'Tha'll fun four raps with her stick if tha doesn't change it. Found, you daft nut.'

'Oh holy mackerel, so it is, Mike. Quick, is there owt else?'

'Put an 'e' on came. Chey, what's "unconcon"?'

'I'm blowed if I know what tha'rt talkin' about!'

'Tha'll be blowed if tha doesn't. Should it be 'unconscious'?'

'Holy Moses, I were goin' at it that fast I didn't have time to cudgitate. Go over it, Mike.'

'That sounds a bit odd to me, Chey – "He had thick golden hair growing down the back of his chest."'

'What's odd about it?'

'The *back* of his chest, Chey.'

'Holy Mother, that would mean down his lungs, wouldn't it? He couldn't have hair growing down his lungs, could he?'

'He could, perhaps – but it's not likely tha'd have heard about it, Chey.'

'An' me thinkin' I'd written the best composition of all time,' said Charlie, 'that 'ud have been framed in letters of gold in the school hall, whereas I'd ha' got my bum smacked. Comes from not cudgitatin', Mike. I'll remember thee in my will.'

(ii)

Half-way across the brewery ground he had a feeling that he hadn't come the right way, and he turned to the left and went down Back Howbert Street. Suddenly he spotted a figure ahead, playing with a ball.

'Howgo, Chey,' he called.

Charlie Criddle didn't speak, but caught the ball and approached him. '"The sledge has withered from the lake",' he spoke dreamily, '"an' no brids sing".'

'The *sedge*, Chey,' he said quickly, 'What the heck's the sledge?'

'Sedge? I know what a sledge is – but what the flappin' Nora is a sedge?'

'Summat on a lake, Chey.'

'Don't be fawse, Mike, it don't become thee. If tha goes round contradictin' folk tha should first know what tha'rt talkin' about.'

'Listen, Chey, a sedge is summat as withers.'

'Scorn withers – is that a sedge? Tha'rt gettin' a billoxed up an' tha knows it. Did ta hear about that chap in the paper as poisoned his wife with a razor?'

'Aye, he gave her arsenic.'

'An' no brids sing. An' no brids sing. I were sayin' that all night long, Mike. It hath me infatuated. What comes after 'I made a garland for her head'?'

' "And bracelets too, and fragrant zone –" '

'Oh Christ aye! "She looked at me as she did love. And made sweet moan." I were cudgitatin' like mad over that bit in bed. I'd have given a fortune to know it. Aye, an' made sweet moan, an' made sweet moan. An' no brids sing, an' no brids sing. An' gave her arse a nick. Who told thee, Mike?'

'It's hairs on, Chey.'

'Ready?' yelled Charlie, flinging the ball into the air. They both raced after it, and then they began kicking it along the street on the way to school. Charlie stopped three times along the way to turn his head upwards and cry out: 'And made sweet moan. And made sweet moan.' The last time he called out: 'That'll plague me tonight, Mike. I can feel it in m veins. "And made sweet moan." '

ACTIVITY 124

The crime novels of Colin Dexter are familiar to millions through the TV dramatisations starring John Thaw as Inspector Morse. The pair of excerpts you are going to examine come from *The Way Through The Woods* (1992).

Interwoven with the story of a murder investigation is a story of a developing relationship between Morse and a pathologist, Dr Laura Hobson. The first excerpt presents their first encounter with each other; the second relates how one of the characters in the book, who has been holding back vital information, gives herself away.

Read the two excerpts and comment on the way Dexter handles the dialogue in relation to the narrative. Again, you will learn much about his technique by inventing a scene of your own and writing it in a similar vein.

Our comments will be found at the end of the chapter.

(i)

'Tell me more about Karin,' continued Morse. ' "Proper" you said, Do you mean "prim and proper" – that sort of thing? You know, a bit prudish; a bit ... straightlaced?'

'Nor, I dorn't mean *that*. As I say it's five or six years back, isn't it? But she was ... well, her mother said she'd always got plenty of boyfriends, like, but she knew, well ... she knew where to draw the line – let's put it like that.'

'She didn't keep a packet of condoms under her pillow?'

'I dorn't think so.' Mrs Evans seemed far from shocked by the blunt enquiry.

'Was she a virgin, do you think?'

'Things change, dorn't they? Not many gels these days who ought to walk up the aisle in white, if you ask me.'

Morse nodded slowly as if assimilating the woman's wisdom, before switching direction again. What was Karin like at school – had Mrs Evans ever learned that? Had she been in the – what was it? – Flikscouten, the Swedish Girl Guides? Interested in sport, was she? Skiing, skating, tennis, basketball?

Mrs Evans was visibly more relaxed again as she replied: 'She was always good at sport, yes. Irma – Mrs Eriksson – she used to write and tell me when her daughters had won things; you know, cups and medals, certificates and all that.'

'What was Karin best at, would you say?'

'Dorn't know really. As I say it's a few years since –'

'I do realize that, Mrs Evans. It's just that you've been so helpful so far – and if you could just cast your mind back and try – try to remember.'

'Well, morst games, as I say, but –'

'Skiing?'

'I dorn't think so.'

'Tennis?'

'Oh, she loved tennis. Yes, I think tennis was her favourite game, really.'

'Amazing, aren't they – these Swedes! They've only got about seven million people there, is that right? But they tell me about four or five in the world's top-twenty come from Sweden.'

Lewis blinked. Neither tennis nor any other sport, he knew, was of the slightest interest to Morse who didn't know the difference between side-lines and touch-lines. Yet he understood exactly the trap that Morse was digging; the trap that Mrs Evans tumbled into straightaway.

'Edberg!' she said. 'Stefan Edberg. He's her great hero.'

'She must have been very disappointed about Wimbledon last year, I should think then?'

'She was, yes. She told me she –'

Suddenly Mrs Evans's left hand shot up to her mouth, and for many seconds she sat immobile in her chair as if she'd caught a glimpse of the Gorgon.

'Don't worry,' said Morse quietly. 'Sergeant Lewis will take it all down. Don't talk too fast for him, though: he failed his forty words per minute shorthand test, didn't you, Sergeant?'

Lewis was wholly prepared. 'Don't worry about what he said, Mrs Evans. You can talk just how you like. It's not as if' – turning to Morse – 'she's done much wrong, is it, sir?'

'Not very much,' said Morse gently; 'not very much at all, have you, Mrs Evans?'

'How on earth did you guess *that* one?' asked Lewis an hour later as the car accelerated down the A483 to Llandovery.

'She'd've slipped up sooner or later. Just a matter of time.'

'But all that tennis stuff. You don't follow tennis.'

'In my youth, I'll have you know, I had quite a reliable back-hand.'

'But how did you –'

'Prayer and fasting, Lewis, Prayer and fasting.'

Lewis gave it up. 'Talking of fasting, sir, aren't you getting a bit peckish?'

'Yes, I am. Hungry *and* thirsty. So perhaps if we can find one of those open-all-day places . . .'

(ii)

SUNDAY is not a good day on which to do business. Or to expect others to be at work – or even to be out of bed. But Dr Laura Hobson was out of bed fairly early that morning, and awaiting Morse at the (deserted) William Dunn School of Pathology building at 9.30 a.m.

'Hello.'

'Hello.'

'You're Inspector Morse?'

'Chief Inspector Morse.'

'Sorry!'

'And you're Dr Hobson?'

'I am she.'

Morse smiled wanly. 'I applaud your grammar, my dear.'

'I am not your "dear". You must forgive me for being so blunt: but I'm no one's "luv" or "dear" or "darling" or "sweetheart". I've got a name. If I'm at work I prefer to be called Dr Hobson; and if I let my hair down over a drink I have a Christian name: Laura. That's my little speech, Chief Inspector! You're not the only one who's heard it.' She was smiling sufficiently as she spoke though, showing small, very white teeth – a woman in her early thirties, fair-complexioned, with a pair of disproportionately large spectacles on her pretty nose; a smallish woman, about 5 foot 4 inches. But it was her voice which interested Morse: the broad north-country vowels in "luv" and "blunt"; the pleasing nairm she had – and perhaps the not unpleasant prospect of meeting her sometime orver a drink with her hair doon . . .

They sat on a pair of high stools in a room that reminded Morse of his hated physics lab at school, and she told him of the simple yet quite extraordinary findings. The report on which Max had been working, though incomplete, was incontestable: the bones discovered in Wytham Woods were those of an adult male, Caucasian, about 5 foot 6 inches in height, slimly built, brachycephalic, fair-haired . . .

But Morse's mind had already leaped many furlongs ahead of the field. He'd been sure that the bones had been those of Karin Eriksson. All right, he'd been wrong. But now he knew whose bones they were – for the face of the man in the photograph was staring back at him, unmistakably. He asked only for a photocopy of Dr Hobson's brief, preliminary report, and rose to go.

The pair of them walked to the locked outer door in silence, for the death of Max was heavy on her mind too.

'You knew him well, didn't you?'

Morse nodded.

'I feel so sad,' she said simply.

Morse nodded again. '"The cart is shaken all to pieces, and the rugged road is at its end."'

ACTIVITY 125

A linguist goes to a party

Deborah Tannen is well known for her contribution to language and gender studies. Two of her books, *You Just Don't Understand* and *From Nine To Five*, focus attention on differences in the ways that men and women talk, and on power aspects of everyday conversations at work and in the home. Prior to these books, she wrote *Conversational Style: Analyzing Talk Among Friends* (Ablex Publishing, 1984), in which she analyses and discusses tape recordings made at a Thanksgiving party she attended in Berkeley, California.

Her work is not only interesting but very accessible. You could easily do a more modest study of your own to be written up as an article or as research for a short story about party talk. First, read our summary of her investigation.

The party she attended was made up of five middle class, university educated Americans and one Londoner. Three of them, including Tannen, were New York Jews; four were male, two female. Three were heterosexual, three homosexual. All were friends of varying degrees of acquaintance. Their conversation could have shifted from one topic, one person to another or it could have been dominated by a variety of topics and by different people. What happened in fact was that the New Yorkers completely dominated the talk from start to finish. Asked about the conversation several months later, the non-New Yorkers recalled the conversation as typical of New Yorkers, and said they felt 'out of their element' and 'couldn't get a word in edgeways'.

Tannen analysed her tapes very closely, and discovered:

- New Yorkers expect shorter pauses between turns taken than most other people do
- New Yorkers said nearly twice as much as the others
- New Yorkers disclose personal details about themselves expecting a similar response
- New Yorkers talk in a 'fast, unrelenting style'

She concluded that despite the fact that the conversation took place in California, and that only three people were New Yorkers, the talk quickly took on 'the high involvement style of native New Yorkers' with its preference for personal topics. When asked later, the New Yorkers thought the other members of the party uncommunicative.

[a statistic: the New Yorkers spoke 17,759 words, the others, 9,097]

Think about parties or occasions you have attended where social talk has been expected, or think about a group of people you know, who tend to dominate conversations.

Write a sketch, or a scene in a novel, written from the point of view of someone who feels out of their element. It could take a dramatic turn of events!

ACTIVITY 126

A novelist reflects on things people say

The following excerpt is the beginning of a short story by Mavis Gallant, entitled *Voices Lost In Snow*. It comes from a collection, *Overhead In A Balloon and Other Stories* (Faber, 1989). The storyteller starts off with some first person reflections on how adults talk to children (see our comments on pragmatic aspects of a child's acquisition of language in Chapter 1).

First, read the passage and comment on how apt it is to your own experience.

Next, look at the final paragraph and explain why the author has not only shifted into the third person but even drawn the reader's

attention to it. It is fairly infrequent for a fiction writer to comment explicitly on her artistic choices. What do you think she means by, 'the only authentic voices I have belong to the dead'?

Finally, write a short story of your own, beginning with a reflection or observation on something you have noticed about the things people habitually or automatically say. Make your story an illustration of your opening reflection. It doesn't have to be about a child and adults; it could be about lovers, an employee and an employer, a student and a teacher, or just friends. Pay special attention to how they talk, and make sure you have worked out a satisfactory ending.

Halfway between our two great wars, parents whose own early years had been shaped with Edwardian firmness were apt to lend a tone of finality to quite simple remarks: 'Because I say so' was the answer to 'Why?,' and a child's response to 'What did I just tell you?' could seldom be anything but 'Not to' – not to say, do, touch, remove, go out, argue, reject, eat, pick up, open, shout, appear to sulk, appear to be cross. Dark riddles filled the corners of life because no enlightenment was thought required. Asking questions was 'being tiresome,' while persistent curiosity got one nowhere, at least nowhere of interest. How much has changed? Observe the drift of words descending from adult to child – the fall of personal questions, observations, unnecessary instructions. Before long the listener seems blanketed. He must hear the voice as authority muffled, a hum through snow. The tone has changed – it may be coaxing, even plaintive – but the words have barely altered. They still claim the ancient right-of-way through a young life.

'Well, old cock,' said my father's friend Archie McEwen, meeting him one Saturday in Montreal. 'How's Charlotte taking life in the country?' Apparently no one had expected my mother to accept the country in winter.

'Well, old cock,' I repeated to a country neighbor, Mr. Bainwood. 'How's life?' What do you suppose it meant to me, other than a kind of weathervane? Mr. Bainwood thought it over, then came round to our house and complained to my mother.

'It isn't blasphemy,' she said, not letting him have much satisfaction from the complaint. Still, I had to apologize. 'I'm sorry' was a ritual habit with even less meaning than 'old cock.' 'Never say that again,' my mother said after he had gone.

'Why not?'

'Because I've just told you not to.'

'What does it mean?'
'Nothing.'
It must have been after yet another 'nothing' that one summer's day I ran screaming around a garden, tore the heads off tulips, and – no, let another voice finish it; the only authentic voices I have belong to the dead: '. . . then she *ate* them.'

A linguist goes to the theatre

For many years, linguistic approaches to literary texts were concerned almost wholly with prose fiction and poetry. Playscripts seemed rather peculiar, hybrid texts, not real conversation on the one hand, and not designed for readers, on the other. They are of course performance texts, speech as action, and as such are ideal for linguistic analysis. It wasn't until methods for describing what goes on in everyday conversation became well established that linguists began to analyse dramatic texts.

Interestingly enough, some of the most useful ideas have come via the work of linguists analysing the ways in which adults talk to children and the ways in which talk goes on in school classrooms. M. C. Ward's *Them Children: A Study in Language Learning* (Holt, Rinehart and Winston, 1972) is one American study that has proved influential, while in Britain, Sinclair and Coulthard's, *Towards An Analysis of Discourse* (OUP, 1975) has proved an important ground-breaking study. We have introduced them in this chapter rather than the last one because we want to demonstrate how a linguist, Deirdre Burton, applies concepts of conversation analysis to dialogue in dramatic texts. In her book, *Dialogue and Discourse* (RKP, 1980), she focuses attention on two plays, one of which is *The Dumb Waiter* by Harold Pinter (1957). It's a short play lasting about 40 minutes. Excerpts are provided in the next activity, but it will help you considerably if you acquire a copy of the play in order to follow up more of Deirdre Burton's analysis.

We strongly recommend you to read the play because Pinter is the dramatist par excellence when it comes to turning everyday, trivial remarks into something puzzling and slightly fantastic, yet disturbingly 'real'.

There is another example of his work in Chapter 5.

The Dumb Waiter is about two characters, Gus and Ben. We are not exactly sure what is going on (as is often the case in real life!) but it is clear from the way the two talk that Gus is undoubtedly dominated by Ben, and that there is something sinister but unspecified in the background. Burton points out, for example, that Ben treats Gus rather like a child and she applies five concepts from Ward's study of adult/child conversations to throw some light on the relationship between Ben and Gus.
The concepts are:

– initiation
– questioning
– requesting speaker's rights

- requesting permission
- volunteering information.

Here are some examples of each of these in action:

GUS: He's laid on some very nice crockery this time, I'll say that. It's sort of striped. There's a white stripe.
(Ben reads)
It's very nice, I'll say that.
(Ben turns the page)

Gus continues to initiate conversation but Ben ignores him.

GUS: What time is he getting in touch?
(Ben reads)
What time is he getting in touch?
BEN: What's the matter with you? It could be any time. Any time.

Routinely, Ben treats Gus's questions as a nuisance.

GUS: I asked you a question.
BEN: Enough.
GUS: I asked you before. Who moved in? I asked you. . . .
BEN: (hunched up) Shut up.

No speaker's rights for Gus!

GUS: I want to ask you something.
BEN: What are you doing out there?

GUS: Eh, I've been meaning to ask you.
BEN: What is it now?

In these instances, and frequently throughout the play, Ben makes Gus out to be a nagging nuisance, which is quite unjustifiable. Deborah Tannen also observes this strategy as one characteristic of many husbands toward their wives.

GUS: That's what I was wondering about.
BEN: What?
GUS: The job.
BEN: What job?
GUS: (tentatively) I thought you might know something.
(Ben looks at him)
I thought perhaps – I mean – have you got any idea who it's going to be tonight?
BEN: Who what's going to be?
(They look at each other)
GUS: (at length) Who it's going to be.
(Silence)
BEN: Are you feeling alright?
GUS: Sure.
BEN: Go and make the tea.
GUS: Yes, sure.

Ben is clearly in possession of information that Gus needs; his unwillingness to volunteer that information puts Gus at considerable disadvantage, a position in which children are frequently placed. Throughout the play this happens, and Gus frequently speaks at length to fill in the silences left by Gus's uncommunicativeness.

Burton also includes a statistical check in her stylistic analysis of the play, observing that Ben utters 66 *directives* in the course of the play, and Gus only four, three of which are ignored by Ben totally. Directives tell people what to do. She divides them into those that are explicit and *unmitigated* (blunt, if you like):

E.g. 'Stop wondering', 'Go and make the tea', 'Let me see that', 'Don't do that', 'Shut up'.

Implicit and mitigated directives (softer, more polite forms) are the following:

E.g. 'What about the tea?' 'You'd better get ready', 'You shouldn't shout like that' 'You'll have to wait'.

Directives are part of Sinclair and Coulthard's descriptive framework which also includes the following concepts applied by Burton:

- **Marker** (words like 'Well' 'OK' 'Now . . .' 'Good' signifying that a speaker is about to initiate something or marking a boundary point in a conversation such as a conclusion or a pause for thought).
- **Summons** (e.g. the use of the addressee's name in order to get attention, or an exaggerated cough).
- **Silent stress** (a pause for effect, often used in conjunction with a marker or a summons).
- **Starter** (a statement, question or command to get an initiation going).
- **Metastatement** (don't be put off by this term! which describes explicit references by a speaker to the conversation itself e.g. 'Shall I go on?' 'I have to ask you a delicate question.' 'Can you hear alright?'). Magnus Magnussen makes a metastatement everytime he says, 'I've started, so I'll finish'.
- **Elicitation** (using a question or a command to get another person to make a response).
- **Accusation** (an implicit or explicit request for an apology or an excuse).
- **Acceptance** (affirmative response in the form of 'Yes' 'I see' 'Getaway!' 'Uhuh' 'Right!').
- **Prompt** (reinforcing, encouraging expressions, e.g. 'Go on' 'Hurry up' 'Yes' [with rising intonation]).
- **Evaluation** (a comment on the appropriateness or truth of what has just been uttered).

ACTIVITY 127

Gambits, ploys and strategies

Look through any literary passages in this book that contain stretches of dialogue and see if you can find other examples of the features listed above. Look out also for instances of the authors themselves making a metastatement, i.e. a statement about the speech itself. Conrad, for example does it in *The Secret Sharer* excerpt when he says: 'my first words were prompted'.

It's not an exhaustive list and you could add one or two of your own. We would add 'recapitulation', which is fairly self-explanatory and 'repetition'. It is interesting to note that Sinclair and Coulthard refer to these features of conversation as 'acts'; they are things people do with words, which makes them useful for describing what people are doing in dramatic dialogue and in conversations in novels. It provides the start of a vocabulary for writing about interactions.

In the previous chapter, we suggested four concept areas in which you could raise questions about texts. So far as stylistic analysis is concerned, it is the raising of questions that most often leads to interesting things to say. In this chapter you have been introduced to some more ideas that may be applied to literary texts. At first you will be looking for features of a text that exemplify these ideas, e.g. use of directives, asking questions or topic initiation. Beware though that you don't just become a feature spotter. If that is all you do, e.g. he asks seven questions, or 'there are no directives', or 'she gives negative evaluations to most of his remarks', then a reader (e.g. examiner) is perfectly justified in asking, 'So what?' You must move on to show how the features you have noticed help you to a fuller understanding and interpretation of the text, and possibly of human behaviour too, a prime concern of literature.

Deirdre Burton's close analysis and quantification of Ben's domination over Gus leads her to notice something at the end of the play that suggests an interesting interpretation. In general, Ben and Gus perform a kind of double act, their roles not unlike those of Laurel and Hardy or Morcambe and Wise, only without the warmth or the knockabout comedy. At the end however, the messages that come from the Dumb Waiter begin to rattle Ben. (A dumb waiter is a small hand operated lift set in a wall for hauling food up from the kitchen to a dining room.) He starts to panic and lose his dominating role. The messages summon Ben to do crazy things which he does, eager to please. When the Dumb Waiter returns again, demanding Chinese food, Ben temporarily treats Gus as an equal, even a superior, asking him for information which neither of them can supply. Burton concludes that after thirty-five minutes of clearly defined dominant and subservient roles, both are now subservient to someone higher up in the organisation, and far from being meaningless, the play seems like a parable about the management of modern organisations. Her interpretation is a good example of the way in which linguistic and literary observations work very well together.

ACTIVITY 128

'Mend your speech a little, lest you mar your fortunes'

In this activity you are going to look in detail at the way people talk to each other in the opening scene of Shakespeare's *King Lear*. Make sure you have a copy of the play to hand. The quotation at the start of this activity is spoken by King Lear, and not only serves as an ironic motto for the whole scene, but also as a reminder of how important it is to get the pragmatics right in real life as well as on the stage.

Remember too, that by 'people' here, we mean:

- the inventions of an author
- re-creations in the mind of a reader
- (on stage) performances by actors.

This may seem rather obvious, but when the art is of such quality as in *King Lear*, it is easy to forget that the characters and what they say are entirely authorial constructions. Sometimes the verb 'authored' is used, which sounds slightly odd but which contains a key idea, namely that somebody 'did it' or 'made it happen'. At the end of *The Dumb Waiter* we find that there is somebody higher up, pulling Ben's strings. Ultimately, the person pulling all the strings is the playwright, Harold Pinter, just as Shakespeare pulls the strings of *King Lear*.

Read the scene through first and then go through again, writing a detailed commentary on the dialogue. You do not need to do this line-by-line, but think of your commentary as a kind of flow chart. Use any terms that you think are useful. We have made a start:

The scene (and the play) begins with Kent, Gloucester and Edmund. Kent speaks the first words of the play accompanied by members of the Gloucester family, and it is interesting to note that this is matched by the very last scene and speeches of the play, in which Kent again is addressing a member of the Gloucester family. This kind of device is called 'framing', whereby, rather in the manner of a picture frame or book ends, the whole of the play is topped and tailed. (Bear in mind too, the popular use of the word 'framed' to mean manipulating an innocent person into a compromising or guilty situation. Has it ever happened to you?!)

Kent makes a political observation which is amplified by Gloucester. His question that follows is a familiar dramatic device for turning attention to another character, the villain Edmund. Yes, Shakespeare can't resist a pun on 'conceive', but notice the light touch with which Edmund's bastardy is introduced. Notice too, the elaborate courtesy of the rest of the conversation, partly to do with the formal, courtly style appropriate to the context, and partly to contrast with later plain speaking. The opening political gossip or chat is brought to an end by the ceremonious arrival of Lear, whose first utterance is a command (unmitigated imperative). The long speech that follows is predominantly in the first person plural (the royal 'we'), but notice the use of the first person singular in, 'Tell me, my daughters …' Could this be a significant lexico-grammatical item, to be explained by a different context or purpose? It may be worth keeping an eye on any pronoun shifts in Lear's speeches.

And so on …

Voices in poetry

The last activity in this chapter turns to poetry.

There follows a series of poetic excerpts arranged in chronological order, in which poets have chosen a conversational or dialogic form in which to express what they wish to say.

Read the poems and note the various ways that poets represent speech in their poems. How does the use of speech forms and characteristics affect your response?

You may find it helpful to make comparisons with other poems in this book which are not dialogic, or which do not make obvious use of features of conversation.

Don't forget the poet's own voice which will be there in every poem, however hidden or elusive. One question you will need to consider, for example, is what is the point of using other people's voices when you have a perfectly good one of your own?

(i) The Book of Job (Bible)
The Book of Job is a long debate in which the exchanges continue for something like 40 chapters of argument initiated by Job's opening speech, 'Let the day perish wherein I was born'.

Chapter 40
Moreover the Lord answered Job, and said,

'Shall he that contendeth with the Almighty instruct him?
He that reproveth God, let him answer it.'

Then Job answered the Lord, and said,

'Behold, I am vile; what shall I answer thee?
    I will lay mine hand upon my mouth.
Once have I spoken; but I will not answer:
    yea, twice; but I will proceed no further.'

Then answered the Lord unto Job out of the whirlwind, and said,

'Gird up thy loins now like a man:
    I will demand of thee, and declare thou unto me.
Wilt thou also disannul my judgment?
    wilt thou condemn me, that thou mayest be righteous?
Hast thou an arm like God?
    or canst thou thunder with a voice like him?

'Deck thyself now with majesty and excellency;
    and array thyself with glory and beauty.
Cast abroad the rage of thy wrath:
    and behold every one that is proud, and abase him.
Look on every one that is proud, and bring him low;
    and tread down the wicked in their place.
Hide them in the dust together;
    and bind their faces in secret.
Then will I also confess unto thee
    that thine own right hand can save thee.

(ii) Ninth century Irish saga (trns. by modern poet, Thomas Kinsella)

Exile of the Sons of Uisliu

What caused the exile of the sons of Uisliu?

It is soon told.

The men of Ulster were drinking in the house of Conchorbor's storyteller, Fedlimid mac Daill. Fedlimid's wife was overseeing everything and looking after them all. She was full with child. Meat and drink were passed round, and a drunken uproar shook the place. When they were ready to sleep the woman went to her bed. As she crossed the floor of the house the child screamed in her womb and was heard all over the enclosure. At that scream everyone in the house started up, ready to kill. Sencha mac Ailella said:

'No one move! Bring the woman here. We'll see what caused this noise.'

So the woman was brought before them. Her husband Fedlimid said:

> 'Woman,
> what was that fierce shuddering sound
> furious in your troubled womb?
> The weird uproar at your waist
> hurts the ears of all who hear it.
> My heart trembles at some great terror
> or some cruel injury.'

She turned distracted to the seer Cathbad:

> 'Fair-faced Cathbad, hear me
> – prince, pure, precious crown,
> grown huge in druid spells.
> I can't find the fair words
> that would shed the light of knowledge
> for my husband Fedlimid,
> even though it was the hollow
> of my own womb that howled.
> No woman knows what her womb bears.'

Then Cathbad said:

> 'A woman with twisted yellow tresses,
> green-irised eyes of great beauty
> and cheeks flushed like the foxglove
> howled in the hollow of your womb.
> I say that whiter than the snow
> is the white treasure of her teeth;
> Parthian-red, her lip's lustre.
> Ulster's chariot-warriors
> will deal many a blow for her.
> There howled in your troubled womb
> a tall, lovely, long-haired woman.
> Heroes will contend for her,
> high kings beseech on her account;
> then, west of Conchorbor's kingdom
> a heavy harvest of fighting men.
> High queens will ache with envy
> to see those lips of Parthian-red
> opening on her pearly teeth,
> and see her pure perfect body.'

Cathbad placed his hand on the woman's belly and the baby wriggled under it. 'Yes,' he said, 'there is a girl there. Derdriu shall be her name. She will bring evil.' Then the daughter was born and Cathbad said:

> 'Much damage, Derdriu, will follow
> your high fame and fair visage:
> Ulster in your time tormented,
> demure daughter of Fedlimid.
>
> And later, too, jealousy
> will dog you, woman like a flame,
> and later still – listen well –
> the three sons of Uisliu exiled.
>
> Then again, in your lifetime,
> a bitter blow struck in Emain.
> Remorse later for that ruin
> wrought by the great son of Roech;
>
> Fergus exiled out of Ulster
> through your fault, fatal woman,
> and the much-wept deadly wound
> of Fiachna, Conchobor's son.
>
> Your fault also, fatal woman,
> Gerrce felled, Illadan's son,
> and a crime that no less cries out,
> the son of Durthacht, Eogan, struck.
>
> Harsh, hideous deeds done
> in anger at Ulster's high king,
> and little graves everywhere
> – a famous tale, Derdriu.'

'Kill the child!' the warriors said.

'No,' Conchobor said. 'The girl will be taken away tomorrow. I'll have her reared for me. This woman I'll keep to myself.'

The men of Ulster didn't dare speak against him.

And so it was done. She was reared by Conchobor and grew into the loveliest woman in all Ireland.

(iii) Twelfth century Scottish ballad

Bonny Barbara Allan

> It was in and about the Martinmas time,[1]
> When the green leaves were a falling,
> That Sir John Graeme, in the West Country,
> Fell in love with Barbara Allan.
>
> He sent his man down through the town,
> To the place where she was dwelling:
> 'O haste and come to my master dear,
> Gin[2] ye be Barbara Allan.'
>
> O hooly,[3] hooly rose she up,
> To the place where he was lying,
> And when she drew the curtain by,
> 'Young man, I think you're dying.'

'O it's I'm, sick, and very, very sick,
And 'tis a' for Barbara Allan':
'O the better for me ye's[4] never be,
Tho your heart's blood were a spilling.

'O dinna ye mind,[5] young man,' said she,
'When ye was in the tavern a drinking,
That ye made the healths[6] gae round and round,
And slighted Barbara Allan?'

He turned his face unto the wall,
And death was with him dealing:
'Adieu, adieu, my dear friends all,
And be kind to Barbara Allan.'

And slowly, slowly raised she up,
And slowly, slowly left him,
And sighing said, she coud not stay,
Since death of life had reft[7] him.

She had not gane[8] a mile but twa,[9]
When she heard the dead-bell ringing,
And every jow[10] that the dead-bell geid,[11]
It cry'd, 'Woe to Barbara Allan!'

'O mother, mother, make my bed!
O make it saft[12] and narrow!
Since my love died for me to-day,
I'll die for him to-morrow.'

[1] November feast of St Martin	[2] If	[3] Slowly	[4] You shall	[5] Do You Not Remember?	[6] Toasts
[7] Bereft; deprived.	[8] Gone.	[9] Two.	[10] Stroke.	[11] Gave; made.	[12] Soft.

(iv) The Knight's Interruption of the Monk's Tale
From *The Canterbury Tales*.

'Stop!' cried the Knight. 'No more of this, good sir!
You have said plenty, and much more, for sure,
For only a little such lugubriousness
Is plenty for a lot of folk, I guess.
I say for me it is a great displeasure,
When men have wealth and comfort in good measure,
To hear how they have tumbled down the slope,
And the opposite is a solace and a hope,
As when a man begins in low estate
And climbs the ladder and grows fortunate,
And stands there firm in his prosperity.
That is a welcome thing, it seems to me,
And of such things it would be good to tell.'
'Well said,' our Host declared. 'By St. Paul's bell,
You speak the truth; this Monk's tongue is too loud.
He told how fortune covered with a cloud –
I don't know what-all; and of tragedy
You heard just now, and it's no remedy,
When things are over and done with, to complain.
Besides, as you have said, it is a pain
To hear of misery; it is distressing.

Sir Monk, no more, as you would have God's blessing.
This company is all one weary sigh.
Such talking isn't worth a butterfly,
For where's the amusement in it, or the game?
And so, Sir Monk, or Don Pierce by your name,
I beg you heartily, tell us something else.
Truly, but for the jingling of your bells
That from your bridle hang on every side,
By Heaven's King, who was born for us and died,
I should long since have tumbled down in sleep,
Although the mud had never been so deep,
And then you would have told your tale in vain;
For certainly, as these learned men explain,
When his audience have turned their backs away,
It doesn't matter what a man may say.
I know well I shall have the essence of it
If anything is told here for our profit.
A tale of hunting, sir, pray share with us.'
    'No,' said the Monk, 'I'll not be frivolous.
Let another tell a tale, as I have told.'
    Then spoke our Host, with a rude voice and bold,
And said to the Nun's Priest, 'Come over here,
You priest, come hither, you Sir John, draw near!
Tell us a thing to make our spirits glad.
Be cheerful, though the jade you ride is bad.
What if your horse is miserable and lean?
If he will carry you, don't care a bean!
Keep up a joyful heart, and look alive.'
    'Yes, Host,' he answered, 'as I hope to thrive,
If I weren't merry, I know I'd be reproached.'
And with no more ado his tale he broached,
And this is what he told us, every one,
This precious priest, this goodly man, Sir John.

Geoffrey Chaucer, 1344–1400

(v) *A Dialogue Between God and the Soul*

Love bade me welcome: yet my soul drew back,
    Guiltie of dust and sinne.
But quick-ey'd Love, observing me grow slack
    From my first entrance in,
Drew nearer to me, sweetly questioning
    If I lack'd any thing.

'A guest,' I answer'd, 'worthy to be here':
    Love said, 'You shall be he.'
'I the unkinde, ungratefull? Ah, my deare,
    I cannot look on thee.'
Love took my hand, and smiling did reply,
    'Who made the eyes but I?'

'Truth Lord, but I have marr'd them: let my shame
    Go where it doth deserve.'
'And know you not,' sayes Love, 'who bore the blame?'
    'My deare, then I will serve.'

'You must sit down, sayes Love, 'and taste my meat':
   So I did sit and eat.

George Herbert, 1593–1633

(vi) The Passionate Shepherd to His Love ...

Come live with me and be my love,
And we will all the pleasures prove
That valleys, groves, hills, and fields,
Woods, or steepy mountain yields.

And we will sit upon the rocks,
Seeing the shepherds feed their flocks,
By shallow rivers to whose falls
Melodious birds sing madrigals.

And I will make thee beds of roses
And a thousand fragrant posies,
A cap of flowers, and a kirtle
Embroidered all with leaves of myrtle.

A gown made of the finest wool
Which from our pretty lambs we pull;
Fair lined slippers for the cold,
With buckles of the purest gold

A belt of straw and ivy buds,
With coral clasps and amber studs;
And if these pleasures may thee move,
Come live with me, and be my love.

The shepherd swains shall dance and sing
For thy delight each May morning
If these delights thy mind may move,
Then live with me and be my love.

Christopher Marlowe, 1564–93

(vii) The Nymph's Reply to the Shepherd

If all the world and love were young,
And truth in every shepherd's tongue,
These pretty pleasures might me move
To live with thee and be thy love.

Time drives the flocks from field to fold,
When rivers rage and rocks grow cold,
And Philomel becometh dumb;
The rest complain of cares to come.

The flowers do fade, and wanton fields
To wayward winter reckoning yields;
A honey tongue, a heart of gall,
Is fancy's spring, but sorrow's fall.

Thy gowns, thy shoes, thy beds of roses,
Thy cap, thy kirtle, and thy posies
Soon break, soon wither, soon forgotten,

In folly ripe, in reason rotten.

Thy belt of straw and ivy buds,
Thy coral clasps and amber studs,
All these in me no means can move
To come to thee and be thy love.

But could you last and love still breed,
Had joys no date nor age no need,
Then these delights my mind might move
To live with thee and be thy love.

[Ralegh's poem was written as a 'reply' to Marlowe's]

Sir Walter Ralegh, 1552–1618

(viii) from *A Dialogue Between the Resolved Soul and Created Pleasure*

PLEASURE   All this fair and soft and sweet,
     Which scatteringly doth shine,
     Shall within one beauty meet,
     And she be only thine.

SOUL   If things of sight such heavens be,
     What heavens are those we cannot see?

PLEASURE   Wheresoe'er thy foot shall go
     The minted gold shall lie;
     Till thou purchase all below,
     And want new worlds to buy.

SOUL   Were't not a price who'd value gold?
     And that's worth nought that can be sold.

PLEASURE   Wilt thou all the glory have
     That war or peace commend?
     Half the world shall be thy slave,
     The other half thy friend.

SOUL   What friends, if to my self untrue?
     What slaves, unless I captive you?

PLEASURE   Thou shalt know each hidden cause,
     And see the future time;
     Try what depth the centre draws,
     And then to heaven climb.

SOUL   None thither mounts by the degree
     Of knowledge, but humility.

CHORUS   *Triumph, triumph, victorious soul;*
     The world has not one pleasure more:
     The rest does lie beyond the pole,
     And is thine everlasting store.

Andrew Marvell 1621–78

(ix) from *A Dialogue Between The Soul and The Body*

BODY Oh, who shall me deliver whole
From bonds of this tyrannic soul?
Which stretched upright, impales me so
That mine own precipice I go;
And warms and moves this needless frame,
A fever could but do the same.
And, wanting where its spite to try,
Has made me live to let me die.
A body that could never rest,
Since this ill spirit it possessed.

SOUL What magic could me thus confine
Within another's grief to pine?
Where whatsoever it complain,
I feel, that cannot feel, the pain.
And all my care itself employs,
That to preserve which me destroys.
Constrained not only to endure
Diseases, but, what's worse, the cure;
And ready oft the port to gain,
Am shipwrecked into health again.

BODY But physic yet could never reach
The maladies thou me dost teach:
Whom first the cramp of hope does tear,
And then the palsy shakes of fear;
The pestilence of love does heat,
Or hatred's hidden ulcer eat.
Joy's cheerful madness does perplex,
Or sorrow's other madness vex;
Which knowledge forces me to know,
And memory will not forgo.
What but a soul could have the wit
To build me up for sin so fit?
So architects do square and hew
Green trees that in the forest grew.

Andrew Marvell 1621–78

(x) from *On the Receipt of My Mother's Picture out of Norfolk, the gift of my cousin Ann Bodham*

OH that those lips had language! Life has passed
With me but roughly since I heard thee last.
Those lips are thine – thy own sweet smiles I see,
The same that oft in childhood solaced me;
Voice only fails, else, how distinct they say,
'Grieve not, my child, chase all thy fears away!'
The meek intelligence of those dear eyes
(Blest be the art that can immortalize,
The art that baffles time's tyrannic claim
To quench it) here shines on me still the same.
  Faithful remembrancer of one so dear,
Oh welcome guest, though unexpected, here!

Who bidd'st me honour with an artless song,
Affectionate, a mother lost so long,
I will obey, not willingly alone,
But gladly, as the precept were her own;
And, while that face renews my filial grief,
Fancy shall weave a charm for my relief –
Shall steep me in Elysian reverie,
A momentary dream, that thou art she.

William Cowper, 1731–1800

(xi) from *The Hunting of the Snark*

The Baker's Tale

THEY roused him with muffins – they roused him with ice –
    They roused him with mustard and cress –
They roused him with jam and judicious advice –
    They set him conundrums to guess.

When at length he sat up and was able to speak,
    His sad story he offered to tell;
And the Bellman cried 'Silence! Not even a shriek!'
    And excitedly tingled his bell.

There was silence supreme! Not a shriek, not a scream,
    Scarcely even a howl or a groan,
As the man they called 'Ho!' told his story of woe
    In an antediluvian tone.

'My father and mother were honest, though poor –'
    'Skip all that!' cried the Bellman in haste.
'If it once becomes dark, there's no chance of a Snark –
    We have hardly a minute to waste!'

'I skip forty years,' said the Baker in tears,
    'And proceed without further remark
To the day when you took me aboard of your ship
    To help you in hunting the Snark.

'A dear uncle of mine (after whom I was named)
    Remarked, when I bade him farewell –'
'Oh, skip your dear uncle!' the Bellman exclaimed,
    As he angrily tingled his bell.

'He remarked to me then,' said that mildest of men,
    "If your Snark be a Snark, that is right:
Fetch it home by all means – you may serve it with greens
    And it's handy for striking a light.

"You may seek it with thimbles – and seek it with care –
    You may hunt it with forks and hope;
You may threaten its life with a railway-share;
    You may charm it with smiles and soap – " '

('That's exactly the method,' the Bellman bold
    In a hasty parenthesis cried,
'That's exactly the way I have always been told
    That the capture of Snarks should be tried!')

' "But oh, beamish nephew, beware of the day,
  If your Snark be a Boojum! For then
You will softly and suddenly vanish away,
  And never be met with again!"

'It is this, it is this that oppresses my soul,
  When I think of my uncle's last words:
And my heart is like nothing so much as a bowl
  Brimming over with quivering curds!

'It is this, it is this –' 'We have had that before!'
  The Bellman indignantly said.
And the Baker replied 'Let me say it once more.
  It is this, it is this that I dread!

'I engage with the Snark – every night after dark –
  In a dreamy delirious fight:
I serve it with greens in those shadowy scenes,
  And I use it for striking a light:

'But if ever I meet with a Boojum, that day,
  In a moment (of this I am sure),
I shall softly and suddenly vanish away –
  And the notion I cannot endure!'

Lewis Carroll, 1832–98

(xii) Tommy

I WENT into a public-'ouse to get a pint o' beer,
The publican 'e up an' sez 'We serve no red-coats here.'
The girls be'ind the bar they laughed an' giggled fit to die,
I outs into the street again an' to myself sez I:
    O it's Tommy this, an' Tommy that, an' 'Tommy, go away';
    But it's 'Thank you, Mister Atkins,' when the band begins to play –
    The band begins to play, my boys, the band begins to play,
    O it's 'Thank you, Mister Atkins,' when the band begins to play.

I went into a theatre as sober as could be,
They gave a drunk civilian room, but 'adn't none for me;
They sent me to the gallery or round the music-'alls,
But when it comes to fightin', Lord! they'll shove me in the stalls!
    For it's Tommy this, an' Tommy that, an' 'Tommy, wait outside';
    But it's 'Special train for Atkins' when the trooper's on the tide –
    The troopship's on the tide, my boys, the troopship's on the tide,
    O it's 'Special train for Atkins' when the trooper's on the tide.

Yes, makin' mock o' uniforms that guard you while you sleep
Is cheaper than them uniforms, an' they're starvation cheap;
An' hustlin' drunken soldiers when they're goin' large a bit
Is five times better business than paradin' in full kit.
    Then it's Tommy this, an' Tommy that, an' 'Tommy, 'ow's yer soul?'
    But it's 'Thin red line of 'eroes' when the drums begin to roll –
    The drums begin to roll, my boys, the drums begin to roll,
    O it's 'Thin red line of 'eroes' when the drums begin to roll.

We arent' no thin red 'eroes, nor we aren't no blackguards too,
But single men in barricks most remarkable like you;
An' if sometimes our conduck isn't all your fancy paints,
Why, single men in barricks don't grow into plaster saints;
   While it's Tommy this, an' Tommy that, an' 'Tommy, fall be'ind,'
   But it's 'Please to walk in front, sir,' when there's trouble in the wind —
   Ther'es trouble in the wind, my boys, there's trouble in the wind,
   O it's 'Please to walk in front, sir,' when there's trouble in the wind.

You talk o' better food for us, an' schools, an' fires, an' all:
We'll wait for extry rations if you treat us rational.
Don't mess about the cook-room slops, but prove it to our face
The Widow's Uniform is not the soldier-man's disgrace.
   For it's Tommy this, an' Tommy that, an' 'Chuck him out, the brute!'
   But it's 'Saviour of 'is country' when the guns begin to shoot;
   An' it's Tommy this, an' Tommy that, an' anything you please;
   An' Tommy ain't a bloomin' fool — you bet that Tommy sees!

                                              Rudyard Kipling, 1865–1936

(xiii) From *The Waste Land*

        'My nerves are bad to-night. Yes, bad. Stay with me.
'Speak to me. Why do you never speak. Speak.
        'What are you thinking of? What thinking? What?
'I never know what you are thinking. Think.'

        I think we are in rats' alley
Where the dead men lost their bones.
        'What is that noise?'
                        The wind under the door.
'What is that noise now? What is the wind doing?'
                        Nothing again nothing.
                                'Do
'You know nothing? Do you see nothing? Do you remember
'Nothing?'

        I remember
Those are pearls that were his eyes.
'Are you alive, or not? Is there nothing in your head?'
                                But
O O O O that Shakespeherian Rag —
It's so elegant
So intelligent
'What shall I do now? What shall I do?'
'I shall rush out as I am, and walk the street
'With my hair down, so. What shall we do tomorrow?
'What shall we ever do?'
                        The hot water at ten.
And if it rains, a closed car at four.
And we shall play a game of chess,
Pressing lidless eyes and waiting for a knock upon the door.

        When Lil's husband got demobbed, I said —

I didn't mince my words, I said to her myself,
HURRY UP PLEASE IT'S TIME
Now Albert's coming back, make yourself a bit smart.
He'll want to know what you done with that money he gave you
To get yourself some teeth. He did, I was there.
You have them all out, Lil, and get a nice set,
He said, I swear, I can't bear to look at you.
And no more can't I, I said, and think of poor Albert,
He's been in the army four years, he wants a good time,
And if you don't give it him, there's others will, I said.
Oh is there, she said. Something o' that, I said.
Then I'll know who to thank, she said, and give me a straight look.
HURRY UP PLEASE IT'S TIME
If you don't like it you can get on with it, I said.
Others can pick and choose if you can't.
But if Albert makes off, it won't be for lack of telling.
You ought to be ashamed, I said, to look so antique.
(And her only thirty-one.)
I can't help it, she said, pulling a long face,
It's them pills I took, to bring it off, she said.
(She's had five already, and nearly died of young George.)
The chemist said it would be all right, but I've never been the same.
You are a proper fool, I said.
Well, if Albert won't leave you alone, there it is, I said,
What you get married for if you don't want children?
HURRY UP PLEASE IT'S TIME
Well, that Sunday Albert was home, they had a hot gammon,
And they asked me in to dinner, to get the beauty of it hot –
HURRY UP PLEASE IT'S TIME
HURRY UP PLEASE IT'S TIME
Goonight Bill. Goonight Lou. Goonight May. Goonight.
Ta ta. Goonight. Goonight.
Good night, ladies, good night, sweet ladies, good night, good night.

T. S. Eliot, 1888–1965.

(xiv) Alabama poem

if trees could talk
   wonder what they'd say
met an old man
   on the road late afternoon
   hat pulled over to shade
   his eyes
   jacket slumped over his
   shoulders
   told me 'girl! my hands seen
   more than all
   them books they got
   at tuskegee[1]'
   smiled at me
   half waved his hand
   walked on down the dusty road
met an old woman
   with a corncob pipe
   sitting and rocking
   on a spring evening

'sista' she called to me
'let me tell you – my feet
seen more than yo eyes
ever gonna read'
smiled at her and kept
on moving
gave it a thought and went
back to the porch
'I say gal!' she called down
'you a student at the institute?
better come here and study
these feet
i'm gonna cut a bunion off
soons I gets up'
i looked at her
she laughed at me
if trees would talk
wonder what they'd tell me

[1]Tuskegee Institute in Alabama.

Nikki Giovanni (b. 1943)

Getting the act together

We have devoted a whole chapter to ways of looking at talk in real life, and this chapter to applying the insights gained to talk in literature. Throughout the book we have stressed that the language resources available to novelists, poets and playwrights are no different from the ordinary resources of a common language available to any users for any purposes. It is the art that makes the difference, together with the contexts in which that art is enjoyed.

To conclude this chapter, we need to draw together more systematically those features that transform the familiar stuff of everyday life into literary art.

Look again at a traditional literary critical classification of the functions of dialogue in fiction:

– it reveals and differentiates character and motive
– it slackens or quickens the action
– it provides contrast or humour
– it pinpoints a moment.

All of these can be observed in the texts considered in this chapter. The characters of Sleary and Mr Gradgrind, and of Ben and Gus, are clearly revealed in the ways in which they speak, while their motivations are implied in what they actually say. Variety of pace in any narrative is desirable, but also necessary if subtle and gradual aspects of relationships are to be conveyed. Dialogue in a novel such as *The Go-Between* takes place in real time, that is to say in the time it would take, more or less, in real life. The things said are the action, whereas the narration of physical events (e.g. the cricket match, not included in the excerpt) can be conveyed equally vividly yet in a very short reading time. The opening scene of *King Lear* is all dialogue yet it is likely that you detected changes of pace at significant moments, e.g. the abrupt turning to other affairs after the banishment of Cordelia.

Contrast is provided by dialogue in all the excerpts here, while the humorous intention of the *Three Men In A Boat* excerpt is surely obvious even to those who do not enjoy this brand of humour.

Pin-pointing, or 'defining' a particular moment is a very important feature of both *Hard Times* excerpts, and especially of the exchanges between Lear and Cordelia.

Clearly then, the four functions are observable in the examples quoted, but we would add three more functions in the light of studies of spontaneous conversation in real life. These are:

– demonstrating relationships between characters as they speak
– providing an additional channel for conveying information to readers/theatre audiences/TV watchers
– creating a distinct sense of group or social identity.

The seven functions can be reorganised as follows:

– it reveals and differentiates character and motive
– it demonstrates relationships through interaction, the roles and status of characters
– it creates distinct impressions of group and social identity and of milieu
– it provides an additional channel for conveying information to audiences
– it quickens or slackens the pace of the action
– it provides contrasts and humour
– it pinpoints significant moments in the plot.

We don't regard this as an exhaustive list, but it is sufficient to provide detailed approaches to plays, narrative fiction and even poetry. You could work systematically through all of them with every text you are required to analyse stylistically, but it is a better practice to keep them all in the back of your mind, while the front of your mind concentrates on the three or four for which you can find clear exemplification.

Below, we have listed a number of terms for useful linguistic concepts that may be applied to conversations in real life. They are *descriptions* of everyday features that have been systematically studied. They are however, only descriptive terms that have caught on after being coined by a respected researcher. They are not laws, nor even fixed terms of measurement, like 'amp', 'volt', 'centimetre', or names for technical objects, e.g. 'fuel injector', ' amplifier', 'violin bow', 'vertibrae', 'software'. They are helpful ideas to be used with a mixture of confidence and caution. Using them is a bit like buying a replacement length of drainpipe and some brackets from B&Q: they are 90 per cent right for the job, but still need modifying to fit your own purposes. It's the bit of modifying that makes all the difference. As you look at these terms, see which ones may be appropriate to any of the seven functions above.

Finally, we have added a selection (from thousands) of adjectives and verbs useful for describing dialogue. As well as terminology (literary or linguistic) a versatile repertoire of mainstream vocabulary is equally useful, both for putting things into words precisely, and for scoring marks on examination papers.

Terminology

Address terms – how you refer to the person you are talking to, e.g. Sir, old cock, mate, Mr Brown, etc

Adjacency pairs – the way many conversations are built up of initiation/response utterances

Agenda – someone's intended topic of conversation, though an agenda can be hidden but implicit

Agreement or affirmative signals – making encouraging noises and using phrase like, 'I'm with you . . .'

Attention getting – sometimes referred to as 'summons', e.g. 'Are you sitting comfortably? Then I'll begin'

Backtracking – interrupting yourself to go back on something; more likely in spontaneous talk

Boundaries – points at which topic changes or natural breaks occur in a conversation; more than adjacency pairs

Closure – the closing or termination of a part or the whole of a conversation; often expresses power

Code – a way of talking that carries implied but shared meanings

Correction – either self correction (often and safe) or correcting other speaker (more confrontational)

Framing – prefacing and concluding what you have to say, putting it in a context

Formulaic expression – something utered automatically as a greeting, an apology, a sympathetic response

Imperative – mitigated (soft), e.g. 'If I could just have a little room . . .' or unmitigated, e.g. 'Get out of the way'

Implicature – a meaning that is implied in a remark or utterance but never stated

Initiator (and Initiating) – a remark or utterance that starts off a conversation or introduces a new topic

Intensifiers – words or phrases (usually adverbial, e.g. 'absolutely') that emphasise an utterance

Marker – a noise, word or phrase that marks a significant stage in a conversation

Negative evaluation – rejecting, scorning, disbelieving, censuring what someone has said

Non-fluency – frequently present in real life, rare and crafted in fiction, especially soap opera scripts

Orientation (and Reorientation) – focusing on the topic, sticking to the point, getting back to the point

Positive evaluation – complimenting, acknowledging, welcoming what someone else has to say

Requests – for clarification, repetition, elaboration

Sympathetic circularity – expressing identification with and friendship toward another speaker, e.g. 'Yes.'

Tag – a question or pronoun, for example, tagged onto the end of a remark, e.g. 'It's nice, isn't it?'

Topic setting – not unrelated to agenda though an agenda may be an intended sequence of topics

Transition relevance – how a conversation moves from one topic to another (relevant) one (coherence)

Turn taking – self explanatory process yet highly sophisticated, rule-governed behaviour

Symmetry – conversations may be between equals or the status of speakers may be asymmetrical, e.g. teacher/pupil, female/male, boss/employee, person with particular knowledge/person without it but needing it, nervous witness/aggressive barrister.

Pauses (or 'stressed silences') – they occur naturally in everyday speech for a variety of reasons; sometimes indicated in literature, sometimes supplied by actors, and sometimes need to be imagined by the reader.

Words in the mainstream of the English vocabulary but which are useful to apply to conversation in your own writing, in commentaries and in stylistics:

Adjectives: conciliatory, hesitant, inquisitorial, exploratory, confrontational, sardonic, measured, ineffectual, deferential, evasive.

Verbs: suggest, imply, exclaim, insinuate, elicit, concede, reiterate, resist

Adverbs: tentatively, confidentially, ingratiatingly, effusively, emphatically, relentlessly, guardedly.

ACTIVITY 129

Not what you say but the way you say it

Write a brief conversation of no more than three or four exchanges that illustrates one of the adjectives, verbs, adverbs above. Don't use the actual word, suggest it. See how successful you have been by asking a partner to identify which word or words you had in mind.

e.g. 'Er . . . excuse me . . . but I er . . . was wondering if . . . if . . .', began the man (tentatively).

'Cat got your tongue, has it?', she snapped. (sardonic tone of voice)

These are just a few possibilities for describing and interpreting people's speech behaviour and the tenor of conversations. For each one there are ten or more synonyms and antonyms, as you would discover in any decent sized thesaurus. You could explore nuances of meaning for the examples we have given you, and begin to develop your active repertoire of words that would bring both life and precision to your description of speech styles and effects. Look, for example, what a rich field of speech styles there is in the opening of *King Lear*. What are the right words to describe the differences in speech between Lear's three daughters? Or the shifts of mood in Lear's own speaking? the imperious, the ceremonious, the complacent, the incredulous, the pained, the angry, the petulant? All descriptions of ways of speaking, yet all indicative too of character and state of mind.

Commentaries on the texts

Activity 118: Hard Times

Notice the repetition of words ('Facts' and 'principle' 'nothing'). There is also grammatical patterning, another kind of repetition ('Plant nothing/root out ... everything' and 'This is the principle/this is the principle' and 'my own children/these children'). Note too the antonyms 'plant' and 'root out'. The address is formal ('sir') and the purpose is a mixture of instruction and sermonising. Gradgrind seems at war with unruly nature (root out everything else) and animal life, i.e. non-rational animals.

In the second excerpt Dickens' descriptions of the scene, and especially of Gradgrind himself, vividly complement the utilitarian use of language.

The third excerpt presents an alternative view of life and the world. Sleary's philosophy of education is more personal and all the more human for including horses. How do you react to his lisp? Is it an endearing imperfection – a bit of non-standard pronunciation – Dickens has highlighted? Buy why? For comic effect? And is that fair, from a modern politically correct point of view? To show Sleary's world of imperfections as preferable to Gradgrind's? Interestingly enough, and 150 years after *Hard Times*, Nescafe also chose to feature a lisp as an attention-getter in one of their national advertisements (shown opposite).

Excerpt four shows Gradgrind in action again: the classroom contrasted with the world of the circus. Pupils have numbers, family names like Sissy are not to be used and the linguistic style of teaching is one of interrogation. Notice that there are four negatives, one after the other: 'Sissy is not a name', 'We don't want to know ...', 'You mustn't tell ...', 'Girl number twenty unable to define a horse'.

The language spoken by Bitzer is the essence of utilitarianism, reduced entirely to facts.

The irony behind Gradgrind's words to Sissy, brought up in a circus, is heavy indeed: 'Now you know what a horse is'.

Activity 120: King Street Junior

Notice that the first remark is an acknowledgement of an unspoken request. Pragmatics includes such behaviour as 'hovering', a familiar enough way of communicating without actually speaking. Making a person speak first is a way of securing attention.

Note the technique of interruption between 'Look Chandra ...' and '... you had a cold' which creates a naturalistic effect in the dialogue. Notice

Figure 8.1 Nescafe advertisement

also the author's use of familiar school phrases: 'Please, sir', 'But sir ...' and 'Yes, sir', followed by an adverbial phrase that leaves no doubt about Chandra's tone of voice or his feelings; 'in a voice low with misery'!

Activity 121: Three Men in a Boat

The first excerpt is a set piece, a little bit of anthropomorphism for adults. Note the rather formal politeness in which the animals speak. It is unusual for a story teller to use a playscript format. What do you think is gained by it? Does the narrative lose anything?

The same technique is used again in the second excerpt. Notice though, that the non-spoken sections don't quite correspond to stage directions. They are the author's comments.

Activity 122: The Go-Between

The conversation between young Leo and Ted seems quite tense. There are a lot of questions for a start. Ted's are probing, Leo's inquisitive in a general way.

Note how complicity is gradually established between them.

Do you think that with very little alteration, the dialogue here would suit a film or TV version of the scene?

Activity 123: One Small Boy

The author uses phonetic spellings to convey something of regional accent. As in the Dickens passage, it adds not only good humour but a touch of familiarity and possibly warmth. Note how the speech is allowed to speak for itself. There are very few comments, adverbial or otherwise, from the author.

The humour consists of three elements:
- portrayal of schooldays (a staple of British comedy)
- accent as part of the characterisation
- language (i.e. the things people say!) is a ready made fount of humour

Activity 124: The Way Through the Woods

The first excerpt illustrates a style of police questioning. Morse sets a trap that works only too well. To what extent do you see Morse and Lewis here as a double act?[*]

In the second excerpt, language itself is highlighted. Do you find Morse's reference to grammar pedantic? Snobbish? The later comments on Dr Hobson's accent (Hobson's Choice?) suggest pleasure, even though Morse has been well and truly put in his place.

[*]Note the narrative gap allowing an abrupt change of scene but a continuation of the conversation.

9 Change and Continuity in English Language and Literature

For the times they are a' changin'

Language is a fact of life, and change is a fact of both life and language. Fashions in dress, car designs, eating habits, dance styles, popular music, graphic decoration, technology, interior décor, household goods and appliances, even humour, sexual mores, patterns of crime, and tastes in films and books are all subject to constant change. Everything is in a state of flux, said the Greek philosopher, Heraclitus, so we should not be surprised that change is in the nature of language too. Sometimes the changes are gradual, such as the hundred years or so it took for late medieval English to drop the pronunciation of initial 'k' in words like 'know', 'knife' and 'knee', or the more recent switch to using 'their' with a singular noun, as in 'Each child must put their coat on their own peg', to avoid the more cumbersome 'his or her' and also to get out of a linguistic gender trap. German speakers, however, still pronounce the initial 'k' in words such as 'knabe' (boy), 'Knie' (knee), 'knochel' (knuckle), 'Knopf' (button). Don't be surprised by this; stranger things have happened in the history of the world's languages. English is after all, an offspring of the Germanic family of languages, and a new generation frequently does things that are different from the ways of their parents. The famous writers of fairy stories, the Brothers Grimm, spent a lifetime studying the sound changes that occurred over centuries of Asian and European ancient history. During that time different peoples wandered and settled, developed their own identity and in turn, modified the sounds and the word content of a common ancestral language (Indo-European), to create the distinctive national languages we know today.

It is the spoken language that is more immediately susceptible to change. In thirty years or so since the 1950s, for example, large numbers of a new generation of speakers in the South-East of England have introduced a 'v' or an 'f' sound into words like 'whether' and 'nothing', replacing the more conventional 'th' sound. This kind of sound change, along with others, has created a new dialect known as Estuary English, in which 'cockney' pronunciations have replaced the traditional pronunciations that an earlier generation in Stewkley (i.e. pre-Milton Keynes) would have used. This 'contemporary' change seems less surprising once you know, for example, that the ancient Sanskrit word for father, 'pitar', migrated into Southern Europe becoming, variously, 'pater', 'padre', 'pere', 'patron', but in northern Europe, 'vater', 'faeder' and 'father' in different languages.

One of the Assessment Objectives (QCA requirement) for A level English Language and Literature is that you should understand 'change over time'. You need to distinguish between two kinds of time: one, the broad scale of worldwide language changes over thousands of years, including the two thousand years, or so, of English language developments (Historical Linguistics); two, contemporary changes taking place today and tomorrow. The fact is that every child is born into a changing language. It sometimes takes ten or twenty tears to notice changes that have occurred, but by then they are almost becoming 'historical'. The important thing is to be alert to changes going on in your own lifetime, your own lifestyle and in your own vocabulary, especially now that electronic media (TV and IT, especially, which are a language change in themselves) influence so much and so instantaneously what we say and how we say it.

Language change, as a topic, is not just about how things used to be, a yesterday world, albeit a fascinating one; it is equally about the ways in which a living language reflects social and cultural changes happening today and tomorrow. The vast scale of historical linguistics is, however, too large for an A level course. A very general outline of the history of English will help you to notice where and how changes occur in a language but the focus of this chapter is on literary texts written from the sixteenth century onwards, the long period known as Modern English. Examinations will not expect you to analyse and discuss Old English texts (the earliest form of English, up to about 1100, and sometimes referred to as Anglo-Saxon) or Middle English (1100 to 1450, the language of Chaucer who died in 1400). Your studies begin with the age and the language of William Shakespeare, but it helps to know that Chaucer's ghost would have encountered some linguistic surprises had he turned up at the first performance of Hamlet (circa 1600), and that had King Alfred's ghost turned up too, he would have found the English of both Chaucer and *Hamlet* incomprehensible.

A highly entertaining as well as reliable account of the history of English, is Bill Bryson's *The Mother Tongue* (Penguin, 1997) – you'll enjoy it! Equally worth reading, from a different perspective, are the first seven chapters of David Crystal's *Encyclopedia of the English Language* (CUP, 1995), and Shelley Martin's, *Language Change* in the Living Language series (Hodder, 1999).

Tradition and continuity

Before turning to some examples of English texts written over the last five hundred years, you need to consider another concept in the title of this chapter, namely 'continuity'. The very fact that texts from Shakespeare's day onwards are still accessible to modern readers means that however much language changes over time, there's an awful lot of it that doesn't. It's a great relief that this is so, else each new generation would have to re-invent the language. Thankfully, there is much that can be taken for granted.

It is important to recognise features of tradition and continuity, especially in literary genres, as it is to notice evidence of language change.

Continuity in language uses (e.g. letter writing, storytelling, versifying, writing plays, text construction of all kinds) is an important aspect of genre studies since it is very frequently the modification, the nuancing and even the subversion of a familiar form or style, that gives a meaning to the text and enjoyment to the reader. This will be evident when you look, later, at a modernised fairy story. The combination of tradition and modernity is one of the factors that make reading English literature a rich and rewarding experience.

ACTIVITY 130

Grammar is good for you

The two texts you are going to investigate first are both non-fiction texts separated by about five hundred years. The first belongs to the 1590s and is the preface to a new grammar book for use in schools. It is an endorsement by Queen Elizabeth the First of the educational value of the book, though whether she wrote it herself or simply put her signature to a statement prepared by a minister, you must decide for yourself, perhaps after some discussion with a history teacher. The second introduces a government booklet on the teaching of grammar, published in 1999.

Consider first the Elizabethan text which will give you an opportunity to do some first-hand historical linguistics. We haven't altered the text in any way though there is a version in modern typeface should you need it (see end of this chapter). It is much better that you re-write it yourself; you'll notice more.

Read/write out the text to get the sense of it. To do this you will need to get the rhythm of the sentences right, so don't be timid about reading out aloud. They are, after all, Elizabethan sentences, not late twentieth century ones.

When you feel that you have got the sense of it,

list the evidence for language change. Remember, you are an expert here, simply because you know exactly what is and isn't late twentieth century English, even though you may not think you know much about Elizabethan English. Just list anything you find. Going through the text line by line is as good a way as any.

The next thing to do is to group your different bits of evidence into four or five ways in which the language has changed. Uses of individual words is an obvious one to start with, but pinpoint what it is about a word that seems 'odd', 'unusual', 'unfamiliar', 'surprising'. Spelling is an even more obvious aspect of change.

Finally, ask yourself some broader sociolinguistic questions about the text. It's very easy to get bogged down in details and to forget other important factors about texts, such as their purpose, authority, intended audience, formal construction, social context – in other words, all the continuity factors. Even when looking at historical texts, you still need to do everything that you would do in modern stylistics, because style is always a relevant matter in texts of any age.

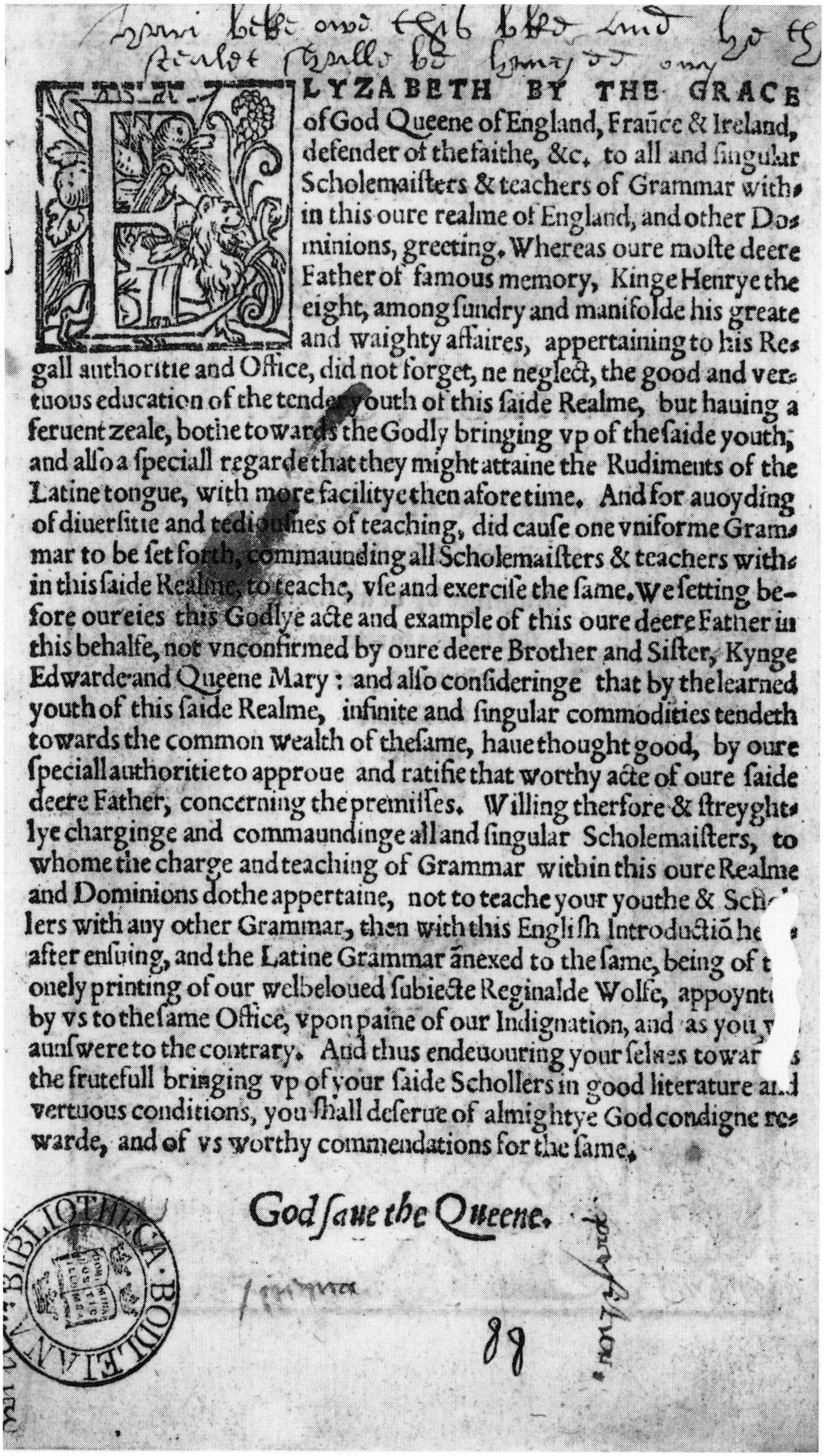

LYZABETH BY THE GRACE of God Queene of England, France & Ireland, defender of the faithe, &c. to all and singular Scholemaisters & teachers of Grammar within this oure realme of England, and other Dominions, greeting. Whereas oure moste deere Father of famous memory, Kinge Henrye the eight, among sundry and manifolde his greate and waighty affaires, appertaining to his Regall authoritie and Office, did not forget, ne neglect, the good and vertuous education of the tender youth of this saide Realme, but hauing a feruent zeale, bothe towards the Godly bringing vp of thesaide youth, and also a speciall regarde that they might attaine the Rudiments of the Latine tongue, with more facilitye then aforetime. And for auoyding of diuersitie and tediousnes of teaching, did cause one vniforme Grammar to be set forth, commaunding all Scholemaisters & teachers within this saide Realme, to teache, vse and exercise the same. We setting before oureies this Godlye acte and example of this oure deere Father in this behalfe, not vnconfirmed by oure deere Brother and Sister, Kynge Edwarde and Queene Mary : and also consideringe that by the learned youth of this saide Realme, infinite and singular commodities tendeth towards the common wealth of thesame, haue thought good, by oure speciall authoritie to approue and ratifie that worthy acte of oure saide deere Father, concerning the premisses. Willing therfore & streyghtlye charginge and commaundinge all and singular Scholemaisters, to whome the charge and teaching of Grammar within this oure Realme and Dominions dothe appertaine, not to teache your youthe & Schollers with any other Grammar, then with this English Introductiõ hereafter ensuing, and the Latine Grammar anexed to the same, being of t onely printing of our welbeloued subiecte Reginalde Wolfe, appoynte by vs to the same Office, vpon paine of our Indignation, and as you r aunswere to the contrary. And thus endeuouring your selues towar s the frutefull bringing vp of your saide Schollers in good literature and vertuous conditions, you shall deserue of almightye God condigne rewarde, and of vs worthy commendations for the same.

God saue the Queene.

Figure 9.1 Endorsement by Queen Elizabeth the First

Now turn to the following text from *Teaching Grammar: not whether but how.* (QCA, 1999). Read it first of all to get to get the sense of it, and then note one or two historical differences in language between the two texts. Use the second text as a reference point or as a measure of how much change has occurred.

In 1998 QCA published *The grammar papers: perspectives on the teaching of grammar in the national curriculum.* The background to that publication was a long-standing controversy about teaching grammar and widespread uncertainty as to how to interpret and implement the national curriculum grammar requirements. The booklet:

- identified key issues in the teaching of grammar;
- clarified the grammar requirements in the English order;
- established clear principles to inform the planning of grammar teaching;
- provided guidance on assessing pupils' knowledge and use of grammar.

Many schools and teachers agreed that the publication succeeded in promoting wide professional discussion of teaching grammar. There is growing consensus about the need for systematic, explicit teaching of grammar. The debate now is less about whether to teach grammar but how best to:

- approach grammar as part of wider approaches to teaching reading and writing;
- highlight grammatical features of texts, sentences and words;
- achieve progression;
- make the teaching of grammar manageable;
- use appropriate technical terms in purposeful contexts.

This booklet reflects the changing debate and addresses concerns about how best to teach grammar. It explores the implications of the principles set out in *The grammar papers* and gives examples of how the principles can be put into practice. It offers further guidance on the teaching of grammar at key stages 3 and 4, but does not attempt to provide complete answers in an area where much remains to be developed. The teachers and trainers who have contributed to the booklet show how the study of grammatical features can illuminate pupils' understanding and appreciation of texts and make clear the choices that are available to them as speakers and writers.

The three chapters in part one deal with the development of pupils' explicit grammatical knowledge. Their starting point is Paper 2 in *The grammar papers*, which sets out the aims and scope of the grammar requirements in the English order.

The aim of the requirements is to ensure that pupils are familiar with grammatical terminology, and can make independent use of their grammatical knowledge when reading and writing. Pupils should be taught:

- the organising principles and structures of language;
- how they contribute to meaning and effect;
- how to use their knowledge of language structures in their reading and writing.

They should also be taught:

- that language changes;
- the sources and causes of linguistic change;
- how meanings are affected by choice of vocabulary and structure;
- to apply their knowledge of language variety.

Central to the development of pupils' explicit grammatical knowledge is the ability to name linguistic features, structures and patterns at word, sentence and whole text level. Familiarity with the grammatical terms enables pupils to identify linguistic features correctly and thus comment more precisely and effectively about language structure and use. Such knowledge helps pupils reflect purposefully on examples, generalise from them and check the accuracy of their conclusions. The overall purpose of language analysis is to develop pupils' understanding of the function of particular linguistic features and patterns in spoken and written texts and to evaluate their effects on readers and listeners. Explicit grammatical knowledge extends the choices available to pupils in speaking and writing, and enables them to evaluate the appropriateness and effectiveness of the choices made by speakers and writers in achieving their purpose.

Consider the sociolinguistic factors surrounding the publication of the second text. What similarities do you detect. Is there any evidence that, despite differences of style, not much changes really, in context, audience and purpose?

A good way to get inside the differences is to write one text in the style of the other. Begin by modernising the Elizabethan text. Initially, you will need to decide whether you are going to retain the royal proclamation format (cf. the modern day Queen's speech at the opening of Parliament), or whether you are going to dispense with it, and introduce the booklet in the more anonymous manner of a modern government bureaucracy. Either approach will raise interesting issues about style of address.

Writing the second text in the style of the first is a trickier business but worth doing, just to see if you can get into the mind and the attitudes behind the language. In educational contexts, the word 'scholars' would have been quite a normal one, forty or fifty years ago.

Complete this activity by compiling two brief lists of:

(i)   aspects of language that change over time
(ii) aspects of genre, form, purpose, audience, text construction, level of formality that continue over time (e.g. the legal and political contexts)

You will find our commentary at the end of the chapter.

The previous activity should have introduced you to the substance of language change and led you to think about the circumstances and significance of those changes. By 'substance' we mean the evidence in texts of the following kinds of change:

- spellings, though these become fewer and fewer as you look at later and later texts
- words whose meanings have changed
- words that are no longer used, whatever their meanings
- phrases and expressions that seem 'old fashioned'
- unusual grammatical forms (e.g. archaic pronoun, a word ending, discontinued word order)
- uses or non-uses of punctuation
- likely differences in pronunciation (which you may have to guess at)

Over the years, etymologists, lexicographers and grammarians have filled libraries with their observations and explanations for these changes. Why has a 'b' appeared in the spelling of 'debt' when previously it was spelled 'dett'? And when did it first appear? How did words like 'Gothic' and

'Impressionism', originally used as insults, come to be respected academic terms for schools of art? What on earth is an 'adze'? What has happened to 'Your obedient servant' as a way of concluding some formal letters? When and why did the pronouns 'you' and 'yours' replace 'thee' and 'thine' in standard English use? And are they still used in dialects? Is the influence of IT changing the ways we punctuate? Where did the rising tone at the end of statements come from? Australia? Cornwall? And what does it mean? We can go a long way to answering these questions and the explanations, often curious, are always interesting because language is just as queer as folks.

You might find that the origins of words and changes in their use has a lifelong fascination for you. The danger at A level is that there isn't time to pursue them, which means that you can end up pointing out changes for the sake of it (a fairly easy thing to do) without going on to something more worthwhile. If your observations amount to noting that somebody, somewhere three hundred years ago, spelled 'only' as 'onlie' and used 'more flowery expressions', the response, 'So what?!' is not entirely unjustified. You need a purpose for studying language change beyond just noticing it, and as good a purpose as any is to feel your way into the mind and the period of a writer by the most immediately available means. Word choice and sentence rhythm and construction are always the best guides to style; they are also extremely susceptible to social and cultural changes. This means that you have to attune your twenty-first century ear, and your sense of rhythm, to language tunes from an earlier age. Actors and directors involved in television versions of classic novels, for example, will tell you that it is no good getting the clothes and the furniture and the hair styles right, if you don't get the voices right.

In 1989 the BBC televised a fictional series about the so-called phoney war. It centred on RAF personnel stationed in France in 1939. The planes were right as were the settings and the events, but one viewer, writing to *Radio Times*, pointed out that what they hadn't got right was the language: the things the airmen said and the way in which they said them. That one lapse in attention to language detail made the series seem inauthentic to someone who had been there.

ACTIVITY 131

Comic cuts

You are going to look at two excerpts from playscripts, but this time in reverse chronological order. The first comes from a TV programme, 'Dad's Army', written in 1969 for the BBC. The second is an excerpt from Shakespeare's *Much Ado About Nothing* (1600).

Concentrate first of all on the 'Dad's Army' text. It comes from a programme called *Sgt. Wilson's Little Secret* and is set in the church hall, where the men are on parade, wearing different kinds of camouflage. The period is of course 1940. The script is not a full shooting script with directions for cameramen and technicians; it has been adapted for the convenience of readers rather than performers.

Read the text and identify any 'modern' features in the writing. What, for example, are the signs that it was written for TV?

CHURCH HALL.

THE MEN ARE ALL DRAWN UP ON PARADE WITH VARIOUS FORMS OF CAMOUFLAGE ON

MAIN   Excellent turnout, men. Don't you think so, Wilson?

WILSON   Yes, absolutely first class, sir.

(MAIN STOPS IN FRONT OF THE FIRST MAN. HE IS COVERED FROM HEAD TO FOOT IN HAY)

MAIN   (ASIDE TO WILSON) Who's this, Wilson?

WILSON   I haven't the faintest idea, sir.

(WALKER PULLS ASIDE THE HAY AND POKES HIS HEAD THROUGH)

WALKER   It's me, sir. I'm a small haystack.

MAIN   Good gracious, that's good, don't you think, Wilson?

WILSON   Awfully good, sir.

(SUDDENLY THERE IS A TERRIFIC SNEEZE FROM YOUNG PIKE WHO IS STANDING BESIDE WALKER. HE SNEEZES AGAIN. HIS EYES ARE RUNNING AND HE IS IN A TERRIBLE STATE)

MAIN   What on earth's the matter with you, boy?

PIKE   I can't stand it, sir, it's my hayfever.

MAIN   Well don't stand next to him then; move to the end of the line.

PIKE   Yes, sir.

(HE MOVES TO THE END OF THE LINE. MAIN MOVES ON TO GODFREY WHO IS WEARING A BEE-KEEPER'S MASK AND VEIL WHICH IS FULL OF HOLES. HE IS ALSO WEARING A LAY OF FLOWERS ROUND HIS NECK)

MAIN   What's this supposed to be, Godfrey?

GODFREY   Well, I tried several things on, sir, and none of them really seemed to suit me.

MAIN   But you're supposed to break up your outline.

GODFREY   I thought it looked pretty broken up as it is, sir.

MAIN   What's that you've got round your face?

GODFREY   It's my bee-keeping mask, sir.

MAIN   But it's full of holes.

GODFREY   It's all right, my bees are quite friendly.

MAIN   (TOUCHING THE 'LAY') But why this? It looks as if you're going on a cruise to the South Seas.

GODFREY   Well, I got the idea from a film I saw at the Odeon last week. It was called the *South of Pago Pago*. It had Dorothy Lamour and Victor Mature in it, it was awfully good.

MAIN   What's that got to do with camouflage?

GODFREY   I don't know really, sir. I just thought it looked rather er . . . open air.

MAIN   I see (HE MOVES ON).

WILSON   He's right, you know, sir, it does look open air.

(MAIN GIVES HIM A GLANCE AND STOPS IN FRONT OF FRAZER, WHO HAS A BATTERED TOP HAT ON HIS HEAD AND A TATTY BIT OF WHITE SHEETING ROUND HIS SHOULDERS LIKE A CLOAK).

MAIN   What are you going as, Frazer? The Phantom of the Opera?

FRAZER   No, this is a winter camouflage, sir, you wear it in the snow.

(HE CROUCHES DOWN. TURNS THE SHEET SO THAT IT FALLS IN FRONT OF HIM. IT HAS THREE BLACK BUTTONS PAINTED ON IT. ON THE BACK OF HIS HEAD HE HAS A SNOWMAN MASK WHICH HE TURNS ROUND. HE REPLACES TOP HAT AND STICK WITH A PIPE IN HIS MOUTH.)

MAIN   Well done, Frazer (HE PASSES ON TO JONES WHO IS WEARING HIS BUTCHERS OUTFIT, STRAW HAT AND APRON) Why aren't you wearing camouflage, Jones?

JONES   I am, sir. I'm camouflaged as a butcher.

MAIN   I don't think I quite follow you.

JONES   Well, sir, I'm standing outside my shop, right. (MAIN NODS) A Jerry soldier comes along, he don't know I'm in the Home Guard, he thinks I'm a butcher, right. (MAIN NODS) Then when he's not looking, whop! Right up with the old cold steel. And that's one thing they don't like, you know, sir.

MAIN   Yes, thank you, Jones, I'm well aware of that fact.

(HE PASSES ON TO PIKE WHO IS WEARING HIS UNIFORM AND NO CAMOUFLAGE)

MAIN   What's the meaning of this, Pike?

PIKE   I've got a note for you, Mr Mainwaring, it's from my mum.

(HE HANDS MAIN THE NOTE. MAIN TAKES IT AND MOVES DOWN WITH WILSON)

MAIN   (READS) 'I don't want young Frank covered in a lot of damp leaves, it will only set off his chest again.' Right, this is the finish, Wilson, I want to speak to you in my office as soon as parade's over.

FADE.

What are the taken-for-granted features of modern, everyday speech?

Do you detect anything in the language that contributes to the authenticity of a 1940 setting?

Some critics would say that the text is dated now, twice dated in fact. Once, by its Home Guard setting, and again, by the fact that it was written in the 1960s. Do you agree?

Before turning to the second text, make some stylistic notes on the text, regardless of when it was written. What sorts of verbal art are at work here?

Look at the opening and closure.

What kind of humour do you detect? You don't have to find it hilariously, or even mildly, funny as a personal response but you should be able to explain how it works on people who do enjoy it.

How is cohesion achieved, i.e. how is the conversation developed through the scene?

Suggest some vocal features that actors would need to bring to different parts.

Now turn to the scene from *Much Ado* (below) in which there are some similarities with the 'Dad's Army' scene. Dogberry, a constable, is addressing the Watch, a collection of Elizabethan 'policemen' charged with keeping the peace and watching over the safety of local folk – a kind of peacetime Home Guard. Verges is his partner in office. Many critics have likened Dogberry to a kindly, bumbling, pompous village bobby – a breath of fresh, comic Warwickshire air in a play set in Sicily. He made Elizabethans laugh, and in the hands of good actors, the whole scene can still make modern audiences laugh aloud. The genre of situation comedy among incompetent local officials has continued to the present day, not only in 'Dad's Army' but in countless novels, plays, films and TV programmes. But you are going to find this example difficult to read even though it is in recognisably modern English. Don't expect to laugh, though you may smile here and there as you get into it. Use the glossary, and remember one important thing: Shakespeare deliberately makes Dogberry and Verges use words that are the opposite of what they mean – it became an old Music Hall gag for years.

Enter DOGBERRY *and his compartner* [VERGES] *with the* WATCH.

Dog.   Are you good men and true?

Verg.   Yea, or else it were pity but they should suffer salvation, body and soul.

Dog.   Nay, that were a punishment too good for them, if they should have any allegiance in them, being chosen for the Prince's watch.   6

Verg.   Well, give them their charge, neighbor Dogberry.

Dog.   First, who think you the most desartless man to be constable?   10

1. Watch.   Hugh Oatcake, sir, or George Seacole, for they can write and read.

Dog.   Come hither, neighbor Seacole. God hath blest you with a good name. To be a well-favor'd man is the gift of fortune, but to write and read comes by nature.   16

2. Watch.   Both which, Master Constable—

Dog.   You have: I knew it would be your answer. Well, for your favor, sir, why, give God thanks, and make no boast of it, and for your writing   20 and reading, let that appear when there is no need of such vanity. You are thought here to be the most senseless and fit man for the constable of the watch; therefore bear you the lanthorn. This is your charge:

you shall comprehend all vagrom men; you are to
bid any man stand, in the Prince's name. 26

2. Watch. How if 'a will not stand?

Dog. Why then take no note of him, but let him
go, and presently call the rest of the watch together,
and thank God you are rid of a knave. 30

Verg. If he will not stand when he is bidden, he
is none of the Prince's subjects.

Dog. True, and they are to meddle with none
but the Prince's subjects. You shall also make no
noise in the streets; for, for the watch to babble 35
and to talk, is most tolerable, and not to be endur'd.

[2.] Watch. We will rather sleep than talk, we
know what belongs to a watch.

Dog. Why, you speak like an ancient and most
quiet watchman, for I cannot see how sleeping 40
should offend; only have a care that your bills be not
stol'n. Well, you are to call at all the alehouses, and
bid those that are drunk get them to bed.

[2.] Watch. How if they will not?

Dog. Why then let them alone till they are
sober. If they make you not then the better 46
answer, you may say they are not the men you took
them for.

[2.] Watch. Well, sir.

Dog. If you meet a thief, you may suspect him,
by virtue of your office, to be no true man; and 51
for such kind of men, the less you meddle or make
with them, why, the more is for your honesty.

[2.] Watch. If we know him to be a thief, shall
we not lay hands on him? 55

Dog. Truly by your office you may, but I think
they that touch pitch will be defil'd. The most peace-
able way for you, if you do take a thief, is to let him
show himself what he is, and steal out of your
company. 60

Verg. You have been always call'd a merciful
man, partner.

Dog. Truly, I would not hang a dog by my will,
much more a man who hath any honesty in him.

Verg. If you hear a child cry in the night, you
must call to the nurse and bid her still it. 66

[2.] Watch. How if the nurse be asleep and will
not hear us?

Dog. Why then depart in peace, and let the
child wake her with crying, for the ewe that will not
hear her lamb when it baes will never answer a calf
when he bleats. 72

Verg. 'Tis very true.

Dog. This is the end of the charge: you,
constable, are to present the Prince's own person. If
you meet the Prince in the night, you may stay him. 76

Verg. Nay, by'r lady, that I think 'a cannot.

Dog. Five shillings to one on't, with any man
that knows the [statues], he may stay him; marry,
not without the Prince be willing, for indeed the
watch ought to offend no man, and it is an offense to
stay a man against his will. 82

Verg. By'r lady, I think it be so.

Dog. Ha, ah ha! Well, masters, good night.
And there be any matter of weight chances, call up
me. Keep your fellows' counsels and your own, and
good night. Come, neighbor. 87

[2.] Watch. Well, masters, we hear our charge.
Let us go sit here upon the church-bench till two, and
then all to bed. 90

Dog. One word more, honest neighbors. I pray
you watch about Signior Leonato's door, for the wedding being there to-morrow, there is a great coil tonight. Adieu! Be vigitant, I beseech you.

Exeunt [*Dogberry and Verges*].

III.iii. Location: A Street.
1. true: loyal.
3. salvation: blunder for *damnation*. Dogberry's and Verges'
words
frequently mean precisely the opposite of what the speaker
intends;
witness *allegiance* (line 5), *desartless* (line 9), *senseless* (line 23).
14. well-favor'd: good-looking.
19. favor: appearance.
24. lanthorn: variant form of *lantern* (by popular etymology from the
fact that lanterns often had sides made of transparent sheets of
horn).
25. comprehend: i.e. apprehend. **vagrom**: i.e. vagrant.

26. stand: stop.
33. meddle: have to do. **36. tolerable**: for *intolerable*.
38. belongs to: are the duties of.
41. bills: hooked blades fastened on long poles.
46–47. make ... answer: ... don't then agree to go home.
51. true: honest. **53. is**: it is.
57. they ... defil'd. A commonplace, derived from the
Apocryphal book Ecclesiasticus (**13:1**).
64. more: for *less*. **66. still**: quiet.
75. present: represent. **79. statues**: i.e. statues.
80. without: unless.
94. coil: fuss, to-do. **vigitant**: i.e. vigilant.

The reason why you will find this activity difficult lies not in your reading ability but in the ways language use has changed between then and now. So much of the humour is linguistic in essence.

Your task here is to try to get inside the scene and imagine the voices and the actions that would reactivate the Elizabethan meanings. You will need to work with one or two partners. Some words and phrases will give you little difficulty, others will be extremely puzzling. It is at the puzzling points that you can learn most about language change, so analyse why there is a difficulty for a modern reader and note what you had to do to 'get at' a meaning.

Finally, you should write on stylistic features of the text as an example of verbal art:

- consider sociolinguistic factors (purpose, audiences, reception, context)
- look at the construction of the scene
- note the interactions
- compare different dialogue functions, e.g. asking questions, exclaiming
- describe the roles assigned to the characters, e.g. proactive, reactive.

Our commentary will be found at the end of this chapter.

One important reason then, for being alert to language change, is to be able to appreciate more fully the text, the writer and their social and cultural contexts – to add another dimension to your own reading. Many changes – words and expressions, for example – are self evident, and studying them for the sake of it can lessen enjoyment and understanding of the text as a whole. In any case, the voices of good writers have a habit of staying alive and of becoming remarkably contemporary.

In the last activity you looked at comic scriptwriting separated by over 350 years. Changes in cultural contexts, nuances of humour, entertainment style and medium required you to make some effort of imagination and research to 'think' yourself into the language of one particular scene in *Much Ado*. Finding an opportunity to watch that scene on video, and seeing how a director and modern actors would play it, will prove very illuminating if you haven't already done so.

In the next activity, you are going to look at excerpts from novels written at about the turn of the eighteenth century into the nineteenth.

ACTIVITY 132

Jane Austen's contemporaries

Jane Austen's voice has never been more alive than in the last 50 years. *Pride and Prejudice* appeared as a set-book in the first days of GCE 'O' level, and has appeared regularly ever since, right through to GCSE in the late 1990s.

In this activity you are going to explore the writing of some of her contemporaries, but first, to get yourself into her style, look at two excerpts from her novels published in 1816 and 1818 respectively.

Read them in the spirit in which they are meant to be read, for curiosity, entertainment, enjoyment and instruction. In Jane Austen's day, it would have been called 'diverting reading'.

Don't concern yourself with looking for 'language change' as such, but note any distinctive features of her prose style, e.g. word choice, phraseology, sentence construction and way of addressing her readers.

Do make sure you 'hear' the excerpts as well as 'read' them. Read them aloud at least once.

from *Emma* (1816)

EMMA could not bear to give him pain. He was wishing to confide in her – perhaps to consult her; cost her what it would, she would listen. She might assist his resolution, or reconcile him to it; she might give just praise to Harriet, or, by representing to him his own independence, relieve him from that state of indecision which must be more intolerable than any alternative to such a mind as his. They had reached the house.

'You are going in, I suppose?' said he.

'No,' replied Emma, quite confirmed by the depressed manner in which he still spoke, 'I should like to take another turn. Mr Perry is not gone.' And, after proceeding a few steps, she added – 'I stopped you ungraciously, just now, Mr Knightley, and, I am afraid, gave you pain. But if you have any wish to speak openly to me as a friend, or to ask my opinion of anything that you may have in contemplation – as a friend, indeed, you may command me. I will hear whatever you like. I will tell you exactly what I think.'

'As a friend!' repeated Mr Knightly. 'Emma, that, I fear, is a word – no, I have no wish. Stay, yes, why should I hesitate? I have gone too far already for concealment. Emma, I accept your offer, extraordinary as it may seem, I accept it, and refer myself to you as a friend. Tell me, then, have I no chance of ever succeeding?'

He stopped in his earnestness to look the question, and the expression of his eyes overpowered her.

'My dearest Emma,' said he, 'for dearest you will always be, whatever the event of this hour's conversation, my dearest, most beloved Emma – tell me at once. Say "No," if it is to be said.' She could really say nothing. 'You are silent,' he cried, with great animation; 'absolutely silent! at present I ask no more.'

Emma was almost ready to sink under the agitation of this moment. The dread of being awakened from the happiest dream was perhaps the most prominent feeling.

'I cannot make speeches, Emma,' he soon resumed, and in a tone of such sincere, decided, intelligible tenderness as was tolerably convincing. 'If I loved you less, I might be able to talk about it more. But you know what I am. You hear nothing but truth from me. I have blamed you, and lectured you, and you have borne it as no other woman in England would have borne it. Bear with the truths I would tell you now, dearest Emma, as well as you have borne with them. The manner, perhaps, may have as little to recommend them. God knows, I have been a very indifferent lover. But you understand me. Yes, you see, you understand my feelings – and will return them if you can. At present, I ask only to hear – once to hear your voice.'

from *Persuasion* (1818)

UPPERCROSS was a moderate-sized village, which a few years back had been completely in the old English style, containing only two houses superior in appearance to those of the yeomen and labourers; the mansion of the squire, with its high walls, great gates, and old trees, substantial and unmodernized, and the compact, tight parsonage, enclosed in its own neat garden, with a vine and a pear-tree trained round its casements; but upon the marriage of the young squire, it had received the improvement of a farm-house, elevated into a cottage, for his residence, and Uppercross Cottage, with its veranda, French windows, and other prettinesses, was quite as likely to catch the traveller's eye as the more consistent and considerable aspect and premises of the Great House, about a quarter of a mile farther on.

Here Anne had often been staying. She knew the ways of Uppercross as well as those of Kellynch. The two families were so continually meeting, so much in the habit of running in and out of each other's house at all hours, that it was rather a surprise to her to find Mary alone; but being alone, her being unwell and out of spirits was almost a matter of course. Though better endowed than the elder sister, Mary had not

Anne's understanding nor temper. While well, and happy, and properly attended to, she had great good humour and excellent spirits; but any indisposition sunk her completely. She had no resources for solitude; and, inheriting a considerable share of the Eliot self-importance, was very prone to add to every other distress that of fancying herself neglected and ill-used. In person, she was inferior to both sisters, and had, even in her bloom, only reached the dignity of being 'a fine girl'. She was now lying on the faded sofa of the pretty little drawing-room, the once elegant furniture of which had been gradually growing shabby under the influence of four summers and two children; and, on Anne's appearing, greeted her with –

'So you are come at last! I began to think I should never see you. I am so ill I can hardly speak. I have not seen a creature the whole morning!'

'I am sorry to find you unwell,' replied Anne. 'You sent me such a good account of yourself on Thursday.'

'Yes, I made the best of it; I always do: but I was very far from well at the time; and I do not think I ever was so ill in my life as I have been all this morning: very unfit to be left alone, I am sure. Suppose I were to be seized of a sudden in some dreadful way, and not able to ring the bell! So Lady Russell would not get out. I do not think she has been in this house three times this summer.'

COMMENTARY

(i) The *Emma* excerpt: no doubt you noted some particular words and expressions e.g.

'I should like to take another turn'
'I ask no more'
'whatever the event of this hour's conversation'
'the agitation of this moment'
'concealment' 'contemplation'

All of these carry resonances from the period in which they were written. They express a considerable degree of decorum, reserve, politeness – ceremoniousness, even – especially in the conversation. But those qualities are also there in the conversation Jane Austen is having with her readers (of necessity, a one-sided mode of address).

The characteristic style of Jane Austen, or of the language of novel writing in that period, are not accounted for by the use of words and expressions alone. You need to look also at the sentence grammar.

The excerpt begins with a simple, declarative sentence (i.e. a statement). Notice the dash and the semi-colon in the second sentence, indicating a concern for exactness. After the semi-colon comes another statement, 'she would listen', premodified by 'cost her what it would'. There have been three modal verbs so far, conveying the hesitancy of the characters and the carefulness of the narrator. Read both sentences aloud and 'feel' the rhythm.

There follows a long sentence of 46 words that are very carefully balanced.

Look at the verb pairs 'assist'/'reconcile' and 'give praise'/'relieve' separated by 'or'.

'She might' is repeated, and note how a semi-colon is used to separate two unequal sections of the sentence. And because the punctuation keeps everything tidy, there is even room to slip in a parenthesis – 'by representing to him his own independence' – as an additional thought.

In all, there are six modal verbs, creating a strong sense of uncertainty, yet the paragraph is rounded off with a matter of fact, five word, simple sentence.

Note the inversion of the more usual contemporary word order, 'said he', but note too, that the inverted form is still used in fiction today, mainly for effect.

Austen interrupts Emma's reply with a comment of her own: 'No', replied Emma, quite . . . spoke, 'I should like . . .' You might try this effect in your own writing.

She also begins a sentence with 'And', yet another example of a great writer doing what some old fashioned pedants tell you not to do. It works here because the prose is already flowing freely; the characters are walking and talking after all.

The hesitancy, anxiety and bursts of conviction in Mr Knightly's speech are conveyed in the discontinuity of his sentences. Listen to his speech patterns. Yet there is also a care for exactness.

In the last two sentences, comment from Jane Austen, there are two adverbs that reinforce the effect of the six modal verbs: 'almost' and 'perhaps'.

All these features add up to what used to be called a 'niceness' in the prose style. Not a niceness in the sense of 'kind and agreeable' but in the sense of 'precise, carefully judged'. It is a quality that delights many readers of Austen, and irritates others.

(ii) The *Persuasion* excerpt: again, you no doubt noticed some words and expressions, e.g.

'in the old English style'
'superior in appearance'
'but upon the marriage of the young squire'
'prettinesses'
'she had no resources for solitude'
'Mary had not Anne's understanding nor temper' (note, not just the 'had not', but the meaning of 'temper')

The first paragraph of the excerpt is one long sentence, supported by no less than 14 commas and 2 semi-colons. It is followed by a short one beginning with 'Here . . .' which links two paragraphs (a common example of narrative cohesion).

Note the repeated 'so continually' and 'so much' creating, once again, that effect of balance in the prose.

You might also have noticed too, the sentences beginning with 'Though . . .' and 'Whist . . .' both conveying a carefully considered (and premodified) view of the character's actions.

The excerpt ends with another example of prose craft. In the *Emma* excerpt, we drew attention to the way in which speech may be interrupted by narative comment; we also noted an effective use of 'And' as a sentence opener. The *Persuasion* excerpt concludes with an unusual way of leading out of narrative into conversation. Think how it might sound if read on the radio by a single presenter.

Many, if not all, of these observations are to do with prose craft, the accumulated tricks of the novelist's trade, available to any writer today. We have tried to show how sentence grammar, sentence construction if you prefer, has a powerful effect on prose style. If you add up all the features listed, lexical, grammatical and rhythmical, you get very close to defining Jane Austen's distinctive style, but you also get an insight into a style of prose fiction as it was written nearly two hundred years ago.

There follow excerpts from novels written close to the time of *Emma* and *Persuasion*. Each excerpt is preceded by some contextual information to help you, but concentrate on the texts themselves and write a running commentary on each one, noting:

- individual words and expressions that sound 'dated' (some people use the word 'archaic')
- how the sentences are constructed and contrasted.

Follow a pattern similar to our commentary on the Austen excerpts, and then write a short piece describing any personal voices you have discovered and summarising what you think is a prose fiction style of the period.

Check your impressions by finding another novel of the same period, and comparing an excerpt. Check also an excerpt from a modern novel, written post 1945, to give you a contrast.

We are not suggesting, incidentally, that the years 1794 to 1818 are a special literary period in their own right; we could have cut a segment of twenty years from anywhere in the history of English literature.

You could pick your own twenty years or so, as a follow up, and compare three novels in that period. Try it out for yourself any wet afternoon at the local public library. It is a good way of getting a feel for both continuity and the nuances of change.

(i) William Godwin (1756–1836) is not well known as a novelist, more's the pity, for *The Adventures of Caleb Williams* (1794) is well worth a read. It is a first person narrative in which Williams tells of his persecution by his employer, a man he knows is guilty of a murder for which others were executed. His employer has him imprisoned on a trumped up charge of theft but he makes his escape, which is where the excerpt begins.

I HAD not stood up in this manner two minutes, before I heard the sound of feet, and presently saw the ordinary turnkey and another pass the place of my retreat. They were so close to me that, if I had stretched out my hand, I believe I could have caught hold of their clothes without so much as changing my posture. As no part of the overhanging earth intervened between me and them, I could see them entire, though the deepness of the shade rendered me almost completely invisible. I heard them say to each other, in tones of vehement asperity, 'Curse the rascal! Which way can he be gone?' The reply was, 'Damn him! I wish we had him but safe once again!' – 'Never fear!' rejoined the first, 'he cannot have above half a mile the start of us.' They were presently out of hearing; for, as to sight, I dared not advance my body, so much as an inch, to look after them, lest I should be discovered by my pursuers in some other direction. From the very short time that elapsed, between my escape and the appearance of these men, I concluded that they had made their way through the same outlet as I had done, it being impossible that they could have had time to come from the gate of the prison, and so round a considerable part of the town, as they must otherwise have done.

I was so alarmed at this instance of diligence on the part of the enemy, that, for some time, I scarcely ventured to proceed an inch from my place of concealment, or almost to change my posture. The morning, which had been bleak and drizzly, was succeeded by a day of heavy and incessant rain; and the gloomy state of the air and surrounding objects, together with the extreme nearness of my prison, and a total want of food, caused me to pass the hours in no very agreeable sensations. This inclemency of the weather however, which generated a feeling of stillness and solitude, encouraged me by degrees to change my retreat, for another of the same nature, but of somewhat greater security. I hovered with little variation about a single spot, as long as the sun continued above the horizon.

Towards evening, the clouds began to disperse, and the moon shone, as on the preceding night, in full brightness. I had perceived no human being during the whole day, except in the instance already mentioned. This had perhaps been owing to the nature of the day; at all events I considered it as too hazardous an experiment, to venture from my hiding-place in so clear and fine a night. I was therefore obliged to wait for the setting of this luminary, which was not till near five o'clock in the morning. My only relief during this interval was to allow myself to sink to the bottom of my cavern, it being scarcely possible for me to continue any longer on my feet. Here I fell into an interrupted and unrefreshing doze, the consequence of a laborious night, and a tedious, melancholy day; though I rather sought to avoid sleep, which, cooperating with the coldness of the season, would tend more to injury than advantage.

(ii) Maria Edgeworth (1768–1849) is credited with writing the first regional novel and the first historical novel in English, both of which were accomplished in *Castle Rackrent* (1820) set in Ireland. It is another first person narrative, this time by the steward of a castle. He has served three generations of its owners, the Rackrent family. The excerpt concerns Sir Condy Rackrent and his wife Isabella, whose extravagant lifestyle brings down the family fortune. Imagining or imitating an Irish accent as you read, would be helpful.

As to affording it, God knows it was little they knew of the matter; my lady's few thousands could not last for ever, especially the way she went on with them, and letters from tradesfolk came every post thick and threefold, with bills as long as my arm of years and years standing; my son Jason had 'em all handed over to him, and the pressing letters were all unread by Sir Condy, who hated trouble and could never be brought to hear talk of business, but still put it off and put it off, saying – settle it any how, or bid 'em call again tomorrow, or speak to me about it some other time. – Now it was hard to find the right time to speak, for in the mornings he was a-bed and in the evenings over his bottle, where no gentleman chuses to be disturbed. – Things in a twelve-month or so came to such a pass, there was no making a shift to go on any longer, though we were all of us well enough used to live from hand to mouth at Castle Rackrent. One day, I remember, when there was a power of company, all sitting after dinner in the dusk, not to say dark, in the drawing-room, my lady having rung five times for candles and none to go up, the housekeeper sent up the footman, who went to my mistress and whispered behind her chair how it was. – 'My lady (says he) there are no candles in the house.' – 'Bless me, (says she) then take a horse, and gallop off as fast as you can to Carrick O'Fungus and get some.' – 'And in the mean time tell them to step into the play-house, and try if there are not some bits left,' added Sir Condy, who happened to be within hearing. The man was sent up again to my lady, to let her know there was no horse to go but one that wanted a shoe. – 'Go to Sir Condy, then, I know nothing at all about the horses, (said my lady) why do you plague me with these things?' – How it was settled I really forget, but to the best of my remembrance, the boy was sent down to my son Jason's to borrow candles for the night. Another time in the winter, and on a desperate cold day, there was no turf in for the parlour and above stairs, and scarce enough for the cook in the kitchen, the little *gossoon* was sent off to the neighbours to see and beg or borrow some, but none could he bring back with him for love or money; so as needs must we were forced to trouble Sir Condy – 'Well, and if there's no turf to be had in the town or country, why what signifies talking any more about it, can't ye go and cut down a tree?' – 'Which tree, please your honour?' I made bold to say. – 'Any tree at all that's good to burn, (said Sir Condy); send offsmart, and get one down and the fires lighted before my lady gets up to breakfast, or the house will be too hot to hold us.' – He was always very considerate in all things about my lady, and she wanted for nothing whilst he had it to give. – Well, when things were tight with them about this time, my son Jason put in a word again about the lodge, and made a genteel offer to lay down the purchase money to relieve Sir Condy's distresses.

(iii) Sir Walter Scott (1771–1832) abandoned his first novel, *Waverley*, some years before it was first published. It tells the story of a British army officer with strong Scottish sympathies at a time of acute political tension between the two countries. His visits to Scottish friends and the girl he loves, come to the attention of his commanding officer who finally accuses him of fomenting mutiny in his regiment. Waverley is a romantic idealist with a great deal to learn about politics.

THESE letters, as might have been expected, highly excited Waverley's indignation. From the desultory style of his studies, he had not any fixed political opinion to place in opposition to the movements of indignation which he felt at his father's supposed wrongs. Of the real cause of his disgrace, Edward was totally ignorant; nor had his habits at all led him to investigate the politics of the period in which he lived, or remark the intrigues in which his father had been so actively engaged. Indeed, any impressions which he had accidentally adopted concerning the parties of the times, were (owing to the society in which he had lived at Waverley Honour) of a nature rather unfavourable to the existing government and dynasty. He entered, therefore, without hesitation, into the resentful feeling of the relations who had the best title to dictate his conduct; and not perhaps the less willingly, when he remembered the tædium of his quarters, and the inferior figure which he had made among the officers of his regiment. If he could have had any doubt upon the subject, it would have been decided by the following letter from his commanding officer, which, as it is very short, shall be inserted verbatim:

SIR,

Having carried somewhat beyond the line of my duty, an indulgence which even the lights of nature, and much more those of Christianity, direct towards errors which may arise from youth and inexperience, and that, altogether without effect, I am reluctantly compelled, at the present crisis, to use the only remaining remedy which is in my power. You are, therefore, hereby commanded to repair to –, the headquarters of the regiment, within three days after the date of this letter. If you shall fail to do so, I must report you to the War Office as absent without leave, and also take other steps, which will be disagreeable to you, as well as to,

> Sir,
> Your obedient Servant,
> J. GARDINER, Lieut.-Col.
> Commanding the – Regt. Dragoons.

Edward's blood boiled within him as he read this letter. He had been accustomed from his very infancy to possess, in a great measure, the disposal of his own time, and thus acquired habits which rendered the rules of military discipline as unpleasing to him in this as they were in some other respects. An idea that in his own case they would not be enforced in a very rigid manner, had also obtained full possession of his mind, and had hitherto been sanctioned by the indulgent conduct of his lieutenant-colonel. Neither had anything occurred, to his knowledge, that should have induced his commanding officer, without any other warning than the hints we noticed at the end of the fourteenth chapter, so suddenly to assume a harsh, and, as Edward deemed it, so insolent a tone of dictatorial authority. Connecting it with the letters he had just received from his family, he could not but suppose, that it was designed to make him feel, in his present situation, the same pressure of authority which had been exercised in his father's case, and that the whole was a concerted scheme to depress and degrade every member of the Waverley family.

(iv) *Nightmare Abbey* (1818) by Thomas Love Peacock (1785–1866) is a satire on the literary fashions of the day – fashions not unlike contemporary fashions for esoteric videos and Point Horror stories. The humour of TV series such as *The Addams Family* and *The Munsters* are a distant echo of the genre. Nightmare Abbey is owned by Mr Glowry and staffed by a motley collection of gloomy servants with names like Diggory Deathshead. His son, Scythrop, is unable to decide which of two women to marry and loses both of them. The excerpt below describes Scythrop.

SHORTLY after the disastrous termination of Scythrop's passion for Miss Emily Girouette, Mr Glowry found himself, much against his will, involved in a lawsuit, which compelled him to dance attendance on the High Court of Chancery. Scythrop was left alone at Nightmare Abbey. He was a burnt child, and dreaded the fire of female eyes. He wandered about the ample pile, or along the garden-terrace, with 'his cogitative faculties immersed in cogibundity of cogitation'. The terrace terminated at the south-western tower, which, as we have said, was ruinous and full of owls. Here would Scythrop take his evening seat, on a fallen fragment of mossy stone, with his back resting against the ruined wall, – a thick canopy of ivy, with an owl in it, over his head, – and the Sorrows of Werther in his hand. He had some taste for romance reading before he went to the university, where, we must confess, in justice to his college, he was cured of the love of reading in all its shapes; and the cure would have been radical, if disappointment in love, and total solitude, had not conspired to bring on a relapse. He began to devour romances and German tragedies, and, by the recommendation of Mr Flosky, to pore over ponderous tomes of transcendental philosophy, which reconciled him to the labour of studying them by their mystical jargon and necromantic imagery. In the congenial solitude of Nightmare Abbey, the distempered ideas of metaphysical romance and romantic metaphysics had ample time and space to germinate into a fertile crop of chimeras, which rapidly shot up into vigorous and abundant vegetation.

He now became troubled with the *passion for reforming the world*. He built many castles in the air, and peopled them with secret tribunals, and bands of illuminati, who were always the imaginary instruments of this projected regeneration of the human species. As he intended to institute a perfect republic, he invested himself with absolute sovereignty over these mystical dispensers of liberty. He slept with Horrid Mysteries under his pillow, and dreamed of venerable eleutherarchs and ghastly confederates holding midnight conventions in subterranean caves. He passed whole mornings in his study, immersed in gloomy reverie, stalking about the room in his nightcap, which he pulled over his eyes like a cowl, and folding his striped calico dressing-gown about him like the mantle of a conspirator.

(v) John Galt (1779–1839) is another lesser known novelist, whose *Annals of the Parish* (1821) describes village life in Scotland. The first person narrator is the Reverend Michael Balwhidder, who tells of the lives and times of his parishoners. The book seems like a documentary because of its social detail, but the narrator and all the characters are fictions invented by Galt. Interestingly, the Oxford English Dictionary cites *Annals of the Parish* as the source of the word 'utilitarian', used to describe the belief that a thing had value only according to its usefulness in creating the greatest good for the greatest number. Dickens satirises this belief in *Hard Times*, especially in the person of Mr Gradgrind. We have chosen a passage that describes the building of a new cotton mill, a potent symbol for the evils of utlitarianism in the poetry of an older contemporary William Blake (1757–1823).

The cottonmill was built, and a spacious fabric it was – nothing like it had been seen before in our day and generation – and, for the people that were brought to work in it, a new town was built in the vicinity, which Mr Cayenne, the same being founded on his land, called Cayenneville, the name of the plantation in Virginia that had been taken from him by the rebellious Americans. From that day Fortune was lavish of her favours upon him; his property swelled, and grew in the most extraordinary manner, and the whole country side was stirring with a new life. For, when the mill was set a-going, he got weaves of muslin established in Cayenneville; and shortly after, but that did not take place till the year following, he brought women all the way from the neighbourhood of Manchester, in England, to teach the lassie bairns in our old clachan tambouring.

   Some of the ancient families, in their turreted houses, were not pleased with this innovation, especially when they saw the handsome dwellings that were built for the weavers of the mills, and the unstinted hand that supplied the wealth required for the carrying on of the business. It sank their pride into insignificance, and many of them would almost rather have wanted the rise that took place in the value of their lands, than have seen this incoming of what they called o'er-sea speculation. But, saving the building of the cottonmill, and the beginning of Cayenneville, nothing more memorable happened in this year, still it was nevertheless a year of a great activity. The minds of men were excited to new enterprises; a new genius, as it were, had descended upon the earth, and there was an erect and outlooking spirit abroad that was not to be satisfied with the taciturn regularity of ancient affairs. Even Miss Sabrina Hooky, the schoolmistress, though now waned from her meridian, was touched with the enlivening rod, and set herself to learn and to teach tambouring, in such a manner as to supersede by precept and example that old time-honoured functionary, as she herself called it, the spinning-wheel, proving, as she did one night to Mr Kibbock and me, that, if more money could be made by a woman tambouring than by spinning, it was better for her to tambour than to spin.

   But, in the midst of all this commercing and manufacturing, I began to discover signs of decay in the wonted simplicity of our country ways. Among the cotton-spinners and muslin weavers of Cayenneville were several unsatisfied and ambitious spirits, who clubbed together, and got a London newspaper to the Cross-Keys, where they were nightly in the habit of meeting and debating about the affairs of the French, which were then gathering towards a head. They were represented to me as lads by common in capacity, but with unsettled notions of religion. They were, however, quiet and orderly; and some of them since, at Glasgow, Paisley, and Manchester, even, I am told, in London, have grown into a topping way.

It seems they did not like my manner of preaching, and on that account absented themselves from public worship; which, when I heard, I sent for some of them, to convince them of their error with regard to the truth of divers points of doctrine; but they confounded me with their objections, and used my arguments, which were the old and orthodox proven opinions of the Divinity Hall, as if they had been the light sayings of a vain man. So that I was troubled, fearing that some change would ensue to my people.

You will find our comments at the end of this chapter.

English prose 150 years on

If you were to compare dictionaries written a century apart, differences between the two would virtually leap off the page. You would find lots of new nouns and lots of new meanings for old words. Changes in English prose fiction are less obviously noticeable, more subtle, but still significant. As you will have seen in the last activity, it is not just a matter of new nouns and word meanings, but also a matter of voice (or tone), rhythm and attitude.

In the next activity you are going to look at another arbitrarily chosen segment of time, the twenty five years or so between the 1950s and the 1970s, but first we should like to look at two passages separated by 165 years. The first text below is a later section of the 'Caleb Williams' story:

I had now reached the border of the heath, and entered upon what is usually termed the forest. Strange as it may seem, it is nevertheless true, that, in this conjuncture, exhausted with hunger, destitute of all provision for the future, and surrounded with the most alarming dangers, my mind suddenly became glowing, animated, and cheerful. I thought that, by this time, the most formidable difficulties of my undertaking were surmounted; and I could not believe that, after having effected so much, I should find any thing invincible in what remained to be done. I recollected the confinement I had undergone, and the fate that had impended over me, with horror. Never did man feel more vividly, than I felt at that moment, the sweets of liberty. Never did man more strenuously prefer poverty with independence, to the artificial allurements of a life of slavery. I stretched forth my arms with rapture; I clapped my hands one upon the other, and exclaimed, 'Ah, this is indeed to be a man! These wrists were lately galled with fetters; all my motions, whether I rose up or sat down, were echoed to with the clanking of chains; I was tied down like a wild beast, and could not move but in a circle of a few feet in circumference. Now I can run fleet as a greyhound, and leap like a young roe upon the mountains. Oh, God! (if God there be that condescends to record the lonely beatings of an anxious heart) thou only canst tell with what delight a prisoner, just broke forth from his dungeon, hugs the blessings of a new-found liberty! Sacred and indescribable moment, when man regains his rights! But lately I held my life in jeopardy, because one man was unprincipled enough to assert what he knew to be false; I was destined to suffer an early and inexorable death from the hands of others, because none of them had penetration enough to distinguish from falsehood, what I uttered with the entire conviction of a full-fraught heart! Strange, that men from age to age should consent to hold their lives at the breath of another, merely that each in his turn may have a power of acting the tyrant according to law! Oh, God! give me poverty! shower upon me all the imaginary hardships of human life! I will receive them all with thankfulness. Turn me a prey to the wild beasts of the desert, so I be never again the victim of man dressed in the gore-dripping robes of authority! Suffer me at least to call life and the pursuits of life my own! Let me hold it at the mercy of the elements, of the hunger of beasts or the revenge of barbarians, but not of the cold-blooded prudence of monopolists and kings!' – How enviable was the enthusiasm, which could thus furnish me with energy, in the midst of hunger, poverty and universal desertion!

The next text comes from *The Runaway* by Morley Callaghan, a Canadian writer. A schoolboy, Michael, is fed up with both his friends, who call him a coward because he fails to do a 'dare', and with his parents who depress him by quarrelling a great deal.

It was then, on the way back to the house, that he felt he had to go away at once. 'I've got to go. I'll die here. I'll write to Dad from the city.'

No one paid any attention to him when he returned to the house. His father and stepmother were sitting quietly in the living-room reading the paper. In his own room he took a little wooden box from the bottom drawer of his dresser and emptied it of twenty dollars and seventy cents, all that he had saved. He listened solemnly for sounds in the house, then he stuffed a clean shirt into his pocket, a comb, and a toothbrush.

Outside he hurried along with his great swinging strides, going past the corner house, on past the long fence and the bridge and the church, and the shipyard, and past the last of the town lights to the highway. He was walking stubbornly with his face looking solemn and dogged. Then he saw the moonlight shining on the hay stacked in the fields, and when he smelled the oats and the richer smell of sweet clover he suddenly felt alive and free. Headlights from cars kept sweeping by and already he was imagining he could see the haze of bright light hanging over the city. His heart began to thump with eagerness. He put out his hand for a lift, feeling full of hope. He looked across the fields at the dark humps, cows standing motionless in the night. Soon someone would stop and pick him up. They would take him among a million new faces, rumbling sounds, and strange smells. He got more excited. His Uncle Joe might get him a job on the boats for the rest of the summer; maybe, too, he might be able to move around with him in the winter. Over and over he kept thinking of places with beautiful names, places like Tia Juana, Woodbine, Saratoga and Blue Bonnets.

When comparing texts with language change in mind, it is always a good idea to make some straightforward stylistic observations first. The fact that you can understand both in your own time is every bit as important, if not more so, than the historical distance between them. After all, Godwin and Callaghan are two different individuals in their own right, and not merely representative of their times.

Here are some noticeable features that distinguish the two texts:

– the first is written in the first person, the second in the third
– there is a greater degree of abstraction in the first, especially in the first part, more concreteness in the second (note that the 'wild beast', 'the

greyhound' and the 'young roe' are figures of speech, preceded by 'as' and 'like', whereas the car headlights, the cows etc. are all real ones in the second; admittedly, the 'chains' in the first seem a real memory)
- a consequence of these lexical features is that the first contains more ideas for the reader to think about, the second, more things for them to see (readers have to visualise the forest in the first piece, through their own imaginations)
- the first piece expresses in a direct way 'narrator emotion' because it is written in the first person, whereas the second, on the face of it, is a 'cooler' narrative (this doesn't rule out of course, the fact that some readers may be all the more moved by the distancing created through writing in the third person. Think what a difference it would make if Callaghan had chosen the first person)
- each piece is about 300 words long, yet the sentences in the first one are twice as long on average (there are 10 full-stops [including an exclamation mark] in the first, 20 in the second)

When doing stylistics with non-fiction texts, questions about a writer's purpose and the social function of the text are crucial first questions. With verbal art (prose fiction, drama, poems) the crucial purpose is not social but artistic. What is the writer's artistic purpose? There may be other purposes bound up with that but the essential, primary purpose that will give the text its value to a reader will be something like:

- to tell a story in a way that 'feels' right for the characters and events
- to avoid cliché expressions and attitudes the writer doesn't want to express
- to make dialogue convincing
- to please, or earn the respect of, the reader
- to say enough
- to generate pity, fear, love, horror, sympathy, disapproval or whatever for a character
- to shape the text into a satisfying whole
- to get the rhythm right
- not to sound like a wally, or a wimp, or a bore, or a pompous idiot, or too miserable (in other words, to get the 'tone of voice' right)
- to find a word that rhymes with 'brilliant' (or whatever).

There are many more purposes writers have cited as important to them.

Without getting into a quite unnecessary argument about which piece is the better, it is not difficult, on the evidence of language use, to make some distinctions between the texts in terms of artistic purpose and effects. (Artistic purposes, by the way, are not necessarily intended; they are often a mixture of accident, habit and intention.)

There are more ideas presented in the Godwin text. You could say that it was more ideologically driven – a political cry for freedom and justice. Both political historians and literary critics recognise Godwin's book as a propaganda novel of its day. And political propaganda novels are still written today, so there is not much change there; the genre has continued. For some readers, Godwin's artistic choice of a first person narrator may be too emotional, too close for comfort. Others may respond to it very sympathetically.

Callaghan's text represents a different genre: a genre stretching, possibly, from *Huckleberry Finn* through *A Catcher In The Rye* and, possibly on, in lighter vein, to *The Diary of Adrian Mole*, taking in along the way, novels like those of Bill Naughton and including Stan Barstow's *Joby*.

Differences and similarities of genre and individual writer's voices, are much more far reaching issues for understanding texts, than issues of language change on their own. The historical details preserve a writer's authentic voice as well as offering clues to the times in which a text was written. The passion, the references to God, chains and liberty, accord with the year 1794, while the sentences sound absolutely right. It should not be too surprising that some of these sentence patterns are still used today in fervent political speeches. Notice such grammatical repetitions as: 'Never did man ... Never did man ...' and 'I stretched forth my arms ... I clapped my hands'.

Discovery of 'old fashioned' sounding features often leads to seeing the very same language features being used in a modern context. The history of Modern English is like that.

The pace of the Godwin passage is a rising tide of personal and political emotion; the pace of the Callaghan passage is one of steady, determined action rising to a note of elation, as Michael feels himself free at last. Any reader today is likely to find this modern fiction. Is it the familiarity of words like 'Dad' and 'his Uncle Joe' and 'get him a job'? Is it the effect of 'he stuffed ...' or 'his heart began to thump'? Is it the short sentences? Is it, after all, the way in which the content evokes the twentieth century and not the nineteenth – the car headlights, the toothbrush, the haze of bright light hanging over the city?

We have nothing to say about the author's nationality, not just because it seems quite irrelevant here, but because it makes much more sense nowadays to think about literature written in English as a worldwide activity, rather than something practised only in the British Isles.

ACTIVITY 133

Below are some short examples of modern fiction in English. They are all in fact, by English, Irish or Scottish writers.

Read each one (listen to it as well!), considering any relevant stylistic issues.

When you have done this, make comparisons of the artistic purposes and effects of each piece. None is long enough for you to generalise safely about the authors, but there is enough verbal art for you to examine.

Finally, comment on any aspects of language that seem 'modern' compared with the early nineteenth century passages in the previous activity.

For this activity we have chosen texts from a segment of time between the 1950s and the 1970s. There is nothing extra special about this period. Texts have been chosen that have a reasonable thematic connection with the earlier ones, and which exemplify similar aspects of the novelist's art: dialogue, character and scene description, selection of events, narrator commentary and reflection.

When you looked at the older texts, you observed things in the language that used to be taken for granted by readers of an earlier generation but which is now noticeable; in this exercise you are trying to identify features that you are used to taking for granted, but which may become noticeable only to a future generation.

(i) from *In at the Birth*

William Trevor (1967)

ONCE upon a time there lived in a remote London suburb an elderly lady called Miss Efoss. Miss Efoss was a spry person, and for as long as she could control the issue she was determined to remain so. She attended the cinema and the theatre with regularity; she read at length; and she preferred the company of men and women forty years her junior. Once a year Miss Efoss still visited Athens and always on such visits she wondered why she had never settled in Greece: now, she felt, it was rather too late to make a change; in any case, she enjoyed London.

In her lifetime, nothing had passed Miss Efoss by. She had loved and been loved. She had once, even, given birth to a child. For a year or two she had known the ups and downs of early family life, although the actual legality of marriage had somehow been overlooked. Miss Efoss's baby died during a sharp attack of pneumonia; and shortly afterwards the child's father packed a suitcase one night. He said goodbye quite kindly to Miss Efoss, but she never saw him again.

In retrospect, Miss Efoss considered that she had run the gamut of human emotions. She settled down to the lively superficiality of the everyday existence she had mapped for herself. She was quite content with it. And she hardly noticed it when the Dutts entered her life.

It was Mr. Dutt who telephoned. He said: 'Ah, Miss Efoss, I wonder if you can help us. We have heard that occasionally you baby-sit. We have scoured the neighbourhood for a reliable baby-sitter. Would you be interested, Miss Efoss, in giving us a try?'

'But who are you?' said Miss Efoss. 'I don't even know you. What is your name to begin with?'

'Dutt,' said Mr. Dutt. 'We live only a couple of hundred yards from you. I think you would find it convenient.'

'Well –'

'Miss Efoss, come and see us. Come and have a drink. If you like the look of us perhaps we can arrange something. If not, we shan't be in the least offended.'

(ii) from *Tigers are Better-Looking*

Jean Rhys (1968)

'MEIN LIEB, Mon Cher, My Dear, Amigo,' the letter began.

I'm off. I've been wanting to go for some time, as I'm sure you know, but was waiting for the moment when I had the courage to step out into the cold world again. Didn't feel like a farewell scene.

Apart from much that it is *better* not to go into, you haven't any idea how sick I am of all the phoney talk about Communism – and the phoney talk of the other lot too, if it comes to that. You people are exactly alike, whatever you call yourselves – Untouchable. Indispensable is the motto, and you'd pine to death if you hadn't someone to look down on and insult. I got the feeling that I was surrounded by a pack of timid tigers waiting to spring the moment anybody is in trouble or hasn't any money. *But tigers are better-looking, aren't they?*

I'm taking the coach to Plymouth. I have my plans.

I came to London with high hopes, but all I got out of it was a broken leg and enough sneers to last me for the next thirty years if I live so long, which may God forbid.

Don't think I'll forget how kind you were after my accident – having me to stay with you and all that. But assez means enough.

I've drunk the milk in the refrigerator. I was thirsty after that party last night, though if you call that a party I call it a wake. Besides, I know how you dislike the stuff (Freud! Bow-wow-wow!!) So you'll have to have your tea straight, my dear.

Goodbye. I'll write you again when times are better.

HANS

There was a postscript:

Mind you write a swell article today, you tame grey mare.

Mr. Severn sighed. He had always known Hans would hop it sooner or later, so why this taste in his mouth, as if he had eaten dust?

A swell article.

The band in the Embankment Gardens played. It's the same old song once again. It's the same old tender refrain.

(iii) from *Tithonus*

George Mackay Brown (1974)

FRAGMENTS FROM THE DIARY OF A LAIRD

THEY are all, especially the women, excited in Torsay today. There is a new child in the village, a little girl. The birth has happened in a house where – so Traill the postman assured me – no one for the past ten years has expected it. The door of Maurice Garth the fisherman and his wife Armingert had seemed to be marked with the sign of barrenness. They were married twenty-one years ago, when Maurice was thirty and Armingert nineteen. One might have expected a large family, five or six a least, from such a healthy devoted pair. (They had both come from tumultuous households to the cold empty cottage at the end of the village.) But the years passed and no young voice broke the quiet dialogue of Maurice and Armingert. To all the islanders it seemed a pity: nothing but beautiful children could have come from their loins.

I was hauling my dinghy up the loch shore this afternoon – it was too bright a day, the trout saw through every gesture and feint – when I saw the woman on the road above. It seemed to me then that she had been waiting to speak to me for some time. I know who she must be as soon as she opened her mouth. The butterings of her tongue, and the sudden knife flashes, had been described to me often enough. She was Maggie Swintoun. I had been well warned about her by the factor and the minister and the postman. Her idle and wayward tongue, they told me, had done harm to the reputation of more than one person in Torsay; so I'm sure that when I turned my loch-dazzled face to her it did not wear a welcoming expression.

'O sir, you'll never guess,' she said, in the rapt secret voice of all news bearers. 'A bairn was born in the village this morning, and at the Garth cottage of all places – a girl. I think it's right that you should know. Dr. Wayne from Hamnavoe took it into the world. I was there helping. I could hardly believe it when they sent for me.'

The face was withdrawn from the loch side. A rare morning was in front of her, telling the news in shop, smithy, manse, and at the doors of all the crofts round about.

I mounted my horse that, patient beast, had been cropping the thin loch-side grass all morning and cantered back to The Hall over the stony dusty road.

Now I knew why a light had been burning at two o'clock in the cottage at the end of the village. I had got up at that time to let Tobias the cat in.

This is the first child to be born in the island since I came to be laird here. I feel that in some way she belongs to me. I stood at the high window of The Hall looking down at the Garth cottage till the light began to fade.

The generations have been renewed. The island is greatly enriched since yesterday.

(iv) from *Brontëburgers*

Victoria Wood (1986)

Guide: Right, I'm your official guide. Now before I show you round, I'll just fill you in on a few details, as we call them. As you can see, we're standing in the hall of the Haworth Parsonage, where Haworth's parson, the Reverend Brontë, lived here with his daughters, the famous Brontë sisters, now, alas, no longer with us – but they have left us their novels, which I've not read, being more of a Dick Francis nut. Now, if you pass by me into the parlour (mind my vaccination) ... This is what was known in those days as a parlour, somewhat similar to our lounge-type sitting-room affair in modern terminology. I'm afraid the wallpaper isn't the original period to which we're referring to, it is actually Laura Ashley, but I think it does give some idea of what life must have been like in a blustery old Yorkshire community of long ago.

That portrait on the wall is actually of Charlotte Brontë, one of the famous Brontë sisters, and of course to us she may seem a rather gloomy-looking individual; but you must remember these days she'd have a perm, or blusher, or I suppose even drugs would have helped her maintain a more cheerful attitude. In fact, she'd probably not be dead if she was alive today. Now if you'd like to hutch through to the Reverend Brontë's study ... This is a typical study in which to do studying – as you can see there's a table, chair ... (oh my poncho, I've been looking for that ...) and I like to imagine this elderly old gentleman hunched over a sermon, probably thinking, 'Where's my cocoa, I suppose those darn girls are in the middle of another chapter,' or something like that he may have been thinking – we just can't be sure ... Of course he died eventually, unfortunately. You must remember this is an extremely exposed part of the United Kingdom, I mean, it's May now, and I'm still having to slip that polo-neck under my bolero.

On the table we see the Reverend Brontë's gloves. They tell us such a lot about him. He had two hands, and he wasn't missing any fingers. We think they were knitted by one of the famous Brontë sisters. I don't suppose their brother Branwell could knit and anyway being an alcoholic he'd never have been able to cast on.

Now if you'd just hutch up the stairs ... We're looking out over the graves to the hills beyond. And, fairly clearly in the distance we can hear the wind 'wuthering'. That's an old Yorkshire word; some other old Yorkshire words are 'parkin' and 'fettle'. The room in which we're now standing it was originally Charlotte's mother's bedroom. In fact Charlotte's mother died in this room, and Charlotte died in here too, so better not stay too long! (Just my joke!) In that glass case you'll see what we call a day dress – that is a dress worn in the day, not at night – we think belonging to Anne or Emily, presumably not Branwell, unless he had more problems than history's prepared to tell us.

A few dates for the date-minded. The Brontë family moved here some time in the nineteenth century, and lived here for quite a number of years. As I say, Charlotte died in this room – those are her slippers. And I like to imagine her in this room, with her slippers on, dying.

Now if you go through the far door, yes, do move my moped ... Now this room was at one time Branwell's room. I think people tend to forget Branwell was fairly artistic himself. Of course, he was lazy, conceited and a dipsomaniac, so these days he'd have probably been in the government.

Now if anybody would like a souvenir to take home as a souvenir, we have Brontë video-games, body-warmers, acrylic mitts, pedestal mats, feminine deodorants and novelty tea-strainers. Snacks and light refreshments are available in the Heathcliff Nosher Bar, so please feel free to sample our very popular Brontëburgers. Or for the fibre-conscious – our Branwell Brontëburgers.

Oh – just a little message for the 'Yorkshire Heritage' coach party. Can they please re-convene at two in the car-park ready for this afternoon's trip which is, I believe, round three dark Satanic mills, Emmerdale Farm, and Nora Batty's front room? Thank you.

Fairy tales with attitude

Among the different approaches to the study of myths and fairy stories, three have featured prominently in modern studies of literature and literary theory. One approach sees myths and fairy stories as psycho-analytical dramas, in which deep seated fears and desires and a sense of loss are expressed, e.g. monsters, quests, lost and step-parents, friends and enemies; another pays attention to their formal structures, e.g. the recurring number three, as in the three bears, the three little pigs and the three billy goats gruff, or the problem>quest>setbacks>final triumph plot; while a third approach sees them as models or reflectors of social values and attitudes. In many modern novels and plays, you can see the ancient themes very much alive and well: from rags to riches (Cinderella and/or Pygmalion), selling your soul to the devil (Faust), the ugly duckling transformed into a swan, young lovers caught between families at war, awakening from a curse to a new life (Sleeping Beauty). In all these it is not difficult to see how the three different approaches complement each other when it comes to interpretation.

In 1994, an American writer, James Finn Garner, published a runaway best seller, entitled, *Politically Correct Bedtime Stories*, (Souvenir Press). It caught the mood of the time, satirising a new language fashion for euphemisms that would give no offence to minority groups, nor reinforce privilege and social injustices.

Much of Garner's success comes from working within a well known, traditional genre, but his comic approach is so subversive it virtually creates a new genre. We are unable to reproduce examples here but we are sure you would find them very enjoyable. If you look, for example at his version of *The Three Little Pigs*, you'll find wickedly funny attention to modern uses of words. Note the p-c use of 'hemisphere' instead of 'world', the 'massive' heart attack, 'socialist democracy' and 'affordable' housing, all indicators of 1990s political preoccupations. The footnote, apart from its assertion of animal rights, also shows that Garner is well versed in the literary theory of fairy stories. The term 'metaphorical construct' is quite a serious idea, warning the reader not to take for granted the values and attitudes embodied in fairy stories.

Garner's version of *Rumpelstiltskin* is hilarious. We have reproduced below a Victorian version on which Garner has based his modern version.

ACTIVITY 134

Rumpelstiltskin

The text below is a translation of the Brothers Grimm story (originally written in German) into early Victorian English, in the storytelling style of the day (1853). The complete stories were published under the title, *Grimms' Household Stories*, an interesting bit of language change in itself.

Read the 1853 version, commenting on how language is used to tell the story (what are the verbal arts?), and on the values and attitudes you find implicit in the language. What dates it?

Now write a modern version of your own and a commentary to it, identifying the contemporary language uses and attitudes that you are satirising. You may find it helpful to look at another author's modern version of *The Three Little Pigs*, see Chapter 11 page 312.

Finally, choose any fairy story (by the Brothers Grimm, Hans Anderson or le Fanu) and update it in any way you wish. Do ensure that you read first a traditional version, to get the language nuances right, rather than just rely on your memory of the plot.

Essentially, this is a transformation exercise, but one with a special eye on language innovations.

Rumpelstiltskin (1853)

THERE was once a poor Miller who had a beautiful daughter; and one day, having to go to speak with the King, he said, in order to make himself appear of consequence, that he had a daughter who could spin straw into gold. The King was very fond of gold, and thought to himself, 'That is an art which would please me very well;' and so he said to the Miller, 'If your daughter is so very clever, bring her to the castle in the morning, and I will put her to the proof.'

As soon as she arrived the King led her into a chamber which was full of straw; and, giving her a wheel and a reel, he said, 'Now set yourself to work and if you have not spun this straw into gold by an early hour to-morrow, you must die.' With these words he shut the room door, and left the maiden alone.

There she sat for a long time, thinking how to save her life; for she understood nothing of the art whereby straw might be spun into gold; and her perplexity increased more and more, till at last she began to weep. All at once the door opened and in stepped a little Man, who, said, 'Good evening, fair maiden; why do you weep so sore?' 'Ah,' she replied, 'I must spin this straw into gold, and I am sure I do not know how.'

The little Man asked, 'What will you give me if I spin it for you?'

'My necklace,' said the maiden.

The Dwarf took it, placed himself in front of the wheel, and whirr, whirr, whirr, three times round, and the bobbin was full. Then he set up another, and whirr, whirr, whirr, thrice round again, and a second bobbin was full; and so he went all night long, until all the straw was spun, and the bobbins were full of gold. At sunrise the King came, very much astonished to see the gold; the sight of which gladdened him, but did not make his heart less covetous. He caused the maiden to be led into another room, still larger, full of straw; and then he bade her spin it into gold during the night if she valued her life. The Maiden was again quite at a loss what to do; but while she cried the door opened suddenly, as before, and the Dwarf appeared and asked her what she would give him in return for his assistance. 'The ring off my finger,' she replied. The little Man took the ring and began to spin at once, and by the morning all the straw was changed to glistening gold. The King was rejoiced above measure at the sight of this, but still he was not satisfied; but, leading the maiden into another still larger room, full of straw as the others, he said, 'This you must spin during the night; but if you accomplish it you shall be my bride.' 'For,' thought he to himself, 'a richer wife thou canst not have in all the world.'

When the maiden was left alone, the Dwarf again appeared, and asked for the third time, 'What will you give me to do this for you?'

'I have nothing left that I can give you.' replied the maiden.

'Then promise me your first-born child if you become Queen,' said he.

The Miller's daughter thought, 'Who can tell if that will ever happen?' and, ignorant how else to help herself out of her trouble, she promised the Dwarf what he desired; and he immediately set about and finished the spinning. When morning came, and the King found all he had wished for done, he celebrated his wedding, and the fair Miller's daughter became Queen.

About a year after the marriage, when she had ceased to think about the little Dwarf, she brought a fine child into the world; and, suddenly, soon after its birth, the very man appeared and demanded what she had promised. The frightened Queen offered him all the riches of the kingdom if he would leave her her child; but the Dwarf answered, 'No; something human is dearer to me than all the wealth of the world.'

The Queen began to weep and groan so much, that the Dwarf compassionated her, and said, 'I will leave you three days to consider; if you in that time discover my name you shall keep your child.'

All night long the Queen racked her brains for all the names she could think of, and sent a messenger through the country to collect far and wide any new names. The following morning came the Dwarf, and she began with 'Caspar,' 'Melchior,' 'Balthassar,' and all the odd names she knew; but at each the little Man exclaimed, 'That is not my name.' The second day the Queen inquired of all her people for uncommon and curious names, and called the Dwarf 'Ribs-of-Beef,' 'Sheep-shank,' 'Whalebone;' but at each he said, 'This is not my name.' The third day the messenger came back and said, 'I have not found a single name; but as I came to a high mountain near the edge of a forest, where foxes and hares say good night to each other, I saw there a little house, and before the door a fire was burning, and round this fire a very curious little Man was dancing on one leg, and shouting, –

> '"To-day I stew, and then I'll bake,
> To-morrow I shall the Queen's child take;
> Ah! how famous it is that nobody knows
> 'That my name is Rumpelstiltskin.'"

When the Queen heard this she was very glad, for now she knew the name; and soon after came the Dwarf, and asked, 'Now my lady Queen, what is my name?'

First she said, 'Are you called Conrade?' 'No.'

'Are you called Hal?' 'No.'

'Are you called Rumpelstiltskin?'

'A witch has told you! a witch has told you!' shrieked the little Man, and stamped his right foot so hard in the ground with rage that he could not draw it out again. Then he took hold of his left leg with both his hands, and pulled away so hard that his right came off in the struggle, and he hopped away howling terribly. And from that day to this the Queen has heard no more of her troublesome visitor.

Literary biography

In Chapter 3, we included in the spectrum of 'literary texts', biographical and travel writing. Both have explicit factual content but some biographies and travel accounts achieve 'literary' status by virtue of the imagination and the verbal art with which they have been conceived and written. In the next activity you are going to look at three seventeenth century biographies that are literary in another sense of that word: they are about people who, among other accomplishments, have reputations as poets.

The three biographies are separated by a period of only 30 years, and are:

The Life of John Donne by Izaak Walton, 1640
The Histories of the Worthies of England by Thomas Fuller, 1662
Brief Lives by John Aubrey, c. 1670

Through exploring some excerpts you should get a feel for the flavour of seventeenth century prose writing. Already you will have noticed that whilst two of the titles could have been published today, the title of Fuller's book conjures up another age altogether. The word 'worthies' might well have been used in Victorian times but the use of the word 'histories' in a biographical context, speaks more of the seventeenth century. The word has itself an interesting history, worth looking up in the OED on CD ROM.

ACTIVITY 135

Telling it as it was

Read the three texts making, first of all, stylistic observations about them. Try to forget, initially, that you are studying language changes, but give some thought to how a seventeenth century reader may have read them. Think about the genre of biography, and the attitude of the biographer to his subject. After all, you can only learn about the subject's life, through the mind of the biographer, which was as true in the seventeenth century.

When you have done this, look more closely at words and expressions in the texts that seem to you to have changed, since the mid-seventeenth century. We have listed below some features of the first text, to get you started on the historical part of this activity.

(i) Izaak Walton on John Donne

I must here look so far back as to tell the reader that at his first return out of Essex to preach his last sermon, his old friend and physician, Dr. Fox, a man of great worth, came to him to consult his health and that after a sight of him and some queries concerning his distempers he told him, 'That by cordials and drinking milk twenty days together there was a probability of his restoration to health'; but he passionately denied to drink it. Nevertheless, Dr. Fox, who loved him most entirely, wearied him with solicitations till he yielded to take it for ten days; at the end of which time he told Dr. Fox, 'He had drunk it more to satisfy him than to recover his health and that he would not drink it ten days longer upon the best moral assurance of having twenty years added to his life, for he loved it not, and was so far from fearing death, which to others is the king of terrors, that he longed for the day of his dissolution.'

It is observed that a desire of glory or commendation is rooted in the very nature of man and that those of the severest and most mortified lives, though they may become so humble as to banish self-flattery and such weeds as naturally grow there, yet they have not been able to kill this desire of glory, but that, like our radical heat, it will both live and die with us; and many think it should be so, and we want not sacred examples to justify the desire of having our memory to outlive our lives. Which I mention, because Dr. Donne, by the persuasion of Dr. Fox, easily yielded at this very time to have a monument made for him; but Dr. Fox undertook not to persuade him how or what monument it should be; that was left to Dr. Donne himself.

A monument being resolved upon, Dr. Donne sent for a carver to make for him in wood the figure of an urn, giving him directions for the compass and height of it, and to bring with it a board of the just height of his body. These being got, then without delay a choice painter was got to be in a readiness to draw his picture, which was taken as followeth: Several charcoal fires being first made in his large study, he brought with him into that place his winding-sheet in his hand and, having put off all his clothes, had this sheet put on him and so tied with knots at his head and feet and his hands so placed as dead bodies are usually fitted to be shrouded and put into their coffin or grave. Upon this urn he thus stood with his eyes shut and with so much of the sheet turned aside as might show his lean, pale, and death-like face, which was purposely turned toward the East, from whence he expected the second coming of his and our Saviour, Jesus. In this posture he was drawn at his just height; and when the picture was fully finished, he caused it to be set by his bed-side, where it continued and became his hourly object till his death and was then given to his dearest friend and executor, Doctor Henry King, then chief residenciary of St. Paul's, who caused him to be thus carved in one entire piece of white marble, as it now stands in that church; and by Doctor Donne's own appointment these words were to be affixed to it as his epitaph:

JOHANNES DONNE

Sac. Theol. Profess.

*Post varia studia quibus ab annis tenerrimis
fideliter, nec infeliciter incubuit,
instinctu et impulsu Sp. Sancti, monitu
et hortatu*

*REGIS JACOBI, ordines sacros
amplexus, anno sui Jesu, 1614, et suæ ætatis 42,
decanatu hujus ecclesiæ indutus 27,
Novembris, 1621,*

*exutus morte ultimo die Martii, 1631,
hic licet in occiduo cinere aspicit eum
cujus nomen est Oriens.**

And now, having brought him through the many labyrinths and perplexities of a various life, even to the gates of death and the grave, my desire is he may rest till I have told my reader that I have seen many pictures of him in several habits and at several ages and in several postures. And I now mention this because I have seen one picture of him, drawn by a curious hand at his age of eighteen, with his sword and what other adornments might then suit with the present fashions of youth and the giddy gaieties of that age;

* 'John Donne, Doctor of Divinity, after various studies, pursued by him from his earliest years with assiduity, and not without success, entered into holy orders under the influence and impulse of the Holy Ghost and by the advice and exhortation of King James, in the year of our Lord 1614, when he

was 42. Having been invested with the Deanery of this church on November 27, 1621, he was stripped of it by death on the last day of March 1631: and here, though himself set in dust, he beholdeth Him whose name is the Rising Sun.'

(ii) Fuller on Edmund Spenser

Edmund Spenser, born in this city, was brought up in Pembroke Hall in Cambridge, where he became an excellent scholar; but especially most happy in English poetry, as his words do declare; in which the many Chaucerisms used (for I will not say affected by him) are thought by the ignorant to be blemishes, known by the learned to be beauties, to his book, which notwithstanding had been more saleable, if more conformed to our modern language.

There passeth a story commonly told and believed, that Spenser presenting his poems to Queen Elizabeth, she, highly affected therewith, commanded the Lord Cecil, her treasurer, to give him a hundred pounds; and when the treasurer (a good steward of the Queen's money) alleged that the sum was too much, 'Then give him,' quoth the queen, 'what is reason'; to which the lord consented. But was so busied, belike, about matters of high concernment that Spenser received no reward; whereupon he presented this petition in a small piece of paper to the queen in her progress:

> I was promised on a time,
> To have reason for my rhyme;
> Form that time unto this season,
> I received nor rhyme nor reason.

Hereupon the queen gave strict order (not without some check to her treasurer) for the present payment of the hundred pounds she first intended unto him.

He afterwards went over into Ireland, secretary to the Lord Gray, Lord Deputy thereof; and though that his office under his lord was lucrative, yet got he no estate; but, saith my author, '*peculiari poetis fato, semper cum paupertate conflictatus est.*' So that it fared little better with him than with William Xilander the German (a most excellent linguist, antiquary, philosopher, and mathematician), who was so poor that (as Thuanus saith) he was thought, '*fami non fame scribere.*'

(iii) Aubrey on Ralegh

He was the first that brought tobacco into England and into fashion. – In our part of North Wilts, e.g. Malmesbury hundred, it came first into fashion by Sir Walter Long.

I have heard my grandfather Lyte say that one pipe was handed from man to man round about the table. They had first silver pipes; the ordinary sort made use of a walnut shell and a straw.

It was sold then for its weight in silver. I have heard some of our old yeomen neighbours say that when they went to Malmesbury or Chippenham market, they culled out their biggest shillings to lay in the scales against the tobacco.

Sir W.R., standing in a stand at Sir Robert Poyntz's part at Acton, took a pipe of tobacco, which made the ladies quit till he had done.

Within these 35 years 'twas scandalous for a divine to take tobacco.

I have heard old Major Cosh say that Sir W. Ralegh did not care to go on the Thames in a wherry boat; he would rather go round about over London Bridge.

He loved a wench well; and one time getting up one of the Maids of Honour up against a tree in a wood ('twas his first Lady) who seemed at first boarding to be somewhat fearful of her honour and modest, she cried: 'Sweet Sir Walter, what do you me ask? Will you undo me? Nay, sweet Sir Walter! Sweet Sir Walter! Sir Walter!' At last, as the danger and the pleasure at the same time grew higher, she cried in the extasy, 'Swisser Swatter Swisser Swatter.' She proved with child, and I doubt not but that this hero took care of them both, as also that the product was more than an ordinary mortal.

My old friend James Harrington, Esq. was well acquainted with Sir Benjamin Rudyerd, who was an acquaintance of Sir Walter Ralegh's. He told Mr. J.H. that Sir Walter Ralegh, being invited to dinner with some great person where his son was to go with him, he said to his son, 'Thou art such a quarrelsome, affronting creature that I am ashamed to have such a bear in my company.' Mr. Walt humbled himself to his father, and promised he would behave himself mightily mannerly. So away they went, and Sir Benjamin, I think, with them. He sat next to his father and was very demure at least half dinner time. Then said he: 'I this morning, not having the fear of God before my eyes but by the instigation of the Devil, went to a whore. I was very eager of her, kissed and embraced her, and went to enjoy her, but she thrust me from her and vowed I should not, *"For your father lay with me but an hour ago."*' Sir Walt, being so strangely surprised and put out of his countenance at so great a tale, gives his son a damned blow over the face. His son, as rude as he was, would not strike his father, but strikes over the face of the gentleman that sat next to him and said, 'Box about, 'twill come to my father anon.' 'Tis now a common-used proverb.

He was scandalized with atheism, but he was a bold man, and would venture at discourse which was unpleasant to the churchmen. I remember my Lord Scudamour said 'twas basely said of Sir W.R. to talk of the anagram of Dog. In his speech on the scaffold, I have heard my cousin Whitney say (and I think 'tis printed) that he spake not one word of Christ, but of the great and incomprehensible God, with much zeal and adoration, so that he concluded that he was an a-Christ, not an atheist.

He took a pipe of tobacco a little before he went to the scaffold, which some formal persons were scandalized at, but I think 'twas well and properly done, to settle his spirits.

[Historical note: the dates for the three poets are, Donne (1572–1631); Spenser (1552–1599); Ralegh 1554–1618).

COMMENTARY   **THE WALTON EXCERPT**

The first sentence begins with a grammatical strategy not unfamiliar today: 'It is observed that . . .'

The effect is both formal and in the passive voice, giving it a formal, impersonal, quasi scientific tone. We don't know specifically who it is that makes the observation, but there is an assumption that the reader will agree. By the time we reach 'most mortified lives' the period voice of the text has begun to make itself heard. 'Mortified' has a religious meaning here (self-denial) and not the modern, slightly comic sense of being, metaphorically, slapped in the face or humiliated. The phrase 'radical heat' is puzzling at first but a little guess work, checked out, suggests that it means 'body warmth', i.e. 'being alive'.

The sentence beginning, 'A monument resolved upon . . .' is another formal expression that continues today in certain kinds of report writing. It is certainly an economical one, and notice again its impersonal, passive voice.

Reading on discovers a number of instances of seventeenth century word choice and word order:

'we want not' = 'we do not need'; 'make for him' (the 'for' seems to have been discontinued in general use today, but not completely); 'just height' = 'right height' today (note though, the modern idiom; It's just right'); 'put off his clothes' ('took off'); 'from whence' (unusual today, but sometimes used for effect); 'caused it to be set'; 'his hourly object' (= 'occupation? objective?'); 'curious' (not its modern meaning); 'residenciary' (archaic term now); 'giddy gaieties' (lovely phrase in its own right, needs no explanation).

The opening words of some sentence opening words are worth noticing: 'Which I mention ...' and several beginning with 'And ...' The punctuation is also worth noticing. Where a modern writer would use commas for a parenthetical remark, Walton uses semi-colons, as in '... die with us; and many think it should be so; and we want not ...' A look in Tom McArthur's *Oxford Companion To The English Language* would tell you that semi-colons were a relatively new form of punctuation, introduced from Italy in the time of Francis Bacon (1561–1626) who used them to mark off direct speech, while others used them for question marks.

These are the kinds of things you can notice in the other texts. Don't worry if you can't explain what you have found; the important thing is that you have noticed the changing nature of language, and know where to look for more information. What matters in the end is that you should be able to appreciate the author's distinctive voice, albeit speaking in the language of the age in which he lived.

Three questions you might ask at the end of this activity, about each of the texts, are:

1 what does the text tell me about its subject?
2 what does it tell me about the biographer?
3 what does it tell me about some examples of seventeenth century English prose?

Poetic voices

In general, written English prose has developed as a formal version of everyday English. The degree of formality and distance from educated, spontaneous speech may be considerable or slight. There are examples in early modern English of extravagantly literary and Latinate writing styles, but in this book we have concentrated on prose texts where it is possible to see, hear and feel a connection with the spoken language of the day.

With poetry, however, it is not quite so straightforward. Poetry makes language work in significantly different ways from our everyday expectations of language. That's the whole point of poetry. When poets say they want their poems to stay close to the language of ordinary people, they are not deceiving themselves. It can be both extraordinary and ordinary at the same time. That is what makes poetic meanings so complex.

ACTIVITY 136

From Queen Elizabeth the First to Margaret Atwood

Below are some excerpts from poems written between c.1570 and 1974. They are not arranged in chronological order. Your task is to read the poems, appreciating each one on its own terms, regardless of when it was written.

When you have done this, arrange the poems in what you think would be their chronological order. Make a note of your linguistic reasons for placing a poem earlier or later than others. Think of your chronological order as a radioscript to be read by different voices with accompanying music and effects.

All the poems were written by women.

Clearly you will try to be as accurate as you can, but don't worry too much about the exact dates. This is not an easy activity, but it will be interesting.

When you have made your decisions, look at the end of the chapter for the actual dates and details. Don't be too concerned at any errors. If any poems surprise you, ask yourself why? Ask also about the assumptions that guided your guesswork, and remember that most people will arrive at a different order from the true chronological order. Why should this be so?

1

Long neglect has worn away
Half the sweet enchanting smile;
Time has turned the bloom to gray;
Mold and damp the face defile.

But that lock of silky hair,
Still beneath the picture twined,
Tells what once those features were,
Paints their image on the mind.
Fair the hand that traced that line,
"Dearest, ever deem me true";
Swiftly flew the finger fine
When the pen that motto drew.

2

I think of the Celts as rather a whining lady
Who was beautiful once but is not so much so now
She is not very loving, but there is one thing she loves
It is her grievance which she hugs and takes out walking.

The Celtic lady likes fighting very much for freedom
But when she has got it she is a proper tyrant
Nobody likes her much when she is governing.

The Celtic lady is not very widely popular
But the English love her oh they love her very much
Especially when the Celtic lady is Irish they love her
Which is odd as she hates them then more than anyone else,
When she's Welsh the English stupidly associate her chiefly
With national hats, eisteddfóds and Old Age Pensions.
(They don't think of her at all when she is Scotch, it is rather a problem.)
Oh the Celtic lady when she's Irish is the one for me
Oh she is so witty and wild, my word witty,

And flashing and spiteful this Celtic lady we love
All the same she is not so beautiful as she was.

3

In such a night when every louder wind
Is to its distant cavern safe confined;
And only gentle Zephyr fans his wings,
And lonely Philomel, still waking, sings;
Or from some tree, famed for the owl's delight,
She, hollowing clear, directs the wanderer right:
In such a night, when passing clouds give place,
Or thinly veil the heavens' mysterious face;
When in some river, overhung with green,
The waving moon and trembling leaves are seen;
When freshened grass now bears itself upright,
And makes cool banks to pleasing rest invite,
Whence springs the woodbind, and the bramble-rose,
And where the sleepy cowslip sheltered grows;

4

Come to me in the silence of the night;
    Come in the speaking silence of a dream;
Come with soft rounded cheeks and eyes as bright
        As sunlight on a stream;
            Come back in tears,
O memory, hope, love of finished years.

Oh dream how sweet, too sweet, too bitter sweet,
    Whose wakening should have been in Paradise,
Where souls brimful of love abide and meet;
        Where thirsting longing eyes
            Watch the slow door
That opening, letting in, lets out no more.

Yet come to me in dreams, that I may live
    My very life again tho' cold in death:
Come back to me in dreams, that I may give
        Pulse for pulse, breath for breath:
            Speak low, lean low,
As long ago, my love, how long ago.

5

This is what you changed me to:
a graypink vegetable with slug
eyes, buttock
incarnate, spreading like a slow turnip,

a skin you stuff so you may feed
in your turn, a stinking wart
of flesh, a large tuber
of blood which munches
and bloats. Very well then. Meanwhile

I have the sky, which is only half
caged, I have my weed corners,

I keep myself busy, singing
my song of roots and noses,

my song of dung. Madame,
this song offends you, these grunts
which you find oppressively sexual,
mistaking simple greed for lust.

I am yours. If you feed me garbage,
I will sing a song of garbage.
This is a hymn.

6

Thou ill-formed offspring of my feeble brain,
Who after birth didst by my side remain,
Till snatched from thence by friends, less wise than true,
Who thee abroad, exposed to public view,
Made thee in rags, halting to th' press to trudge,
Where errors were not lessened (all may judge).
At thy return my blushing was not small,
My rambling brat (in print) should mother call,
I cast thee by as one unfit for light,
Thy visage was so irksome in my sight;
Yet being mine own, at length affection would
Thy blemishes amend, if so I could:
I washed thy face, but more defects I saw,
And rubbing off a spot still made a flaw.
I stretched thy joints to make thee even feet,
Yet still thou run'st more hobbling than is meet;
In better dress to trim thee was my mind,
But nought save homespun cloth i' th' house I find.
In this array 'mongst vulgars may'st thou roam.
In critic's hands beware thou dost not come,
And take thy way where yet thou art not known;
If for thy father asked, say thou hadst none;
And for thy mother, she alas is poor,
Which caused her thus to send thee out of door.

7

It is ten years, now, since we rowed to Children's Island.
The sun flamed straight down that noon on the water off Marblehead.
That summer we wore black glasses to hide our eyes.
We were always crying, in our spare rooms, little put-upon sisters,
In the two, huge, white, handsome houses in Swampscott.
When the sweetheart from England appeared, with her cream skin and Yardley
    cosmetics,
I had to sleep in the same room with the baby on a too-short cot,
And the seven-year-old wouldn't go out unless his jersey stripes
Matched the stripes of his socks.

O it was richness! – eleven rooms and a yacht
With a polished mahogany stair to let into the water
And a cabin boy who could decorate cakes in six-colored frosting.
But I didn't know how to cook, and babies depressed me.
Nights, I wrote in my diary spitefully, my fingers red
With triangular scorch marks from ironing tiny ruchings and puffed sleeves.

When the sporty wife and her doctor husband went on one of their cruises
They left me a borrowed maid named Ellen, "for protection,"
And a small Dalmatian.

8

What was he doing, the great god Pan,
     Down in the reeds by the river?
Spreading ruin and scattering ban,
Splashing and paddling with hoofs of a goat,
And breaking the golden lilies afloat
     With the dragonfly on the river.

He tore out a reed, the great god Pan,
     From the deep cool bed of the river;
The limpid water turbidly ran,
And the broken lilies a-dying lay,
And the dragonfly had fled away,
     Ere he brought it out of the river.

High on the shore sat the great god Pan
     While turbidly flowed the river;
And hacked and hewed as a great god can,
With his hard bleak steel at the patient reed,
Till there was not a sign of the leaf indeed
     To prove it fresh from the river.

9

At length, by so much importunity pressed,
Take, C –, at once, the inside of my breast;
This stupid indifference so often you blame
Is not owing to nature, to fear, or to shame;
I am not as cold as a Virgin in lead,
Nor is Sunday's sermon so strong in my head;
I know but too well how time flies along,
That we live but few years and yet fewer are young.

But I hate to be cheated, and never will buy
Long years of repentance for moments of joy.
Oh was there a man (but where shall I find
Good sense and good nature so equally joined?)
Would value his pleasure, contribute to mine,
Not meanly would boast, nor would lewdly design,
Not over severe, yet not stupidly vain,
For I would have the power though not give the pain;

No pedant yet learnéd, not rakehelly gay
Or laughing because he has nothing to say,
To all my whole sex obliging and free,
Yet never be fond of any but me;
In public preserve the decorum that's just,
And show in his eyes he is true to his trust,
Then rarely approach, and respectfully bow,
Yet not fulsomely pert, nor yet foppishly low.

10

When I was fair and young, and favor gracéd me,
Of many was I sought, their mistress for to be;

But I did scorn them all, and answered them therefore,
   "Go, go go seek some otherwhere!
     Importune me no more!"

How many weeping eyes I made to pine with woe,
How many sighing hearts, I have no skill to show;
Yet I the prouder grew, and answered them therefore,
   "Go, go go seek some otherwhere!
     Importune me no more!"

Then spake fair Venus' son, that proud victorious boy,
And said, "Fine dame, since that you be so coy,
I will so pluck your plumes that you shall say no more,
   'Go, go go seek some otherwhere!
     Importune me no more!'"

When he had spake these words, such change grew in my breast
That neither night nor day since that, I could take any rest.
Then lo! I did repent that I had said before,
   "Go, go go seek some otherwhere!
     Importune me no more!"

Are English sentences getting shorter?

Before looking at our last activity on Modern English – a survey of prose texts from the 1590s to the 1990s – we would like you to think in more detail about sentences. Essentially you have been considering in this chapter, changes in English style. Word choice and the use of particular expressions and idioms have considerable influence on the reader, but equally, sentence type and construction exert a strong influence too. It can be argued that sentence grammar is the greatest influence of all on style. After all, if you haven't 'sentenced' or 'verbed', nobody is quite sure what you are actually saying!

The question in our sub-title above is a serious one but we do not wish to imply that the language is in some way decaying. It is nevertheless true, that if you were to choose any 'classic' nineteenth century novel and compare it with a serious novel written in the second half of the twentieth century, you would find a significant difference in average sentence length. You can easily test this, looking at sample pages from the beginning, middle and ends of novels, and even short stories. It is interesting too, to compare your findings with somebody else's.

There can be little doubt that the new twentieth century media, especially film and telecommunications, has had considerable influence on writers and on the language itself. The cinema, for example, has influenced narrative construction and time sequences, charcater portrayals and dialogue styles. More recently IT appears to be influencing grammatical aspects of style and the very term 'computer literacy' has added a new dimension to traditional notions of reading and writing.

In *The Descent of Language* (1993), Rod Mengham has this to say:

In contemporary written English, the number of words in an average sentence is about twenty, while in standard programming jargon the average would be half a dozen. The average number of grammatical rules according to which the sentences of a computer language are constructed is little more than a hundred, as compared to the thousands that are available and that are continually represented in contemporary usage. A fundamental reduction of scope and expressive power ... is not (an) inevitable outcome of sustained exposure to computer usage, but it is ... increasingly likely with the growth in computer literacy. For many students nowadays (the) means of processing data ... discourages, rather than encourages, an individual ability to give a shape to their knowledge.

Well! A solemn warning, worth debating. A good place to start looking for data would be e-mail messages. Is it possible to detect a general style and how much evidence is there of individuality?

We want to pick up on the idea of 'giving a shape' to your own thoughts. Where A level English courses have an Original Writing component, you are given a sustained opportunity to do just that, in the form of stories, articles, poems, radioscripts, etc, etc.

The word 'shape' is never very far away from the notion of what a sentence is. Sentences are 'thought shapers'; they are a product of joined up thinking, or you hope they are! Sometimes they write themselves, for good or ill; sometimes you have to pore over them to get them right.

The following activity concentrates on sentences.

ACTIVITY 137

Shaping sentences, shaping meanings
This activity will take you through a series of mini-activities, at the end of which you should have a clearer idea of the role of sentences in prose style and in language development. Before starting however, we should like to make three grammatical points:

1 There have always been only four sentence functions (statement, question, command, exclamation), most written ones performing the first three functions.
2 Clauses are the units writers think in, and the key element is the verb, around which all the other words are wrapped. Sentences consist of: a single clause ('I like fish and chips') = a simple sentence
   or
   two or more clauses, joined usually by 'and' or 'then' or 'but' (I like fish and chips, and I like meat pies, too) = a compound sentence
   or
   two or more clauses joined by a word like 'although', 'if', 'because', 'when', 'whilst',

'unless', 'before', 'after' (*I like fish and chips* because *they are tasty,* although *I don't eat them too often*) = a complex sentence (not specially complicated, but the ideas are linked with more meaning than just 'and' or 'then'). You could call a clause an 'idea unit'; sentences contain one or more connected 'idea units'.
In the Appendix on page 283, we have set out examples of the seven kinds of clause structures used in the English language.

3 Apart from key words such as the verbs and connectives (e.g. and, when, however, although, etc.) there are other key features of sentences you should get into the habit of noticing (both in your reading and in your own writing):

   - the initial word (which sets the sentence off on its grammatical flight path)
   - the length of the sentence
   - the rhythm and emphasis (word stress) of the sentence
   - internal punctuation and how it shapes the sentence and the rhythm

– how a sentence relates to the preceding and the succeeding ones.

Now look at two sequences of verse, fifty lines each, and answer the questions that follow. The first is the complete poem by Anne Finch from which you have already examined an excerpt. The second is the opening section of Alexander Pope's *The Rape of the Lock,* written one year earlier (1712). Both are typical of Augustan poetry, yet there are distinct stylistic differences between them. Finch's poem stands on its own so far as context is concerned but you need to know the circumstances of Pope's poem, which is considerably longer and has a very specific historical/biographical context. The poem is based on an actual incident in which a young man had cut off a lock of a girl's hair, angering both her and her family. The style of the poem is referred to as 'mock heroic' because the poet deliberately treats a trivial incident as though it were a great epic.

A Nocturnal Reverie

Anne Finch, Countess of Winchilsea (1661–1720)

In such a night, when every louder wind
Is to its distant cavern safe confined;
And only gentle Zephyr fans his wings,
And only Philomel,[1] still waking, sings;
5   Or from some tree, famed for the owl's delight,
She, hollowing clear, directs the wanderer right:
In such a night, when passing clouds give place,
Or thinly veil the heavens' mysterious face;
When in some river, overhung with green,
10 The waving moon and trembling leaves are seen;
When freshened grass now bears itself upright,
And makes cool banks to pleasing rest invite,
Whence springs the woodbind, and the bramble-rose,
And where the sleepy cowslip sheltered grows;
15 Whilst now a paler hoe the foxglove takes,
Yet checkers still with red the dusky brakes.[2]
When scattered glow-worms, but in twilight fine,
Show trivial beauties watch their hour to shine;[3]
Whilst Salisbury stands the test of every light,
20 In perfect charms, and perfect virtue bright:
When odors, which declined repelling day,[4]
Through temperate air uninterrupted stray;
When darkened groves their softest shadows wear,
And falling waters we distinctly hear;
25 When through the gloom more venerable shows
Some ancient fabric,* awful in repose,   * building
While sunburnt hills their swarthy looks conceal,
And swelling haycocks thicken up the vale:
When the loosed horse now, as his pasture leads,
30 Comes slowly grazing through the adjoining meads,
Whose stealing pace, and lengthened shade we fear,
Till torn-up forage in his teeth we hear:
When nibbling sheep at large pursue their food,
And unmolested kine rechew the cud;
35 When curlews[5] cry beneath the village walls,
And to her straggling brood the partridge calls;
Their shortlived jubilee the creatures keep,
Which but endures, whilst tyrant man does sleep;

When a sedate content the spirit feels,
40   And no fierce light disturbs, whilst it reveals;
But silent musings urge the mind to seek
Something, too high for syllables to speak;
Till the free soul to a composedness charmed,
Finding the elements of rage disarmed,

1. The nightingale.
2. Thickets; tall ferns or bracken.
3. I.e., show lesser beauties that, unlike Lady
    Salisbury of the following line, they must
    make the most of their limited
    opportunities to shine.
4. When the aromas ('odors') of field and
    wood, which refused to come forth
    ('declined') under the not, 'repelling' rays
    of the sun ('day').
5. A kind of shore bird not unlike a sandpiper.

Opening of The Rape of the Lock

Alexander Pope 1688–1744

What dire offence from amorous causes springs,
What mighty contests rise from trivial things,
I sing—This verse to CARYLL, Muse! is due;
This, even Belinda may vouchsafe to view:
Slight is the subject, but not so the praise,
If she inspire, and he approve my lays.
  Say what strange motive, Goddess! could compel
A well-bred Lord to assault a gentle Belle?
O say what stranger cause, yet unexplored,
Could make a gentle Belle reject a Lord?
In tasks so bold, can little men engage,
And in soft bosoms dwells such mighty rage?
  Sol through white curtains shot a timorous ray,
And oped those eyes that must eclipse the day:
Now lapdogs give themselves the rousing shake,
And sleepless lovers, just at twelve, awake:
Thrice rung the bell, the slipper knocked the ground,
And the pressed watch returned a silver sound.
Belinda still her downy pillow prest,
Her guardian Sylph prolonged the balmy rest.
'Twas he had summoned to her silent bed
The morning dream that hovered o'er her head.
A youth more glittering than a birth-night beau
(That even in slumber caused her cheek to glow)
Seemed to her ear his winning lips to lay,
And thus in whispers said, or seemed to say:
  'Fairest of mortals, thou distinguished care
Of thousand bright inhabitants of air!

If e'er one vision touched thy infant thought,
Of all the nurse and all the priest have taught,
Of airy elves by moonlight shadows seen,
The silver token, and the circled green,
Or virgins visited by angel powers,
With golden crowns and wreaths of heavenly flowers,
Hear and believe! thy own importance know,
Nor bound thy narrow views to things below.
Some secret truths, from learnèd pride concealed,
To maids alone and children are revealed:
What though no credit doubting wits may give?
The fair and innocent shall still believe.
Know, then, unnumbered spirits round thee fly,
The light militia of the lower sky;
These, though unseen, are ever on the wing,
Hang o'er the box, and hover round the Ring.
Think what an equipage thou hast in air,
And view with scorn two pages and a chair.
As now your own, our beings were of old,
And once enclosed in woman's beauteous mould;
Thence, by a soft transition, we repair
From earthly vehicles to these of air.

(i)   How many sentences are there in each sequence? (Count the full stops)

(ii) What difference does the number of sentences make to the effect of each poem?

(iii) Summarise in sentences of your own, the sequence of points made in Pope's poem

(iv) What do you think are the points being made by Anne Finch? Could the 'point' of the poem have been left until the last four lines? (Note the echo of the first line.)

(v)   Anne Finch calls her poem a 'reverie' (pleasantly wandering thoughts). How far is this idea reflected in the grammar of the poem and its punctuation?

(vi) Pope doesn't just make statements in his poem; there are other sentence functions. What are they?

(vii) Which poem seems more energetic? more argumentative? Why?

(viii) Write a paragraph summarising grammatical differences of style between two poems written one year apart. How, for example, would you describe the mood of each poem and the tone of voice coming across?

Now look at a poem from the early nineteenth century, 1818. It is a sonnet by Shelley; fourteen lines shaped into four sentences, or four sentences shaped into a sonnet, whichever you prefer. Below is a version of the poem completely unpunctuated. Add the punctuation you think Shelley might have used.
Your 'solution' to this puzzle won't necessarily be wrong, but you are likely to be surprised by the original version. We haven't bothered to change capital letters. The punctuated version is at the end of the chapter.

Ozymandias

I met a traveller from an antique land
Who said Two vast and trunkless legs of stone
Stand in the desert near them on the sand
Half sunk a shattered visage lies whose frown
And wrinkled lip and sneer of cold command
Tell that its sculptor well those passions read
Which yet survive stamped on these lifeless things
The hand that mocked them and the heart that fed
And on the pedestal these words appear
My name is Ozymandias king of kings
Look on my works ye Mighty and despair
Nothing beside remains round the decay
Of that colossal wreck boundless and bare
The lone and level sands stretch far away

(i) It is vital that you hear the poem to get the rhythm right, and then you will begin to feel where the punctuation should go, and what kind.

(ii) Beware line eight; it's an odd one to get right.

(iii) When you have completed this task, and checked Shelley's punctuation, write a paragraph on what the four sentence shapes contribute to the poem.

Now to prose sentences.

The following appeared in a travel brochure, 1990. It illustrates a familiar grammatical feature of modern advertising. What do you think it is? There may be other things you notice too.

Have a little pick-me-up before you get back to work. Iberia's Business Class always welcomes you with a glass of sherry. A taste of Spanish sunshine to whet your appetite for the delicious meal ahead. And afterwards relax and take advantage of our unique multilingual, on-board library. Efficient and professional but warm and hospitable. That's how we think business should be.

Question: Why are verbless (or minor) sentences so popular?
Now, another look at what punctuation does to meaning.

The following sentence can be punctuated in six different ways:

People in the north are more friendly and helpful than those in the south

Find the different versions without altering the word order. Again, listening to different ways of saying these words will help. Two ways of punctuating it will radically alter the sentence function, four other ways will add a different nuance of meaning but not change the function.

The 'answers' are at the end of the chapter (*see* 'Answers' number 1).
Punctuation doesn't 'make' the grammar; it is there to 'mark' the grammar. It is especially helpful in reading long sentences. Look at the following examples in which novelists are shaping thoughts that carry a good deal of

information. The first is from *The Secret Sharer* by Joseph Conrad, the second from *The Takeover* by Muriel Spark.

Supply what you think is appropriate punctuation, and then compare your versions with the authors' (see 'Answers' numbers 2 and 3 at the end of the chapter). Conrad's is one sentence; Spark's is three.

> the why and wherefore of the scorpion how it had got on board and came to select his room rather than the pantry which was a dark place and more what a scorpion would be partial to and how on earth it managed to drown itself in the ink well of his writing desk had exercised him infinitely
>
> [Conrad]

> her husband was intent on listening to a Beethoven symphony on the gramophone and frowned across the room at Maggie to keep her voice down he made an irritable gesture with his hand to accompany the frown he was not in the least disenthralled with Maggie he only wanted to savour the mighty bang crash and terror of sound which would soon be followed by the sweet never mind so adorable to his ears of the finale he was a sentimental man Maggie and Mary lowered their voices
>
> [Spark]

Getting into the rhythm, the punctuation, the grammar of a writer's prose style is a way of getting into a writer's style.

The Long and the Short of it

There is a certain kind of long sentence known as the 'periodic' sentence. The term means 'completed', not in the sense that it ends with a full stop, but that it is 'rounded of' in a satisfying way. The original model is Latin, and the alternative term 'Ciceronian' is sometimes used after the Roman orator, Cicero.

Sometimes these sentences are compared with Chinese boxes in which a series of smaller iunits are embedded in larger ones. You will find lots of periodic sentences in a lot of eighteenth

century prose, the Augustan Age of English Literature, hence the term 'Augustan sentences', yet another alternative.

Here is an example from Henry Fielding's *Joseph Andrews* (1742). It has been de-punctuated; the original version is at the end of the chapter (*see* 'Answers' number 4).

Punctuate the sentence, looking out especially for what happens between the first 'who' and 'had the curiosity', a typical feature of the periodic sentence.

Don't be thrown by the eighteenth century use of 'owing' early in the sentence; a modern meaning would be: 'due to' or 'brought about by'.

> this discovery was now luckily owing to the presence of Joseph at the opening of the saddle bags who having heard his friend say he carried with him nine volumes of sermons and not being of that sect of philosophers who can reduce all the matter of the world into a nutshell seeing there was no room for them in the bags where the parson had said they were deposited had the curiosity to cry out bless me sir where are your sermons

This kind of sentence is not at all usual today; it is a feature that almost guarantees the historic age of a text. But it isn't quite extinct. Here is an example from a novel written in 1988 by

Dan Jacobson (*Adult Pleasures*), the original version is at the end of the chapter (see 'Answers' number 5).

never to feel wholly that you wish to feel and to wish it all the more intensely for that very reason never to be able to believe in the veracity of whatever feelings you do have and to make threatening gestures towards anyone who has his own doubts about them to be aware of a sickening gap between assertion and inner state every time you open your mouth not least when you open your mouth precisely to deny that there is such a gap whether or not it is a crime to feel the throes and pangs of that kind of insincerity I do not know

(i)   What is there in the language of these two sentences that separates them by nearly 250 years?

(ii) Both sentences are constructed in a periodic way (notice how the point of the second is delayed until the very end). What effect is achieved on the reader, regardless of period?

Finally a look at a sentence from Alex Garland's, *The Beach*, written in 1996 and already regarded as a cult book. We tried to find the longest sentence; here it is:

Almost all the buildings had been converted into guest-houses, there were long-distance-telephone booths with air-con, the cafes showed brand-new Hollywood films on video, and you couldn't walk ten feet without passing a bootleg-tape stall.

Compare it with the Jacobson sentence. What does one do that the other doesn't? Do they create different moods in the reader?

ACTIVITY 138

Islands and shipwrecks

In this last activity you are going to look at a series of texts spanning four hundred years. We have linked them by the theme of islands and shipwrecks. Take your time over this activity, since new examination papers in English language and literature will require you to make close comparisons between texts.

Read each one as a stylistic exercise first (enjoy it, too!), and then identify features of language change over time. These will include outmoded words, words that appear to have changed their meaning, idioms and expressions no longer current, spelling, word order and sentence construction.

The texts are arranged in chronological order; you don't have to do any guessing this time.

Consider also, elements of continuity in the language, and whether you think the genres represented are still in evidence today.

(i) From a letter written by William Strachey, dated 15 July, 1610. It became known as the *True Repertory of the Wrack.*

Our Governour was at this time below at the Capstone, both by his speech and authoritie heartening every man unto his labour. It [a huge sea] strooke him from the place where hee sate, and groveled him, and all us about him on our faces, beating together with our breaths all thoughts from our bosomes, else, then that wee were now sinking . . . During all this time, the heavens look'd so blacke upon us, that it was not possible the elevation of the Pole might be observed: nor a Starre by night, nor Sunne beame by day was to be seene. Onely upon the Thursday night Sir George Summers being upon the watch, had an apparition of a little round light, like a faint Starre, trembling, and streaming along with a sparkling blaze, halfe the height upon the Maine Mast, and shooting sometimes from Shroud to Shroud, tempting to settle as it were upon any of the foure Shrouds: and for three or foure houres together, or rather more, halfe the night it kept with us; running sometimes along the Maine-yard to the very end, and then returning. At which, Sir George Summers called divers about him, and shewed them the same, who observed it with much wonder, and carefulnesse: but upon a sodaine, towards the morning watch, they lost the sight of it, and knew not what way it made. The superstitious Sea-men make many constructions of this Sea-fire, which neverthelesse is usuall in stormes: the same (it may be) which the Græcians were won't in the Mediterranean to call Castor and Pollux, of which, if one onely appeared without the other, they tooke it for an evill signe of great tempest . . .

East and by South we steered away as much as we could to beare upright, which was no small carefulnesse nor paine to doe, albeit we much unrigged our Ship, threw over-boord much luggage, many a Trunke and Chest (in which I suffered no meane losse) and staved many a Butt of Beere, Hogsheads of Oyle, Syder, Wine, and Vinegar . . . But see the goodnesse and sweet introduction of better hope, by our mercifull God given unto us. Sir George Summers, when no man dreamed of such happinesse, had discovered, and cried Land . . . We were inforced to runne her ashoare, as neere the land as we could, which brought us within three quarters of a mile of shoare . . .

We found it to be the dangerous and dreaded Iland, or rather Ilands of the Bermuda: whereof let mee give your Ladyship a briefe description, before I proceed to my narration. And that the rather, because they be so terrible to all that ever touched on them, and such tempests, thunders, and other fearefull objects are seene and heard about them, that they be called commonly, The Devils Ilands, and are feared and avoyded of all sea travellers alive, above any other place in the world. Yet it pleased our mercifull God, to make even this hideous and hated place, both the place of our safetie, and meanes of our deliverance.

And hereby also, I hope to deliver the world from a foule and generall errour: it being counted of most, that they can be no habitation for Men, but rather given over to Devils and wicked Spirits; whereas indeed wee find them now by experience, to bee as habitable and commodious as most Countries of the same climate and situation: insomuch as if the entrance into them wer as easie as the place it selfe is contenting, it had long ere this beene inhabited, as well as other Ilands. Thus shall we make it appeare, That Truth is the daughter of Time, and that men ought not to deny every thing which is not subject to their owne sense . . .

Sure it is, that there are no Rivers nor running Springs of fresh water to bee found upon any of them: when wee came first wee digged and found certaine gushings and soft bublings, which being either in bottoms, or on the side of hanging ground, were onely fed with raine water, which neverthelesse soone sinketh into the earth and vanisheth away . . . A kinde of webbe-footed Fowle there is, of the bignesse of an English green Plover, or Sea-Meawe, which all the Summer wee saw not . . . Their colour is inclining to Russet, with white bellies (as are likewise the long Feathers of their wings Russet and White) these gather themselves together and breed in those Ilands which are high, and so farre alone into the Sea, that the Wilde Hogges cannot swimme over them, and there in the ground they have their Burrowes, like Conyes in a Warren, and so brought [?wrought] in the loose Mould, though not so deepe: which Birds with a light bough in a darke night (as in our Lowbelling), wee caught. I have beene at the taking of three hundred in an houre, and wee might have laden our Boates. Our men found a prettie way to take them, which was by standing on the Rockes or Sands by the Sea side, and hollowing, laughing, and making the strangest outcry that possibly they could: with the noyse whereof the Birds would come flocking to that place, and settle upon the very armes and head of him that so cryed, and still creepe neerer and neerer, answering the noyse themselves: by which our men would weigh them with their hand, and which weighed heaviest they tooke for the best and let the others alone, and so our men would take twentie dozen in two houres of the chiefest of them; and they were a good and well relished Fowle, fat and full as a Partridge . . . The Tortoyse is reasonable toothsom (some say) wholsome meate. I am sure our Company liked the meate of them verie well, and one Tortoyse would goe further amongst them, then three Hogs. One Turtle (for so we called them) feasted well a dozen Messes, appointing sixe to every Messe. It is such a kind of meat, as a man can neither absolutely call Fish nor Flesh, keeping most what in the water . . .

(ii) *Robinson Crusoe*

Daniel Defoe

September 30, 1659. I, poor miserable Robinson Crusoe, being ship wreck'd, during a dreadful storm, in the offing, came on shore on this dismal unfortunate island, which I call'd the Island of Despair, all the rest of the ship's company being drown'd, and my self almost dead.

All the rest of that day I spent in afflicting my self at the dismal circumstances I was brought to, viz. I had neither food, house, clothes, weapon, or place to fly to, and in despair of any relief, saw nothing but death before me, either that I should be devour'd by wild beasts, murther'd by savages, or starv'd to death for want of food. At the approach of night, I slept in a tree for fear of wild creatures, but slept soundly tho' it rain'd all night.

October 1. In the morning I saw to my great surprise the ship had floated with the high tide, and was driven on shore again much nearer the island, which as it was some comfort on one hand, for seeing her sit upright, and not broken to pieces, I hop'd, if the wind abated, I might get on board, and get some food and necessaries out of her for my relief; so on the other hand, it renew'd my grief at the loss of my comrades, who I imagin'd if we had all staid on board might have sav'd the ship, or at least that they would not have been all drown'd as they were; and that had the men been sav'd, we might perhaps have built us a boat out of the ruins of the ship, to have carried us to some other part of the world. I spent great part of this day in perplexing my self on these things; but at length seeing the ship almost dry, I went upon the sand as near as I could, and then swam on board; this day also it continu'd raining, tho' with no wind at all.

From the 1st of October to the 24th. All these days entirely spent in many several voyages to get all I could out of the ship, which I brought on shore, every tide of flood, upon rafts. Much rain also in these days, tho' with some intervals of fair weather: but, it seems, this was the rainy season.

Oct. 20. I overset my raft and all the goods I had upon it, but being in shoal water, and the things being chiefly heavy, I recover'd many of them when the tide was out.

Oct. 25. It rain'd all night and all day, with some gusts of wind, during which time the ship broke in pieces, the wind blowing a little harder than before, and was no more to be seen, except the wreck of her, and that only at low water. I spent this day in covering and securing the goods which I had sav'd, that the rain might not spoil them.

Oct. 26. I walk'd about the shore almost all day to find out a place to fix my habitation, greatly concern'd to secure my self from an attack in the night, either from wild beasts or men. Towards night I fix'd upon a proper place under a rock, and mark'd out a semi-circle for my encampment, which I resolv'd to strengthen with a work, wall, or fortification made of double piles, lin'd within with cables, and without with turf.

From the 26th to the 30th, I work'd very hard in carrying all my goods to my new habitation, tho' some part of the time it rain'd exceeding hard.

The 31st, in the morning I went out into the island with my gun to see for some food, and discover the country, when I kill'd a she-goat, and her kid follow'd me home, which I afterwards kill'd also because it would not feed.

November 1. I set up my tent under a rock, and lay there for the first night, making it as large as I could with stakes driven in to swing my hammock upon.

Nov. 2. I set up all my chests and boards, and the pieces of timber which made my rafts, and with them form'd a fence round me, a little within the place I had mark'd out for my fortification.

Nov. 3. I went out with my gun and kill'd two fowls like ducks, which were very good food. In the afternoon went to work to make me a table.

Nov. 4. This morning I began to order my times of work, of going out with my gun, time of sleep, and time of diversion, viz.: every morning I walk'd out with my gun for two or three hours if it did not rain, then employ'd my self to work till about eleven a-clock, then eat what I had to live on, and from twelve to two I lay down to sleep, the weather being excessive hot, and then in the evening to work again. The working part of this day and of the next were wholly employ'd in making my table, for I was yet but a very sorry workman, tho' time and necessity made me a compleat natural mechanick soon after, as I believe it would do any one else.

(iii) *The Coral Island*
R. M. Ballantyne

'But what has become of the wreck, Jack? I saw you clambering up the rocks there while I was watching Ralph. Did you say she had gone to pieces?'

'No, she has not gone to pieces, but she has gone to the bottom,' replied Jack. 'As I said before, she struck on the tail of the island and stove in her bow, but the next breaker swung her clear, and she floated away to leeward. The poor fellows in the boat made a hard struggle to reach her, but long before they came near her she filled and went down. It was after she foundered that I saw them trying to pull to the island.'

There was a long silence after Jack ceased speaking, and I have no doubt that each was revolving in his mind our extraordinary position. For my part I cannot say that my reflections were very agreeable. I knew that we were on an island, for Jack had said so, but whether it was inhabited or not I did not know. If it should be inhabited, I felt certain, from all I had heard of South Sea islanders, that we should be roasted alive and eaten. If it should turn out to be uninhabited, I fancied that we should starve to death. 'Oh!' thought I, 'if the ship had only struck on the rocks we might have done pretty well, for we could have obtained provisions from her, and tools to enable us to build a shelter, but now – alas! alas! we are lost!' These last words I uttered aloud in my distress.

'Lost! Ralph?' exclaimed Jack, while a smile overspread his hearty countenance. 'Saved, you should have said.'

'Do you know what conclusion *I* have come to?' said Peterkin. 'I have made up my mind that it's capital – first rate – the best thing that ever happened to us, and the most splendid prospect that every lay before three jolly young tars. We've got an island all to ourselves. We'll take possession in the name of the king; we'll go and enter the service of its inhabitants. Of course we'll rise, naturally, to the top of affairs. You shall be king, Jack; Ralph, prime minister, and I shall be –'

'The court jester,' interrupted Jack.

'No,' retorted Peterkin, 'I have no title at all. I shall merely accept a highly responsible situation under government, for you see, Jack, I'm fond of having an enormous salary and nothing to do.'

'But suppose there are no natives?'

'Then we'll build a charming villa, and plant a lovely garden round it, stuck all full of the most splendiferous tropical flowers, and we'll farm the land, plant, sow, reap, eat, sleep, and be merry.'

'But to be serious,' said Jack, assuming a grave expression of countenance, which I observed always had the effect of checking Peterkin's disposition to make fun of everything, 'we are really in rather an uncomfortable position. If this is a desert island, we shall have to live very much like the wild beasts, for we have not a tool of any kind, not even a knife.'

'Yes, we have *that*,' said Peterkin, fumbling in his trousers pocket, from which he drew forth a small penknife with only one blade, and that was broken.

'Well, that's better than nothing; but come,' said Jack, rising, 'we are wasting our time in *talking* instead of *doing*. You seem well enough to walk now, Ralph, let us see what we have got in our pockets, and then let us climb some hill and ascertain what sort of island we have been cast upon, for, whether good or bad, it seems likely to be our home for some time to come.'

(iv) *Treasure Island*

R L Stevenson 1850–94

I was now, it seemed, cut off upon both sides; behind me the murderers, before me this lurking nondescript. And immediately I began to prefer the dangers that I knew to those I knew not. Silver himself appeared less terrible in contrast with this creature of the woods, and I turned on my heel, and, looking sharply behind me over my shoulder, began to retrace my steps in the direction of the boats.

Instantly the figure reappeared, and, making a wide circuit, began to head me of. I was tired, at any rate; but had I been as fresh as when I rose, I could see it was in vain for me to contend in speed with such an adversary. From trunk to trunk the creature flitted like a deer, running manlike on two legs, but unlike any man that I had ever seen, stooping almost double as it ran. Yet a man it was, I could no longer be in doubt about that.

I began to recall what I had heard of cannibals. I was within an ace of calling for help. But the mere fact that he was a man, however wild, had somewhat reassured me, and my fear of Silver began to revive in proportion. I stood still, therefore, and cast about for some method of escape; and as I was so thinking, the recollection of my pistol flashed into my mind. As soon as I remembered I was not defenceless, courage glowed again in my heart; and I set my face resolutely for this man of the island, and walked briskly towards him.

He was concealed by this time, behind another tree trunk; but he must have been watching me closely, for as soon as I began to move in his direction he reappeared and took a step to meet me. Then he hesitated, drew back, came forward again, and at last, to my wonder and confusion, threw himself on his knees and held out his clasped hands in supplication.

At that I once more stopped.

'Who are you?' I asked.

'Ben Gunn,' he answered, and his voice sounded hoarse and awkward, like a rusty lock. 'I'm poor Ben Gunn, I am; and I haven't spoke with a Christian these three years.'

I could now see that he was a white man like myself, and that his features were even pleasing. His skin, wherever it was exposed, was burnt by the sun; even his lips were black; and his fair eyes looked quite startling in so dark a face.

Of all the beggar-men that I had seen or fancied, he was the chief for raggedness. He was clothed with tatters of old ship's canvas and old sea cloth; and this extraordinary patchwork was all held together by a system of the most various and incongruous fastenings, brass buttons, bits of stick, and loops of tarry gaskin. About his waist he wore an old brass-buckled leather belt, which was the one thing solid in his whole accoutrement.

'Three years!' I cried. 'Were you shipwrecked?'

'Nay, mate,' said he – 'marooned.'

I had heard the word, and I knew it stood for a horrible kind of punishment common enough among the buccaneers, in which the offender is put ashore with a little powder and shot, and left behind on some desolate and distant island.

'Marooned three years agone,' he continued, ' and lived on goats since then, and berries, and oysters. Wherever a man is, says I, a man can do for himself. But, mate, my heart is sore for Christian diet. You mightn't happen to have a piece of cheese about you, now? No? Well, many's the long night I've dreamed of cheese – toasted, mostly – and woke up again, and here I were.'

(v) *Lord of the Flies*

William Golding, 1911–

The boy with fair hair lowered himself down the last few feet of rock and began to pick his way towards the lagoon. Though he had taken off his school sweater and trailed it now from one hand, his grey shirt stuck to him and his hair was plastered to his forehead. All round him the long scar smashed into the jungle was a bath of heat. He was clambering heavily among the creepers and broken trunks when a bird, a vision of red and yellow, flashed upwards with a witch-like cry; and this cry was echoed by another.

'Hi!' it said, 'wait a minute!'

The undergrowth at the side of the scar was shaken and a multitude of raindrops fell pattering.

'Wait a minute,' the voice said, 'I got caught up.'

The fair boy stopped and jerked his stockings with an automatic gesture that made the jungle seem for a moment like the Home Counties.

The voice spoke again.

'I can't hardly move with all these creeper things.'

The owner of the voice came backing out of the undergrowth so that twigs scratched on a greasy wind-breaker. The naked crooks of his knees were plump, caught and scratched by thorns. He bent down, removed the thorns carefully, and turned round. He was shorter than the fair boy and very fat.
He came forward, searching out safe lodgements for his feet, and then looked up through thick spectacles.

'Where's the man with the megaphone?'

The fair boy shook his head.

'This is an island. At least I think it's an island. That's a reef out in the sea. Perhaps there aren't any grown-ups anywhere.'

The fat boy looked startled.

'There was that pilot. But he wasn't in the passenger tube, he was up in the cabin in front.'

The fair boy was peering at the reef through screwed-up eyes.

'All them other kids,' the fat boy went on. 'Some of them must have got out. They must have, mustn't they?'

The fair boy began to pick his way as casually as possible towards the water. He tried to be offhand and not too obviously uninterested, but the fat boy hurried after him.

'Aren't there any grown-ups at all?'

'I don't think so.'

The fair boy said this solemnly; but then the delight of a realized ambition overcame him. In the middle of the scar he stood on his head and grinned at the reversed fat boy.

'No grown-ups!'

The fat boy thought for a moment.

'That pilot.'

The fair boy allowed his feet to come down and sat on the steamy earth.

'He must have flown off after he dropped us. He couldn't land here. Not in a plane with wheels.'

'We was attacked!'

'He'll be back all right.'

The fat boy shook his head.

'When we was coming down I looked through one of them windows. I saw the other part of the plane. There were flames coming out of it.'

He looked up and down the scar.

'And this is what the tube done.'

The fair boy reached out and touched the jagged end of a trunk. For a moment he looked interested.

'What happened to it?' he asked. 'Where's it got to now?'

'That storm dragged it out to sea. It wasn't half dangerous with all them tree trunks falling. There must have been some kids still in it.'

He hesitated for a moment then spoke again.

'What's your name?'

'Ralph.'

The fat boy waited to be asked his name in turn but this proffer of acquaintance was not made; the fair boy called Ralph smiled vaguely, stood up, and began to make his way once more towards the lagoon. The fat boy hung steadily at his shoulder.

'I expect there's a lot more of us scattered about. You haven't seen any others have you?'

Ralph shook his head and increased his speed. Then he tripped over a branch and came down with a crash.

The fat boy stood by him, breathing hard.

'My auntie told me not to run,' he explained, 'on account of my asthma.'

'Ass-mar?'

'That's right. Can't catch me breath. I was the only boy in our school what had asthma,' said the fat boy with a touch of pride. 'And I've been wearing specs since I was three.'

(vi) *The Beach*

Alex Garland

We set off immediately after breakfast: half a bar of chocolate each and cold noodles, soaked in most of the water from our canteens. There wasn't any point in hanging around. We needed to find a freshwater source, and according to Mister Duck's map, the beach was on the other side of the island.

At first we walked along the beach, hoping to circle the coast, but the sand soon turned to jagged rocks, which turned to impassable cliffs and gorges. Then we tried the other end, wasting precious time while the sun rose in the sky, and found the same barrier. We were left with no choice but to try inland. The pass between the peaks was the obvious goal so we slung our bin-liners over our shoulders and picked our way into the jungle.

The first two or three hundred metres from the shore were the hardest. The spaces between the palm trees were covered in a strange rambling bush with tiny leaves that sliced like razors, and the only way past them was to push through. But as we got further inland and the ground began to rise, the palms became less common than another kind of tree – trees like rusted, ivy-choked space rockets, with ten-foot roots that fanned from the trunk like stabilizer fins. With less sunlight coming through the canopy, the vegetation on the forest floor thinned out. Occasionally we were stopped by a dense spray of bamboo, but a short search would find an animal track or a path cleared by a fallen branch.

After Zeph's description of the jungle, with Jurassic plants and strangely coloured birds, I was vaguely disappointed by the reality. In many ways I felt like I was walking through an English forest, I'd just shrunk to a tenth of my normal size. But there were some things that felt suitably exotic. Several times we saw tiny brown monkeys scurrying up the trees, Tarzan-style lianas hung above us like stalactites – and there was the water: it dripped on our necks, flattened our hair, stuck our T-shirts to our chests. There was so much of it that our half-empty canteens stopped being a worry. Standing under a branch and giving it a shake provided a couple of good gulps, as well as a quick shower. The irony of having kept my clothes dry over the swim, only to have them soaked when we turned inland, didn't escape me.

After two hours of walking we found ourselves at the bottom of a particularly steep stretch of slope. We virtually had to climb it, pulling ourselves up on the tough fern stems to keep us from slipping down on the mud and dead leaves. Étienne was the first to get to the top and he disappeared over the ridge, then reappeared a few seconds later, beckoning enthusiastically.

'Hurry up!' he called. 'Really, it is amazing!'

'What is it' I called back, but he'd disappeared again.

I redoubled my efforts, leaving Françoise behind.

The slope led to a football-pitch-sized shelf on the mountainside, so flat and neat that it seemed unnatural in the tangle of the surrounding jungle. Above us the slope rose again to what appeared to be a second shelf, and past that it continued straight up to the pass.

Étienne had gone further into the plateau and was standing in some bushy plants, gazing around with his hands on his hips.

'What do you think?' he said. I looked behind me. Far below I could see the beach we had come from, the island where our hidden rucksacks lay, and the many other islands beyond it.

'I didn't know the marine park was this big,' I replied.

'Yes. Very big. But that is not what I mean.'

I turned back to the plateau, putting a cigarette in my mouth. Then, as I patted down my pockets looking for my lighter, I noticed something strange. All the plants in the plateau looked vaguely familiar.

'Wow,' I said, and the cigarette dropped from my lips, forgotten.

'Yes.'

'. . . Dope?'

Étienne grinned. 'Have you ever seen so much?'

'Never . . .' I pulled a few leaves from the nearest bush and rubbed them in my hands.

Étienne waded further into the plateau. 'We should pick some, Richard,' he said. 'We can dry it in the sun and . . .' Then he stopped. 'Wait a moment, there is something funny here.'

'What?'

'Well, it is just so . . . These plants . . .' He crouched down, then looked round at me quickly. His lips had begun to curve into a smile, but his eyes were wide and I could literally see colour draining from his face. 'This is a field,' he said.

I froze. 'A field?'

'Yes. Look at the plants.'

'But it can't be a field. I mean, these islands are . . .'

'The plants are in rows.'

'Rows . . .'

We stared at each other. 'Jesus Christ,' I said slowly. 'Then we're in deep shit.'

NOTES AND COMMENTARIES　**1　QUEEN ELIZABETH'S PREFACE IN MODERN TYPEFACE.**

ELYZABETH BY THE GRACE of God Queene of England & Ireland, defender of the faithe, & to all and singular Scholemaisters & teachers of Grammar within this oure realme of England, and other Dominions, greeting. Whereas oure moste deere Father of famous memory, Kinge Henrye the eight, among sundry and manifoldee his greate and waighty affaires, appertaining to his Regall authoritie and office, did not forget, ne neglect, the good and vertuous education of the tender youth of this saide Realme, but hauing a feruent zeale, bothe towards the Godly bringing up of the saide youth, and also a seciall regarde that they might attaine the Rudiments of the Latine tongue, with more facilitye than aforetime. And for auoyding of diversitie and xxxxxxnes of teaching, did cause one uniforme Grammar to be set (forth) commaunding all Scholemaisters &

teachers within this saide Realme to teache, use and exercise the same. We setting before our eies this Godlye acte and axample of this oure deere Father in this behalfe, not vncnfirmed by oure deere Brother and Sister, Kynge Edward and Queen Mary: and also consideringe that by the learned youth of this saide Realme, the infinite and singular commodities tendeth towards the common wealth of the same, have thought good, by oure speciall authoritie to approve and ratifie that worthy acte of oure saide deere Father, concerning the premisses. Willing therefore & streyghtlye charginge and commaundinge all and singular Scholemaisters, to whom the charge and teaching of Grammar within this oure Realme and Dominions dothe appertaine, not to teache your youthe & Schollers with any other Grammar, than with this English Introduction hereafter ensuing, and the Latine Grammar anexed to the same, being of the onely printing of our welbeloved subiecte Reginalde Wolfe, appoyntedd by vs to the same office, vpon paine of our Indignation, and as you xxx answere to the contrary. And thus endeuouring yourselves towards the frutefull bringing vp of your saide Schollers in good literature and vertuous conditions, you shall deserve of almightye God condigne rewarde, and of vs worthy commendations for the same.

God save the Queene.

2 COMMENTARIES ON TEXT
Elizabeth the First's preface to a grammar book

There are a number of observations to be made on the spellings. Remember that before the age of printing, all documents were hand written for a relatively small number of people able to read. Spelling was very much a matter of individual choice by the scribe, guided by personal and local pronunciation and by some conventions for familiar and important words. Printing proved to be the biggest single factor in standardising English spelling and this text is an example of early printing practices in Elizabethan England. You will have noticed the elongated 's' (not the same as the modern 'f' character which has a cross bar), and an apparent confusion between 'u' and 'n'. Notice also the use of 'u' for 'v'. It should also be noted how many spellings are consistent with modern spellings. You could easily calculate just what proportions of spellings have and have not changed. You could also sort out the variant spellings according to where in each word the variation occurs. Use the following categories: word endings; vowel sounds (including those that use two vowel letters); consonants (e.g. doubled final consonant). Where would you put the use of 'I' for a 'j'?
You might also be surprised by the use of the ampersand (&) in an official document, especially by its use as a symbol for 'etc' in the opening section. The etymologies of some words need to be investigated in the OED: e.g. manifold, singular, condigne.
But there are very few difficulties of vocabulary for a modern reader. One specialist word, 'anexed' (now spelt 'annexed'), is still used in modern official documents in exactly the same way as it is here.
You are likely however to have found the flow, or the cohesion, more difficult to follow. Clearly the grammatical style is different from that of

today. It begins with a formal salutation from on high, and then, through a long series of preliminaries, ends with a promise of reward or indignation, depending on whether the royal command has been acted upon. It is in fact an unequivocal endorsement of an educational measure. 'Scholemaisters' who ignore it will 'answere to the contrary'. The legal register is very noticeable.

When sociolinguistic features of this text are examined there is a distinct continuity between this text and the 1999 text on teaching grammar. We are left in no doubt about the political significance of the document it prefaces and of the authority that lies behind it. The use of the first person plural (the royal 'we') and the references to 'oure most deere Father' tell of an age in which monarchy enjoyed much more personal and direct power than today. She is endorsing a document brought to her attention, no doubt, by a minister, and in consequence both the preface and the grammar book itself take on the force of a policy document. There is no mistaking the power embedded in the formally polite language.

One final point: throughout the text, the emphasis has been on grammar, and Latin grammar in particular (remember, this is the age that saw the development of 'grammar schools'), yet at the end it shifts to 'good literature'. How do you explain this implicit connection between grammar and good literature? Moreover, what exactly do you think is meant by 'vertuous conditions'?

Teaching Grammar **(1999)**

It is pointless to comment on the spelling, since English spelling has been standardised for the past three hundred years or so. The typeface and layout is of course distinctly modern. Notice the bullet points, which raise an interesting question. Could Queen Elizabeth's preface be bullet pointed in the modern manner? Have a go, but you will need to change her grammatical constructions.

Notice how both documents establish an historical context for what they introduce. The 1999 document also leaves the reader in no doubt about the authority that lies behind it. Note the phrase, 'the grammar requirements in the English order'. This is a reference to the National Curriculum, binding by law on modern schools, hence the use of the word 'order'. In one document, a royal 'command', in the other a Parliamentary 'order'. These are important sociolinguistic features discernible in the style of both texts.

The style of this document might be described as late twentieth century bureaucratic English. This should not be taken as an insult, for it is written with clarity and elegance. It is less imperious in tone, and much more impersonal. There is also an acknowledgement of the schoolmasters (now called 'teachers') as participants in educational development, willingly or otherwise. Note the references to 'growing consensus' and 'changing debate', and the statement, 'Many schools and teachers agree . . . .'

Quite often, the study of language changes in the period of Modern English raises the question, 'How much has really changed?' Certainly, if these two texts are looked at as examples of language and power, then it would be fair to reply, 'Not much'. Yet in their contexts there are significant differences. The complete document was written by a team of writers and the introductory remarks are made by an editor, albeit in the employ of the government's regulatory body, QCA. Note too, that whereas the 'vertuous conditions' are taken for granted in the earlier document, the editor of the 1999 booklet spells out very clearly in the final paragraph what 'vertuous conditions' might be in the modern sense.

As already noted the two documents, whilst both exercises in political control, nevertheless illustrate significant structural changes in British politics away from royal patronage of education toward government control through parliamentary legislation.

Finally, there is one very significant language change between the publication of these documents, and that is the shift from schools dominated by Latin grammar to modern schools where it is still grammar that is a prime concern, but this time, the grammar of the English language.

The 'Dad's Army' sketch

The words, the grammar and the meanings here are all recognisably late twentieth century English but there is also an element of nostalgia appropriate to a series set in the war years of the 1940s. Wilson's genteel expressions such as 'absolutely first class' and 'awfully good' are examples. If not exactly out-of-date yet, the word 'boy' as used by Mainwaring (Main) harks back to the attitudes of another age.

When modern readers read a text of this kind it is highly likely that they will already have visualised locations, characters and actions before even the first word of the text. Such is the pervasive influence of television. The interactions between scriptwriters and actors becomes very close in a long running series so that the text is not so much a playscript written to be played by any actors, as an extension of the characters as developed by a particular set of actors. Consequently we can hear quite distinctly the tones of voice in which the dialogue is spoken. The scene depicts a silly enough situation with good comic possibilities, but much of the humour lies in our ability to imagine (from having seen and heard the series) exactly how the actors/characters speak to each other. The text is in fact extraordinarily dependent upon its true medium, television, and in this case the reader supplies as much if not more than the words on the page can communicate.

Much Ado About Nothing, Act 3 Scene 3

Whereas with the *Dad's Army* text, the modern reader is entirely at home with the humour, like it or not, the modern reader has to do a great deal of work with Act Three, Scene Three of *Much Ado About Nothing* to even begin to understand it, let alone laugh at it. The play itself is a romantic comedy about young love and the sex war between men and women. It is thematically related to *The Taming of the Shrew* and contrasts in its down to earth realism with *Romeo and Juliet,* a romantic tragedy. The Kenneth Branagh film (1993) was very successful visually and quite popular with a wide audience, yet Act Three, Scene Three was cut by half and depended entirely on clowning rather than verbal humour. Branagh's adaptation completely opted out of trying to make the words funny. What's the problem? Well, there's more than one problem. To start with there is the Elizabethan comic idiom, that is to say, the style of comic dialogue. Idioms are problematical anyway because they never actually mean what the words mean (e.g. Be careful you don't buy a pig in a poke!).

The scene opens in a mock philosophical vein, 'Are you good men and true?' Verges' reply continues the vein but uses the word 'salvation' instead of 'damnation', the very opposite. A number of word meanings are confused in this scene, e.g. allegiance = betrayal; desartless = deserving; senseless = sensible; statues = statutes; vigitant = vigilant. Getting words wrong is still a feature of popular comedy but it helps if the idiom is familiar. We may find it difficult to genuinely laugh at these jokes, and modern actors may find it difficult to perform them, but they are valuable evidence of what Elizabethan audiences expected in comedy, and there can be no doubt that Shakespeare knew how to make his audiences laugh. The nearest the 'Dad's Army' sketch gets to this kind of verbal humour is Godfrey's phrase, 'rather er . . . open air' taken up later by Sgt Wilson, much to Captain Mainwaring's annoyance.

The direction. 'Main. Gives him a glance' is enough for the actor, Arthur Lowe, to know what sort of a look to give, and familiarity with the idiom and the character means that the reader has no difficulty imagining the look. As ever, so many nuances in language can be taken for granted, but not across four hundred years.

Imagine the language problems and the culture shock that an Elizabethan playgoer would experience watching 'Dad's Army' on the telly!

It is not difficult though to respond to the humour of the situation: preferring sleep rather than being on watch, and giving villains a wide berth rather than arresting them. These things are the traditional stuff of comedy, as is Corporal Jones' daft idea of camouflaging himself as a butcher when he is a butcher anyway. Once into the idiom, it is likely that an Elizabethan would appreciate the absurd humour of his explanation.

The combination of unfamiliar comic idiom, deliberate verbal confusion, the strong likelihood of topical references and shared feelings between actors on the night and the contemporary audience more than account for the present day reader's (and actor's) difficulties but they also demonstrate how much of the 'atmosphere' the attitudes and the 'feel' of another age can be encoded in its literature for a future generation.

Putting aside the clowning with language by two preposterous local 'bobbies', there are a number of words and phrases not common nowadays but clearly part of everyday vocabulary in Shakespeare's day: nay; give then their charge; well favor'd = good looking; lanthorn; knave; none but; not to be endur'd; we will rather sleep than talk; alehouses; get them to bed; stay a man against his will; masters; call up me; I beseech you; and so on.

Jane Austen's contemporaries

Comments on the excerpts from Godwin, Edgeworth, Scott, Peacock and Galt follow the same sequence. First, choices of words and phrases; secondly, sentence construction; thirdly, overall style of the text.

(i) The Adventures of Caleb Williams

'Presently' is likely to be the first signal to a modern reader that the text is from another age, followed by the word 'turnkey' and possibly the phrase, 'the place of my retreat'. Other words reinforce the impression: vehement asperity; no very agreeable sensations; but safe; presently (used a second time).

Apart from the brief conversation of the turnkeys, the sentences have an even, measured character of fairly equal length. In the first paragraph there is a noticeable alternation between 'I' and 'they' sentences in keeping with the dramatic character of the situation. This is a general stylistic point rather than an observation on the language of the period, but there is another grammatical feature that is less noticeable today. Look at the following phrases:

The place of my retreat
The deepness of the shade
The appearance of these men
The gate of the prison
This instance of diligence
My place of concealment
The gloomy state of the air
The extreme nearness of my prison
A total want of food
This inclemency of the weather
A feeling of stillness and solitude
Another of the same nature ... of somewhat greater security

Do you think a modern writer (or you) would use this construction so frequently? What effect does it have?

The text is in two paragraphs, the first of which contains short bursts of talk, which sound more old fashioned than the narrative:

'Curse the rascal! Which way can he be gone?' The reply was, 'Damn him! I wish we had him but safe once again!' – 'Never fear!' rejoined the first, he cannot have above half a mile the start of us.'

Consider how Ian Fleming would have written the situation. Would he have used a word like 'rejoined'?

Have a go at writing the scene in the style of Ian Fleming or Robert Harris or Catherine Cookson.

(ii) Castle Rackrent

A stylistic feature that needs to be taken into account regardless of the period in which this text was written, is the author's decision to create a first person narrator who speaks with an Anglo-Irish turn of phrase.

The phrase 'my lady' certainly dates the text but a dialect phrase like 'thick and threefold' survives to this day. In fact, throughout the text, you have to balance phrases of yesterday's standard written expression with dialectal or everyday speech: could never be brought to hear (SE) and bid 'em call again; to the best of my remembrance (SE) and 'he was a-bed'; none could he bring back with him (SE) and 'send offsmart'.

The informal phrases of everyday conversation are more noticeable than any individual words, though 'gossoon' and 'play-house' need investigating, while 'chuses' appears to be a phonetic spelling of a distinctive feature of Irish pronunciation.

The excerpt begins with a long sentence in which the punctuation indicates both run-on speech and pauses. Notice how many sentences are preceded by a dash. A good deal of the account is technically reported speech but is reported in such a way that it sounds immediate. Notice the number of times phrases like (says he) and (said my lady) are placed in brackets to separate them from the flow of the narrator's dramatic recounting.

We find a similarity between the overall stylistic effect of this writing and Alan Bennet's *Talking Heads* in which a single narrator chats, muses, thinks aloud, buttonholes, 'goes on' – whatever you call it – a captured but willing listener.

(iii) Waverley

Some words in this text are not at all unfamiliar in their meaning but are unfamiliar in their context: 'highly excited Waverley's imagination'; 'desultory style of his studies'; 'which shall be disagreeable to you'; 'unpleasing to him' (sounds very Jane Austenish, this one!). On the other hand, 'Edward's blood boiled ...' sounds distinctly modern and conversational.

The sentence constructions seem more like those in the Godwin text than that of Maria Edgeworth. They are of similar length, have a measured rhythm and are about equal length. Do you find the of-construction as frequent? There is a noticeable use of parenthesis in the Scott text, not excessive but noticeable. Read the text from 'Edward's blood boiled' and notice the following:

In a great measure
To his knowledge
Without any warning than the hints we noticed at the end of the fourteenth chapter
As Edward deemed it
In his present situation

Why is parenthesis a useful sentence strategy?

If the stylistic effect of the Edgeworth text is strongly affected by strong echoes of direct speech, the letter has as important a role in this text, since it presents us directly with an individual voice even if the character isn't present. It doesn't over-ride Edward Waverley's voice but it is a strong presence. There is however another equally strong voice in the text and that is Scott's own. It is almost a self-consciousness about novel writing, and Waverley was after all, his first novel, published anonymously. Notice how the novelist narrator, as opposed to Edward Waverley, seems to address the reader directly on two occasions: once, when he comments 'the following letter ... as it is very short, shall be inserted verbatim', and secondly, when he refers to 'the hints we noticed at the end of the fourteenth chapter', a very unusual remark.

(iv) Nightmare Abbey

In this text, the novelist is having such a good time with the rather exotic vocabulary that it appears much more stylised than any of the others in this group. Expressions like 'ample pile', 'the mantle of a conspirator', 'leading-strings' and 'distempered ideas' sound 'dated' but the overwhelming impression is one of a writer taking great delight in spinning phrases, many of them Graeco–Latin in origin. The vocabulary is highly suited to the literary attitudes and behaviour that are being satirised. There are strong semantic fields of horror, melancholy, philosophy and romantic mystery. We must not take this text as typical of the language of Peacock or of his day, but as an indication of how extravagant it could be. Phrases to savour are 'necromantic imagery', 'vigorous and abundant vegetation' and (in the author's own italics), *'passion for reforming the world'*. Peacock doesn't take any of his chosen vocabulary seriously, nor should the reader, ancient or modern. Notice how one ridiculous phrase is put in inverted commas, 'his cogitative faculties immersed in cogibundity of cogitation'.

Fashions of language are frequently satirised today; James Finn Garner does it in his *Politically Correct Bedtime Stories*. You could try it yourself. Choose an aspect of modern life, e.g. New Age mysticism, animal liberation, the body beautiful (male or female), science fiction enthusiasm, aggressive modern management, collect some of its characteristic language and human behaviour and write a satirical piece that is modern in style but in the Peacock genre.

The sentences in this text may seem to you to have, despite long and strange words, an energy and spirit typical of satire (compare the tone with that of Pope, writing a century earlier in *The Rape of the Lock*). Peacock has a tendency to introduce paragraphs with relatively short, pithy sentences and then to elaborate his point in longer ones. This is noticeable in paragraphs two and three, and if you were to read on, you would notice it even more.

So far as the whole text is concerned, there seems to be a shift in paragraph three to a tougher more distinctly modern kind of satirical writing. Notice how the final remark is about language itself.

(iv) Annals of the Parish

Galt is describing the effects on a Scottish community of a cotton mill, recently built on the river bank. A new energy and prosperity has come to the people of the region. Words like 'commercing' and 'manufacturing' have historical significance. Words like 'bairn' and 'clachan' tell of the text's Scottish origin.

Some constructions are not familiar now;

They were represented to me as lads by common in capacity.
. . . and got a London newspaper to the Cross-Keys. . .

Some sentences are very long, having the running-on characteristic of a monologue or a particularly full diary entry. Notice the first sentence of the last paragraph, beginning, 'It seems . . . '

As a whole the text is a combination of detailed social observation and comment and a little fiction. Mainly though, it reads like a documentary and has considerable historical value for that reason.

3   THE CHRONOLOGICAL SEQUENCE OF THE POEMS IS:

'When I was fair and young . . .', Queen Elizabeth the First, c. 1570
'Thou ill-formed offspring . . .' (*The Author to her Book*), Anne Bradstreet, 1678
'In such a night . . .' (*A Nocturnal Reverie*), Anna Finch, 1713
'At length, by so much importunity . . .' (*The Lover: A ballad*), Lady Mary Wortley Montagu, 1747
'Long neglect has worn away', Emily Brontë, 1837
'Come to me in the silence of the night' (*Echo*), Christina Rossetti, 1854
'What was he doing, the great god Pan' (*A Musical Instrument*), Elizabeth Barrett Browning, 1862
'I think of the Celts . . .' (*The Celts*), Stevie Smith, 1954
'It is ten years now . . .' (*The Babysitters*), Sylvia Plath, 1960
'This is what you changed me to' (*Pig Song*), Margaret Atwood, 1974

4 THE AUTHORS' ORIGINAL PUNCTUATIONS ARE AS FOLLOWS:

I met a traveller from an antique land
Who said: Two vast and trunkless legs of stone
Stand in the desert. Near them, on the sand,
Half sunk, a shattered visage lies, whose frown,
And wrinkled lip, and sneer of cold command,
Tell that its sculptor well those passions read
Which yet survive, stamped on these lifeless things,
The hand that mocked them and the heart that fed;
And on the pedestal these words appear;
'My name is Ozymandias, king of kings:
Look on my works, ye Mighty, and despair!'
Nothing beside remains. Round the decay
Of that colossal wreck, boundless and bare
The lone and level sands stretch far away.

The 'Answers'

1　People in the north are more friendly and helpful than those in the south.

People in the north are more friendly, and helpful, than those in the south.

People in the north are more friendly (and helpful) than those in the south.

People in the north are more friendly – and helpful – than those in the south.

People in the north are more friendly and helpful than those in the south?

People in the north are more friendly and helpful than those in the south!

2.　The why and wherefore of the scorpion – how it had got on board and came to select his room rather than the pantry (which was a dark place and more what a scorpion would be partial to), and how on earth it managed to drown itself in the ink-well of his writing desk – had exercised him infinitely.

3.　Her husband was intent on listening to a Beethoven symphony on the gramophone and frowned across the room at Maggie to keep her voice down; he made an irritable gesture with his hand to accompany the frown; he only wanted to savour the mighty bang-crash and terror of sound which would soon be followed by the sweet 'never mind', so adorable to his ears, of the finale. He was a sentimental man. Maggie and Mary lowered their voices.

4.　This discovery was now luckily owing to the presence of Joseph at the opening of the saddle bags; who, having heard his friend say he carried with him nine volumes of sermons, and not being of that sect of philosophers who can reduce all the matter of the world into a nutshell, seeing there was no room for them in the bags, where the parson had said they were deposited, had the curiosity to cry out, 'Bless me, sir, where are your sermons?'

5. Never to feel wholly what you wish to feel – and to wish it all the more intensely for that very reason; never to be able to believe in the veracity of whatever feelings you do have – and to make threatening gestures towards anyone who has his own doubts about them; to be aware of a sickening gap between assertion and inner state every time you open your mouth – not least when you open your mouth precisely to deny that there is such a gap ... whether or not it is a crime to feel the 'throes' and 'pangs' of that kind of insincerity I do not know.

Appendix

The seven clause structures for English sentences are as follows:

1. SV (The little girl) (was eating).
2. SVO (The little girl) (was eating) (all the apples).
3. SVC (The little girl) (was) (greedy).
4. SVOO (The little girl) (gave) (her dog) (an apple).
5. SVOC (The little girl) (got) (her feet) (wet).
6. SVA (The little dog) (lay) (on her feet).
7. SVOA (The little girl) (loved) (the little dog) (lying on her feet).

S = Subject noun or noun phrase; V = Verb; O = Object of the verb's action; C = Complement; A = Adverbial

Objects can *directly* receive the action of the verb e.g. 'all the apples'.

Objects can also *indirectly* receive the verb e.g. 'her dog'. Don't confuse the 'apple' (which is the direct object) with the 'dog' (which is the indirect object) even though the 'dog' comes first in the sentence. Indirect objects often precede direct ones.

All these clauses are simple sentences. Join them together with 'and' or 'then' and you get compound sentences. Join them with an 'although' or 'because' or 'when' etc and you get complex sentences. Subordinating conjunctions can also come at the beginning of a complex sentence. 'And' is a coordinating conjunction; words like 'although', 'because', 'when', 'if', 'until' etc are subordinating conjunctions.

And that is how English sentences are built up.

Note here some slightly unusual ones. What kind of clauses are being constructed here?

Over the moon they jumped.
Away flew the umbrella.
What I would say to you is this:. . .
There are a number of issues here.
It is a well known fact, that. . .
It's good, isn't it?
They're hopeless, they are.

10 Genre

LIZA Well; I must go. (*They all rise. Freddy goes to the door*). So pleased to have met you. Goodbye. (*She shakes hands with Mrs Higgins*)
MRS HIGGINS Goodbye
LIZA Goodbye, Colonel Pickering.
PICKERING Goodbye, Miss Doolittle. (*They shake hands*).
LIZA (*nodding to the others*) Goodbye, all
FREDDY (*opening the door for her*) Are you walking across the Park, Miss Doolittle? If so –
LIZA (*perfectly elegant diction*) Walk! Not bloody likely. (*Sensation*) I am going in a taxi. (*She goes out*)
Pickering gasps and sits down. Freddy goes out on the balcony to catch another glimpse of Eliza.
MRS EYNSFORD HILL (*suffering from shock*) Well, I can't get used to the new ways.

It seems surprising to us today that this excerpt from Bernard Shaw's play *Pygmalion* caused one of the greatest theatre sensations of all time. *The Daily Sketch* front page of 11 April 1914 reveals why:

PYGMALION MAY CAUSE SENSATION TONIGHT

Mr Shaw Introduces A
Forbidden Word.

WILL 'MRS PAT' SPEAK IT?

Has The Censor Stepped In, Or
Will The Phrase Spread?

Has the Censor interfered?
If not, tonight's performance of Bernard Shaw's
Pygmalion at His Majesty's Theatre may cause
one of the greatest sensations of our theatrical
history.
If the Censor has not interfered the audience will either
laugh immoderately or – well, anything may
happen.
Is an expression which hitherto no respectable
newspaper has dared to print permissible when
uttered on stage?
Mrs Patrick Campbell in the new Shaw comedy plays
the part of Liza Doolittle, a flower girl, whom
a professor of phonetics turns into a lady.
But before her education is quite complete she uses
language which is – at present – barred in
drawing rooms, though she has heard her
instructor use the word so often that she does not
know it is not etiquette to use it.

The word 'bloody' which seems so relatively inoffensive to us was clearly not one that was acceptable as an utterance on the public stage in Britain in 1914, despite the fact that it was a word known to and used by many people at that time, as *The Daily Sketch* makes plain. It was a word that broke too many social conventions for it to be allowed even as a word in a play. It was these very stiff and snobbish conventions that Shaw was making fun of in the play itself. Liza was, at the time, a flower seller in Covent Garden with a broad Cockney accent. Professor Henry Higgins, an expert on accents and phonetics, met her and decided that he would try to transform her into someone who would learn 'how to speak beautifully' and 'to behave like a duchess'. The scene we are concerned with takes place when Higgins puts his experiment to the test by introducing Liza into polite society for the very first time. All is going well until she utters the fateful word. What is interesting from our point of view is the reaction of the others on hearing her: *Pickering gasps* and Mrs Eynsford Hill (*suffering from shock*) says 'Well, I can't really get used to the new ways.'

Liza's use of 'bloody' has broken the social rules (or 'etiquette' as *The Daily Sketch* put it) of how people should behave and speak in the upper-middle class world of pre-World War 1 Britain. That it was merely social and linguistic convention and, therefore, subject to change can be seen by the fact that you, even if you are upper-middle class yourself, are unlikely to be able to take very seriously at all the fuss that it caused. There will, of course, be a number of social and linguistic conventions that you do observe and we will be exploring these later.

Liza's use of the word broke the rules or norms that were shared by the members of Mrs Eynsford Hill's circle and class and if these 'rules' were ever broken or disregarded by one of its members, this breach had to be justified. Liza had not yet fully understood these conventions at this stage in the play; Professor Higgins needs, therefore, to continue her linguistic and social education.

Though you may well smile at what seems to be absurd sensitivity about the word 'bloody', you ought to remember that there are plenty of words used today that would cause similar, if not more extreme, reactions. Though 'fuck' has become more acceptable in print, in public and on stage, it wasn't that long ago that its first use on television by drama critic, Kenneth Tynan, caused similar outrage in the popular press to that generated by Shaw's play. We probably wouldn't have dared use it in a text book such as this ten years ago. There are still swear words we wouldn't include and their use in the press or on TV might still cause an uproar. For instance, a late evening programme called *Something for the Weekend,* which deliberately sets out to shock and titillate its viewer, included an item in which young men and women were asked what they thought were their parents' favourite sexual positions and their parents were asked to confirm or deny their children's ideas and an item in which girls were asked to select what they thought were their boyfriends' penises from an identity parade of these organs. Despite the somewhat tasteless and explicit nature of these items no one on the programme, neither 'contestants' nor the presenter, were able to bring themselves to use everyday words to refer to either the act or the organs in question. Euphemisms abounded! The fact that you will be very easily able to guess what these were should demonstrate that their use or non-use in certain contexts is very much a matter of convention. Who knows, by the time a later edition of this book comes to be written, conventions may well have changed and we would have no compunction in using them! It is, of course, not only swear words that are subject to convention. You, for instance, would be very unlikely to use words such as *spastic* or *mongol* for people who have cerebral palsy or Down's Syndrome, though the two words were quite recently in common use and did not cause as much offence as they at present do.

Can you think of other words that are now unacceptable because of changing conventions? The movement towards political correctness should yield you plenty of examples. *Nigger, cripple* . . . .?

Language is not, of course, the only aspect of life that is subject to convention. One of the most noticeable and one that is most subject to comment is the dress code. There are many unwritten 'rules' as to what is suitable to wear on particular occasions. We all have a pretty good idea as to what we should wear on such formal occasions as interviews or funerals; similarly there are dress codes for informal occasions: clubbing or attending college, for example. Some of these rules, as you will know, are not unwritten. School and military uniforms are perhaps the most prominent, but woe betide you if you attempt to enter some gentlemen's clubs in London without wearing a tie. Two further points about dress need to be made. First, dress changes over the years so that, obviously, twenty-first century girls do not wear the same kind of clothes as did their nineteenth century counterparts. Second, even within the dress codes of today, variation is possible. For example, men's suits can vary as to whether they are structured or unstructured, single or double breasted, narrow- or wide-fitting trousers, with or without turn-ups and so on. Variations can be found in other clothes as well. You'll all be familiar with the infinite number of variations that can be played upon the basic school uniform, much to the annoyance of generations of head and deputy head teachers.

But what has all this got to do with language? Quite a lot! Let's say four young men were attending an interview for a managerial job. They all wear suits, but each of the suits is different. We can then say that all of the four recognise that the appropriate *register* for the occasion is the register of suits, but within that register there is permitted a variety of *styles*, so that the style of suit chosen by each candidate will reflect something of their personality. You'll be familiar with register and style as important linguistic terms. So, just as there are different dress registers for different social occasions, but permitted stylistic variation within these registers, the same is true for language. There are registers for geography textbooks, historical biographies, sports reporting, prayers, travel brochures and so on, but within each of these is some allowable stylistic variation. So we can recognise all football reports as football reports or all historical biographies as historical biographies, but can also identify and describe the differences between a match report written by one individual and another or between two biographies of Churchill, for instance. It's only when the registers are broken, as with Liza Doolittle, that we are disturbed.

Genre

Register (together with 'permitted' stylistic variation) is one of the important defining characteristics of a 'genre'. What, then is 'genre'? Two definitions:

- a term in literature and the arts for a particular type of performance, such as the novel or symphonic music (*The Oxford Companion to the English Language*)
- genres are kinds, categories or types of cultural product and process – including texts (Rob Pope, *The English Studies Book*)

You'll notice two things referred to in each of these definitions:

- a genre is a type or a kind of something
- a genre is not just restricted to literature.

So we can say at this stage, then, that as a genre is a type of text, there must be a number of ways in which a text can be identified as belonging to a particular genre. Just as there are a number of characteristics that allow us to group together all birds as birds, all fish as fish and all mammals as mammals, so there will be a set of defining characteristics that allow us to say that some texts are films, some novels, some poems and so on. It's no coincidence that *genre* stems from the Latin word *genus*, which we still use today to label our classification and categorisation of species of plants, animals, insects and fish. A genre can thus be identified by a set of 'rules' and conventions. The writer (or constructor) will be aware of these conventions which govern how he or she will construct the text in order to achieve its aims. If the text is to be a written one then these conventions will, in the main, be linguistic. As we saw earlier, Liza inadvertently broke the social–linguistic conventions of her day. Some writers, of course, deliberately break the rules to create particular effects.

Before we move on to look at specifically 'literary' genres, we are going to consider some examples of what might be called non-traditional genres.

ACTIVITY 139

TV programmes such as *Coronation Street, East Enders, Brookside, Emmerdale, Neighbours* and *Home and Away* are all currently very popular and they all share certain characteristics. Amongst these are:

- they are episodic
- each episode lasts approximately 25–30 minutes

- there are a limited number of locations in which the action takes place
- each episode contains a number of separate storylines.

In groups, discuss and draw up a list of the other characteristics shared by these programmes and others of their type.

COMMENTARY Because they are such popular programmes, you should have had little difficulty in drawing up quite a long list. You'll probably have included such things as the types of characters who appear, the structure of the episodes, the kind of dialogue used and so on. You have, therefore, defined the characteristics and conventions of the genre, TV soaps.

ACTIVITY 140

Having looked for the features that such programmes have in common, you are now ready to explore the features that make each one of them distinct. You are going to look at the stylistic variation between them. Remind yourself of what we said about style on p 286.

Working in the same groups, choose any two TV soaps. Using the list you drew up in the previous activity as headings for your categories, compare, in detail, the differences between your chosen two programmes.

ACTIVITY 141

Draw up a list of other TV genres and discuss what the characteristics of each one are. You could consider, for example, game shows, the

news, gardening programmes, cookery programmes, football, children's cartoons . . .

COMMENTARY You'll have realised from your work on the three previous activities that genre study has moved away from its traditional concentration on literature texts and that all sorts of things are now considered as texts. In this book, naturally, we have been concentrating on 'literary' and 'non-literary' spoken and written texts in English. So, for example, we can talk about the genres of love sonnets, detective novels and revenge tragedy or the genres of application forms, problem-page letters and shopping lists. In spoken language we can talk about the genres of sermons, job interviews, courtroom exchanges or answerphone messages. By extension then, we can talk about the genres of everything from out-of-town shopping centres to suburban post offices or from car design to chocolate-bar wrappers. The important thing for you to remember when discussing genre is that there should be some basic similarity of form and function in those things considered to be representative of a particular genre (the *register*, if you like), but that there will be differences between one representative of the genre and another (the *style*). *Coronation Street* and *East Enders* are both soaps, but there are differences between them. *Othello* and *Macbeth* are both Shakespearean tragedies but there are differences between them.

In order, then, to recognise and analyse a genre, the most important thing you need to be able to do is to see the similarities and differences between texts. This is not as difficult as it might sound. The next activity will demonstrate this.

ACTIVITY 142

Here are ten fragments from written texts. Each text fragment has been chosen because it is typical of its genre. For each fragment decide:

- what genre of text is represented
- what enabled you to recognise the genre
- what other features you would expect the genre to exhibit.

1 GSOH
2 Once upon a time
3 To Whom It May Concern
4 Almighty and Everlasting God
5 http
6 Welcome to the Isle of Man
7 Shall I compare thee to a summer's day
8 WOLVES: Stowell 7, Muscat 7, Bazeley 7
9 Crooning clergyman Ralph Boydell has given up his job ... to be a pop star
10 A bizarre murder leaves two teenagers dead in a desert arroyo, their naked bodies side by side, face up under the New Mexican sun.

COMMENTARY

The fact that you were likely to have found little difficulty in assigning most of these texts to a particular genre demonstrates that as experienced readers you are very familiar with a wide range of genres and their associated features. For example, GSOH will have alerted you to the fact that this was an extract from a 'Lonely Hearts' advertisement in which you would expect to find, amongst other features: further abbreviations (WLTM; NS); an indication of the age, sex and interests of the advertiser together with certain euphemisms for sexual/romantic activities and a rather 'shorthand' style of writing that omits such word classes as pronouns and articles in order to save money by having fewer words to pay for. Of course, these are not the only features that characterise this particular genre.

ACTIVITY 143

Here are a number of examples of the 'Lonely Hearts' genre, taken from two very different publications. What similarities and differences are there between these examples of the same genre?

Private Eye

ASSERTIVE, HANDSOME M/entrepreneur, 40, seeking younger, svelte, erotically unassertive F/partner – 07050 398943.

POTENTIAL sugar daddy (39. GSOH. NS) seeks struggling student/nurse/similar to occasionally distract him from workaholic lifestyle. Photo appreciated. ALA. Box 0790.

PROFESSIONAL attached male, late 40s, 6ft, medium build, not too bad looking, with sensitive yet assertive nature, seeks younger, slimish responsive female for occasional evenings of intense but uncomplicated pleasure. Discretion assured and expected. West London/ Thames valley/ Home Counties. Box 0890.

CITY EXECUTIVE female, 45, late developer, seeks mentor Box 0490.

SLIM MALE – 50, tactile – seeks slim lady for discreet love, fun. Photograph please. S East. Box 1890.

CONSIDERATE, ATTRACTIVE, AFFLUENT COMPANY DIRECTOR 42 in celibate marriage, would love to meet one special female, maybe in similar situation. for secret daytime affair LONDON Box 1790.

LA PERLA LADY, fun 30's, sought by tall, stylish, solvent, ex-city broker. 40, studying in Cambridge and London Box 1890.

RESOLUTE MATURE male, requires dutiful mature female who requires direction. Ideal candidate will be middle aged and will initially correspond politely with photograph. Cleveland/Teeside. Box 2890.

CLASSICAL FLAUTIST, idealistic, somewhat unusual, wants man with character to appreciate her depths. Happens to be voluptuous blonde. Box 2790.

ENJOY HILLWALKING, ballet, theatre? Single man (N/S. 49) seeks woman for love, romance and friendship in the 21st century Manchester/NW. Box1990.

SINGLE MALE (40, blond hair, blue-eyes, n/s) seeks attractive soul mate (35–40) with a sense of romance, for friendship and possible long-term relationship. Interests include classical music (19c Romantics and Renaissance polyphony), the Great War, family history and the Quakers. Photo appreciated. Yorks area. Box 3090.

Country Walking

NORTH EAST LADY, 52, WLTM intelligent male who likes laughing, books, theatre, walking, gardening & animals. BOX NO. 2327.

GAY FEMALE PROFESSIONAL, South Manchester/Cheshire. Attractive, slender, active, 40. Seeks similar intelligent female, 30's to 40's, for walking fells/lows, cultural pursuits, occasional daft kids stuff, friendship/relationship. BOX NO. 2328.

VERY FIT MALE, 42, 6'1" WLTM similar lady for walks, companionship, Herts or surrounding area. BOX NO. 2329.

DORSET LADY, single, 35ish, seeks N/S genuine male 30–45 WGSH for outdoor pursuits, friendship, fun!! BOX NO. 2330.

FEMALE WALKAHOLIC, young 50, N/S, slim, tall, optimist, WLTM cheerful male for weekend walks in North Yorkshire, for friendship initially. BOX NO. 2331.

KEEN 33, happy walker, WLTM someone like myself for friendship/relationship to make walks interesting. BOX NO. 2332.

NORTH EAST MALE, 30's, sincere, trustworthy WLTM lady for walks and friendship. BOX NO. 2333.

MALE, 52, 6ft, divorced WLTM female for walking, days out etc, Herts, London, Anywhere ALA. BOX NO. 2334.

ATTRACTIVE, THOUGHTFUL, young 50s Devon lady, seeks educated, interesting male friend to share concerts, walks, laughter. BOX NO. 2335.

HAMPSHIRE PROFESSIONAL man 45, seeks N/S lady 35–45 for walks, cycling, picnics, fun and friendship. BOX NO. 2336.

EAST MIDLANDS LADY, N/S seeks male companion 48ish for weekday walks, enjoys theatre, classical music. BOX NO. 2337.

MANCHESTER FEMALE, 48 tall N/S WLTM female for friendship or man for walks, evenings out, travel and romance. BOX NO. 2338.

YORKS MALE, 58, loves walking, country pubs, sunsets, N/S GSOH needs lady to escort. BOX NO. 2339.

Sometimes, of course, you may not be familiar enough with the conventions of a genre and not be able to recognise when these conventions are inadvertently broken. To return to the clothes analogy for a moment: the person who arrives for his or her important job interview dressed in a faded pair of jeans and a T-shirt is unlikely to be appointed. They either do not know or deliberately choose to ignore the dress code for that particular context. Similarly, you will be able to think of lots of contexts where faded jeans and T-shirt would be entirely appropriate and where interview dress would be totally out of place. The same is true, as you saw with Liza Doolittle, of what can be said in certain situations. It's not the done thing to tell dirty jokes at a funeral nor to chat about your latest boyfriend at an interview! Most people recognise and adhere to the speech conventions of an interview or a funeral, but sometimes speakers or writers do not know the conventions of a particular genre.

ACTIVITY 144

What genre conventions is the writer of the following extract unaware of?

> Lear's decision, in the opening scene of the play, to divide his kingdom between his daughters is a clear abdication of his responsibilities as King and a contemporary audience would have immediately recognised it as such. To compound his folly, Lear is determined to allocate territory to his daughters on the basis of their answers to the unanswerable question: 'Which of you shall we say doth love us most?'. Lear, throughout this scene, is depicted by Shakespeare as a stupid old git who is clearly off his trolley.

Later in this chapter, we shall be looking at some examples of writers who deliberately break and mix conventions of genre.

Literary genres

There are three traditional literary genres. Indeed, the criteria that are laid down for your A level subject of English Language and Literature explicitly state that you must study texts from the three literary genres of prose, poetry and drama. These, then, are what most people would see as the main literary genres but, whilst they are obviously useful in general terms and helpful in distinguishing between the characteristics of, say, *Macbeth*, *Huckleberry Finn* and Wordsworth's *Daffodils*, they are best regarded as mega-genres, each of which can be broken down into quite a large number of sub-genres. Imagine a filing cabinet labelled 'Poetry'. Within that filing cabinet you would find a large number of files, all of which come under the general heading of 'Poetry', but each of which would be labelled with a particular category of poetry, such as ballad, sonnet and haiku, for example. The same would be true of the filing cabinets labelled 'Prose' and 'Drama'. The division of mega-genres into sub-genres can sometimes cause difficulty, but it's a difficulty that's not a new one. Shakespeare in *Hamlet* makes fun of the many ways in which the drama of his time could be classified and categorised when he makes the rather pedantic Polonius, in a famous speech to Hamlet, list the various genres as:

tragedy, comedy, history, pastoral, pastoral-comical, historical-pastoral, tragical-historical, tragical-comical-historical-pastoral, scene individable or poem unlimited.

Before you laugh too much at Polonius' difficulty, you should try the next activity.

ACTIVITY 145

For each of the three main or mega-genres we have given you three sub-genres and examples of texts that could be classified in this way. Your task is to research, by using either literary histories, literary encyclopaedias or the Internet, and discover other sub-genres of prose, poetry and drama, together with some example texts for each.

Poetry	ballad *Sir Patrick Spens; The Rime of the Ancient Mariner* (Coleridge) sonnet *Ozymandias* (Shelley); *On His Blindness* (Milton) epic *Paradise Lost* (Milton); *The Iliad* (Homer)
Prose (novel)	social realist *Great Expectations* (Dickens); *Middlemarch* (G. Eliot) detective *The Moonstone* (W. Collins); *Farewell, My Lovely* (Raymond Chandler) magical realist *Midnight's Children* (Salman Rushdie); *Nights at the Circus* (Angela Carter)
Drama	comedy *The Importance of Being Ernest* (Oscar Wilde); *She Stoops to Conquer* (Oliver Goldsmith) melodrama *Maria Marten* absurd *Waiting for Godot* (Samuel Beckett); *The Bald Prima Donna* (Eugene Ionesco)

COMMENTARY　You may well have noticed already one difficulty in trying to classify a genre. We said that there were three main genres – poetry, prose and drama – and, indeed there are; however, in the activity, we were forced to put *novel* in brackets following *prose*. This was because the novel is the literary prose genre that you'll probably be most familiar with, though the short story may well be another. However, the novel is but a sub-genre of prose, although a very large one and you need also to remember that literary prose can encompass diaries, letters, sermons, journals – and that this does not exhaust the list of potential sub-genres. In a sense, what you have been doing is to put genre labels on a variety of literary texts. There are, however, two very important things to remember about genre:

- Whenever you try to pin a genre label on a particular text, you will often find that more than one label can be used. In this sense, many texts can be seen as 'mixed'. We'll be taking a look at this later in the chapter, but just to give you one example: Wilfred Owen's *Anthem for Doomed Youth* can be characterised and categorised not only as a sonnet, but also as an elegy and as an anti-war poem.
- Genres are constantly changing. For example, as has been recently

pointed out 'the romance was initially a chivalric tale of love and war in the Romance languages (hence the name); but subsequently it came to be the name for any story with a love (but not erotic or pornographic) interest.' Interestingly, H. G. Wells called his novel *The Time Machine* a 'scientific romance'. We, today, would classify it as 'science fiction'.

Odd ones out

We are not going to be able to cover all the possible literary sub-genres in one short chapter. To do so would require a large number of volumes, let alone part of one chapter! We can only look at one or two genres here.

ACTIVITY 146

Below, you will find four short extracts from novels published between 1855 and 1902. Each extract is concerned with some aspect of a city. Three of the extracts are taken from novels which can be classified as belonging to the 'social realism' genre.

Discuss which extract you think does not belong to this genre. What are your reasons?

1 Stoke-on-Trent

Moor Road, which climbs over the ridge to the mining village of Moorthorne and passes the new Park on its way, was crowded with people going up to criticize and enjoy this latest outcome of municipal enterprise in Bursley: sedate elders of the borough who smiled grimly to see one another on Sunday afternoon in that undignified, idly curious throng; white-skinned potters, and miners with the swarthy pallor of sub-terranean toil; untidy Sabbath loafers whom neither church nor chapel could entice, and the primly-clad respectable who had not only clothes but a separate deportment for the seventh day; housewives whose pale faces, as of prisoners free only for a while, showed a naive and timorous pleasure in the unusual diversion; young women made glorious by richly-coloured stuffs and carrying themselves with the defiant independence of good wages earned in warehouse or painting-shop; youths oppressed by stiff new clothes bought at Whitsuntide, in which the bright necktie and the nosegay revealed a thousand secret aspirations;

Arnold Bennett, *Anna of the Five Towns* (1902)

2 Manchester

For several miles before they reached Milton, they saw a deep lead-coloured cloud hanging over the horizon in the direction in which it lay. It was all the darker from contrast with the pale gray-blue of the wintry sky; for in Heston there had been the earliest signs of frost. Nearer to the town, the air had a faint taste and smell of smoke; perhaps, after all, more a loss of the fragrance of grass and herbage than any positive taste or smell. Quick they were whirled over long, straight, hopeless streets of regularly-built houses, all small and of brick. Here and there a great oblong many-windowed factory stood up, like a hen among her chickens, puffing out black 'unparliamentary' smoke, and sufficiently accounting for the cloud which Margaret had taken to foretell rain. As they drove through the larger and wider streets, from the station to the hotel, they had to stop constantly; great loaded lorries blocked up the not over-wide thoroughfares. Margaret had now and then been into the city in her drives with her aunt. But there the heavy lumbering vehicles seemed various in their purposes and intent; here every van, every wagon and truck, bore cotton, either in the raw shape in bags, or the woven shape in bales of calico. People thronged the footpaths, most of them well-dressed as regarded the material, but with a slovenly looseness which struck Margaret as different from the shabby, threadbare smartness of a similar class in London.

Elizabeth Gaskell, *North and South* (1855)

3 London

Forthwith came a change over the waters, and the serenity became less brilliant but more profound. The old river in its broad reach rested unruffled at the decline of day, after ages of good service done to the race that peopled its banks, spread out in the tranquil dignity of a waterway leading to the uttermost ends of the earth. We looked at the venerable stream not in the vivid flush of a short day that comes and departs for ever, but in the August light of abiding memories. And indeed nothing is easier for a man who has, as the phrase goes, 'followed the sea' with reverence and affection, than to evoke the great spirit of the past upon the lower reaches of the Thames. The tidal current runs to and fro in its unceasing service, crowded with memories of men and ships it had borne to the rest of home or to the battles of the sea. It had known and served all the men of whom the nation is proud, from Sir Francis Drake to Sir John Franklin, knights all, titled and untitled – the great knights-errant of the sea. It had borne all the ships whose names are like jewels flashing in the night of time, from the *Golden Hind* returning with her round flanks full of treasure, to be visited by the Queen's Highness and thus pass out of the gigantic tale, to the *Erebus* and *Terror*, bound on other conquests – and that never returned. It had known the ships and the men. They had sailed from Deptford, from Greenwich, from Erith – the adventurers and the settlers; kings' ships and the ships of men on 'Change; captains, admirals, the dark 'interlopers' of the Eastern trade, and the commissioned 'generals' of East India fleets. Hunters for gold or pursuers of fame, they all had gone out on that stream; bearing the sword and often the torch, messengers of the might within the land, bearers of a spark from the sacred fire. What greatness had not floated on the ebb of that river into the mystery of an unknown earth! ... The dreams of men, the seed of commonwealths, the germs of empires.

The sun set; the dusk fell on the stream, and lights began to appear along the shore. The Chapman lighthouse, a three-legged thing erect on a mud-flat, shone strongly. Lights of ships moved in the fairway – a great stir of lights going up and going down. And farther west on the upper reaches the place of the monstrous town was still marked ominously on the sky, a brooding gloom in sunshine, a lurid glare under the stars.

Joseph Conrad, *Heart of Darkness* (1902)

4 Chicago

Minnie's flat, as the one-floor resident apartments were then being called, was in a part of West Van Buren Street inhabited by families of laborers and clerks, men who had come, and were still coming, with the rush of population pouring in at the rate of fifty thousand a year. It was on the third floor, the front windows looking down into the street, where, at night, the lights of grocery stores were shining and children were playing. To Carrie, the sound of the little bells upon the horsecars, as they tinkled in and out of hearing, was as pleasing as it was novel. She gazed into the lighted street when Minnie brought her into the front room, and wondered at the sounds, the movement, the murmur of the vast city which stretched for miles and miles in every direction.

Theodore Dreiser, *Sister Carrie* (1900)

COMMENTARY There are a number of features that 'social realism' novels share. For example, they often:

- include realistic descriptions of the environment in which the events of the novel are set
- are concerned with the everyday lives, loves and tragedies of ordinary people
- deal with the complex socio-economic and class relationships within a particular community
- focus on the particular social problems or injustices that the author wishes to draw the readers' attention to
- were written in the late nineteenth or early twentieth century.

Amongst other novelists who could be considered 'social realists' are Charles Dickens, Thomas Hardy and George Eliot, though it was not a genre confined to writers in England or America. Emile Zola, in France, with his novels about miners and prostitutes is a social realist par excellence as is Guy de Maupassant in his very popular short stories.

There are other features of the social realist genre that are not immediately obvious when reading the novels! These include:

- they are frequently set on examination syllabuses
- they are frequently dramatised on TV and radio
- they generate a large number of the sub-genre of 'study notes'.

It was, and still is, a massively influential genre. For instance, most A level English students writing a fictional narrative will slip into this genre.

A group of English poets writing between 1590 and 1650, including John Donne, George Herbert and Andrew Marvell are frequently known as the 'Metaphysical Poets'. Characteristics of this genre of poetry include:

1 A line of argument or persuasion running through the poem.
2 Concise expression and syntax, sometimes accompanied by a deliberate roughness of versification.
3 Lines of varying length.
4 Simple verse forms.
5 The use of conceits – striking and ingenious metaphors and comparisons.
6 A display of wit and learning.
7 Brilliant, abrupt openings.
8 A strong sense of drama.
9 A subject matter of love or religion, with the profane and spiritual interwoven.

Discuss the following extracts from poems. Which would you characterise as being

metaphysical? Which of the nine characteristics apply to them?

1 He who bends to himself a joy
   Does the wingèd life destroy
   But he who kisses the joy as it flies
   Lives in eternity's sunrise.

2 A little learning is a dangerous thing;
   Drink deep, or taste not the Pierian spring;
   There shallow draughts intoxicate the brain,
   And drinking largely sobers us again.

3 For Godsake hold your tongue, and let me love,
      Or chide my palsie, or my gout,
   My five grey haires, or ruin'd fortune flout,
         With wealth your state, your mind with Arts improve,
            Take you a course, get you a place,
            Observe his honour, or his grace,
   Or the Kings reall, or his stamped face
         Contemplate, what you will, approve,
            So you will let me love.

4 Redemption

HAVING been tenant long to a rich Lord,
      Not thriving, I resolved to be bold,
      And make a suit unto him, to afford
A new small, rented lease, and cancell th' old.
In heaven at his manour I him sought:
      They told me there, that he was lately gone
      About some land, which he had dearly bought
Long since on earth, to take possession.
I straight return'd, and knowing his great birth,
      Sought him accordingly in great resorts;
      In cities, theatres, gardens, parks, and courts:
At length I heard a ragged noise and mirth
      Of theeves and murderers: there I him espied,
      Who straight, *Your suit is granted, said*, & died.

5 The flowers left thick at nightfall in the wood
   This Eastertide call into mind the men,
   Now far from home, who, with their sweethearts, should
   Have gathered them and will do never again.

6 DEATH, be not proud, though some have called thee
   Mighty and dreadful, for thou art not so;
   For those whom thou think'st thou dost overthrow
   Die not, poor Death, nor yet canst thou kill me.
   From rest and sleep, which but thy pictures be,
   Much pleasure – then, from thee much more must flow;
   And soonest our best men with thee do go,
   Rest of their bones and soul's delivery.
   Thou'rt slave to fate, chance, kings and desperate men,
   And dost with poison, war, and sickness dwell;
   And poppy or charms can make us sleep as well,

And better than thy stroke. Why swell'st thou then?
One short sleep past, we wake eternally,
And death shall be no more. Death, thou shalt die.

ACTIVITY 148

As we said, there are a vast number of literary genres. Here are ten you are quite likely to come across in your studies. Each member of the group should take one of these genres and research the answers to these questions:

- What are the main characteristics of the genre?
- What are some important examples of the genre?

Having researched the answers, you should then present them to the rest of the group and illustrate your findings with reference to and illustrations from specific examples of your genre.
You'll notice that the genres below focus on either form, period or content, though these are, of course, not entirely separable.

1 The Comedy of Manners
2 Shakespearean tragedy
3 The sonnet
4 Romantic poetry about nature
5 The mock-heroic
6 Free verse
7 Lyric
8 Satire
9 Feminist fiction
10 Restoration comedy.

You can, of course, choose a genre in consultation with your teacher that is relevant to your own particular course of study.

There are some genres that you are unlikely to encounter in traditional literary studies, though they play a very important part in many people's reading. Amongst the most famous of these must be the Mills and Boon series of escapist romantic novels. These books sell in large numbers to a fairly traditional and conservative audience, mainly female, and the publishers insist that the writers of books follow quite rigid genre requirements. The publishers know what type of book their readers expect and to ensure that the writers produce such novels, they are issued with a set of guidelines that must be adhered to.

Here are the guidelines for two of Mills and Boon's current, popular series.

Presents™ 50,000–55,000 words

Pick up a *Presents* novel and you enter a world full of spine-tingling passion and provocative, tantalising romantic excitement! Although grounded in reality, these stories offer compelling modern fantasies to readers all around the world, and there is scope within this line to develop relevant, contemporary issues which touch the lives of today's woman. Each novel is written in the third person and features spirited, independent heroines – who aren't afraid to take the initiative! – and breathtakingly attractive, larger-than-life heroes. The conflict between these characters should be lively and evenly matched, but always balanced by a developing romance which may include explicit lovemaking. *Presents* novels capture the drama and intensity of a powerful, sensual love affair.

Medical Romance™ 50,000–55,000 words

These are present day romances in a medical setting. There should be a good balance between the romance, the medicine, and the underlying story. At least one of the main characters should be a medical professional, and developing the romance is easier if the hero and heroine work together. Medical detail should be accurate but preferably without using technical language. An exploration of patients and their illnesses is permitted, but not in such numbers as to overwhelm the growing love story. Settings can be anywhere in the world.

ACTIVITY 149

Produce a detailed plot synopsis for either a *Presents* or a *Medical Romance* novel. This could, of course, become the basis of a piece you submit for coursework, either for original writing or for text transformation.

ACTIVITY 150

Research another genre of popular fiction: thrillers, detective, fantasy, westerns, horror, for example. Draw up the 'Guidelines' for these that a publisher could send to a prospective author.

Non-literary genres

If it was difficult to consider all the possible 'literary' genres in this chapter, it is impossible when we move to the 'non-literary'. These range from advertisements, brochures, chatlines, delivery notes, e-mails, fanzines, guarantees, headlines, invitations, jokes, kissograms, leaflets, mail-shots . . .. You can complete the (more difficult) half of the alphabet for yourself!

Cross-dressing

Eddie Izzard, Lily Savage, Dame Edna Everage, Danny la Rue and pantomime dames amuse us because they break convention. Because they all dress as women, whilst their audience is left in no doubt that they are, in fact, men is one of the sources of their humour though not, of course, the only one. We find it funny that these actors adopt the dress code of the opposite sex. Conventions and code are deliberately broken in the interests of entertainment, humour and social commentary. Because of how they dress and act, we are forced to see things in a different light.

Earlier in this chapter, we made a comparison between the codes and conventions of dress and linguistic and genre conventions. We can now take the comparison a stage further and see that there is cross-dressing in genre as well as on stage!

Read this poem by Adrian Henri, then answer the two following questions.

1 What two genres is he deliberately mixing?
2 What is the effect of this genre mixing?

The New, Fast, Automatic Daffodils
(New variation on Wordsworth's *Daffodils*)

I wandered lonely as
THE NEW, FAST DAFFODIL
    FULLY AUTOMATIC
that floats on high o'er vales and hills
The Daffodil is generously dimensioned to accommodate four adult
    passengers
10,000 saw I at a glance
Nodding their new anatomically shaped heads in
    sprightly dance
Beside the lake beneath the trees
    in three bright modern colours
red, blue and pigskin
The Daffodil de luxe is equipped with a host of useful
    accessories
including windscreen wiper and washer with joint
    control
A Daffodil doubles the enjoyment of touring at home
    or abroad

in vacant or in pensive mood
SPECIFICATION:
    Overall width 1.44m (57")
    Overall height 1.38m (54.3")
    Max. speed 105 km/hr (65m.p.h.)
    (also cruising speed)

DAFFODIL
    RELIABLE – ECONOMICAL
DAFFODIL
    THE BLISS OF SOLITUDE
DAFFODIL
    The Variomatic Inward Eye
Travelling by Daffodil you can relax and enjoy every
    mile of the journey.

COMMENTARY

You will have recognised that what Adrian Henri is doing in this piece is to mix excerpts from Wordsworth's famous poem *Daffodils* with the text of an advertisement for a Dutch car called the Daffodil. So, for example, the first line of Henri's poem 'I wandered lonely as' is a shortened version of Wordsworth's opening 'I wandered lonely as a cloud', but Henri removes the simile of 'cloud' to replace it by a quotation from the advert 'THE NEW FAST DAFFODIL FULLY AUTOMATIC'. If you are not already familiar with Wordsworth's poem, you will easily be able to get hold of a copy and see how Henri has interlinked the two texts to create an entirely new one. One of the results of this interlinking is to make us read both source texts in a new light and to see one thing in terms of another. You saw earlier that this is what the cross-dressing comics achieved. A more literary term in place of 'cross-dressing' for what Adrian Henri is doing in his poem is 'intertextuality'. This means that a text (or genre) is referred to, either directly or obliquely, by the writer of the new text and that for a full appreciation or understanding of the new text, its reader should be familiar with the earlier text or genre referred to. In this particular example of 'The New, Fast, Automatic Daffodils', if you did not know Wordsworth's original poem, which is about the restorative power of Nature, then Henri's new poem would be almost meaningless to you and therefore his implied ironic comments on our highly commercial culture would be lost, because you wouldn't be able to compare the socio-cultural meaning of the two source texts. Literature is full of examples of intertextuality: Pope's *The Rape of the Lock* depends on its readers being familiar with the conventions of Greek and Roman epics such as *The Iliad* and *The Aeneid;* a full appreciation of James Joyce's *Ulysses* requires a knowledge of another Greek epic, *The Odyssey*. Such examples could be multiplied almost indefinitely. Intertextuality can also be found in films (*Apocalypse Now* is a reworking of Joseph Conrad's *Heart of Darkness* (see page 294); in painting (Manet's *Dejeuner sur l'Herbe* is based on a composition by the Renaissance artist, Raphael) and in most other art forms. Even a Mickey Mouse telephone could be seen as an example of cross-dressing or intertextuality.

ACTIVITY 152

The next four texts, taken from novels, are examples of writers deliberately choosing to use the register conventions of another genre as part of their own novel.

1 Identify the genre (or, in the case of Extract 3, the genres) that the writer is using.

2 What are the linguistic features that enabled you to identify the genre?

3 What is the effect of the writer including this genre as part of the novel?

1 *This is the opening of Toni Morrison's* The Bluest Eye *which chronicles the life of a poor black American family in the 1940s. One of the children, Pecola, prays each night for blue eyes like those of her privileged blond, white schoolfellows.*

> Here is the house. It is green and white. It has a red door. It is very pretty. Here is the family. Mother, Father, Dick, and Jane live in the green-and-white house. They are very happy. See Jane. She has a red dress. She wants to play. Who will play with Jane? See the cat. It goes meow-meow. Come and play. Come play with Jane. The kitten will not play. See Mother. Mother is very nice. Mother, will you play with Jane? Mother laughs. Laugh, Mother, laugh. See Father. He is big and strong. Father, will you play with Jane? Father is smiling. Smile, Father, smile. See the dog. Bowwow goes the dog. Do you want to play with Jane? See the dog run. Run, dog, run. Look, look. Here comes a friend. The friend will play with Jane. They will play a good game. Play, Jane, play.

2 *An extract from an early chapter of* Waterland *by Graham Swift, which is set in the fen country of eastern England*

> About the Fens
> Which are a low-lying region of eastern England over 1,200 square miles in area, bounded to the west by the limestone hills of the Midlands, to the south and east by the chalk hills of Cambridgeshire, Suffolk and Norfolk. To the north, the Fens

advance, on a twelve-mile front, to meet the North Sea at the Wash. Or perhaps it is more apt to say that the Wash summons the forces of the North Sea to its aid in a constant bid to recapture its former territory. For the chief fact about the Fens is that they are reclaimed land, land that was once water, and which, even today, is not quite solid.

3 *John dos Passos' USA is a huge novel that is a savagely satirical portrait of twentieth century America from coast to coast and at every social level. One of his techniques is to blend non-fiction with fiction.*

Newsreel LXVIII

WALL STREET STUNNED

This is not Thirtyeight, but it's old Ninetyseven
You must put her in Center on time

MARKET SURE TO RECOVER FROM SLUMP

DECLINE IN CONTRACTS

POLICE TURN MACHINE GUNS ON COLORADO

MINE STRIKERS KILL 5 WOUND 40

Sympathizers appeared on the scene just as thousands of office workers were pouring out of the buildings at the lunch hour. As they raised their placard high and started an indefinite march from one side to the other, they were leered and hooted not only by the office workers but also by workmen on a building under construction

NEW METHODS OF SELLING SEEN

RESCUE CREWS TRY TO UPEND ILL-FATED CRAFT

WHILE WAITING FOR PONTOONS

He looked 'round an' said to his black greasy fireman
Jus' shovel in a little more coal
And when we cross that White Oak Mountain
You can watch your Ninety-seven roll

I find your column interesting and need advice. I have saved four thousand dollars which I want to invest for a better income. Do you think I might buy stocks?

POLICE KILLER FLICKS CIGARETTE AS HE GOES

TREMBLING TO DOOM

4 The Last of the Menu Girls *is a short story by Denise Chavez, a Latino writer from the south-western USA.*

NAME: Rocio Esquibel
AGE: Seventeen
PREVIOUS EXPERIENCE WITH THE SICK AND DYING: My Great Aunt Eutilia
PRESENT EMPLOYMENT: Work-study at Altavista Memorial

I never wanted to be a nurse. My mother's aunt died in our house, seventy-seven years old and crying in her metal crib: "Put a pillow on the floor. I can jump," she cried. "Go on, let me jump. I want to get away from here, far away."

COMMENTARY All these texts demonstrate the notion of 're-registration', a term used by the linguist, Ron Carter. He defines 're-registration' as meaning that no single word or stylistic feature or register will be barred from admission to a literary context. Registers such as legal language or the language of instructions are recognised by the neat fit between language form and specific function, but any language at all can be deployed to literary effect by the process of re-registration. In other words, as you saw in the four extracts, literary language (whether in prose, poetry or drama) can use registers from any non-literary genre and turn them to its own purposes.

Of course, 'cross-dressing' or genre mixing occurs in not just literary texts and, perhaps, the genre in which it most frequently occurs is in advertising. There seems to be no limit to the genres that advertising copywriters can turn (or re-register) for their own purposes. You have already seen one example of this on page 80. Here is a further one.

Enquiry warns fat cats to curb sminting excesses
Nick Ninelives
Business Correspondent

SENIOR executives have come under renewed attack today with the publication of the latest findings of the Mackinnon Report into top level sminting. After two months of intense investigations, it seems that no boardroom in the country has been spared from the all seeing eye of Sir Archibald Mackinnon. The report's main recommendations involve a complete ban on sminting options and a ceiling on sminting 'sweeteners' – the practice whereby senior executives are offered substantial sminting opportunities to induce them to leave one firm and join another. CBI spokesperson, Albert Hatt reacted strongly to the views of industry: 'Naturally, we don't want top executives to appear greedy. At the same time, we all know how enjoyable a good smint can be. And if it's been well earned, then why should it be denied? We're currently examining the report in detail and shall be tabling counter proposals at our next Downing Street meeting in a few weeks time.'

Meanwhile, Sir Archibald was remaining tight lipped: 'Everything, I have to say can be found in the report; the fact that I have been known to smint myself from to time should have no bearing whatsoever on the matter.'

Makes your mouth a much nicer place.

ACTIVITY 153

Identify, in detail, the features of the newspaper genre which this advert is using. Is there anything to indicate that it is not a genuine newspaper story?

ACTIVITY 154

Working in groups, collect as many examples of advertisements as you can that 're-register' the codes and conventions of other genres. You could use these either as the basis for a classroom wall display or as the basis for a piece of coursework.

Changing genres

Legal documents, advertisements, letters, graffiti, sermons, recipes . . . the list of genres is huge. However, most of the genres we have just listed – and we could have added many more – have one thing in common: such genres have existed for a very long time. You can find examples of Roman legal documents, eighteenth century adverts, medieval letters, graffiti in ancient native American settlements, Elizabethan sermons and recipes from the nineteenth century Mrs Beeton, the Delia Smith of her day. Many genres with which we are familiar today possess an ancient genealogy. You can find many further examples in Shelley Martin's book in the 'Living Language' series, *Language Change* (Hodder & Stoughton, 1999). Of course, technology and socio-cultural changes have introduced new genres. You won't find many nineteenth century e-mails or many Elizabethan answerphone messages, though the hit TV series *Blackadder* gains much of its comedy from just this anachronistic mixing of genres. You could try writing a series of e-mails between Sir Walter Ralegh or Sir Francis Drake and Elizabeth I!

And, as we saw earlier, the three main literary genres continue to spawn many new sub-genres such as feminist sci-fi novels. But, apart from such developments, it's true to say that genre is one of the aspects of language that changes least. (It has this in common with grammar! Whilst lexis is frequently changing, our grammar now is relatively stable.) The reasons for genres not changing much are fairly obvious. For example, people will always need to eat, so recipes will always be needed. People will always fall foul of the law, so legal documents will always be needed and so on ....

So genres are fairly stable. Of course, this is not the whole story. Though the genres themselves remain stable because their audiences and purposes remain the same, the style and content change considerably. You might well be sick if you ate food prepared according to a Roman recipe and, presumably, you're pleased not to be faced with the prospect of being hanged or transported for relatively minor breaches of the law as your eighteenth century counterparts were!

As you will see in this next activity, even over quite a short period of time, the style and content of some genres have changed quite markedly, though the genres still exist.

ACTIVITY 155

The book review is a genre with a long and distinguished history. Here are three reviews of novels taken from *The Guardian*. The first is a review of Virginia Woolf's *To the Lighthouse* and was published on 20 May 1927. The two following reviews were published on 18 December 1999.

What similarities and differences are there between the reviews of 1927 and 1999?

SENSITIVES
To the Lighthouse, by Virginia Woolf

London: The Hogarth Press, pp. 320. 7s 6d

One hopes not to fumble unforgivably in dealing with a book so fine in workmanship as Mrs Woolf's, so delicate in such intentions as we have divined. The background in Skye, with the natives negligible, the canvas being peopled by the Ramsay family and their visitors, a sophisticated and cultivated set. But the subtle lonely land and sea scape counts; for it isolates them, giving them more significance, perhaps, than might be their due were they merely characters in a story. They have another use. The book is a study of sensitives by sensitivists. Minds are opened – especially Mrs. Ramsay's and the plain spinster Lily Briscoe's – for us to watch the hints, impressions, reflections, flashes from other minds and beings, now dancing up and down like a swarm of gnats, again for a moment fixed and coloured spectrum-wise before the final rapid blend of sympathetic comprehension. Thus Mr Ramsay, the vain egotist, albeit pathetic and of a fiery unworldliness, we know chiefly through the brilliant intuitions of his beautiful, clear-souled, and indulgent wife, a non-intellectual;

and her we are vividly aware of mainly through the partial intuitions of devoted friends, who helplessly see her victim yet content. But Lily, unlucky in life and as an artist, is the most gifted with this uncanny power. She has the compensation, if it be one, that her mind is all alive with human experiences, enlightenments, and humours – that she owns her world if she cannot bend it to her will or fantasy. As we look at the party grouped friendliwise in their summer quarters, though humour is playing about them lightly all the time, we receive an impression of the intense loneliness of each. There may be more than one symbolic meaning attached to the lighthouse of the title – and of the opening and closing incidents. Is it the isolated watching mind? Is it the thing remote, so passionately desired, which turns to nothingness when we are forced to pursue it by the arrogant will of another? A deep and reticent homage to beauty speaks under the recorded irritations and frustrations of the passing day; while an austere resignation follows hard on natural yearnings after the permanent and the perfect, for 'our penitence deserves a glimpse only, and our toil respite only.'

The Breeders Box,
by Timothy Murphy (Abacus, £7.99)

Purple jacket, streamlined lettering, chunky cartoon graphics of slouching clubbers . . . *The Breeders Box* gives off all the right vibes yet has more in common with *Bleak House* than *The Acid House* – and the appeal of neither. We follow siblings Jess, Flip and Tigger through their emotionally charged teens and 20s, the latter spent largely in Flip's fabulous club in SoHo. Laughter, tears, weddings, funerals – all the sentimental standbys are here. Except that because this is a 'now' novel, our protagonists go through life's moments with a hangover. A welcome spark of cynicism comes from a drag queen, Urethra Franklin, but even she is bravely hiding tears, behind her 40-watt smile.

Married Alive,
by Julie Burchill (Orion, £6.99)

Inevitably, this echoes her first Bolly-and-bathos blockbuster, although you could also read it as the diary of Helen Fielding's Jude, or quite possibly Shazzter. But Julie B has a style so idiosyncratic that it lifts *Married Alive* above the crowd of chick-books from the first line. 'I woke up around midday, sick as the proverbial.' The 'I' here is Nicole, whose happy, shagful marriage begins to creak when she takes in Liza, her foul-mouthed and stroppy gran. Not a lot actually happens, but fans of Burchill's journalism will enjoy the book's wit and razor-sharp insight – not to mention its tendency to go off on amusing 800-word tangents at frequent intervals.

ACTIVITY 156

Three further genres that are commonly found in newspapers follow. Each is taken from early twentieth century editions of *The Guardian*. Obtain a current edition of the paper and compare the way that the genres have changed. The areas you should look at include:

- content
- layout and presentation
- the voice used to address the reader
- the type of reader envisaged
- levels of formality of the lexis
- grammatical structures
- any examples of language play
- the overall structure of the article

1 Film review

New Chaplin Film

Charlie Chaplin is the sole justification for a large part of the kinema's repertory. On the steadiness of his success hang, with precarious clutches, numbers of weak little screen comedians whose humour is wholly blatant.

At the Deansgate Picture House this week there is a new Chaplin comedy. It is called *The Adventurer* and portrays the hero in the role of an escaped convict. Like all his recent films it is exceedingly well produced, and the acting of the lesser people avoids any risk of the film being a one-man show.

As regards Charlie himself, it is a little disappointing. There are scenes of him running, monkey-like, up the sheer slopes of a sandy cliff, of high dives and splendid swimming. He doesn't carry the expressive cane, nor does he wear the bowler hat that was bought for him when he was ten and is now an indifferent fit. He does things which we've never seen him do before, and most of the time the camera is too far away from him to catch the full significance of his expressions. But there are one or two perfect moments in the film, as, for instance when the freed convict wakes up and finds himself clad in a sleeping suit, striped like the ominous garments of Sing-Sing, and with the bars of his bedstead behind him.

29 January 1918

2 Sports report

Boxing
Championship.
Police Stop the Fight

The great prize fight for the heavy-weight championship of the world between the negro Johnson and Tommy Burns took place at Sydney (New South Wales) on Saturday morning and resulted in the defeat of Burns on points after 14 rounds. The fight, the Central News correspondent telegraphs, furnished one of the most disgusting spectacles of the kind ever witnessed in this country. The men took into the ring with them to an extraordinary degree a violent personal animosity, and hatred, which was manifested throughout in insulting cries whenever damage was inflicted, as well as by continual insults and gibes. Although the price of admission was very high, from 18,000 to 20,000 people paid to see the match.

The fighting was fierce throughout, and over and over again the referee had to exercise his authority to get the desperate men apart. As early as the fourth round it became apparent that Johnson could not fail to win; and from that point forward Burns did not get in a single really effective blow, while in every round Johnson battered his adversary, who, by the end of the eighth round, presented a shocking figure.

'In the eleventh round,' the correspondent continues, 'a sneering remark by the negro' seemed to drive Burns almost to madness, and he rushed at his opponent with the recklessness of a wounded wild beast. The round was about the severest of the fight, both men hitting out and snarling with the utmost ferocity. Burns, as usual, got by far the worst of it, and was as near being laid out as at any time during the fight. At the fourteenth round the police, represented by several superior officers, who had been closely watching the proceedings throughout, intervened in the interest of public decency, declaring that it was impossible to allow Burns to be further knocked.

Burns, in an interview, said he did his best and fought hard, but Johnson was too big for him and his reach too long.

28 December 1908

3 Parliamentary report

Reform Bill Passed
Women's Vote Won

The Representation of the People Bill, which doubles the electorate, giving the Parliamentary vote to about six million women and placing soldiers and sailors over

19 on the register (with a proxy vote for those on service abroad), simplifies the registration system, greatly reduces the cost of elections, and provides that they shall all take place on one day, and by a redistribution of seats tends to give a vote the same value everywhere, passed both Houses yesterday and received the Royal assent.

7 February 1918

Nobody knows the trouble I've seen

What do these three extracts have in common?

1 If you want to show you take your British fashion heritage seriously, you must dress the Brit right down to your very arse, whilst avoiding the unacceptably inelegant image of a fat, ale-stained Neanderthal in Union Jack boxer shorts.
2 Whoever said spots vanish on the arrival of adulthood was a smug, clear-skinned liar. Blackheads, blemishes, whiteheads will invade any prone complexion that doesn't take preventative action. This doesn't mean stripping your skin of everything ol' Ma Nature put there, nor is it a licence to squeeze spots between grubby vice-like fingers and have all sorts of crap on the bathroom mirror.
3 Are *you* getting enough?
   How to have unstoppable confidence and power with women ... At last available in the UK – the classic 'pick-up' books of all time.

Apart from the fact that they are all taken from the same issue of the young men's magazine *Loaded*, they all also bear witness to some of the predicaments supposedly faced by the modern male. Wearing the wrong underwear, still suffering from zits well past the teenage years and feeling that you're unattractive to women are just some of the problems that seem to burden the modern man. In fact, the predicaments faced by the modern male, possibly exacerbated by the feminist movement, form the staple of many genres. The focus of this short section of the chapter is on the way that one topic, in this case the situation of the modern male, is dealt with in different genres. We could, obviously, have chosen a myriad of topics, but space precludes us from doing this.

ACTIVITY 157

You will need to work in groups for this activity. Each member of the group should take responsibility for one modern genre in which male problems or predicaments form part, if not all of the content. Here are some suggestions as to the genres you may want to consider – but you are free to include others, if you wish. Make sure that you consider at least two examples of your chosen genre.

- TV cartoons (*The Simpsons, King of the Hill*)
- magazines (*Loaded, FHM, Esquire*)
- TV sit-coms (*Men behaving Badly, Friends, Frasier*)
- novels (*Diary of Adrian Mole, Fever Pitch*)
- advertisements.

You should research one of these genres in order to make a presentation to the rest of the group or class. Focus on

- the type of problems or predicaments supposedly faced and their causes
- the type of audience envisaged by the writers
- the solutions, if any, that are put forward
- the characteristics of the genre.

By the end of all the presentations, you should be in a position to answer these questions;

- are the problems/predicaments/solution/ audience the same, whatever the genre?

- what effect does the genre have on the way the predicaments etc of the modern man are presented?
- are the predicaments genuine or merely media creations?

The role or predicament of the male and its treatment in a variety of genres is by no means a modern phenomenon.

This next activity will involve you in looking at how this theme is treated in a variety of texts, each of which has been regarded as belonging to the mainstream of English literature.

In each of these 'classic' texts, the leading character can be said to be partly responsible for his own problems, either because of his character or because of his having a grand idea which went badly wrong. For example, King Lear's decision to divide his kingdom between his daughters proved to have disastrous consequences both for Lear himself and for his kingdom. The Ancient Mariner's decision to shoot the albatross was another such one that had far-reaching consequences.

ACTIVITY 158

Choose one of the following texts and show how the writer examines and presents the role of its leading male character. You should consider the social, cultural and historical contexts at the time the work was written in addition to considering what it has to say to a modern reader of either gender. Needless to say, this is quite a substantial activity and is likely to provide you with a great deal of material for coursework submissions.

1 Falstaff in *Henry IV* (*Parts 1 and 11*) — Shakespeare
2 Lear in *King Lear* — Shakespeare
3 Tom in *Tom Jones* — Henry Fielding
4 The Ancient Mariner in *The Rime of the Ancient Mariner* — Samuel Taylor Coleridge

5 Juan in *Don Juan* (*Cantos 1–1V*) — Lord Byron
6 Nicholas in *Nicholas Nickleby* — Charles Dickens
7 David in *David Copperfield* — Charles Dickens
8 Kipps in *Kipps* — H. G. Wells
9 Mr Polly in *The History of Mr Polly* — H. G. Wells
10 Mr Pooter in *Diary of a Nobody* — George and Weedon Grossmith

Two for the price of one!

Earlier in this chapter we suggested that Wilfred Owen's poem *Anthem for Doomed Youth* could be categorised in a number of ways (p 292) and, of course, this is not the only text that could be categorised in more than one way. The aim of this final section of the chapter is to show you that assigning a text to a particular genre can sometimes be debatable as (i) genres are not always as stable as we would like to think and (ii) genres sometimes share some of the same or similar characteristics.

ACTIVITY 159

Here are the openings of two modern texts. One is factual; one is fictional. Which is which?

In groups, discuss the similarities and differences between the texts and try to assign each to its 'proper' genre.

> Half the world was in mortal terror of him. He had a sixty-inch chest, twenty-three-inch arms, and when the Anadrol and Bolasterone backed up in his bloodstream, his eyes went as red as the laser scope on an Uzi. He threw people through windows, and chased them madly down Hempstead Turnpike when they had the temerity to cut him off. And in the gym he owned in Farmingdale, the notorious Mr America's, if he caught you looking at him while he trained, you generally woke up, bleeding, on the pavement outside. Half out of his mind on androgens and horse steroids, he had this idea that being looked at robbed him of energy, energy that he needed to leg-press two thousand pounds.
>
> Nonetheless, one day a kid walked up to him between sets and said, 'I want to be just like you, Steve Michalik. I want to be Mr America and Mr Universe.'
>
> Paul Solotaroff, *The Power and the Gory* (1991)

> Charlie Croker, astride his favorite Tennessee walking horse, pulled his shoulders back to make sure he was erect in the saddle and took a deep breath ... Ahhhh, that was the ticket ... He loved the way his mighty chest rose and fell beneath his khaki shirt and imagined that everyone in the hunting party noticed how powerfully built he was. Everybody; not just his seven guests but also his six black retainers and his young wife, who was on a horse behind him near the teams of La Mancha mules that pulled the buckboard and the kennel wagon. For good measure, he flexed and fanned out the biggest muscles of his back, the latissimi dorsi, in a Charlie Croker version of a peacock or a turkey preening.
>
> Tom Wolfe, *A Man in Full* (1998)

COMMENTARY

You'll have noticed a number of similarities between the two passages. We won't mention them all in this commentary, but amongst them are:

- third person point-of-view
- use of specific, placing detail (*Tennessee walking horse, La Mancha mules, Hempstead Turnpike, Farmingdale*)
- use of specialised technical terminology (*latissimi dorsi; Anadrol; Bolasterone*)
- striking comparisons (*in a Charlie Croker version of a peacock or turkey preening; as red as the laser scope on an Uzi*).

The important point to note is that the texts, despite their being in what people might regard as diametrically opposed genres, have far more in common than any differences there are between them. The boundaries between genres, as between almost everything in language and literature studies, are often fuzzy and blurred and not as clear-cut as we might have supposed or wished.

ACTIVITY 160

Go to a library, bookshop or your own shelves. Choose a book at random from 'fiction' or 'non-fiction'. Argue a case for the book being categorised as belonging to the other section.

ACTIVITY 161

It's possible to interpret the same text as though it belonged to completely different genres. For each of the following short texts we have suggested a number of different ways of reading them.

1 What support can you find in each text for our different suggested interpretations or 'ways of reading'?

2 What additional 'ways of reading' these texts might there be?

(a)

The cuckoo is a merry bird,
She sings as she flies;
She brings us good tidings,
And tells us no lies.

She sucks little birds' eggs
To make her voice clear,
That she may sing Cuckoo!
Three months in the year.

(*Romantic poem about the natural world; child's poem; a William Blake* Song of Innocence)

(b)

eyes left
eyes right
there's more to this than meets the eye
in the eye of the beholder
in the mind's eye
in the wind's eye
in the eye of the storm

(*poem; part of a sci-fi short story; advertisement; thesaurus*)

(c)

His face was round and plump; his nose small, not flat like the Negroes', a very good mouth, thin lips, and his fine teeth well set, and white as ivory. After he had slumbered, rather than slept, about half-an-hour, he waked again, and comes out of the cave to me, for I had been milking my goats, which I had in the enclosure just by. When he espied me, he came running to me, laying himself down again upon the ground, with all the possible signs of an humble, thankful disposition, making a many antic gesture to show it. At last he lays his head flat upon the ground, close to my foot, and sets my other foot upon his head, as he had done before; and after this, made all the signs to me of subjection, servitude, and submission imaginable, to let me know how he would serve me as long as he lived; I understood him in many things and let him know I was very pleased with him; in a little time I began to speak to him and teach him to speak to me; and first, I made him know his name should be Friday, which was the day I saved his life; I called him so for the memory of the time; I likewise taught him to say 'Master,' and then let him know that was to be my name; I likewise taught him to say 'yes' and 'no' and to know the meaning of them.

(*journal/autobiography; post-colonial novel; language textbook*)

(d)

It is such a beautiful day I had to write you a letter
From the tower, and to show I'm not mad:
I only slipped on the cake of soap of the air
And drowned in the bathtub of the world.
You were too good to cry much over me.
And now I let you go. Signed, The Dwarf.

I passed by late in the afternoon
And the smile still played about her lips
As it has for centuries. She always knows
How to be utterly delightful. Oh my daughter,
My sweetheart, daughter of my late employer, princess,
May you not be long on the way!

(psychiatric 'confession'; modern poem; part of a detective story)

(e)

   During the past few months, Biff had become quite a frequent
visitor to Carol's apartment.
   He never failed to marvel at the cool, corrected elegance of
the place as contrasted with its warm, rippling, honey-blonde
occupant. The apothecary jars,
                         Chippendale furniture,
                                              and wall-to-wall
carpeting were strangely out of keeping with Carol's habitual
'Hiya good lookin'' as she came forward to greet him, wrapped
in one of those big fuzzy bathrobes and drying her hair on a
Turkish towel. Or were his calculations somehow awry? Was
there, deep within this warm, vital-seeming presence a steel
vein so thin as to be almost invisible? Or was this, too, a
mistake?

(magazine journalism; modern poem; romantic novel; advertisement)

Suggest different 'ways of reading' any of the
texts you are studying as part of your course or
any of the texts in this book (or the book itself!)

11 Text Transformations

In this chapter, not surprisingly given its title, you are going to look at how to transform texts. But what do we mean by this and, perhaps more importantly, why are we doing it? The dictionary tells us that to 'transform' something means to change the appearance, substance or character of an original. You'll probably be familiar from your childhood with 'Transformer' toys by which, by a clever series of mechanical moves, an innocent looking lorry could be changed into a fearsome intergalactic warrior complete with death ray guns, or a family car could become a rocket launcher. Well, you'll be pleased to know that you're not going to be involved in designing and building such Transformers in this chapter but, just as these Transformer toys change their appearance, their purpose or function, though not usually their intended 'audience', so we're going to be looking at the ways original literary texts can be altered, re-arranged, re-ordered, re-shaped, re-cast, adapted or converted into something new. But whilst the point of the transformed toys is that the source toy should not be recognisable, in literary transformations, the audience should always be aware of the original source. The source text may undergo any one or more of a number of changes. The text may, for example, change its

genre	*a novel may be adapted for radio or TV; a bible story may be retold in the style of a tabloid newspaper.*
plot	*alternative endings might be provided (as in John Fowles' novel* The French Lieutenant's Woman *or the happy ending to* King Lear *written in the eighteenth century by Nahum Tate in which Cordelia does not die).*
mood	*a 'tough' text could be rewritten 'tenderly' or a humorous text more seriously.*
perspective	*parts of a story could be re-told from another character's point of view. For example, parts of* Great Expectations *could be narrated from Magwitch's point of view, not Pip's.*
characterisation	*central characters could be given different personalities. For example, Jack in* Jack and the Beanstalk *could be depicted as a ne'er-do-well rather than as a lucky idiot.*

However, the transformation will not be so great or so radical that all sight of the original is lost. To recognise the original text in the transformation is, of course, part of the pleasure for the listener or reader. Young children take delight in re-tellings or re-workings of familiar fairy stories or nursery rhymes, but this pleasure or delight is not lost when the child becomes an adult. There are adult equivalents of the child's fun and excitement on hearing *Now I'm going to tell you the story of* Goldilocks and the Four Bears or *Let's listen to* The Three Billy Goats Glum.

Because it is impossible to cover all types of transformation in one short chapter, most of this chapter will be concerned with the adaptation of texts for one specific medium: radio. We don't, however, want to suggest to you that these are the only transformations you should consider. So, before you move on to radio adaptations, you are going to look briefly at some other kinds of transformation.

Fairy stories

Everybody knows the
story of the Three Little Pigs.
Or at least they think they do.
But I'll let you in on a little secret.
Nobody knows the real story,
because nobody has ever heard
my side of the story.

I'm the wolf. Alexander T. Wolf.

You can call me Al.

I don't know how this whole Big Bad Wolf thing got started, but it's all wrong.

Maybe it's because of our diet.

Hey, it's not my fault wolves eat cute little animals like bunnies and sheep and pigs. That's just the way we are. If cheeseburgers were cute, folks would probably think you were Big and Bad, too.

But like I was saying, the whole Big Bad Wolf thing is all wrong.

The real story is about a sneeze and a cup of sugar.

This is the real story.

Way back in Once Upon a Time time,
I was making a birthday cake
for my dear old granny.
I had a terrible sneezing cold.
I ran out of sugar.

So I went next door to ask if I could borrow a cup of sugar.
Now the guy next door was a pig.
And he wasn't too bright, either.
He had built his whole house out of straw
Can you believe it? I mean who in his right mind would build a house of straw?

If you haven't read *The True Story of the 3 Little Pigs* by *A Wolf* (as told to Jon Scieszka) of which that was the first few pages, you have missed out on one of the most delightful of modern children's books. The familiar story is retold by the Wolf, *Alexander T Wolf* but, in the words of the Paul Simon song, *You can call me Al.* The wolf gives his very plausible version of events and by the end of *the real story* has persuaded us that *I was framed.* We won't spoil it by telling you how he *was* framed, but this children's story is a very good example of a text transformation. A new perspective is offered on a familiar story and because the audience will know the original source, enjoyment in this new version is increased. There are, too, added pleasures for sophisticated adult readers that a child may not pick up. *You can call me Al* is one of these.

ACTIVITY 162

Transform a traditional story (fairy story, folk tale or nursery rhyme, for example) by changing one or more of genre, plot, mood, perspective or characterisation. Your transformation should be written for today's children, but the original tale must be kept firmly in mind. Here are ten suggested titles, but you are, of course, free to choose your own.

The Frog Prince Continued

The Secret of Snow White
Revenge of the Ugly Sisters
Whatever Happened to Humpty Dumpty?
The Confessions of Goldilocks
The Return of the Pied Piper
I Married Robin Hood
Sleeping Beauty: The Nightmare Continues
Little Miss Muffet Strikes Back
The Strange Case of Hansel and Gretel.

Politically correct?

ACTIVITY 163

Read the ending of J. F. Garner's version of 'Little Red Riding Hood' (taken from his *Politically Correct Bedtime Stories*, Souvenir Press, 1994 – we were unable to reproduce the extract here). Look at pages 2 to 4 starting from

"Red Riding Hood walked along the main path . . ." to the end of the story. After reading this transformed tale, discuss, in groups, the following:

1 What kind(s) of transformations have taken place?
2 What assumptions does the writer make about his audience?

3 What are the targets of his satire?
4 Write your own politically correct bedtime story.

Adaptation

Some of the most popular television programmes in recent times have been adaptations of classic novels, sometimes into a one off play or, more usually, into a four or six episode serial. The nineteenth century novels, *Middlemarch* by George Eliot, *Vanity Fair* by William Makepeace Thackeray and *Wives and Daughters* by Mrs Gaskell have all been very successfully adapted and transformed into television serials. Jane Austen's and Charles Dickens' novels are forever being transformed and televised. And it's not just the classic nineteenth century 'blockbuster' novels that are used. Highly successful have been Evelyn Waugh's *Brideshead Revisited* published in 1945, Paul Scott's *Jewel in the Crown* (1973), David Lodge's *Nice Work* (1988) and Jeanette Winterson's *Oranges Are Not The Only Fruit* (1991). Detective fiction has provided a rich source for adaptation: Sherlock Holmes, Hercule Poirot, Miss Marple, Lord Peter Wimsey, Brother Cadfael, Inspector Morse, Dalziel and Pascoe, Chief Inspector Wexford and a host of others all began life in the pages of novels or short stories.

Nor is it just for television that novels are adapted. The movies, too, make use of novels for much of their source material. You only have to think of *The Godfather, The Client, Jaws, Carrie, The Postman Only Rings Twice,* Alfred Hitchcock's *The Birds* and *Strangers on a Train* and hosts of other movies to realise how important transformation of novels is. Think, too, of the numerous film versions of Shakespeare's plays: Kenneth Branagh's *Henry V* and *Much Ado About Nothing,* Roman Polanski's *Macbeth* and Franco Zefferelli's *Romeo and Juliet* are just some of the most recent. And just a little further back, Laurence Olivier's *Richard III* and his *Henry V* are amongst the very best films of all time.

Shakespeare himself was a great transformer of original texts. Very few of his plays, even the most famous ones, have entirely original plots. For example, his history plays, such as *Richard II, Henry IV (Parts I and II)* and *Henry V* have their source in his reading of an Elizabethan history book called Holinshed's *Chronicles.* This also provided some of the source material which Shakespeare transformed into two of his greatest plays, *Macbeth* and *King Lear.* His reading from an Elizabethan translation of a Roman history book led to *Antony and Cleopatra* and *Julius Caesar;* Italian stories provided the source of *Romeo and Juliet;* Elizabethan poetry the source of *As You Like It* and a Roman comedy by Plautus the source of *The Comedy of Errors.* So we can see that Shakespeare was perhaps our best and best-known text-transformer. But he was by no means the first. Chaucer in *The Canterbury Tales* 250 years before Shakespeare transformed texts and only 50 or so years after Shakespeare's death, John Milton transformed parts of the Bible into *Paradise Lost.* So, you can see text transformation has a long pedigree.

Here is the opening of *Macbeth* in which Macbeth and Banquo, returning from their recent victory in battle, meet three witches on a heath. It is preceded by the extract from Holinshed's *Chronicles* (1587) that provided the source for the scene. Read the extracts carefully and answer the questions that follow them.

Shortly after happened a strange and uncouth wonder, which afterward was the cause of much trouble in the realm of Scotland, as ye shall after hear. It fortuned as Makbeth and Banquho journeyed towards Fores, where the king as then lay, they went sporting by the way together without other company save only themselves, passing through the woods and fields, when suddenly in the middest of a laund, there met them three women in strange and ferry apparel, resembling creatures of an elder world, whom when they attentively beheld, wondering much at the sight, the first of them spake and said: 'All hail Makbeth, Thane of Glammis' (for he had lately entered into that dignity and office by the death of his father Sinell). The second of them said: 'Hail Makbeth, Thane of Cawder.' But the third said: 'All hail Makbeth, that hereafter shalt be King of Scotland.'

Then Banquho: 'What manner of women (saith he) are you that seem so little favourable unto me, whereas to my fellow here, besides high offices, ye assign also the kingdom, appointing forth nothing for me at all?' 'Yes' (saith the first of them), 'we promise greater benefits unto thee than unto him; for he shall reign indeed, but with an unlucky end; neither shall he leave any issue behind him to succeed in his place, where contrarily thou indeed shalt not reign at all, but of thee those shall be born which shall govern the Scottish kingdom by long order of continual descent.' Herewith the foresaid women vanished immediately out of their sight.

Enter Macbeth and Banquo

MACBETH
So foul and fair a day I have not seen.

BANQUO
How far is't called to Forres? What are these,
So withered and so wild in their attire,
That look not like the inhabitants o'the earth,
And yet are on't? Live you? Or are you aught
That man may question? You seem to understand me
By each at once her choppy finger laying
Upon her skinny lips. You should be women;
And yet your beards forbid me to interpret
That you are so.
   MACBETH Speak if you can! What are you?

FIRST WITCH
All hail, Macbeth! Hail to thee, Thane of Glamis!

SECOND WITCH
All hail, Macbeth! Hail to thee, Thane of Cawdor!

THIRD WITCH
All hail, Macbeth, that shalt be king hereafter!

BANQUO
Good sir, why do you start, and seem to fear
Things that do sound so fair? – I'the name of truth,
Are ye fantastical, or that indeed
Which outwardly ye show? My noble partner

You greet with present grace, and great prediction
Of noble having and of royal hope
That he seems rapt withal. To me you speak not.
If you can look into the seeds of time
And say which grain will grow and which will not,
Speak then to me who neither beg nor fear
Your favours nor your hate.

FIRST WITCH
Hail!

SECOND WITCH
Hail!

THIRD WITCH
Hail!

FIRST WITCH
Lesser than Macbeth, and greater.

SECOND WITCH
Not so happy, yet much happier.

THIRD WITCH
Thou shalt get kings, though thou be none.
So all hail, Macbeth and Banquo!

FIRST WITCH
Banquo and Macbeth, all hail!

MACBETH
Stay, you imperfect speakers! Tell me more!
By Sinell's death I know I am Thane of Glamis;
But how of Cawdor? The Thane of Cawdor lives
A prosperous gentleman. And to be king
Stands not within the prospect of belief –
No more than to be Cawdor. Say from whence
You owe this strange intelligence; or why
Upon this blasted heath you stop our way
With such prophetic greeting? Speak, I charge you!
Witches vanish

1 Is the order of the events the same?
2 Has Shakespeare added anything to Holinshed's account?
3 Has he removed anything? If so, why do you think he did this?
4 How has he altered the speech and dialogue of Holinshed?
5 What makes Shakespeare's version more dramatic?

ACTIVITY 165

Here is the account given in North's *Plutarch* (1599) of the death of Cleopatra, the Queen of Egypt. Her lover, Antony has just died, Egypt has been conquered by Octavius Caesar and Cleopatra has no wish to live longer. Iras and Charmion are her servants.

Transform this extract into a scene (or scenes) from a play. If you want to compare your version with Shakespeare's, you should read Act 5 Scene 2 of *Antony and Cleopatra* from line 240 to the end of the play.

Nowe whilest she was at dinner, there came a contrieman, and brought her a basket. The souldiers that warded at the gates, asked him straight what he had in his basket. He opened the basket, and tooke out the leaves that covered the figges, and shewed them that they were figges he brought. They all of them marvelled to see so goodly figges. The contrieman laughed to heare them, and bad them take some if they would. They beleved he told them truely, and so bad him carie them in. After Cleopatra had dined, she sent a certaine table written and sealed unto Caesar, and commaunded them all to go out of the tombes where she was, but the two women, then she shut the dores to her. Caesar when he received this table, and began to read her lamentation and petition, requesting him that he would let her be buried with Antonius, founde straight what she ment, and thought to have gone thither him selfe: howbeit he sent one before in all hast that might be, to see what it was. Her death was very sodaine. For those whom Caesar sent unto her ran thither in all hast possible, and found the souldiers standing at the gate, mistrusting nothing, nor understanding of her death. But when they had opened the dores, they founde Cleopatra starke dead, layed upon a bed of gold, attried and araied in her royall robes, and one of her two women, which was called Iras, dead at her feete: and her other woman called Charmion halfe-dead, and trembling, trimming the diademe which Cleopatra ware upon her head. One of the souldiers seeing her, angrily sayd unto her: Is that well done Charmion? Verie well sayd she againe, and meete for a Princes discended from the race of so many noble kings. She sayd no more, but fell downe dead hard by the bed. Some report that this Aspicke was brought unto her in the basket with figs, and that she had commaunded them to hide it under the figge leaves, that when she shoulde thinke to take out the figges, the Aspicke shoulde bite her before she should see her: howbeit, that when she would have taken away the leaves for the figges, she perceived it, and said, Art thou here then? And so, her arme being naked, she put it to the Aspicke to be bitten.

aspicke asp (a poisonous snake)

We asked two questions at the beginning of the chapter and have gone some way to answering the first of them by giving you lots of examples of text transformations. We still, however, have to answer the second of these questions as to why we have to concern ourselves with them. Two very immediate answers to the question are that, first, text transformation will allow you to demonstrate your skill in achieving a number of the Assessment Objectives for A level English language and Literature, in particular AO6, which requires you to 'demonstrate expertise and accuracy in writing for a variety of specific purposes and audiences' and to draw on your 'knowledge of literary texts and features of language to explain and comment' on the choices you have made. The second immediate answer is that text transformation is a coursework component of the subject for at least one of the examination boards. More importantly, in the process of transforming texts, you will learn a lot that is central to the study of language and literature. In particular you will

- learn about a number of literary and non-literary genres
- gain a detailed knowledge and understanding of at least one literary text
- learn a lot about language
- learn that many literary texts feed on other literary texts as much as they feed on the writer's experience of life
- improve your ability to write for specific audiences and for specific purposes

■ learn how to select, shape and rewrite material in order to achieve your purpose.

And, of course, you'll be in very good company. Shakespeare, Chaucer and Milton are not bad company to be seen in, we suggest!

To give you an idea of the possible ways in which texts can be adapted, here are some examples taken from the syllabus of one examination board.

The Pardoner's Tale	Chaucer	➜	a modern morality play
One of the *Tales from Ovid*	Ted Hughes	➜	a radio play
Volpone	Ben Jonson	➜	script for a puppet show
Light Shining in Buckinghamshire	Caryl Churchill	➜	short story
Little Dorrit	Charles Dickens	➜	series of readings for radio
Moon Tiger	Penelope Lively	➜	film script

Radio Daze

As we said earlier, we won't be able to cover all the possible ways of transforming texts in this short chapter, so we are going to concentrate on the ways that writers adapt and transform literary texts for just one medium – the radio. You may well be surprised at the variety of ways in which texts are transformed and presented on the radio. For example, in just one week, BBC radio broadcast:

3 stage plays	transformed into radio plays
2 short stories	adapted and abridged for reading
2 novels	transformed into drama serials
3 novels	adapted and abridged for serial reading
1 novel	transformed into a comedy series
1 novel	transformed into a one-off play
1 poem	adapted for serial reading

You can see from this list of just one week's programmes that text transformation is alive and well in at least one medium!

ACTIVITY 166

Look in the current issue of *Radio Times* and compile a list of the text transformations (a) for radio and (b) for television. Note also how many films, not specifically made for television, are based on original literary texts.

You'll probably find, as we did, that many of the transformations are of novels or short stories. These, of course, bring their own problems for adapters. One of the most successful adaptations of recent times has been the dramatisation of J. R. R. Tolkien's *Lord of the Rings*. Those of you who know the work will realise just what a massive undertaking this was. The novel is over a thousand pages long and has a huge number of characters, so the problems for the adapter (or transformer) are legion. This is what Brian Sibley has written about some of the problems he had to solve:

Here are just a few facts about the first appearance in the book of some of the major characters (page numbers refer to the one-volume paperback edition): Frodo does not speak until p. 46: ('Has he [Bilbo] gone?'); Sam and Frodo do not appear together until the eavesdropping scene on p. 76; Merry has only two sentences until he meets his companions at the ferry on p. 110; and Collum does not speak – apart from his reported exchange with Déagol – until p. 638! In order to resolve such difficulties – which would clearly be more of a problem for listeners who did not know the book – it seemed necessary to invent some passages of dialogue. A scene was written in which Sam delivers replies to the party invitations to Bilbo and Frodo at Bag End, and another in order to establish Merry before he sets out for Crickhollow. And as no-one can have failed to notice, the first episode began with the arrest of Gollum on the borders of Mordor and his subsequent interrogation in Barad-Dûr (an event reported by Gandalf and referred to in *Unfinished Tales*).

ACTIVITY 167

Read the following extracts and then, in small groups, discuss the questions. The first extract is the Merry/Frodo passage from the book; the second is the radio script for this episode.

1 What information is given in the radio script that is not found in the extract from the book?

2 How does the adaptation establish Merry's light-hearted personality?

1

On September 20th, two covered carts went off laden to Buckland, conveying the furniture and goods that Frodo had not sold ... The thought that he [Frodo] would so soon have to part with his young friends weighed on his heart. He wondered how he would break it to them ...

The next morning they were busy packing another cart with the remainder of the luggage. Merry took charge of this, and drove off with Fatty ... 'Someone must get there and warm the house before you arrive,' said Merry. 'Well, see you later – the day after tomorrow, if you don't go to sleep on the way!'

2

FRODO: Well, Merry, is everything ready?

MERRY: Yes: two cart-loads yesterday, full to overflowing, and now another one. I'm beginning to wonder if your new home will be big enough!

FRODO: Well, I've sold everything I could bear parting with to Lobelia, but some things I just had to take to remind me of Bilbo and Bag End.

MERRY: Well, I'd best be off ... If I leave now I can get to Crickhollow and warm the house before you arrive – that is, if you're quite sure you want to walk rather than go by cart ...

FRODO: Quite sure.

MERRY: Then I'll see you the day after tomorrow – if you don't go to sleep on the way!

FRODO: (LAUGHING) I'll try not to!

CART STARTS OFF, THEN STOPS

MERRY: (CALLING BACK) I'll tell you one thing, Frodo, you had better settle when you get to Buckland, because I for one am not helping you to move back again!

FRODO: What on earth makes you think Lobelia would ever sell Bag End back to me?

CART STARTS OFF ONCE MORE

MERRY: She might – at a profit! Farewell, Frodo – and good walking!

CART DRIVES OFF

FRODO: (TO HIMSELF) Poor Merry, what will you say when you learn the truth of all this!

COMMENTARY A variety of information is conveyed by the dramatisation that is not found in the extract from the book. We learn that Merry and Frodo are going to Crickhollow, that Bag End has been sold to Lobelia and we are also given a reminder of the existence of Bilbo Baggins. Of course, the adapter has not invented this information (though he has had to invent the dialogue that conveys it); he has merely transferred it from another point in the novel to here where he thinks it would be the most effective. Merry is given invented dialogue that reflects his name. For example, he stops the cart and calls back to Frodo:

I'll tell you one thing, Frodo, you had better settle when you get to Buckland, because I for one am not helping you to move back again!

So, how do you start to transform a text for radio?

Perhaps the most important thing to get clear in your mind is the 'angle' that you are going to take on a text. Some of the questions that you will need answers to in order to ascertain this 'angle' are:

- what makes me want to work on *this* text? What is *my* idea about it? What is *my* artistic purpose in wanting to transform it?
- what do I think are the most important messages or themes in the text?
- can I do justice to some or all of these in my transformation?
- will I include all the events/episodes of the original?
- will I maintain the order of the events/episodes as narrated in the original?
- from whose point(s) of view is the story going to be told?
- am I going to maintain the mood of the original?
- will I include, adapt or jettison any sub plot(s)?
- will I combine, jettison any of the characters from the original?
- will I need to bring anything up to date for a modern audience?

There are four other important things a writer needs to have clear. You need to know

- the audience you are writing for
- the characteristics of the programme aimed at that audience
- the text you are transforming
- the techniques of writing for radio.

1 The audience

The BBC holds very detailed information on the audiences for every type of programme that is broadcast on radio. It is obviously very necessary to have such information because if the programmes were targeting the wrong kind of listener, then very quickly audience figures would plummet. There's no point in making a superb and imaginative programme if no one is listening! To give you an idea of just how detailed is this information, here are the audience profiles for two of Radio 4's well-established drama slots. The first is the audience profile for the afternoon Drama slot, broadcast Monday–Friday from 1415–1500. The second is for the Classic Serial slot, broadcast on Sundays from 1500–1600 with a repeat the following Saturday evening.

1

There are currently around 400,000 listeners at 14.15; this may increase following *The Archers* move to 14.00. Most are listening at home, although the car audience is growing towards the end. Many will have come back to Radio 4 for *The Archers* at 14.00. The audience is mainly middle-aged and retired women with very few retired men listening at this point. Some middle-aged working men are listening in cars. The audience is less AB than is typical for Radio 4.

Many listeners are resuming domestic activity (housework, gardening, shopping etc.) after the lunch-time break. Those who remain listening feel they can give a lot of attention to the radio and are more indulgent about listening – some plan activities such as sewing/ironing/paperwork to fit the play. 14.45 is a time when some parents/grandparents are getting ready to pick children up from school.

2

At this time the audience is declining – there is a loss of 330,000 listeners between 15.00 and 15.30 and a further 230,000 between 15.30 and 16.00. The biggest switch-off is at 15.30 when 170,000 leave.

The audience has a relatively young profile with a below-average age of 51 by 16.00. More women than men listen and there is a good mix of social grades. The proportion listening in cars grows from 10–15 percent across the slot while 700,000 Radio 4 listeners are listening to other stations.

Gardening continues to be the main activity – some are reading books, others are out visiting friends and family. Those at home want radio to take their mind off the tasks in hand – drama is seen as very appropriate.

You'll notice that information is provided on

- the size of the audience (and how this changes during the time the programme is broadcast)
- the age, social class and gender mix of the audience
- the activities they will be engaged in whilst listening.

The information is provided not only for the BBC itself, but also for prospective writers (or text transformers). You can see, then, just how important it is for you to have clearly in mind the audience on whose behalf you will be transforming texts. It's no use just saying 'I'm writing for adults' or 'I'm writing for readers of women's magazines'. These are far too vague and your transformation will consequently have less chance of being successful. You need to be as precise and clear as possible when targeting your audience. If this involves you in research before putting pen to paper, then so be it. But there is a further pay-off in doing this research. You'll be able to write much more meaningfully about your intended audience in your commentary.

ACTIVITY 168

Research the audience profile for other radio programmes with which you are familiar. You could use BBC publications or the Internet for this.

2 The programme

The editors and producers of radio programmes have not only a very clear idea of their audience, they also give writers very detailed instructions about the type of script that that they are looking to accept. Here, for instance, is the Editorial Guide for the Classic Serial slot. This, of course, is highly relevant to text transformation.

This slot is exclusively for dramatisations of works of narrative fiction that have achieved classic status. 'Classic' should mean that the work has won acclaim from succeeding generations of readers. Books that are cult successes, famous for their 'kitsch' element or not part of the mainstream, would not be appropriate. Beyond this, the definition of 'classic' should be as wide as possible to include works from around the world, from the twentieth century and neglected writing. Offers might range from the popular British works of the nineteenth century, e.g. the recent successes of *North and South* by Elizabeth Gaskell or *Agnes Grey* by Anne Bronte to contemporary international masterpieces from authors such as Gabriel Garcia Marquez or Gunter Grass.

If a book from the last 20 years is dramatised there should be some sense of event attached to the choice – perhaps that Radio 4 is predicting a classic of the future.

There could be occasions when the source work is not a novel – perhaps a collection of short stories (e.g. *Dubliners*), epic work (e.g. *The Iliad*) or traditional tales (e.g. Aesop/Grimm).

Imaginative and creative treatments of the texts are welcome though they should be in direct proportion to the fame of the book. For example, a radical treatment of a little known novel would not be ideal.

A strong, clear story is important, as is a plot structure that would work well when abridged – too many flash backs, time-shifts or changes in POV (*point of view*) are not ideal.

There are a number of important points to note here. Not only can writers choose to transform a variety of modern and nineteenth century novels, but they are not restricted to the novel alone. Short stories, epic poems and traditional tales are also potential candidates for transformation. The editors also welcome 'imaginative and creative treatments' and we will examine one of these later in this chapter. Note, too, the need for a strong story line in the adaptation and also the likelihood that the story would need to be abridged. Again, as with audience, it's obvious that you must do a great deal of planning and preparation before you begin the actual writing of the transformation.

3 The text

It almost goes without saying that you must know very thoroughly indeed any text that you wish to transform. If it's a novel or short story that you are going to be working on, then these are some of the features that must become almost second nature to you:

- the structure of the plot (whether there is just one plot or a number of sub-plots and how these relate to each other)
- those scenes which are key and those which are less central
- the setting(s) and period(s) in which the action takes place
- the point of view from which the story is narrated
- the language style of the narrative
- the characters: what they do; how they relate to each other; they way they speak; what happens to them; which ones develop and change and which ones remain static; which ones are central and which peripheral to the plot.

There's quite a lot to consider here and we've only looked at one genre! It's obvious you can't begin the work of text transformation without this detailed knowledge and understanding of your source text. How you obtain this is a matter of choice, but you're unlikely to gain it on just a very quick and sketchy reading of the novel. You really need to immerse yourself in the work. Andrew Davies who has adapted many classic novels for television including *Vanity Fair, Pride and Prejudice* and *Wives and Daughters* follows this method:

If it's been recorded unabridged by 'Cover to Cover' or one of those things, I try to avoid sitting down in front of it. I buy the cassette and go for long drives in the car and listen to it because that way you can't skip . . . so that's the first step anyway . . . either by reading or by listening to it. I listen to it two or three times until I'm pretty well soaked in the thing.

Then I start dividing it into chunks. I suppose the first thing I do when I'm soaking myself in it is also putting myself into it as well . . . thinking, 'What do I think of this?' 'Do I have a particular angle on it?' or 'Am I just trying to present it as it is?'

You'll notice that Andrew Davies stresses the need to have a 'particular angle' on the text.

Whether you follow Andrew Davies' method or one of your own, you can see that thorough preparation is essential. Again, there is a bonus for you in that not only will your thorough preparation mean a successful transformation, but you'll also have important insights to communicate in your commentary.

4 The techniques

Not only do you need to know the text you are transforming, but you also have to be very familiar with the techniques and characteristics of the genre into which you are transforming your text. It might be a film script, a newspaper article, a son-et-lumière presentation or, as here, a radio drama. Whatever genre you are working in, you must ensure that your transformation conforms to its conventions. In other words, your transformation must work! For instance, with radio drama you should:

- not use dialogue to *describe* too much
- avoid having too many characters of the same age who sound similar

- give characters their own distinctive voice (or idiolect)
- include strong elements of suspense and drama
- have an arresting or intriguing opening (otherwise listeners will switch off).

ACTIVITY 169

Here's the opening of a radio play by Timothy West, *The Gun that I Have in my Right Hand is Loaded*. Read it carefully and list as many things as you can that would make it very unsuccessful as radio drama. What are the 'creaky' bits?

(BRING UP MUSIC THEN CROSSFADE TO
TRAFFIC NOISES. WIND BACKED BY SHIP'S
SIRENS, DOG BARKING, HANSOM CAB,
ECHOING FOOTSTEPS, KEY CHAIN, DOOR
OPENING, SHUTTING)

LAURA: (*off*) Who's that?

CLIVE: Who do you think, Laura, my dear? Your husband.

LAURA: (*approaching*) Why, Clive!

RICHARD: Hello, Daddy.

CLIVE: Hello, Richard. My, what a big boy you're getting. Let's see, how old are you now?

RICHARD: I'm six, Daddy.

LAURA: Now Daddy's tired, Richard, run along upstairs and I'll call you when it's supper time.

RICHARD: All right, Mummy.

(RICHARD RUNS HEAVILY UP WOODEN STAIRS)

LAURA: What's that you've got under your arm, Clive?

CLIVE: It's an evening paper, Laura.
(PAPER NOISE)
I've just been reading about the Oppenheimer smuggling case. (*effort noise*) Good gracious, it's nice to sit down after that long train journey from the insurance office in the City.

LAURA: Let me get you a drink, Clive darling.
(LENGTHY POURING, CLINK)

CLIVE: Thank you, Laura, my dear.
(CLINK, SIP, GULP)
Aah! Amontillado, eh? Good stuff. What are you having?

LAURA: I think I'll have a whisky, if it's all the same to you.
(CLINK, POURING, SYPHON)

CLIVE: Whisky, eh? That's a strange drink for an attractive auburn-haired girl of twenty nine. Is there ... anything wrong?

LAURA: No, it's nothing, Clive, I –

CLIVE: Yes?

LAURA: No, really, I–

CLIVE: You're my wife, Laura. Whatever it is, you can tell me. I'm your husband. Why, we've been married – let me see – eight years, isn't it?

LAURA: Yes, I'm sorry Clive, I ... I'm being stupid. It's ... just ... this.
(PAPER NOISE)

CLIVE: This! Why, what is it, Laura?

LAURA: It's ... it's a letter. I found it this morning in the letter box. The Amsterdam postmark and the strange crest on the back ... it ... frightened me. It's addressed to you. Perhaps you'd better open it.

CLIVE: Ah ha.
(ENVELOPE TEARING AND PAPER NOISE)
Oh, dash it, I've left my reading glasses at the office. Read it to me, will you, my dear.

LAURA: Very well.
(PAPER NOISE)
Let's see. 'Dear Mr Barrington. If you would care to meet me in the Lounge Bar of Berridge's Hotel at seven-thirty on Tuesday evening the twenty-first of May, you will hear something to your advantage.

You'll be relieved to know that the play is a send up of the conventions of radio drama. To see just what has gone wrong with this play, these guidelines for aspiring radio writers issued by the BBC should prove illuminating.

GEOFF, CAROL, ALICE, ROGER AND RICHARD ARE
IN A CROWDED PUB WITH SOME OTHER FRIENDS – *NO!*

The only means of establishing a character's presence is to have them speak or be referred to by name. If there are too many characters in a scene the listener will lose track.

GEOFF (LOOKING ANGRILY AT IRENE,
HIS PALE FACE FLUSHED) 'I WILL NOT' – *NO!*

'Stage directions' for the producer's or actor's benefit are to be avoided. If it is important it should be there in dialogue.

A CAR PULLS UP. ENGINE OFF. DOOR OPENS AND SHUTS.
FEET WALK TO THE FRONT DOOR. KEY IN THE LOCK.
DOOR OPENS. FEET WALK DOWN THE HALL TO THE
KITCHEN. 'I'M HOME DARLING'. – *NO!*

Sound effects should be used sparingly. They should work with the dialogue. Out of context they will mean little. Effects are useful in setting a scene, but the signpost must be subtle.

GEOFF'S BREATHING IN THE 'PHONE BOX BECOMES MORE
LABOURED. PAINFUL. BEHIND HIM A SYMPHONY ORCHESTRA.
AT FIRST QUIETLY, PLAYS MAHLER'S FIFTH. BRING UP INTERIOR ALBERT
HALL. – *YES. THINK IN SOUND!*

A variety of sound is essential for holding the listener's attention and engaging their imagination. This variety can be achieved by altering the lengths of sequences, number of people speaking, space of dialogue, volume of sound, background acoustics and location of action. On radio, one room sounds very much like another if they're about the same size, but the difference between an interior and an exterior acoustic is quite considerable. The contrast between a noisy sequence with a number of voices and effects and a quiet passage of interior monologue, is dramatic and effective.

The best way to become familiar with the conventions and the possibilities of the radio medium is to listen to as much of it as you can.

ACTIVITY 170

Rewrite Timothy West's script in Activity 169
so that it could be taken seriously as the opening
of an episode in a TV or radio detective series.

David Copperfield

The novels of Charles Dickens are always popular choices for radio adaptation.
Indeed, even as this chapter is being written, Radio 4 is broadcasting a
dramatisation of *Nicholas Nickleby* in fifteen minute episodes. We, however,
are going to look in detail at an earlier dramatisation of *David Copperfield*.

ACTIVITY 171

The first of the following texts is a transcription
of the opening of Episode One of *David
Copperfield*; the second is the passage from the
novel on which it is based. The extract from the
radio programme lasted 87 seconds on air. Read
the two passages carefully and discuss the
questions which follow.

1

WIND BLOWING. KNOCK AT DOOR. DOOR OPENS.

BETSEY: Mrs David Copperfield?

MRS C: Yes.

BETSEY: Miss Trotwood, your late husband's aunt. You have heard of her, I dare say?

MRS C: I, I have had that pleasure.

BETSEY: Now you see her.

MRS C: Yes. Please come in here, Miss Trotwood. (WIND STOPS) There is a fire.

BETSEY: Thank you.

MRS C: (*cries*)

BETSEY: Don't do that. Come, come. Take off your cap and let me see you. Why,
         bless my heart, you're a baby.

MRS C: I'm afraid I'm but a childish widow and I'll be but a childish mother, if I live.

BETSEY: Why Rookery in the name of heaven?

MRS C: Do you mean the house, ma'am? The name was Mr Copperfield's choice.
         When he bought the house he liked to think there were rooks in it.

BETSEY: And where are the birds?

MRS C: There haven't been any since we lived here. We thought it was a rookery, but
         the nests were very old ones.

BETSEY: David Copperfield all over. Takes the birds on trust because he sees the nests.

MRS C: (*sobs*) Mr Copperfield is dead, if you dare to speak unkindly of him, I'll ...
         (*sobs*)

BETSEY: Come, child. Sit down. You've gone pale. There. When do you expect?

MRS C: I can't stop trembling. I don't know what's the matter. I shall die.

BETSEY: No you won't. Have some tea.

2

My mother was sitting by the fire, but poorly in health, and very low in spirits, looking
at it through her tears, and desponding heavily about herself and the fatherless little
stranger, who was already welcomed by some grosses of prophetic pins in a drawer
up-stairs, to a world not at all excited on the subject of his arrival; my mother, I say,
was sitting by the fire, that bright, windy March afternoon, very timid and sad, and

very doubtful of ever coming alive out of the trial that was before her, when, lifting her eyes as she dried them, to the window opposite, she saw a strange lady coming up the garden.

My mother had a sure foreboding at the second glance, that it was Miss Betsey. The setting sun was glowing on the strange lady, over the garden-fence, and she came walking up to the door with a full rigidity of figure and composure of countenance that could have belonged to nobody else.

When she reached the house, she gave another proof of her identity. My father had often hinted that she seldom conducted herself like any ordinary Christian; and now, instead of ringing the bell, she came and looked in at that identical window, pressing the end of her nose against the glass to that extent that my poor dear mother used to say it became perfectly flat and white in a moment.

She gave my mother such a turn, that I have always been convinced I am indebted to Miss Betsey for having been born on a Friday.

My mother had left her chair in her agitation, and gone behind it in the corner. Miss Betsey, looking round the room, slowly and inquiringly, began on the other side, and carried her eyes on, like a Saracen's Head in a Dutch clock, until they reached my mother. Then she made a frown and a gesture to my mother, like one who was accustomed to be obeyed, to come and open the door. My mother went.

'Mrs. David Copperfield, I think.' said Miss Betsey; the emphasis referring, perhaps, to my mother's mourning weeds, and her condition.

'Yes,' said my mother, faintly.

'Miss Trotwood.' said the visitor. 'You have heard of her, I dare say?'

My mother answered she had had that pleasure. And she had a disagreeable consciousness of not appearing to imply that it had been an overpowering pleasure.

'Now you see her,' said Miss Betsey. My mother bent her head, and begged her to walk in.

They went into the parlour my mother had come from, the fire in the best room on the other side of the passage not being lighted – not having been lighted, indeed, since my father's funeral; and when they were both seated, and Miss Betsey said nothing, my mother, after vainly trying to restrain herself, began to cry.

'Oh tut, tut, tut!' said Miss Betsey, in a hurry. 'Don't do that! Come, come!'

My mother couldn't help it notwithstanding, so she cried until she had had her cry out.

'Take off your cap. child,' said Miss Betsey, 'and let me see you.'

My mother was too much afraid of her to refuse compliance with this odd request, if she had any disposition to do so. Therefore she did as she was told, and did it with such nervous hands that her hair (which was luxuriant and beautiful) fell all about her face.

'Why, bless my heart!' exclaimed Miss Betsey. 'You are a very Baby!'

My mother was, no doubt, unusually youthful in appearance even for her years; she hung her head, as if it were her fault, poor thing. and said, sobbing, that indeed she was afraid she was but a childish-widow, and would be but a childish mother if she lived. In a short pause which ensued, she had a fancy that she felt Miss Betsey touch her hair, and that with no ungentle hand; but, looking at her, in her timid hope, she found that lady sitting with the skirt of her dress tucked up, her hands folded on one knee, and her feet upon the fender, frowning at the fire.

'In the name of Heaven,' said Miss Betsey, suddenly, 'why Rookery?'

'Do you mean the house, ma'am?' asked my mother.

'Why Rookery?' said Miss Betsey. 'Cookery would have been more to the purpose, if you had had any practical ideas of life, either of you.'

'The name was Mr. Copperfield's choice,' returned my mother. 'When he bought the house, he liked to think that there were rooks about it.'

The evening wind made such a disturbance just now, among some tall elm-trees at the bottom of the garden, that neither my mother or Miss Betsey could forbear glancing that way. As the elms bent to one another, like giants who were whispering secrets, and after a few seconds of such repose, fell into a violent flurry, tossing their wild arms about, as if their late confidences were really too wicked for their peace of mind, some weather-beaten ragged old rooks'-nest burdening their higher branches, swung like wrecks upon a stormy sea.

'Where are the birds?' asked Miss Betsey.

'The . . .?' My mother had been thinking of something else.

'The rooks – what has become of them?' asked Miss Betsey.

'There have not been any since we have lived here,' said my mother. 'We thought – Mr. Copperfield thought – it was quite a large rookery; but the nests were very old ones, and the birds have deserted them a long while.'

'David Copperfield all over!' cried Miss Betsey. 'David Copperfield from head to foot! Calls a house a rookery when there's not a rook near it, and takes the birds on trust, because he sees the nests!'

'Mr. Copperfield,' returned my mother, 'is dead, and you dare to speak unkindly of him to me –'

My poor dear mother, I suppose, had some momentary intention of committing an assault and battery upon my aunt, who could easily have settled her with one hand, even if my mother had been in far better training for such an encounter than she was that evening. But it passed with the action of rising from her chair; and she sat down again very meekly, and fainted.

When she came to herself, or when Miss Betsey had restored her, whichever it was, she found the latter standing at the window. The twilight was by this time shading down into darkness; and dimly as they saw each other, they could not have done that without the aid of the fire.

'Well?' said Miss Betsey, coming back to her chair, as if she had only been taking a casual look at the prospect; 'and when do you expect –'

'I am all in a tremble,' faltered my mother. 'I don't know what's the matter. I shall die, I am sure!'

'No, no, no,' said Miss Betsey. 'Have some tea.'

1 The novel is written in the first person. How does the adapter deal with this in the extract?

2 Identify precisely the material from the first six paragraphs of the passage from the novel which is used in the dramatisation.

3 What material is omitted from these first six paragraphs?

4 How does the dramatisation provide information about the speakers' identity and circumstances?

5 What narrative material is transformed into dialogue?

6 Not all of Dickens' dialogue is used, presumably because of pressures of time. Identify what is omitted and discuss whether anything of significance is lost.

COMMENTARY   Perhaps the first thing to say is that, though this is the beginning of the radio dramatisation, it is not the very beginning of the novel. There have already been some three pages in which David Copperfield reflects on the peculiar circumstances of his birth, tells of the earlier death of his father and introduces his great-aunt, Betsey Trotwood. You'll remember that abridging is one of the skills stressed in the BBC guide we looked at earlier and we can see it in operation throughout this extract. A short part of the first paragraph of the novel is used a little later in the dramatisation, but again, you'll remember that too many time shifts are to be avoided. It can be quite awkward, though not impossible, to rely on a first person narrator in a dramatisation, but the adapter overcomes this potential difficulty here by deciding to use no narrator at all. Later, David Copperfield does narrate parts of his own story.

The extract begins with Betsey Trotwood's knock on the door. Her first words indicate the identity of David's mother-to-be. Note, too, how the adapter has to add *Your late husband's aunt* to Betsey's announcement of her own name. You'll have noticed that other sound effects are employed to convey *that bright, windy, March afternoon* but that some incidents are ignored: *my mother had left her chair in her agitation, and gone behind it in the corner* and that some of Dickens' descriptions and comparisons are impossible to convey on radio: *she came walking up to the door with a full rigidity of figure and composure of countenance that could have belonged to nobody else* and *she seldom conducted herself like any ordinary Christian,* though the distinctly different voices of the two actors playing Betsey Trotwood and Mrs Copperfield do suggest the differing characters and ages of the two women. The decision to dispense with the services of a narrator at this point means that some incidents must be conveyed through invented dialogue. There is an example of this when David's mother-to-be *sat down again very meekly, and fainted* and *Miss Betsey had restored her.* The dramatisation covers this by *Come, child. Sit down. You've gone pale. There.* Before picking up Dickens' dialogue with *when do you expect?*

ACTIVITY 172

Write the script for this next extract from the novel. It is the passage immediately following the end of the previous extract. You should ensure your script lasts for 90 seconds air time, the length of the original dramatisation.

'Oh dear me, dear me, do you think it will do me any good?' cried my mother in a helpless manner.

'Of course it will,' said Miss Betsey. 'It's nothing but fancy. What do you call your girl?'

'I don't know that it will be a girl, yet, ma'am,' said my mother innocently.

'Bless the Baby!' exclaimed Miss Betsey, unconsciously quoting the second sentiment of the pincushion in the drawer up-stairs, but applying it to my mother instead of me, 'I don't mean that. I mean your servant.'

'Peggotty,' said my mother.

'Peggotty!' repeated Miss Betsey, with some indignation. 'Do you mean to say, child, that any human being has gone into a Christian church, and got herself named Peggotty,'

'It's her surname,' said my mother, faintly. 'Mr Copperfield called her by it, because her Christian name was the same as mine."

'Here Peggotty!' cried Miss Betsey, opening the parlour-door.
'Tea. Your mistress is a little unwell. Don't dawdle.'

Having issued this mandate with as much potentiality as if she had been a recognised authority in the house ever since it had been a house, and having looked out to confront the amazed Peggotty coming along the passage with a candle at the sound of a strange voice, Miss Betsey shut the door again, and sat down as before; with her feet on the fender, the skirt of her dress tucked up, and her hands folded on one knee.

'You were speaking about its being a girl,' said Miss Betsey. 'I have no doubt it will be a girl. I have a presentiment that it must be a girl. Now, child, from the moment of the birth of this girl –'

'Perhaps boy,' my mother took the liberty of butting in.

'I tell you I have a presentiment that it must be a girl,' returned Miss Betsey. 'Don't contradict. From the moment of this girl's birth, child, I intend to be her friend. I intend to be her godmother, and I beg you'll call her Betsey Trotwood Copperfield. There must be no mistakes in life with this Betsey Trotwood. There must be no trifling with her affections, poor dear. She must be well brought up, and well guarded from reposing any foolish confidences where they are not deserved. I must make that my care.'

There was a twitch of Miss Betsey's head, after each of these sentences, as if her own old wrongs were working within her, and she repressed any plainer reference to them by strong constraint. So my mother suspected, at least, as she observed her by the low glimmer of the fire: too much scared by Miss Betsey, too uneasy in herself, and too subdued and bewildered altogether, to observe anything very clearly, or to know what to say.

'And was David good to you, child?' asked Miss Betsey, when she had been silent for a little while, and these motions of her head had gradually ceased. 'Were you comfortable together?'

'We were very happy,' said my mother. 'Mr. Copperfield was only too good to me.'

'What, he spoilt you, I suppose!' returned Miss Betsey.

'For being quite alone and dependent on myself in this rough world again, yes, I fear he did indeed,' sobbed my mother.

'Well! Don't cry!' said Miss Betsey. 'You were not equally matched, child – if any two people can be equally matched – and so I asked the question. You were an orphan, weren't you?'

'Yes.'

'And a governess?'

'I was nursery-governess in a family where Mr. Copperfield came to visit. Mr. Copperfield was very kind to me, and took a great deal of notice of me, and paid me a good deal of attention, and at last proposed to me. And I accepted him. And so we were married,' said mother simply.

'Ha! Poor Baby!' mused Miss Betsey, with her frown still bent upon the fire. 'Do you know anything?'

'I beg your pardon, ma'am,' faltered my mother.

'About keeping house, for instance,' said Miss Betsey.

'Not much, I fear,' returned my mother. 'Not so much as I wish. But Mr. Copperfield was teaching me –'

('Much he knew about it himself!') said Miss Betsey in a parenthesis

The Whitsun Weddings

Though the focus so far in this chapter has been on dramatisations of novels for radio, you are not, of course, restricted either to novels and short stories as your source text nor are you restricted to dramatisations as the only genre into which you can transform these texts. The list on page 318 should have given you an indication of the possibilities open to you in text transformation.

We want now, therefore, to look at a different way of using a source text, other than as a straight dramatisation. In this example, the writer has used

Philip Larkin's famous poem *The Whitsun Weddings*, published in 1964, as a springboard for a verse drama, again for radio. The programme begins with Philip Larkin himself reading the start of the poem. The persona, or character who is the narrator in the poem, is making a railway journey at Whitsun and gradually becomes aware of the numerous wedding parties on the platforms of the stations at which the train stops on its journey to London. The reading is accompanied by sound effects of a steam train. As the reading of the poem pauses, another voice begins to speak and it gradually becomes apparent that this is the voice of one of the brides speaking some 41 years after her Whitsun wedding. Her daughter then speaks before Larkin's reading of his poem continues.

The Whitsun Weddings

LARKIN

That Whitsun, I was late getting away:
  Not till about
One-twenty on the sunlit Saturday
Did my three-quarters-empty train pull out,
All windows down, all cushions hot, all sense
Of being in a hurry gone. We ran
Behind the backs of houses, crossed a street
Of blinding windscreens, smelt the fish-dock; thence
The river's level drifting breadth began,
Where sky and Lincolnshire and water meet.

All afternoon, through the tall heat that slept
  For miles inland,
A slow and stopping curve southwards we kept.
Wide farms went by, short-shadowed cattle, and
Canals with floatings of industrial froth;
A hothouse flashed uniquely: hedges dipped
And rose: and now and then a smell of grass
Displaced the reek of buttoned carriage-cloth
Until the next town, new and nondescript,
Approached with acres of dismantled cars.

At first, I didn't notice what a noise
  The weddings made
Each station that we stopped at: sun destroys
The interest of what's happening in the shade,
And down the long cool platforms whoops and skirls
I took for porters larking with the mails,
And went on reading. Once we started, though,
We passed them, grinning and pomaded, girls
In parodies of fashion, heels and veils,
All posed irresolutely, watching us go,
As if out on the end of an event
  Waving goodbye
To something that survived it.

MOTHER
Never been so glad to get on a train in my life.
I wore a – something turquoise.
I don't think it ever saw the light of day again, that little outfit.
No, I'm afraid I failed on ladyhood, handbags, heels.

Not *lady* then, *female*? *Female* is an adjective best applied to wildlife,
Now we see the female returning to the nest with a currant loaf and fresh-killed
library books.
F65 – sounds like a fighter jet.
Woman 65 – What? Found on moon? Eaten alive by supermarket trolley?
Woman 65 – sat at kitchen table, waxed cloth, wiped clean;
Surroundings: baking trays, calendar featuring birds of prey.
I don't suppose I've made much impression on this life.
But everyone remembers a good – read *dreary*, read *lonely*
Seeks 'bicycle and English Mist'
(PUFFING OF TRAIN)

DAUGHTER
And just kids! My Mum, she jumped on the first train out of the backstreets, a kid of
24. Then she promptly had two of her own. Well, you can understand it. Not many
options, those days. Marriage – a job for life. Total safety. When I think how clueless
I was, the state I was in at 24, just out of university, floundering, working out how to
live, how the world works, could barely look after myself, never mind a family. I've
got to admire her, holding it together. I'd have been banging off the walls, head in the
gas oven.
(PUFFING OF TRAIN)

It's important to note from your point of view as text transformers that the
writer has used *The Whitsun Weddings* not only as the starting point for the
play but has ensured that (a) the text of the poem is used throughout and
that (b) the events and characters in the play are always suggested by the
content of the poem. Text transformation is *not* the same as producing a
piece of original or creative writing. As we said at the start of this chapter,
the transformation should not be so great or so radical that all sight of the
original is lost. It must be a re-working of an original text.

A very good example of the way that a story can be re-worked is the Faust
legend. In its original version, this is a medieval legend of a man who sold
his soul to the Devil. This man later became identified with a Dr Faustus, a
sixteenth century German wandering necromancer or black magician. In its
most famous English transformation, Christopher Marlowe's play *The
Tragical History of Dr Faustus*, Faustus becomes, not a mere magician, but a
man striving for infinite power, ambitious to be 'great Emperor of the
world'. Perhaps the most famous transformation of the story is by the
German dramatist, Goethe, and in his hands it becomes a two part drama,
that begins with the Devil obtaining permission from God to try to effect
the ruin of the soul of Faust, God being confident that the Devil will fail.
We see Faust's soul finally borne away to Heaven by angels, but not before
he has undergone in the course of the drama disillusion, despair, remorse
and purification, at the end pursuing the service of mankind, not himself.
That the Faust story is a very powerful one can be seen in the many
transformations the story has undergone, including two operas, Berlioz's
The Damnation of Faust and Gounod's *Faust* and the song lyrics of at least
one modern German pop group.

ACTIVITY 173

Here are the remaining lines of Larkin's poem. Read them carefully so that you have a feel for the poem as a whole.

Choose one of the following transformations to work on.

1 Imagine that Larkin's carriage contained mostly women travellers. Inter-mix readings from the poem with *Talking Heads* style monologues from one or more of these women:

an elderly widow; a woman having an affair; a lesbian; a teenage bride, now in her 20s; a spinster; a bigamist.

2 Imagine that one of the following were reflecting on his or her experience of marriage and feelings as the train pulled out of the station. You could use different time perspectives and shifts if you wished:

fathers with broad belts under their suits mothers loud and fat an uncle shouting smut

3 Continue the radio play from the point at which we left off.

4

    Struck, I leant
More promptly out next time, more curiously,
And saw it all again in different terms:
The fathers with broad belts under their suits
And seamy foreheads; mothers loud and fat;
An uncle shouting smut; and then the perms,
The nylon gloves and jewellery-substitutes,
The lemons, mauves, and olive-ochres that

Marked off the girls unreally from the rest.
    Yes, from cafes
And banquet-halls up yards, and bunting-dressed
Coach-party annexes, the wedding-days
Were coming to an end. All down the line
Fresh couples climbed aboard: the rest stood round;
The last confetti and advice were thrown,
And, as we moved, each face seemed to define
Just what it saw departing: children frowned
At something dull; fathers had never known

Success so huge and wholly farcical;
    The women shared
The secret like a happy funeral;
While girls, gripping their handbags tighter, stared
At a religious wounding. Free at last,
And loaded with the sum of all they saw,
We hurried towards London, shuffling gouts of steam.
Now fields were building-plots, and poplars cast
Long shadows over major roads, and for
Some fifty minutes, that in time would seem

Just long enough to settle hats and say
    I nearly died,
A dozen marriages got under way.
They watched the landscape, sitting side by side
– An Odeon went past, a cooling tower
And someone running up to bowl – and none
Thought of the others they would never meet

Or how their lives would all contain this hour.
I thought of London spread out in the sun
Its postal districts packed like squares of wheat:

There we were aimed. And as we raced across
   Bright knots of rail
Past standing Pullmans, walls of blackened moss
Came close, and it was nearly done, this frail
Travelling coincidence; and what it held
Stood ready to be loosed with all the power
That being changed can give. We slowed again,
And as the tightened brakes took hold, there swelled
A sense of falling, like an arrow-shower
Sent out of sight, somewhere becoming rain.

12 Critical Approaches

This final chapter is about reading. 'Critical approaches', like 'stylistics' is just another word for reading. But of course we do not mean casual, take it or leave it reading, we mean something more comprehensive and systematic than that. Casual reading is firing on only one or two cylinders: getting the plain sense of the text and forming a general impression of whether it interests you or not. Critical approaches are a collection of study strategies, linguistic and literary critical, that will enable you to read not only what is on the lines, but between the lines (inferences and symbolic meanings, for example) and beyond the lines (context and evaluation of the text, for example).

The Assessment Objectives for English Language and Literature require A-level candidates to 'respond to literary and non-literary texts, using literary and linguistic concepts and approaches' and to 'use and evaluate different literary and linguistic approaches to the study of written and spoken language, showing how these approaches inform their readings'. This chapter will set out the range of concepts and approaches that may be used and also indicate how different approaches might be evaluated. There will be nothing new introduced, since we are summarising material to which you have already been introduced in the previous chapters. We are also concentrating on written texts for convenience, and because we have in any case devoted two chapters to analysing and evaluating talk.

There are no separate activities in this chapter because the whole chapter is one big activity in which you will make comparisons between three different texts.

First though, an outline or map of just what 'critical concepts and approaches' consist of.

Critical concepts and approaches to written texts may be grouped under two headings:

– cultural context
– stylistics.

Cultural context covers all the factors that bring a text into being, influence how it is received and read and used, and all the circumstances surrounding the text. Here are some fairly familiar perspectives in which a text may be read:

– its historical period

- its socio-economic origins (e.g. 'educated, middle-class socialist' attitudes) including the social class and experiences written about
- its place in the evolution of a particular genre, e.g. novel, sonnet, newspaper article, scientific treatise
- its place in the life of the writer and the writer's beliefs and attitudes (biographical approach)
- its bearing on a prominent theme written about in other periods, other genres (literary and non-literary)
- its psychoanalytical undercurrents (e.g. as an example of repressed sexuality, or of anxiety)
- its reflection of dominance and/or liberation in male/female politics
- its cultural influence on other kinds of writing and social activity
- its adaptability into other media, and (if a play) its performance history.

You could view a potted history of literary criticism in three phases:

First, from ancient times to the nineteenth century – the focus was on the writer as inspired individual, and on the circumstances of his life (Coleridge's poem *The Aeolian Harp* represents the divinely inspired poet as a stringed instrument hanging in the breeze and singing the song that blows through it).

Secondly, in the first half or so of the twentieth century, the focus was on the text itself, the only thing that remains after the death of its author. Meaning lies in the text, only in the text and in nothing but the text, not in the writer: this was the view of an American group known as the New Critics. It was the shift of attention from authors to texts that was new. In England, critics such as I. A. Richards and F. R. Leavis developed this view into an English literary critical tradition which was highly influential up to about 1970, but has now been largely discredited because of the narrow and elitist role it assigned to readers.

Thirdly, the modern age (from the 1960s onwards) – in which the focus has shifted again, this time to the reader as the meaning maker. Modern readers bring the sensibilities and the ideas of their own age to the texts of another age. This approach is known as reader response criticism and has a much wider and more democratic view of what the reading process is. Whilst acknowledging the prime importance of writers, it recognises the important role of readers as accomplices in the making of meanings.

In this book we have tried to show how writers (dead or alive), texts and readers (mostly alive!) are linked in a variety of fascinating linguistic and literary ways.

These are the broadest critical approaches, depending to a large extent on both comparisons between texts and on readers' knowledge beyond the texts themselves, which could include knowledge of historical period, genre and social contexts, for example. It is important however that some connection can be established between the knowledge beyond the text and language features in the text. For the latter you must turn to stylistics.

Stylistics takes into account social functions and cultural contexts but is primarily concerned with evidence in the language itself: the lexico-grammar, the phonology, features of semantics and pragmatic factors. It is in the pragmatic features that the connections between cultural context approaches and stylistics are most clearly seen.

Some interconnections between all these approaches can be understood by examining the poem below:

What Is Our Life?

What is our life? A play of passion.
Our mirth, the music of division.
Our mothers' wombs the tiring houses be,
Where we are dressed for this short comedy.
Heaven the judicious, sharp spectator is,
That sits and marks still who doth act amiss.
Our graves that hide us from the searching sun
Are like drawn curtains when the play is done:
Thus march we, playing, to our latest rest;
Only we die in earnest. That's no jest!

Consider it stylistically first.

It begins by answering its own question (*grammar*). The second line does the same thing but by ellipsis (*grammar*). The meaning of 'division' and 'tiring' need checking ('division' = rapid musical passage resembling laughter, or possibly music between acts of a play; 'tiring' = 'attiring' = 'dressing rooms') (*etymology*). 'Judicious' and 'sits' introduces a legal semantic field while 'spectator', 'act', 'curtains' 'play' and 'jest' continue theatrical semantic field introduced in the first line (*lexis* and *semantics* of metaphor). Note also that there is figurative power in the lexical contrast between 'life' and 'womb' at the beginning of the poem and 'death' and the 'grave' at the end. Similarly the brevity of the opening question sentence is balanced by the brevity of the final three word sentence (*grammar*). There's also a pun on the words 'play' and 'playing'. It's likely that 'still' and 'latest' have changed meanings since the poem was written (*lexis* and *semantics*). 'Still' = 'continually', 'latest' = 'last' (*etymology*).

The rhyming scheme (*phonology*) consists of unvaried rhyming couplets, so lightly done that there is no monotony to detract from the tone of mocking irony.

On the evidence of this stylistic analysis alone, it is clear that a great poem does not need back up from cultural context and biography. And this *is* a great poem. You can see that it helped to follow up your modern intuition that this is not a modern poem and that the original word meanings turned out to be Elizabethan. But given that it is such a fine poem, who would not be grateful to know even more about it by exploring the poem's biographical and historical contexts? So, here goes!

It was written by Sir Walter Ralegh (1552–1618) while imprisoned in the Tower of London, awaiting execution. He was sentenced to death on a trumped charge of treason in 1603 and lived on Death Row for fifteen years.

Just as ICT provides us with so many images and so much vocabulary for modern ideas, so the great age of Elizabethan and Jacobean drama provided them with a rich field of theatrical language and metaphor, as you can see in the poem. It was also a great age for English music, also evident in the poem

Ralegh wrote another poem while imprisoned *Nature, That Washed Her Hands In Milk*, the last verse of which is:

Oh, cruel Time! which takes in trust
Our youth, our joys, and all we have
And pays us but with age and dust;
Who in the dark and silent grave
When we have wandered all our ways
Shuts up the story of our days.

After Ralegh's execution, this last stanza was circulated as a separate little poem with a note saying that the lines had been written on the night before he was beheaded. Two lines had also been added:

And from which earth, and grave, and dust
The Lord will raise me up, I trust.

You didn't *need* to know all that, but once you have discovered these historical circumstances of its composition, the interaction of contextual approaches and stylistic analysis support each other giving a poem written four hundred years ago, if anything, greater poignance and meaning.

AND FINALLY, THE TITANIC, CULTURAL ICON AND MYTH FOR THE LATE 1990s

On the next pages are three texts about the Titanic disaster in 1912. The first is a report in *The Daily Telegraph* for 16 April 1912, which the poet Thomas Hardy would have known. The second is Thomas Hardy's poem, *The Convergence of the Twain*, written shortly after the sinking. The third is a historian's account of the event written in the 1980s (*The Sway of the Grand Saloon: a social history of the North Atlantic* by John Malcolm Brinnin).

APPALLING DISASTER
to
THE TITANIC.

FEARED LOSS
OF
1,683 LIVES.

SUNK IN COLLISION
WITH
AN ICEBERG.

675 REPORTED SAVE

2,358 ON BOARD.

NEW YORK, Monday.

The Titanic sank at 2.20 this morning,
No lives were lost.

NEW YORK, Monday.
The following statement has been given out by the White Star officials:
Capital Haddock, of the Olympic, sends a wireless message that the Titanic sank at 2.20 a.m. (Monday) after all the passengers and crew had been lowered into lifeboats and transferred to the Virginian.
The steamer Carpathia, with several hundred passengers from the Titanic, is now on her way to New York. – *Reuter.*
At 1.45 a.m. we received the following additional message from New York, despatched at 8.40 p.m. Monday:
The White Star officials now admit that many lives have been lost. – *Reuter*

NEW YORK, Monday (8.45 p.m.)
The following despatch has been received here from Cape Race:
The steamer Olympic reports that the steamer Carpathia reached the Titanic's position at daybreak, but found boats and wreckage only.
She reported that the Titanic foundered about 2.20 a.m., in lat. 41deg 16min, long. 50deg 14 min.

The message adds:
All the Titanic's boats are accounted for. About 675 souls have been saved of the crew and passengers. The latter are nearly all women and children.
The Leyland Liner California is remaining and searching the vicinity of the disaster.
The Carpathia is returning to New York with the survivors. – *Reuter.*

NEW YORK, Monday (9.10 p.m.).
The Titanic's survivors on board the Carpathia are stated at the White Star offices to include all the first-class passengers.
She is expected to reach New York on Friday morning. – *Reuter.*

NEW YORK, Monday (9.50 p.m.).
The White Star officials now admit that probably only 675 out of the 2,200 passengers on board the Titanic have been saved. – *Reuter.*

NEW YORK, Monday, (9.35 p.m.).
Mr. Franklin now admits that there has been "horrible loss of life." He says he has no information to disprove the press despatch from Cape Race that only 675 passengers and crew had been rescued.
The monetary loss could not be estimated to-night, but he intimated that it would run into millions. "We can replace money," he added "but not lives." – *Reuter.*

REPORTED DROWNED.

MR. STEAD AND COL. ASTOR AMONG THE LOST.

At four o'clock this morning we received the following additional telegrams:
NEW YORK, Monday.
Colonel J. J. Astor is reported to have been drowned. His wife is believed to have been saved.
Mr. W. T. Stead, Mr. Bruce Ismay, Mr. A. G. Vanderbilt, and Major Butt, Aide-de-Camp to Mr. Taft, are believed to be among the lost.
The latest reports clearly indicate that an un-precedented catastrophe has taken place.

All the above telegrams are given in the order in which they were received in London in the early hours of this morning.
It is as yet impossible to estimate the full magnitude of the disaster, the statements being in many respects contradictory, but it is gravely to be feared that great loss of life has been involved.

RACE TO THE RESCUE.

EXCITEMENT IN NEW YORK.

From Our Own Correspondent.
NEW YORK, Monday Afternoon.

Despatches to the White Star Line's New York office report that the Titanic, at 4.30 this afternoon, was being towed to Halifax by the Allan liner Virginian. The sea was calm and the weather conditions fair.
Her passengers are on board the Cunarder Carpathia and the Allan liner Parisian, which are proceeding to Halifax. They will be brought to New York overland.
It is added that the transfer was made safely, in calm weather.
The White Star liner Baltic was reported at three p.m. as hurrying to overtake the other vessels with the purpose of taking the Titanic's passengers from them. This second transshipment is likely to be made early this evening, and the passengers may reach Halifax more quickly.

The Convergence of the Twain

Lines on the Loss of the *Titanic* by Thomas Hardy (1912)

1

In a solitude of the sea
Deep from human vanity,
And the Pride of Life that planned her, stilly couches she.

2

Steel chambers, late the pyres
Of her salamandrine fires,
Cold currents thrid, and turn to rhythmic tidal lyres.

3

Over the mirrors meant
To glass the *opulent*
The seaworm crawls – grotesque, slimed, dumb, indifferent.

4

Jewels in joy designed
To ravish the sensuous mind
Lie lightless, all their sparkles bleared and black and blind.

5

Dim moon-eyed fishes near
Gaze at the gilded gear
And query: "What does this vaingloriousness down here?" ...

6

Well: while was fashioning
The creature of cleaving wing,
The Immanent Will that stirs and urges everything

7

Prepared a sinister mate
For her – so gaily great –
A Shape of Ice, for the time far and dissociate.

8

And as the smart ship grew
In stature, grace, and hue,
In shadowy silent distance grew the Iceberg too.

9

Alien they seemed to be:
No mortal eye could see
The intimate welding of their later history.

10

Or sign that they were bent
By paths coincident
On being anon twin halves of one *august* event,

11

Till the Spinner of the Years
Said "Now!" And each one hears,
And consummation comes, and jars two hemispheres.

The Sinking of the Titanic
from *The Sway of the Grand Saloon: A Social History of the North Atlantic*
by John Michael Brinnin

'For ten lethal seconds on the night of April 14, 1912, the starboard hull of the greatest ship of the high seas came into contact with the submerged shelf of a drifting island of ice. Smudged with a bit of paint from the shipyards of Belfast, the iceberg then slid back into the dark and floated away on the Labrador Current. Her engines stopped, her signals silent as she continued to travel on the momentum of 46,000 tons, the ship began to fill, to lurch into a list that would never be righted. Through a gash three hundred feet long, torrents of sea water were already pouring in. 'All of a sudden the starboard side came in upon us,' said one of the stokers. 'It burst like a big gun going off; the water came pouring in and swilled our legs.'

'The encounter was as brief as a glancing blow; the meeting of ice and steel a matter of dreadful efficiency. Three hours later the 822-foot-long *Titanic* stood almost vertical, a weird black and white column in the middle of the ocean. Then she dived down, head first. Trapped in the dark companionways and wooden dormitories of the third-class quarters, hundreds of emigrants were first overwhelmed, then entombed. On the upright afterdecks, passengers clinging to stanchions and ventilators were washed from the ship like insects from the trunk of a tree. The water temperature was 28 degrees Fahrenheit.

'Adrift in lifeboats, some seven hundred other people heard the tumbling crash of boilers and engines dragging the ship under, then a vast silence like a sudden intake of breath, then 'one long continuous wailing chant' as their shipmates succumbed to the cold or drowned among pieces of wreckage. To one man in a lifeboat, the sound they made was like that of 'locusts on a mid-summer's night.' To another, their was 'a cry that called to heaven for the very injustice of its own existence; a cry that clamored for its own destruction.' An accident at sea was already on its way to becoming a metaphor: the arm of a wrathful God lifted against the vanity of earthly riches and the presumptions of science.

'In simple fact, the loss of the *Titanic* was a maritime disaster without equal. But in the broad resonance of its notoriety, the sinking of the *Titanic* became an event in the psychological make-up of a generation. 'The pleasure and comfort which all of us enjoyed upon this floating palace,' said one passenger, 'seemed an ominous feature to many of us, including myself, who felt it almost too good to last without some terrible retribution inflicted by the hand of an angry omnipotence.' In the space of three appalling hours, vague guilts and elusive anxieties that had dogged one hundred years of material progress came into focus.

'The unsinkable ship, the most superb technological achievement of her time, the dreamed-of sign and symbol that man's mechanical skill would carry him into a luminous new world of power, freedom, and affluence, had become, in the words of one contemporary dirge, 'the most imposing mausoleum that ever housed the bones of men since the Pyramids rose from the sand.' Nothing had gone wrong. Everything had gone wrong. The odds on a ship such as the *Titanic* hitting an iceberg and foundering under the blow were calculated at a million to one. With devastating and absolute precision the *Titanic* and her officers had in the space of four days surmounted these odds. Designed to survive anything that man or nature could bring to bear against her, the great ship could not survive even the first voyage of the twenty-five or thirty long years of seagoing for which she was built.

'Courts of inquiry on both sides of the Atlantic would sift every detail, rehearse every movement, accuse, exonerate, and recommend. Yet all of their columns of facts would be swamped by an overwhelming sense of incredulity, all their tediously rational explanations would be surrendered with a primitive bow toward the irrational. To the man in the street, not one of the answers to the more than twenty-five thousand questions asked in court about the loss of the *Titanic* would do. The only explanation was Fate, a bolt from the sky that conclusively demolished two of his most important articles of faith: an awed belief in the sovereignty of science, a generous conviction that the rights and privileges of wealth were both real and deserved. When scores of the richest and most influential men on earth, men 'to whom life itself seemed subservient and obedient,' could freeze to death clinging to pieces of wreckage in the middle of the ocean, something in the order of things was amiss. The unfolding marvels of science and the Olympian preserves of privilege were suddenly made human, vulnerable, and hardly worth his affection or his fealty.'

There are no doubt other texts in your mind too, the 1997 film and the soundtrack song by Celine Dion. This is what modern culture is like: the event itself, Hardy, history, documentary and a romantic/tragic film all rolled into one. We would like you to do some sorting out.

Look at the three texts and analyse their stylistic features. How different are the three accounts? How do they 'tell' the story? What different kinds of reflections are there? What sorts of meanings are being constructed by journalist, poet and historian?

In the poem for example, you could explain the pivotal significance of lines 15 and 16. How can it be an 'august' event? What is the significance of the word 'hemispheres'? How do free will, accident, fate and chance come into all this? Is it just coincidence that each set of three lines is reminiscent of a liner's silhouette, or is there another reason for the layout of the lines?

When you have looked in detail at the language of the texts, turn to cultural contextual factors, considering also what the James Cameron film contributes to your appreciation of the texts. What does the soundtrack song contribute?

What social or spiritual themes do you detect? How is the element of drama handled in the different accounts? What different purposes are evident in the texts? Where do you find persuasion or argument, for example? Which text means most to you?

Acknowledgements

The publishers would like to thank the following for their kind permission to reproduce copyright material:

Copyright Text:
Loot by Joe Orton © Methuen, 1973; 'Opening The Cage' by Edwin Morgan from *Collected Poems* © Carcanet Press Limited; *The Tombs of Atuan* by Ursula Le Guin © Inter-Vivos Trust for the Le Guin Children; *Killshot* by Elmore Leonard (Viking, 1989) copyright © Elmore Leonard, Inc., 1989; 'Mr Humphreys and his Inheritance' by M. R. James in *Ghost Stories,* Penguin Books Ltd 1984; *Learning How to Mean* by Michael Halliday © Edward Arnold, 1970; *Focus on Meaning* by Joan Tough © Cassell & Co, 1972; *If We Taught Kids to Speak Like We Teach Them to Write* reproduced by kind permission of Andrew Stibbs; 'Especially When The October Wind' by Dylan Thomas, from *Collected Poems* © JM Dent; *The Writing Systems of the World* by Florian Coulmas © 1989 Blackwell Publishers; Letter to the Times, *The Times Newspaper, 1913*; *Brideshead Revisited* copyright © Evelyn Waugh, 1945, reproduced by permission of PFD on behalf of the Estate of Evelyn Waugh; *The Dumb Waiter* by Harold Pinter © Faber and Faber, 1960; *Jancis Robinson's Wine Course* by Jancis Robinson, reproduced with permission of BBC Worldwide Limited. Copyright © Jancis Robinson, 1999; 'A Bird Came Down the Walk' reprinted by permission of the publishers and the Trustees of Amherst College from *The Poems of Emily Dickinson*, Ralph W. Franklin, ed., Cambridge, Mass.: The Belknap Press of Harvard University Press, Copyright © 1998 by the President and Fellows of Harvard College. Copyright © 1951, 1955, 1979 by the President and Fellows of Harvard College; *Acid* by James Kelman, Vintage; *Beloved* by Toni Morrison, Heather Schroeder International Creative Management Inc.; *Buffalo Bill's Defunct* by e e cummings, Harcourt Brace, US; 'Me Cyaan Believe It' by Michael Smith from *It A Come*, Race Today, 1986; *Riddley Walker* by Russell Hoban, © Jonathan Cape, 1980; *Rosencrantz and Guildenstern are Dead* by Tom Stoppard © Faber and Faber, 1967; 'Punishment' from *North* by Seamus Heaney © Faber and Faber, 1975; Lolita by Vladimir Nabokov, Copyright © 1955 by Vladimir Nabokov. Reprinted by permission of Vintage Books, a Division of Random House Inc.; *The Great American Novel* by Philip Roth © Jonathan Cape, 1973; *Trainspotting* by Irvine Welsh © Secker & Warburg; *Trout Fishing in America* by Richard Brautigan, Vintage. Reprinted by permission of the Peters Fraser & Dunlop Group Ltd; *XXII* and untitled by William Carlos Williams, New Directions Incorporated, USA; 'Lovebirds' taken from *Standing Female Nude* by Carol Ann Duffy published by Anvil Press Poetry, 1985; 'Dead Boy' by John Crowe Ransom, from *Selected Poems*, © Carcanet Press Limited; *Collected Stories* by Tobias Wolffe, Bloomsbury Publishing, 1988; *The Soft Voice of the Serpent* by Nadine Gordimer, A. P. Watts Ltd on behalf of Felix Licensing BV, 1975; *Docherty* by William McIlvanney, Allen and Unwin, 1975; *Me Tarzan* and *The Queen's English* © Tony Harrison; 'No Dialects Please' by Merle Collins, from *Watchers and Seekers* edited by Rhonda Cobham & Merle Collins, first published in Great Britain by The Woman's Press Ltd, 34 Great Sutton Street, London, EC1V 0LQ; 'Trouble in the Works' by Harold Pinter, from *Plays 2* © Faber and Faber, 1977; *The Inimitable Jeeves* by PG Wodehouse, Penguin Books Ltd, 1924; *Trainspotting* by Irvine Welsh © Secker & Warburg; *Small World* by David Lodge © Secker & Warburg; *Farewell My Lovely* by Raymond Chandler (Penguin Books, 1940) copyright 1940 by Raymond Chandler. *Casino Royale, The Spy Who Loved Me, Moonraker* by Ian Fleming, reproduced with the permission of Ian Fleming (Gildrose) Publications Ltd. *Casino Royale* Copyright © Gildrose Publications Ltd, 1953, *The Spy Who Loved Me* Copyright © Gildrose Publications Ltd, 1962, *Moonraker* Copyright © Gildrose Publications Ltd, 1955; *Enigma* by Robert Harris © Arrow Books Ltd, 1995; *Mission to Monte Carlo* © Barbara Cartland 1983; *My Land of The North: memories of a Northern Childhood* by Catherine Cookson, copyright © 1986, 1999, published by Headline Book Publishing; *The Mallen Streak* by Catherine Cookson, published by Corgi, copyright © Catherine Cookson, 1973; *A Century of Pop: A Hundred Years of Music that Changed the World*, Octopus Publishing Group Ltd; *Joseph Conrad* by Neville Newhouse, Evans Brothers, 1966; *The Secret Sharer* by Muriel Spark, Penguin Books Ltd; *King Street Junior* by Jim Eldridge, reproduced with the permission of BBC Worldwide Limited. Copyright © Jim Eldridge, 1988; *The Go-Between* by LP Hartley, Penguin Books Ltd, 1980; *One Small Boy* by Bill Naughton, Longman, 1957; *The Way Through the Woods* by Colin Dexter © Macmillan, 1992; 'Voices Lost in the Snow' from *Overhead in a Balloon and Other Stories* by Mavis Gallant © Jonathan Cape, 1989; 'The Waste Land' from *Collected Poems 1909–1962* by TS Eliot, published by Faber and Faber; 'Alabama Poem' by Nicki Giovanni, William Morrow and Company; *Teaching Grammar: not whether but how* © QCA, 1999; 'Sergeant Wilson's Little Secret' an episode of *Dad's Army*, BBC; *Tigers Are Better Looking* by Jean Rhys, Penguin Books Ltd, 1968; *Tithonus: Fragments from the diary of a laird* by George Mackay Brown, John Murray (Publishers) Ltd; 'Bronteburgers' by Victoria Wood from *The Third Book of Humorous Stories*, Octopus, 1986; *The Celts* by Stevie Smith, reproduced by kind permission of the James MacGibbon Estate; 'The Babysitters' from *Collected Poems* by Sylvia Plath © Faber and Faber; 'Pig Song' by Margaret Atwood from *Collected Poems 1965–1975*, Little Brown; *The Takeover* by Muriel Spark © Penguin; *Adult Pleasures* by Dan Jacobson, André Deutsch, 1988; *The*